W9-BTL-507

CHICKEN

over 400 fabulous recipes for all occasions

Edited by Simona Hill

BARNES
& NOBLE
BOOKS

NEW YORK

This edition published by Barnes & Noble, Inc.,
by arrangement with Anness Publishing Limited

2003 Barnes & Noble Books

M 10 9 8 7 6 5 4 3

ISBN 0-7607- 4945-0

© Anness Publishing Limited 2003

All rights reserved. No part of this publication may be reproduced, stored in a retrieval
system, or transmitted in any way or by any means, electronic, mechanical, photocopying,
recording or otherwise, without the prior written permission of the copyright holder.

Publisher: Joanna Lorenz
Managing Editor: Helen Sudell
Editor: Simona Hill
Designer: Nigel Partridge
Illustrator: Anna Koska and Lucinda Ganderton
Editorial Reader: Penelope Goodare
Production Controller: Ben Worley

Printed and bound in China
Previously published as The Ultimate Chicken Cookbook

Contents

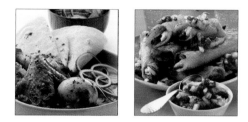

INTRODUCTION

Chicken is possibly the most versatile cooking ingredient of all, and it is used all around the world. It is nourishing, low in fat, and, if you buy good-quality produce, it is full of flavor too. Included here are recipes using chicken as well as Cornish hens, guinea fowl, and turkey, to provide you with a wide choice of poultry dishes using a range of cooking techniques. Because the book has an international flavor, the recipes use a selection of ingredients, herbs, and spices from different countries. Some of the more unusual ingredients will need to be bought at specialist food stores, but most are readily available in supermarkets.

The book opens with a comprehensive introduction to choosing, buying, and storing chicken, turkey, and other poultry, along with guides to preparation and serving methods and cooking times. This collection of recipes has been gathered from around the globe so that you can enjoy chicken at its best.

Chicken and Other Small Poultry

Perhaps because they are small and easy to keep chickens have been domesticated for thousands of years. The chickens we eat today are descended from jungle fowl that were first domesticated in India more than 4,000 years ago.

The idea of hens pecking about a farmyard conjures up an idyllic image, but in reality chickens and other poultry were just as often kept in small domestic backyards. Originally, chickens were farmed for their eggs and killed for their meat only when they were past their laying best. Many birds were undernourished and forced to scavenge in every unhygienic nook and cranny. So the chicken or rooster that eventually made it to the average dinner table was likely to be quite a sad culinary offering, with little meat and the necessity for hours of boiling, rendering minimal flavor to all but the stock.

It wasn't until the last 150 years that attitudes toward chicken rearing changed. Chickens were bred for pleasure and the number of breeds increased. Chicken became an expensive luxury food and a roast bird was an occasional treat. Modern, intensive farming methods over the last few decades have brought chicken to many more

Above: The conditions in which a chicken is reared will affect the quality of the meat.

tables, not only as an occasional treat, but also as an everyday food. However, intensive-rearing methods often meant that quantity superseded quality as birds were fattened quickly, and flavor and texture diminished. As the conditions in which many hens are reared have been exposed and the resulting hygiene and health problems realized, so public outcry has forced a reversal toward

traditional methods of farming, and organic poultry has become more widely available.

Farmers have developed different breeds for a specific purpose, whether it is high egg yields or improved meat quality, and their breeding methods are geared to meet market demands.

Where farming methods are strictly regulated, organic poultry often offers better quality, more flavorful meat. As a rule, the better the conditions under which poultry are reared, the better the end product. Whether the end concern is the welfare of the poultry or the quality of the meat, the means to both are the same: if you want quality chicken, buy those that have been well reared.

Nutrition

Chicken and other small poultry are rich in high-quality protein, providing all the essential amino acids required by the body for growth. The meat provides B-group vitamins, especially niacin. It also provides iron (more in the leg meat than the breast meat) as well as the minerals copper and selenium. The white meat is low in fat (the fat is found in and under the skin) and contains a lower proportion of saturated fat than meat.

Left: Corn-fed chickens are easy to pick out because of their yellow skin but identifying a free-range (middle top) or organic (right) chicken is not so easy. A reputable supplier is the key to obtaining good quality meat.

Right: For a roast, look for a plump breast and creamy skin.

Buying

Poultry can be bought fresh, chilled, or frozen. When choosing, look for birds with a clear, soft skin (there should be no blemishes or bruises). A soft, thin skin shows that the bird is young; the tougher the skin, the older the bird. A fresh chicken should have a plump breast and the skin should be creamy in color. The top of the breastbone should be pliable.

A bird's weight is taken after plucking and drawing and, in some instances, may include the giblets (neck, gizzard, heart, and liver) packaged separately. The bigger the bird, the better its value because the proportion of meat to bone will be higher.

As well as whole birds, chicken is available in a choice of cuts, such as quarters, legs, wings, thighs, breast portions, and drumsticks. Portions may be on the bone or boneless, with or without skin. Sliced, diced, and ground chicken breast portions are also available. Stir-fry strips, marinated cuts, and stuffed portions are all sold fresh or frozen.

Storing

Always keep poultry chilled, as bacteria thrive in warmth. Select poultry toward the end of a shopping session and avoid leaving it in a warm car before going home. Unpack and chill it promptly. Store poultry in the refrigerator until you are ready to cook it.

Place poultry loose in a deep dish and cover it closely. Check prepacked poultry to make sure that the packs are sealed before placing them in the refrigerator. Store in the coldest part of the refrigerator; the lowest part is best, where the chicken cannot accidentally drip onto other foods. Use loose poultry within about two days of purchase.

Raw, fresh poultry can be frozen whole or in portions. If they are included, remove the giblets from a whole bird before freezing. Wrap chicken portions tightly in plastic wrap or freezer wrap. Pack the portions in a freezer bag and seal. Once it has been taken out of the freezer, the best way to thaw poultry is to do so slowly in the refrigerator. Place in a suitable container, cover closely, and leave overnight. Always thaw poultry completely before cooking. Never try to thaw a frozen chicken in hot water, as this will toughen the flesh and is dangerous, as it encourages bacteria to multiply.

Handling

Poultry is particularly susceptible to bacterial growth. This can cause food poisoning if the poultry is eaten without its being thoroughly cooked first, or if it is allowed to contaminate other foods. Contamination occurs when the raw chicken meat touches other foods, or if liquid from the chicken drips onto other foods.

Before preparing raw poultry, assemble all the utensils and dishes you will need. Measure out all the other ingredients you are using, then unpack, and cut, coat, or prepare the poultry.

When making a meal that includes dishes that are to be served uncooked, such as salads or desserts, or ready-cooked foods, such as cooked fish or meat, it is a good idea to prepare these foods first before handling the raw poultry to avoid any risk of cross-contamination.

Thoroughly wash utensils, surfaces, and hands after handling and cooking poultry. Use a cutting board that can be washed at a high temperature, and always keep a cutting board just for preparing raw poultry. Remember to wash utensils used to lift or stir part-cooked poultry before using them with cooked poultry.

Cook Well, Eat Well

It is very important to cook poultry properly to make sure that any bacteria are destroyed. To check if poultry is cooked, pierce the thickest area of the meat with a thin metal skewer or sharp knife. If there is any sign of pink in the flesh or if the juices are not clear, then the chicken or poultry is not properly cooked and it must be returned to the heat or the oven for further cooking.

Types of Small Poultry

There is now a great variety of poultry available in stores and supermarkets. A recipe will usually make it clear what type of bird you need to choose.

Cornish hen
This is the name given to a young chicken, four to six weeks old and weighing 12 ounces–1½ pounds. They are bred for flavor and tenderness. Each bird provides enough meat for an individual portion. Cornish hens, which are also sometimes called spring chickens, have a tender, delicate flavor. They can be roasted, when they benefit from a moist stuffing, and they can also be butterflied and broiled, pan-fried, or cooked on the barbecue.

Broiling chicken
A variation on the Cornish hen, these are larger, older birds that weigh about 2 pounds. Broiling chickens usually have enough meat for two people. Like Cornish hens, the meat is tender and has a delicate flavor.

Rock Cornish hen
This small North American cross-breed was developed from White Rock and Cornish chickens and is sometimes called a Rock Cornish game hen. These small birds are four to six weeks old and can weigh up to 2½ pounds. The flesh is white and flavorful, although the ratio of bone to meat is high.

Roasting chicken
Sometimes simply called a roast, this is a young rooster or hen about 12 weeks old. Roasting chickens usually weigh about 3 pounds, but may be as big as 7 pounds. Older

Above: Cornish hen

Below: Broiling chicken

birds (up to 20 weeks old) are up to 10 pounds in weight and are available from specialist butchers.

Stewing chicken
Also known as a boiling chicken, hen, or fowl, a chicken for stewing requires long, slow simmering as the flesh is tough, but its flavor is excellent. As a guide to age, the older the chicken, the harder and more rigid the breastbone. Stewing chicken are not readily

available these days as demand is low, so they have to be sourced from a specialist supplier. They are used for making pies, fricassées, ballottines and galantines, and, most often of all, in soups, stews, and casseroles.

Capon
This is a young rooster that has been castrated and then fattened on a special diet to make it plump and flavorful. Hormonal castration is prohibited in many countries, including Britain. Capons are large birds and can weigh 6–10 pounds. In the past, they were often cooked for celebration meals at Christmas and Thanksgiving in

Below: Roosters are not often eaten, although castrated birds, or capons, are available in some countries.

Right: A stewing or boiling chicken.

Above: Capon

centuries, but which originally came from the coast of Guinea in West Africa. They are tender with slightly dry flesh that resembles pheasant. The flesh is not distinctly game-like in flavor, but it leans more in that direction than toward chicken. Guinea fowl are generally cooked as for chicken or

pheasant, but at a rather higher temperature—for example the birds should be barded and roasted in an oven preheated to 450°F for 25–30 minutes. The birds can also be braised or casseroled.

Below: An oven-ready guinea fowl.

place of turkey. They have a fairly large proportion of white meat to dark, but are expensive.

Guinea fowl
These are domestic fowl, which have been raised in Europe for

---

CUTS OF CHICKEN
A wide range of different portions is available, on and off the bone. Choose the cut to suit your taste and the recipe.

Quarters include either the leg or the wing joint, the latter including a large portion of breast meat. The leg joint includes both the thigh and drumstick.

Below: Chicken breast portion (top) and a chicken supreme, which includes part of the wing bone.

Right: Wing

Above: Chicken portions include the leg quarter (top middle), drumsticks (left), and thighs (right).

Other portions include **thighs**, which are small, neat cuts, **drumsticks**, which take quite a surprisingly long time to cook, and **wings**, which have very little meat. **Breast portions** are sold on the bone and boneless, both available skinned or unskinned; these portions include only the white meat. **Supremes** include the wing bone.

Part-boned breast portions still have the short piece of bone leading into the wing and the fine strip of breastbone. **Liver** is often used in pâtés, risottos, soups, and terrines.

Above: The whole leg is useful for casseroles and poaching. Left: Liver

Preparing Chicken and Other Small Poultry

These techniques are suitable for chicken as well as other poultry, such as guinea fowl and Cornish hens, and game, such as pheasant.

Cutting up a bird

Many recipes specify particular cuts of poultry or game. Although you can buy them ready-prepared, if you have the right equipment, it is fairly straightforward to cut up a bird to suit the recipe. Use a large, sharp knife and poultry shears for cutting through meat and bone. The following gives four small portions from each side of the bird, eight in total—two wings, two breast portions, two drumsticks, and two thighs.

1 Put the bird breast side up on a cutting board. Remove the leg by cutting through the skin and then through the thigh joint. Repeat with the leg on the other side.

2 Following the line of the breastbone and using poultry shears, cut the breast in half.

3 Turn the bird over and cut out the backbone, leaving the wings.

4 Cut each breast in half, leaving a portion attached to the wing.

5 Cut through the knee joint.

6 Cut off the wing tip.

Preparing a bird for roasting

Little preparation is needed to roast a bird, but the following techniques will produce better results.

Removing the wishbone

Breast meat is carved more easily if this arched neck bone is removed.

1 Using a sharp knife pull back the skin from the neck cavity and carefully cut around the wishbone.

2 Scrape off the meat from the wishbone, then cut it away at the base, and pull it out.

Make a Lucky Wish

It is traditional for two people to pull the wishbone until it snaps. Each person is allowed to use their little finger to hold the end of one side of the bone. The person who ends up with the larger arched top of the bone is entitled to make a wish.

Trussing with skewers
This is a quick method for a larger bird that has a greater quantity of meat so it keeps its shape better.

1 Push one metal skewer through both sections of the wing, into the skin of the neck, and straight out through the wing on the other side.

2 Push the second skewer through the thighs and the tail cavity.

Trussing with string
Tying a bird with string keeps it neat and helps it to cook evenly.

1 Season the bird and tuck the wing tips and neck flap underneath.

2 Tie string around the legs and under the flap of skin.

3 Bring it toward the neck end.

4 Turn the bird over and wrap the string around the wings.

5 Pull tightly and tie neatly.

Butterflying a bird
This is a method of splitting and flattening a whole bird so that it can be broiled or roasted.

1 Tuck the wings under the bird. Remove the wishbone. Split the bird along each side of the backbone. Remove the backbone.

2 Place the bird on a cutting board breast side uppermost. Press down firmly with the heel of one hand on the middle of the breast to flatten the bird against the board.

3 Push a metal skewer through the wings and breast. Push a second skewer through the thighs.

Tunnel boning a bird

This is a method of part-boning a bird from the breast to the joints. The skin is left in one piece and the bird is ready to stuff. This is easy with a larger bird, but can be difficult with small birds.

1 Pull back the skin around the neck, then cut out the wishbone.

2 Feel inside the cavity for the wing joint, then use a sharp knife to cut the breastbone from the meat and skin from one side of the bird.

3 Pull out the curved bone. Cut the meat from the bone until you reach the wing joint.

4 Cut through the wing joint using the tip of the knife. Repeat on the other side of the bird. Pull the meat back from the carcass and cut away the flesh, keeping the knife close to the bone. Sever the leg joints when you reach them, leaving the bones attached to the leg meat.

5 Cut and ease the skin away from the breastbone, then turn the bird so that the skin is on the outside. The finished bird retains the joints, but the central part of the body is completely boneless.

Stuffing

Chickens and other poultry can be stuffed before roasting to improve the flavor and keep the meat moist. Stuffings are usually based on

---

Stuffing Tips

～

Do not stuff the body cavity of a large bird because this could inhibit heat penetration, and harmful bacteria may not be destroyed. For smaller birds, use stuffing that is cool or at room temperature, not hot or chilled. Pack it loosely in the neck end of the bird and cook any leftovers separately—stuffing balls can be cooked around the edges of the roast poultry. Stuff poultry just before cooking.

---

bread crumbs with flavorings such as onions and herbs added. Rice, meat, and nuts can also be used. Stuffing swells during cooking so pack the bird loosely.

Basic Herb Stuffing

This simple stuffing will keep your chicken moist and flavorsome.

1 small onion, finely chopped
1 tablespoon butter
2 cups fresh bread crumbs
1 tablespoon chopped fresh parsley
1 teaspoon mixed dried herbs
1 egg, beaten
salt and ground black pepper

1 Cook the onion gently in the butter until tender. Transfer to a bowl and let cool.

2 Add the remaining ingredients and then mix thoroughly. Season well with salt and pepper.

Preparing boneless breast portions

If you prepare breast portions from a whole chicken, the remainder can be cut and used for stock.

1 Cut the bird into portions, but keep the breasts whole.

2 Use your fingers to pull the skin and thin membrane from the breast. Slice the meat off the rib bone and any remaining breastbone.

3 Cut the thin, white central tendons from the breast.

4 Trim off any pieces of fat and untidy edges from the meat.

Preparing scallops
A chicken breast yields two scallops. A turkey breast can be sliced into several scallops, depending on the size of the breast.

1 Place the skinless, boneless breast portion flat on a cutting board and, using a large, sharp knife, carefully slice in half horizontally. To cut a thin, even slice, hold your hand flat on top of the chicken as you cut, to prevent it from moving.

2 Arrange the chicken between sheets of baking parchment and beat out gently until thin and flat, using a meat mallet or rolling pin.

Cutting strips for stir-frying
Use a flattened scallop for stir-fry strips (see above).

Cut the scallop into fine strips. When cut across the grain in this way, the meat cooks quickly.

Skinning and boning thighs
When boned, chicken thighs yield a neat nugget of well-flavored meat.

1 Use a knife to loosen the skin, then pull it away from the meat.

2 Cut the flesh lengthwise along the main thigh bone, then cut the bone out, trimming the meat close to the bone. Continue cutting out the bones, leaving the meat open and flat.

Making kebabs
The thigh meat is ideal for kebabs. Skin and bone the thigh (as above).

1 Cut the meat across the grain into four pieces, using a sharp knife.

2 Thread the meat on to skewers. Add pieces of vegetable (try mushrooms, small onions, red and green bell pepper); they will cook in the same time as the chicken.

Cooking Chicken and Other Small Poultry

Young, tender birds can be poached, roasted, broiled, cooked on the barbecue, griddled, or fried in a shallow pan or, once coated in bread crumbs or batter, in deep oil. If you do have an older bird, it should be cooked by long, gentle, and moist methods such as braising and stewing.

Roasting

Small poultry, such as chickens, Cornish hens, and guinea fowl, are easy to roast and require the minimum of attention. For a larger bird that requires longer cooking the breast should be covered loosely with foil. Remove the foil for the final 15 minutes' cooking time to complete the browning.

1 Rub the breast and the top of the bird generously with butter. Season with salt and pepper, and add herbs or other flavorings if required.

2 Place the bird breast side down in the roasting pan for the first 30 minutes of the cooking time.

3 Turn and baste the bird, then cook for the calculated time, basting the bird every 15 minutes.

4 When the bird is cooked (see Careful Cooking), remove from the oven, and cover the bird tightly with foil. Let rest in a warm place for 10–15 minutes before carving and serving.

Roasting Times

Preheat the oven to 400°F, or 450°F for guinea fowl. Calculate cooking times using the weight of the bird (including stuffing.)
Chicken: allow 20 minutes per 1 pound, plus 20 minutes.
Cornish hen: allow 50–60 minutes total roasting time.
Guinea fowl: allow 15 minutes per 1 pound, plus 15 minutes.
Rock Cornish hen: allow 40 minutes per 1 pound, plus 20 minutes.

Broiling

This is a quick-cooking method for smaller birds and portions. For even, thorough cooking, split a whole bird in half or butterfly it. Rub flavoring ingredients into the bird 1–2 hours in advance to let the flavors steep.

1 Preheat the broiler. Brush the meat with oil and season well.

2 Place skin side up on a rack in a broiling pan and cook below the heat source so the meat cooks through before it over-browns.

3 Allow about 40 minutes cooking for Cornish hens, turning often.

Griddling skinless breast fillets

This is a healthy way of cooking, allowing fat to drain away between the ridges of the pan and preventing the meat from being greasy.

1 Lightly brush the breast portions with a little vegetable oil.

2 Preheat the griddle until almost smoking, then lay the fillets on it—don't overload the pan, or the meat will steam rather than brown.

3 Cook until the meat is well browned underneath, and firm and white inside. Turn the portions over. Cook until well browned and the meat is white throughout.

Cooking on a barbecue

make sure that the barbecue is properly heated and fueled with enough charcoal to burn hot and long enough to cook the poultry thoroughly. Position the barbecue rack away from the hot coals so that the meat has plenty of time to cook before the skin is overcooked.

1 Cut slashes into thick portions. This will make sure that they cook through. Make two or three cuts across larger drumsticks or poultry quarters. There is no need to slash small drumsticks or breast meat.

2 Marinating poultry before cooking adds flavor and keeps it moist during cooking. Combine olive oil, chopped garlic, chopped fresh herbs, and chopped fresh red or green chiles in a deep, nonmetallic container.

3 Add the poultry to the marinade and turn the pieces to coat them. Cover and chill for at least 30 minutes or for up to 24 hours.

4 To cook, place the portions on the barbecue rack, brush with marinade, and cook over the hot coals. Turn the pieces frequently to make sure that they cook evenly, brushing with more of the marinade to keep the meat moist.

Careful Cooking

Checking cooking progress: Pierce the thickest area of meat with the point of a small, sharp knife. Check the juices—if there is any sign of pink, the meat is not cooked. Then check the meat at the base of the cut, when cooked it will be firm and look white; if it is pink and soft, the bird is not cooked. Use this test on portions and whole birds. On a whole bird, the area behind the thigh takes longest to cook.

Barbecues: Chicken tastes excellent when cooked on a barbecue, but it does require attention to make sure that it is cooked through. One solution is to poach the portions gently in just enough stock to cover until they are only just cooked—this will take about 20–30 minutes. Let cool in the stock, then transfer to the marinade, and chill overnight. Slash the meat and cook until thoroughly reheated and well browned.

Pan-frying

Scallops and boneless breast portions cook quickly, so they are ideal for pan-frying over high heat. Breast meat on the bone takes longer and must be evenly cooked through. Denser thigh and leg meat on the bone require careful cooking and turning. With larger pieces, reduce the heat to low once the chicken is browned. Cook it very slowly so that it does not over-brown, and always make sure that it is cooked through.

1 Heat a little olive oil in a large, nonstick skillet.

2 Add the pieces to the hot oil in the skillet and cook until they are lightly browned underneath.

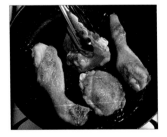

3 Turn the portions and cook until they are lightly browned on the second side. Reduce the heat and continue cooking gently until the meat is cooked. Boneless thighs take 15–20 minutes. Drumsticks take at least 30 minutes.

Stir-frying

Fine strips of poultry cook quickly and are tender. Try diced or thinly sliced pieces.

1 Cut breast portions crosswise into thin, even-size strips.

2 Heat the empty wok or a large, heavy skillet until hot before adding a little oil to the pan. Heat the oil until it is very hot.

3 Add the meat (in batches, if necessary—take care as the oil will spit) and stir-fry over high heat until brown, about 3–5 minutes. Cooking times depend on amounts of meat, oil, and the type of pan.

Casseroling

This moist cooking method allows the herbs, spices, and aromatics to steep the light meat. Whole birds, portions, and pieces of meat can be casseroled.

1 Brown the poultry all over. Remove from the pan, then soften chopped onion, carrot, and celery in the fat remaining in the pan.

2 Replace the poultry, add the wine, stock, canned tomatoes, or water. Season, then bring it to simmering point. Cover, then simmer on the stovetop or cook in a preheated oven at 350°F.

Casserole Cooking Times
~

Whole bird: allow 20 minutes per 1 pound, plus 20 minutes.
Large portions: 45–60 minutes.
Breast fillets: about 30 minutes.
Chunks or diced poultry: 20–40 minutes, depending on size.

Poaching whole poultry

This is a gentle method that brings out the delicate flavor of a bird. Serve the cooked bird hot with a light cream sauce, or let cool in its cooking liquid. The bird can then be cut up, or the meat can be carved from the bones. Poached chicken is tender and juicy, and ideal for using in salads or cold dishes. To cook a whole bird you will need a large pan or flameproof casserole, flavorings, and plenty of cooking liquid.

1 Truss the bird neatly and tightly with string and then place it in a large pan or flameproof casserole.

2 Pour in enough liquid to come just to the top of the bird. Heat gently until the liquid is just starting to simmer. Using a large spoon, carefully skim off any scum that rises to the surface of the liquid during the first few minutes of cooking, before adding any flavoring ingredients, spices, or herbs.

3 Add the chosen flavorings to the pan or casserole. A selection of the following work well: sliced onions, carrot sticks, a bouquet garni, a strip of pared lemon rind, six black peppercorns, and a sprinkle of salt.

4 Bring the liquid back to simmering point, reduce the heat if necessary and then cover the pan. Cook for 1½ hours, or until tender.

5 Use a large slotted spoon to lift the bird from the pan. Transfer it to a large dish and use poultry shears and a sharp knife to cut it into serving portions or use as required.

**Flavorings for
Poached Small Poultry**

Water is the essential base and makes a good stock. Dry white wine or hard cider may be used—about half and half with water. Dry sherry or vermouth can be added in small quantities to intensify the flavor. Carrots and onions are another essential; leeks, fennel, and turnips can also be added. Use herbs such as tarragon or thyme with bay leaves and parsley. Add them to the cooking liquid or, freshly chopped, to a plain cream sauce for serving with the poached poultry.

Chicken Stock

Good stock gives a fuller flavor to soups and casseroles than bouillon cubes. (Turkey can be used instead of chicken.)

Makes about 10 cups

2½–3 pounds chicken wings, backs, and necks
2 onions, unpeeled and quartered
17 cups cold water
2 carrots, coarsely chopped
2 celery stalks, coarsely chopped
a small handful of fresh parsley
a few fresh thyme sprigs or
    1 teaspoon dried thyme
2 bay leaves
10 black peppercorns, lightly crushed

1 Put the chicken and onions in a pan and cook over medium heat. Stir occasionally until browned.

2 Add the water and stir in the sediment on the base. Bring to a boil and skim. Add the other ingredients. Partially cover the pan and gently simmer for 3 hours.

3 Strain the stock into a bowl and let cool, then chill. When cold, remove any fat from the surface. Store in the refrigerator and use within a few days or freeze.

Stock Tips

• Stock can be made from the carcasses of any roasted poultry cooked with vegetables and flavorings. Freeze carcasses in plastic bags until you have three or four, then make the stock.
• No salt is added to stock because as it reduces, the flavor becomes concentrated and the saltiness increases.

Turkey

The turkey is the largest game bird in North America. Turkeys were first domesticated by the Aztecs in Mexico. When the Spanish conquered the Aztecs they brought some of the domesticated birds back to Europe.

For the Pilgrim Fathers who landed at Massachusetts in 1620, wild turkeys were an invaluable source of food. The Pilgrims survived the winter with the help of the native population, who shared their stores of berries, nuts, and corn to supplement the settlers' diet of wild turkey. In November 1621, on the first anniversary of their arrival in North America, the Pilgrims entertained the Native Americans with a feast. The feast is said to have lasted three days and turkey was later established in the United States as the traditional bird for Thanksgiving celebrations.

Well before turkey became popular in Europe, large birds, such as the bustard and peacock, were served, as well as the goose and smaller fowl. Unlike the unfamiliar vegetables that were brought from the Americas to Europe and treated with suspicion and caution, Europeans recognized the benefits of cooking and eating such large birds, so turkey soon became part of affluent feasts. In England, the birds were raised in Norfolk and Suffolk, then herded on foot into London. Gradually the turkey took over from the goose as a popular Christmas treat.

Inevitably, turkey's popularity led to the bird being farmed more intensively. Turkeys were first reared for their meat on a large scale in the late 1940s, and modern intensive breeding and rearing have created birds with an even larger proportion of breast meat.

Above: The turkeys that are farmed today are descended from game birds native to North America.

Nutrition

Turkey meat is lean and a source of high-quality protein. It provides B-group vitamins, particularly niacin, and is a good source of phosphorous, potassium, iron, zinc, and magnesium.

Buying

Turkeys are available fresh, chilled, or frozen. When buying a whole bird, look for soft evenly colored skin and plump, well-rounded breast and legs. Avoid

birds that are bruised, with blemishes, or torn skin. Although there are likely to be small cavities left from plucking (particularly on dark-feathered birds), there should not be any patches of feathers. The bird should smell fresh.

Turkeys vary enormously in weight, from about 6 pounds to over 25 pounds. A hen turkey matures much more quickly than a male turkey (known as a stag or tom). Turkeys can grow up to vast sizes, such as 40 pounds, but the average weights available are 10–14 pounds.

Storing

Place the turkey in a large, deep dish and cover it completely with plastic wrap. Keep it in the coolest part of the refrigerator, making sure that it (or any drip from the bird) does not come into contact with other foods.

Handling

When you have been preparing raw turkey you should always wash your hands thoroughly before handling other foods to avoid cross-contamination.

Left: Bronze turkeys like this have a wonderful flavor.

Right: The majority of turkeys are white-feathered birds, like this Norfolk turkey.

TYPES OF TURKEY

Intensive farming methods mean that turkeys are specially bred so that they will have plenty of meat. Both free-range and organic birds are available. However, free-range labels alone are not a guarantee of good quality. For the best tasting turkey, seek out a source of organic birds from a reputable farm.

Bronze birds

These are dark-feathered birds and the skin may be spotted with dark stubble remaining after plucking. Norfolk Bronze is a popular breed and Norfolk Black is a very plump-breasted bird. American Bronze is another traditional breed. Cambridge turkeys are traditional in Britain and they have been crossed with American Bronze to breed the Cambridge Bronze.

White birds

In North America the White Holland is a popular breed. The majority of British turkeys are white, and traditional breeds include the Norfolk turkey. However, the superior-flavored bronze and dark-feathered birds are becoming more popular.

CUTS OF TURKEY

As well as whole birds, there is a variety of prepared cuts of turkey available.

Part-boned breast

This is a large roasting cut consisting of the whole breast, meat and bone, with skin on. Usually taken from large birds, these can weigh as much as a small turkey and provide a large number of portions.

Boneless breast

This is usually taken from one side of the breast, and neatly rolled or shaped with the skin around the outside. Take care to distinguish between a boneless breast and a joint of "re-formed" meat, made up of scraps and off-cuts molded into a roast.

Turkey drumstick

The leg of the bird is usually enough to provide a meal for four people. Turkey drumsticks have plenty of sinew running through the brown meat. They are better browned, then braised until the meat is tender, when they make full-flavored casseroles.

Diced turkey

Used mainly for pies and casseroles, this is often darker meat from the thigh or leg.

Stir-fry turkey

These thin strips of white breast meat cook very quickly.

Ground turkey

This is good for pies, meat sauces, and burgers.

Left: A Norfolk Black, which has a very plump breast and a full flavor.

Preparing Turkey for Roasting

Turkeys are generally sold cleaned and ready for stuffing or cooking. Methods of preparing small poultry also apply to turkey, for example, trussing and tunnel boning are both relevant. The same rules also apply to hygiene when handling turkey. In addition, there are a few points to check before stuffing or roasting a large bird.

Preparation checks

Use tweezers to remove any feathers remaining on the skin. Then use a long lighted match to singe off any tiny feathers or hairs, allowing the smoke to burn away before drawing the flame across the surface of the skin. Birds with dark plumage have dark "stubble", which may look unpleasant, but these small pits from which the feathers have been removed will melt away during the roasting process.

It is also a good idea to check inside the neck end of the bird for any lumps of excess fat and pull or cut them off.

Preparing the stuffings

Stuffing can be made in advance, but the turkey should not be stuffed until just before it is placed in the oven. It is important to remember to weigh the stuffing and add this to the weight of the bird to calculate the cooking time. Truss the bird, then cook for the calculated time; never shorten the cooking time because the meat appears cooked—time must always be allowed for cooking the stuffing.

Stuffings and fillings are highly flavored mixtures of ingredients. They are added to plain foods to introduce complex flavors. Ground meat, such as veal, pork, or bulk pork sausage, is a traditional main ingredient. Mixtures are also often based on bread crumbs or rice. Alternatively, the stuffing may not be bound into a mixture that can be sliced or spooned out easily, but consist of loose combinations of chopped fruits or vegetables.

Cooking stuffing separately

Stuffing can be cooked separately from the turkey because not everyone likes the flavoring. Also, bear in mind that stuffing will increase the overall cooking time. So for a very large bird, cooking the stuffing in a separate tray can help time-wise and it reduces anxiety about the bird being cooked through and ready on time.

Also any leftover stuffing can be rolled into small balls about the size of walnuts. Place these in a separate baking pan or add them to the roasting pan, for the final 15 minutes' cooking time, and then serve with the carved meat.

Flavoring variations

A popular method is to place aromatics, such as onions or citrus fruits, in the body cavity and to add the stuffing under the skin covering the breast. All these aromatics can be added to the body cavities so the flavors suffuse the meat as it cooks: A large onion cut in half and each half studded with four to six cloves. An orange and a lemon cut into quarters with three bay leaves, four sage sprigs, and three thyme sprigs. A cinnamon stick or a blade of mace for a festive hint.

If you prefer to add stuffing to the breast, you can loosen the skin over the breast meat and insert stuffing underneath it. It is a good idea to add stuffing here, even when stuffing the cavity, as this protects the delicate breast meat during long cooking.

STUFFING RECIPES AND METHODS

There are a number of traditional recipes that will add moistness and flavor to the cooked meat. All of the recipes can be adapted to suit different tastes and occasions.

Bulk Pork Sausage and Chestnut Stuffing

This is a favorite for stuffing turkey. You can buy bulk pork sausage with a high proportion of meat, to make the best stuffing. Use fresh chestnuts in season, or look for ready-prepared, vacuum-packed chestnuts in the supermarket.

1 Peel 2 pounds fresh chestnuts, by slitting the peel and pulling it off. Remove the brown skin inside the shell. Cook the chestnuts in boiling water for 10–15 minutes. Drain, then crumble into a large bowl.

2 Melt 2 tablespoons butter in a pan and add two finely chopped onions. Cook for 10 minutes, until the onions are soft.

3 Add the onions to the chestnuts and mix. Return the pan to the heat and add 1 pound bulk pork sausage. Cook over medium-low heat, stirring until the pork sausage is crumbly and well browned.

4 Add to the chestnut mixture with 2 cups fresh white bread crumbs. Season and add chopped fresh herbs. Beat an egg and add it to the stuffing to bind the ingredients.

Variations for Bulk Pork Sausage and Chestnut Stuffing

This stuffing is often left plain, especially when combined with sage and onion stuffing, but complementary herbs can be added.

Parsley and thyme: add 1 tablespoon chopped fresh thyme and 3 tablespoons chopped fresh parsley.

Tarragon and parsley: add 2 tablespoons chopped fresh tarragon and 2 tablespoons chopped fresh parsley.

Marjoram and orange: add 1 tablespoon dried marjoram and the grated rind of 1 orange.

Sage and parsley: add 3 tablespoons chopped fresh sage and 3 tablespoons chopped fresh parsley.

Sage and Onion Stuffing

This is a classic stuffing, which is suitable for all types of poultry.

1 Melt 2 tablespoons butter in a pan. Add four chopped onions and cook for 10–15 minutes, or until soft. Let cool.

2 Add the onions to 2 cups fresh white bread crumbs and 4 tablespoons chopped fresh sage. Season, then add one beaten egg and about ½ cup stock to bind the stuffing.

Stuffing the body cavity

This stuffing can be prepared in advance and chilled separately from the bird.

1 Rinse the body cavity under cold running water, then drain it well. (Wash the sink afterward.) Then dry the turkey, inside and out, with paper towels.

2 Insert the stuffing, packing it lightly, using your hands.

Stuffing the neck end

It is traditional to stuff the neck end with sage and onion stuffing. Remove the wishbone to make carving the breast easier.

1 Fold back the flap of skin at the neck end and then use a small, knife to cut out the wishbone, working right around the bone and cutting the meat as close to the bone as possible. Cut the bone free at the base on both sides.

2 Press the stuffing inside the shallow neck cavity.

3 Turn the bird over onto its breast and pull the neck skin over the stuffing.

4 Truss the bird to keep the flaps of skin at the neck and body cavities in place. If necessary, use a metal skewer to secure the skin while trussing the bird with string. Weigh the bird and the stuffing, and use both weights to calculate the cooking time.

Cooking and Serving Turkey

Turkey and chicken are fairly similar in taste and consistency so turkey can be cooked by several methods used for chicken. Turkeys have a slightly stronger flavor so it is usually just a question of preference. However, when choosing, bear in mind that thighs and leg meat can be a little tough because they contain more sinew.

Roasting

Turkeys are easy to roast, but require a little more attention than smaller birds. Check that the oven shelves are in the correct position before heating the oven.

1 Put the prepared, stuffed bird on a rack in a large roasting pan.

2 Smear the breast with butter. Season well and place in the oven.

Thawing Frozen Turkey

Turkey must be thawed completely before cooking. Place it on a rack in a dish, so that the liquid that drips from the bird as it thaws runs into the dish. Cover with plastic wrap. Place in the refrigerator.
For a 10-pound bird: allow 2–3 days in the refrigerator.
For a 15-pound bird: allow 3–4 days in the refrigerator.

3 Baste frequently during cooking. When the breast has browned, cover the bird with foil and continue cooking and basting.

4 To check if the meat is cooked, insert a metal skewer into the thickest part of the thigh. If the juices run clear, it is cooked. If they run pink, it is not ready. Return it to the oven and check again after 20 minutes. Remove the foil for the final 20 minutes of cooking to finish browning the skin and give it a crisp texture.

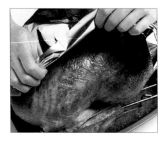

5 Remove it from the oven and cover with foil. Let rest for about 15 minutes before carving.

Roasting Times for Turkey

Preheat the oven to 350°F. Calculate the cooking time, according to the weight of the bird (including the stuffing weight). It is difficult to estimate the exact cooking time when roasting large birds, as the shape and proportion of breast meat and the quantity and position of stuffing all influence the finished result.
For birds up to 10 pounds: allow 20 minutes per 1 pound plus an extra 20 minutes.
For birds over 10 pounds: allow 18 minutes per 1 pound, plus an extra 20 minutes.
For birds over 15 pounds: allow 15 minutes per 1 pound, plus an extra 20 minutes.

Carving turkey

A sharp carving knife is essential.

1 Remove the trussing string. Hold the bird with a carving fork. Cut off the legs, then cut these in half, or carve the meat from the bones.

2 Make a horizontal cut across the breast just above the wing. Carve slices off the breast, then repeat on the other side. Arrange the slices on a warmed serving platter. Add the leg joints or meat to the platter.

Stir-frying turkey

Fillets of turkey breast are best for stir-frying, as thigh and leg meat can be slightly tough. Combine turkey with Asian ingredients, or stir-fry strips of meat with onions, mushrooms, and a dash of sherry for a lightly sauced dish.

1 Cut the breast meat across the grain into thin, even strips.

2 Heat a little oil in a wok or large, heavy skillet. Sunflower, corn, or peanut oils are useful for stir-frying, as they can be heated to a high temperature without smoking. Olive oil gives a good flavor, but it burns easily.

3 Stir-fry the turkey until golden brown. Cook the turkey in batches, if necessary, and remove the strips from the pan, continue until all the pieces are browned. Stir-fry the vegetables in the same pan, then return the turkey to the pan to finish cooking for a few minutes before serving.

Pan-frying turkey

This is a useful method for cooking fillets of turkey breast or fine scallops. It is also the first stage for braising or casseroling poultry. Small, neat portions of turkey thigh are ideal for casseroles.

1 Heat a little olive oil in a skillet. Add the turkey pieces and cook, turning occasionally, for about 15 minutes, or until the meat is golden on all sides.

2 Once the turkey has turned golden brown, season it well, and reduce the heat, then cover the skillet and continue cooking gently for 15–20 minutes, or until the meat is cooked through and succulent. Serve immediately.

Stewing and braising

Prepared diced turkey or portions cut from the thigh are good choices of turkey cuts for stewing or braising. Drumsticks can also be cooked by this method, rendering them succulent and flavorsome.

1 Brown the pieces of turkey as for pan-frying. Instead of using a skillet, a flameproof casserole can be used for browning and simmering or oven cooking.

2 When the pieces are browned, use a slotted spoon to remove them from the pan and set them aside.

3 Cook thickly sliced vegetables in the fat remaining in the casserole. As a simple base, try one onion and two carrots. Add other ingredients to taste, such as one sliced fennel bulb, two sliced celery stalks, two sliced garlic cloves, a bay leaf, and parsley, sage, or thyme.

4 Replace the turkey and pour in enough stock just to cover. Bring to simmering point, then reduce the heat, and cover the pan. Simmer on the stovetop for about 1 hour or place in a preheated oven at 350°F for 1–1½ hours.

Wines to Serve with Turkey

You can drink some of the same wines with turkey as you enjoy with chicken. However, turkey does have a stronger flavor and it can take a fuller, fruitier wine. Try a bright fruity red from the Côtes du Rhône or a lightly oaked white Burgundy.

THE
RECIPES

A range of recipes suitable for all occasions: light soups for lunches, quick meals
for midweek suppers, salads for summer evenings, and feasts for special dinners
as well as roasts, pastries, and pies, pasta, rice, and grain dishes, simple one-pot
dishes, barbecues, tasty stir-fries, and spicy meals.

SOUPS & APPETIZERS

A good chicken stock is often used as a base for many tasty soups, but in this chapter chicken plays a star role. There are hearty chicken soups for lunch or supper and light soups that are perfect for a first course.

This selection of first courses and appetizers uses imaginative ingredients and methods of cooking and preparation. With unusual examples from all around the world, you are sure to find something that is just right for any occasion.

Cream of Chicken Soup

A rich and flavorful creamy chicken soup makes a fabulous lunch served with crusty bread. It is essential to use a really strong, homemade chicken stock for this recipe to give the soup a full flavor.

INGREDIENTS

Serves 6

$^1/_4$ cup butter

2 onions, chopped

2 medium potatoes, chopped

1 large carrot, diced

1 celery stalk, diced

3 cups chicken stock

$^1/_4$ cup all-purpose flour

$^2/_3$ cup milk

6 ounces cooked chicken

$1^1/_4$ cups light cream

salt and ground black pepper

fresh parsley leaves,
   to garnish

1 Melt the butter in a large pan and cook the onions, potatoes, carrot, and celery gently for 5 minutes, but do not let the vegetables turn brown.

2 Add the stock and simmer gently for 30 minutes. Season with salt and pepper to taste. Process in a food processor or blender until smooth and then return to the pan. Blend the flour with the milk and stir into the soup. Cook over low heat, stirring, until the soup thickens.

3 Meanwhile, chop the chicken finely. Add the soup and heat through for 5 minutes. Add $^1/_3$ cup of the cream and simmer gently for 5 minutes more.

4 Serve in individual bowls topped with a swirl of the remaining cream and garnished with ground black pepper and parsley leaves.

Corn and Chicken Soup

This popular classic Chinese soup is a delicious warming dish and is very easy to make.

INGREDIENTS

Serves 4–6

1 skinless, boneless chicken breast portion
   (about 4 ounces), cubed
2 teaspoons light soy sauce
1 tablespoon Chinese rice wine
1 teaspoon cornstarch
4 tablespoons cold water
1 teaspoon sesame oil
2 tablespoons peanut oil
1 teaspoon grated fresh ginger root
4 cups chicken stock
15-ounce can creamed corn
8-ounce can corn kernels
2 eggs, beaten
2–3 scallions, green parts only, cut into
   tiny rounds
salt and ground black pepper

1 Grind the chicken in a food processor, taking care not to overprocess it. Transfer the chicken to a bowl and stir in the soy sauce, rice wine, cornstarch, water, sesame oil ,and seasoning. Cover with plastic wrap and let stand for about 15 minutes to absorb the flavors.

2 Heat a wok over medium heat. Add the peanut oil and swirl it around to coat the wok. Add the ginger and stir-fry for a few seconds. Then add the stock, creamed corn, and corn kernels. Bring to just below boiling point.

3 Spoon about 6 tablespoons of the hot liquid into the chicken mixture until it forms a smooth paste, and stir. Return to the wok. Gradually bring the liquid to a boil, stirring constantly, then simmer for 2–3 minutes, or until cooked.

4 Pour the beaten eggs into the soup in a slow, steady stream, using a fork or chopsticks to stir the top of the soup in a figure-eight pattern. The egg should set in lacy shreds. Serve immediately with the scallions sprinkled over the soup.

Chicken, Leek and Celery Soup

This makes a substantial main course soup when served with fresh crusty bread. You will need nothing more than a salad and cheese or just fresh fruit to follow.

INGREDIENTS

Serves 4–6

1 chicken, about 3 pounds
1 small head of celery, trimmed
1 onion, coarsely chopped
1 fresh bay leaf
a few fresh parsley stalks
a few fresh tarragon sprigs
10 cups cold water
3 large leeks
5 tablespoons butter
2 potatoes, cut into chunks
$2/3$ cup dry white wine
2–3 tablespoons light
   cream (optional)
salt and ground black pepper
$3^1/2$ ounces pancetta, broiled
   until crisp, to garnish

1 Cut the breast portions off the chicken and set aside. Chop the rest of the chicken carcass into 8–10 pieces and place in a pan.

2 Chop four or five of the outer stalks of the celery and add them to the pan with the onion. Tie the bay leaf, parsley, and tarragon together and add to the pan. Pour in the cold water to cover the ingredients and bring to a boil. Reduce the heat and cover, then simmer for $1^1/2$ hours.

3 Remove the chicken from the pan, and then cut off, and reserve the meat. Strain the stock, then return it to the pan, and boil rapidly until it has reduced to about $6^1/4$ cups.

4 Meanwhile, set about 5 ounces of the leeks aside. Slice the remaining leeks and the remaining celery, reserving any celery leaves. Chop the celery leaves and set aside to garnish the soup.

5 Melt half the butter in a large, heavy pan. Add the sliced leeks and celery, cover, and cook over low heat for about 10 minutes, or until softened but not browned. Add the potatoes, wine and 5 cups of the chicken stock.

6 Season to taste with salt and pepper, bring to a boil, then reduce the heat to low. Part-cover the pan and simmer the soup gently for 15–20 minutes, or until the potatoes are cooked.

7 Meanwhile, skin the reserved chicken breast portions and cut the flesh into small pieces. Melt the remaining butter in a skillet, add the chicken, and cook for about 5–7 minutes, or until tender.

8 Thickly slice the remaining leeks, add to the skillet, and cook, stirring occasionally, for 3–4 minutes, or until just cooked.

9 Process the soup with the cooked chicken from the stock in a food processor or blender. Taste and adjust the seasoning; add more stock if the soup is very thick.

10 Stir in the cream, if using, and the chicken and leek mixture. Reheat the soup and ladle into warm bowls. Crumble the pancetta over the soup and sprinkle with the chopped celery leaves.

Chicken, Avocado, and Garbanzo Soup

Chile gives the chicken, garbanzos, and creamy avocado a delicious kick. Enjoy this substantial soup for lunch or dinner on its own.

INGREDIENTS

Serves 6

6 1/4 cups chicken stock
1/2 chipotle chile, seeded
2 skinless, boneless chicken breast portions
1 medium avocado
4 scallions, thinly sliced
14-ounce can garbanzo beans, drained
salt and ground black pepper

1 Pour the stock into a pan and add the chile. Bring to a boil, add the chicken, lower the heat, and simmer for 10 minutes.

2 Remove the pan from the heat and lift out the whole chicken portions with a slotted spoon. Let cool a little.

3 Using two forks, shred the chicken into small pieces. Set the shredded chicken aside.

4 Pour the chicken stock into a food processor or blender. Process the mixture until smooth, then return to the pan.

5 Cut the avocado in half, remove the skin and pit, then slice the flesh into 3/4-inch pieces. Add it to the stock, with the scallions and garbanzos. Return the shredded chicken to the pan, season with salt and ground black pepper to taste, and heat gently.

6 When the soup is heated through, ladle into warm soup bowls and serve.

Chicken and Leek Soup with Prunes

This recipe is based on a traditional Scottish soup, Cock-a-leekie. The unusual combination of prunes and leeks is surprisingly delicious.

INGREDIENTS

Serves 6

1 chicken, about 4^1/$_2$ pounds

2 pounds leeks

1 fresh bay leaf

a few fresh parsley stalks and thyme sprigs

1 large carrot, thickly sliced

10 cups chicken stock

generous ^{1}/$_2$ cup pearl barley

^{1}/$_2$ cup ready-to-eat prunes

salt and ground black pepper

chopped fresh parsley, to garnish

1 Cut the breast portions off the chicken and set aside. Place the remaining chicken carcass in a large pan. Cut half the leeks into 2-inch lengths and add to the pan. Tie the bay leaf, parsley, and thyme together and add to the pan with the carrot and stock. Bring to a boil, then reduce the heat, and cover. Simmer for 1 hour. Skim off any scum when the water first boils and during simmering.

2 Add the chicken portions and cook for another 30 minutes. Let cool, then strain the stock. Reserve the chicken portions and meat from the carcass. Discard the skin, bones, vegetables, and herbs. Skim the fat from the stock, then return the stock to the pan.

3 Meanwhile, rinse the pearl barley thoroughly in a strainer under cold running water, then cook it in a large pan of boiling water for about 10 minutes. Drain, rinse well, and drain thoroughly.

4 Add the pearl barley to the stock. Bring to a boil, then lower the heat, and cook gently for 15–20 minutes. Season the soup.

5 Add the prunes. Slice the remaining leeks and add them to the pan. Bring the ingredients to a boil, then simmer very gently for 10 minutes, or until the leeks are just cooked and tender.

6 Slice all the chicken meat and add to the soup. Reheat, then ladle the soup into deep plates, and sprinkle with chopped parsley.

Mulligatawny Soup

A good chicken stock makes the base for this popular spicy soup. It was adapted from a Tamil recipe—known as milakutanni *(pepper water)—during the days of the British Raj in India.*

INGREDIENTS

Serves 4

1/4 cup butter or 4 tablespoons oil

2 large chicken pieces, about
   12 ounces each

1 onion, chopped

1 carrot, chopped

1 small turnip, chopped

about 1 tablespoon curry powder, to taste

4 cloves

6 black peppercorns, lightly crushed

1/4 cup red lentils

3 3/4 cups chicken stock

1/4 cup golden raisins

salt and ground black pepper

2 Add the onion, carrot, and turnip to the pan and cook, stirring occasionally, until lightly colored. Stir in the curry powder, cloves, and peppercorns, and cook for 1–2 minutes. Add the lentils.

3 Pour in the stock and bring to a boil. Add the golden raisins and chicken with any juices from the plate. Cover and simmer gently for about 1 1/4 hours.

4 Remove the chicken from the pan and discard the skin and bones. Chop the flesh, return to the soup, and reheat. Check and adjust the seasoning before serving the soup in warm bowls.

1 Melt the butter or heat the oil in a large pan and brown the chicken over a medium heat. Transfer the chicken to a plate.

COOK'S TIP

Red split lentils will give the best color for this dish, although green or brown lentils could be used if you like.

Chicken and Lentil Soup

A chunky soup that will make a good lunchtime dish.

INGREDIENTS

Serves 4

2 tablespoons butter or margarine

1 large carrot, chopped

1 onion, chopped

1 leek, white part only, chopped

1 celery stalk, chopped

1$^{1}/_{2}$ cups chopped mushrooms

3 tablespoons dry white wine

4 cups chicken stock

2 teaspoons dried thyme

1 bay leaf

$^{1}/_{2}$ cup brown or green lentils

2 cups diced cooked chicken

salt and ground black pepper

1 Melt the butter or margarine in a large pan. Add the carrot, onion, leek, celery, and chopped mushrooms. Cook over low heat for 3–5 minutes, or until softened.

2 Stir in the wine and chicken stock. Bring to a boil and skim off any foam that rises to the surface. Add the thyme and bay leaf. Reduce the heat, cover, and simmer for 30 minutes.

3 Add the lentils and continue cooking gently, covered, for another 30–40 minutes, or until they are just tender, occasionally stirring the soup.

4 Stir in the diced chicken and season to taste with salt and pepper. Cook until just heated through. Ladle the soup into warm bowls and serve hot.

Greek Chicken and Egg Soup

Avgolemono soup is a great favorite in Greece and is a fine example of how a few ingredients, if carefully chosen and cooked, can make a marvelous-tasting dish. It is essential to use a well-flavored stock.

INGREDIENTS

Serves 4

3³/4 cups chicken stock

generous ¹/3 cup long grain rice, soaked and drained

3 egg yolks

2–4 tablespoons lemon juice

2 tablespoons finely chopped fresh parsley

salt and ground black pepper

lemon slices and parsley sprigs, to garnish

1 Pour the stock into a pan, bring to simmering point, then add the drained rice. Half-cover and cook for about 12 minutes, or until the rice is just tender. Season with salt and pepper.

2 Whisk the egg yolks in a bowl, then add about 2 tablespoons of the lemon juice to the eggs, whisking constantly until the mixture is smooth and bubbly. Add a ladleful of stock with the rice and whisk again.

3 Remove the stock and rice from the heat and gradually add the egg mixture, whisking constantly. The soup will turn a lemon color and will thicken slightly.

4 Taste and add more lemon juice if necessary. Stir in the parsley. Serve the soup immediately, without reheating, garnished with lemon slices and parsley sprigs.

Pasta Soup with Chicken Livers

This is a mouthwatering soup that can be served as either a first or main course. Even those who do not normally like chicken livers may well change their minds when they taste this delicious soup.

INGREDIENTS

Serves 4–6

4 ounces chicken livers, thawed if frozen

1 tablespoon olive oil

pat of butter

4 garlic cloves, crushed

3 sprigs each of fresh parsley, marjoram,
     and sage, chopped

leaves from 1 fresh thyme sprig, chopped

5–6 fresh basil leaves, chopped

1–2 tablespoons dry white wine

2 × 11-ounce cans condensed
     chicken consommé

2 cups fresh shelled or
     frozen peas

$^1/_2$ cup dried pasta shapes, such
     as farfalle

2–3 scallions, sliced

salt and ground black pepper

1 Cut the livers into small pieces. Heat the oil and butter in a skillet, add the garlic and herbs, with salt and pepper to taste, and cook gently for a few minutes. Add the livers, increase the heat to high, and stir-fry for a few minutes, or until they change color and become dry. Pour the wine over the livers. Cook until it evaporates, then remove the livers from the heat, and taste for seasoning.

2 Tip both cans of condensed chicken consommé into a large pan and add water to as directed on the can labels. Add an extra can of water, then stir in a little salt and pepper to taste, and bring the soup to a boil.

3 Add the fresh or frozen peas to the pan and simmer for about 5 minutes, then add the pasta, and bring the soup back to a boil, stirring constantly. Simmer, stirring frequently, until the pasta is only just *al dente*: about 8 minutes, or according to the instructions on the packet.

4 Add the cooked chicken livers and scallions and heat through gently for 2–3 minutes. Taste and adjust the seasoning if necessary. Serve hot, in warm bowls.

Chicken Soup with Dumplings

This traditional soup is served with matzo dumplings. It is a hearty and comforting meal, ideal for those recovering from sickness, and is traditionally often known as the Jewish antibiotic.

INGREDIENTS

Serves 6–8

1 chicken, about $2^1/_4$–$3^1/_4$ pounds, cut
    into portions
2–3 onions
12–17 cups water
3–5 carrots, thickly sliced
3–5 celery stalks, thickly sliced
1 small parsnip, cut in half
2–3 tablespoons coarsely chopped
    fresh parsley
2–3 tablespoons chopped fresh dill
1–2 pinches ground turmeric
2 chicken bouillon cubes
2 garlic cloves, finely chopped (optional)
salt and ground black pepper

For the dumplings
$^3/_4$ cup medium matzo meal
2 eggs, lightly beaten
3 tablespoons vegetable oil or rendered
    chicken fat
1 garlic clove, finely chopped (optional)
2 tablespoons chopped fresh parsley, plus
    extra to garnish
$^1/_2$ onion, finely grated
1–2 pinches of chicken bouillon cube or
    powder (optional)
about 6 tablespoons water

1 Put the chicken pieces in a very large pan. Keeping them whole, cut a large cross in the stem end of each onion and add to the pan with the water, carrots, celery, parsnip, parsley, half the fresh dill, the turmeric, salt, and ground black pepper.

2 Cover the pan and bring to a boil, then immediately lower the heat to a simmer. Skim and discard the scum that surfaces. (Scum will continue to form but it is only the first scum that rises that will detract from the clarity and flavor of the soup.)

3 Add the crumbled bouillon cubes and simmer gently for 2–3 hours. Skim off the fat or chill the soup and remove the layer of solid fat that forms.

4 To make the dumplings, in a large bowl combine the matzo meal with the eggs, oil or fat, chopped garlic, if using, parsley, onion, salt, and pepper. Add only a little chicken bouillon cube or powder, if using, as these are salty. Add the water and mix together until the mixture is about the consistency of a thick, soft paste.

5 Cover the matzo batter and chill for 30 minutes, during which time the mixture will become firm.

6 Bring a pan of water to a boil and have a bowl of water next to the stove. Dip two tablespoons into the water, then take a spoonful of the matzo batter. With wet hands, roll it into a ball, then slip it into the boiling water, and reduce the heat so that the water simmers. Continue with the remaining matzo batter, working relatively quickly, then cover the pan, and cook for 15–20 minutes.

7 Remove the dumplings from the pan with a slotted spoon and transfer to a plate for about 20 minutes to firm up.

8 To serve, reheat the soup, adding the remaining dill and the garlic, if using. Put two to three dumplings in each bowl, pour in the soup, and garnish with parsley.

Pumpkin, Rice, and Chicken Soup

This is a warm, comforting soup, mildly spiced with cardamom. It makes an ideal fall lunch or supper when pumpkins are readily available.

INGREDIENTS

Serves 4

1 wedge of pumpkin, about 1 pound

1 tablespoon sunflower oil

2 tablespoons butter

6 green cardamom pods

2 leeks, chopped

generous ¹/2 cup basmati rice, soaked

1¹/2 cups milk

salt and ground black pepper

strips of pared orange rind,
    to garnish

multigrain or whole-wheat bread,
    to serve

For the stock

2 chicken quarters

1 onion, quartered

2 carrots, chopped

1 celery stalk, chopped

6–8 peppercorns

3³/4 cups water

1 First make the chicken stock. Place the chicken quarters, onion, carrots, celery, and peppercorns in a large pan. Pour in the water and gradually bring to a boil. Skim the surface if necessary, then lower the heat, cover, and simmer gently for 1 hour.

2 Strain the chicken stock into a clean, large bowl, discarding the vegetables. Skin and bone the chicken pieces and cut the flesh into strips.

3 Skin the pumpkin and remove all the seeds and pith, so that you have about 12 ounces of flesh. Cut the flesh into 1-inch cubes.

4 Heat the oil and butter in a pan and cook the cardamom pods for 2–3 minutes, or until slightly swollen. Add the leeks and pumpkin. Cook, stirring, for 3–4 minutes over medium heat, then lower the heat, cover, and cook for 5 minutes more, or until the pumpkin is quite soft, stirring once or twice.

5 Measure 2¹/2 cups of the reserved chicken stock and add to the pumpkin mixture. Bring to a boil, then lower the heat, cover with a lid, and simmer gently for 10–15 minutes, or until the pumpkin is soft.

6 Pour the remaining stock into a measuring cup and make up with water to 1¹/4 cups. Drain the rice and put it into a pan. Pour in the stock, bring to a boil, then simmer for about 10 minutes, or until the rice is tender. Season with salt and pepper to taste.

7 Remove the cardamom pods, then process the soup in a food processor of blender until smooth. Pour back into a clean pan and stir in the milk, chicken, and rice (with any stock that has not been absorbed). Heat gently until simmering. Garnish with the strips of pared orange rind and ground black pepper, and serve with multigrain or whole-wheat bread.

Rich Minestrone

Served with crusty Italian bread, this delicious soup makes a filling meal.

INGREDIENTS

Serves 4–6

1 tablespoon olive oil

2 chicken thighs

3 fatty bacon strips, chopped

1 onion, finely chopped

a few fresh basil leaves, shredded

a few fresh rosemary leaves, finely chopped

1 tablespoon chopped fresh flat
  leaf parsley

2 potatoes, cut into $1^1/2$-inch cubes

1 large carrot, cut into $^1/2$-inch cubes

2 small zucchini, cut into $^1/2$-inch cubes

1–2 celery stalks, cut into $^1/2$-inch cubes

4 cups chicken stock

$1^3/4$ cups fresh shelled or
  frozen peas

scant 1 cup stellette or other dried tiny
  soup pasta

salt and ground black pepper

coarsely shaved Parmesan cheese,
  to serve

fresh basil leaves, to garnish

1 Heat the oil in a large pan, add the chicken, and cook for about 5 minutes on each side. Remove with a slotted spoon and set aside.

2 Lower the heat, add the bacon, onion, and herbs to the pan, and stir. Cook for 5 minutes. Add the potatoes, carrot, zucchini, and celery, and cook for 5–7 minutes.

COOK'S TIP

For extra flavor, add any Parmesan rind to the soup.

3 Return the chicken thighs to the pan, add the stock, and bring to a boil. Cover and cook over low heat for 35–40 minutes, stirring the soup occasionally.

4 Remove the chicken thighs with a slotted spoon and place them on a board. Stir the peas and pasta into the soup and bring back to a boil. Simmer, stirring frequently, until the pasta is *al dente*: 7–8 minutes, or according to the instructions on the packet.

5 Meanwhile, remove and discard the chicken skin, then remove the meat from the bones, and cut it into $^1/2$-inch pieces. Return the meat to the soup and heat through. Taste for seasoning and ladle into warm bowls. Sprinkle Parmesan shavings over it, garnish with one or two basil leaves, and serve.

Italian Minestrone

Use a leftover carcass from a roast chicken to make this tasty Italian soup. The sprinkling of salty ricotta salata at the finish is typical of Puglian cooking.

INGREDIENTS

Serves 4

1 roast chicken carcass

1 onion, quartered lengthwise

1 carrot, coarsely chopped

1 celery stalk, coarsely chopped

a few black peppercorns

1 small handful mixed fresh herbs, such as parsley and thyme

1 chicken bouillon cube

about 6$^1/4$ cups water

$^1/2$ cup tubetti, or other soup pasta

salt and ground black pepper

$^1/2$ cup coarsely grated or crumbled ricotta salata, (see Cook's Tips), and

2 tablespoons fresh mint leaves, to serve

1 Break the carcass into pieces and place in a large pan. Add the onion, carrot, celery, peppercorns, and herbs, then crumble in the bouillon cube and add a good pinch of salt. Cover the chicken generously with cold water and bring to a boil over high heat.

2 Lower the heat, half-cover the pan, and simmer gently for about 1 hour. Remove the pan from the heat and let cool completely, then strain the liquid through a colander or strainer into a clean large pan.

3 Remove any meat from the carcass, cut it into bitesize pieces, and set aside. Discard the carcass and flavoring ingredients.

4 Bring the stock in the pan to a boil, and add the pasta. Simmer, stirring frequently, until only just *al dente*: 7–8 minutes, or according to the instructions on the packet.

5 Add the pieces of chicken and heat through for a few minutes, by which time the pasta will be ready. Taste for seasoning. Serve hot in warm bowls, sprinkled with the ricotta salata and mint.

COOK'S TIPS

• Ricotta salata is a salted and dried version of ricotta cheese. It has a firmer texture, and can be diced, crumbled, and even grated. It is available from some delicatessens, good cheese stores, and large supermarkets. If you can't find it, use feta cheese.

• Use other small, hollow pasta shapes for this soup, if you like.

Christmas Tortellini

These tortellini are served on the day after Christmas in Emilia-Romagna, Italy. Traditionally, they were made with ground leftover capon from Christmas Day, but nowadays chicken or turkey is often used.

INGREDIENTS

Serves 6–8

1³/4 cups all-purpose flour, plus extra
   for dusting
2 extra large eggs, beaten
1 tablespoon oil
9 cups beef stock, made with
   bouillon cubes or diluted
   canned consommé
salt and ground black pepper
freshly grated Parmesan cheese,
   to serve

For the filling
2 tablespoons butter
2¹/4 cups ground chicken
   or turkey
1 teaspoon chopped fresh rosemary
1 teaspoon chopped fresh sage
freshly grated nutmeg
1 cup chicken stock
4 tablespoons freshly grated
   Parmesan cheese
3¹/2 ounces mortadella sausage, very
   finely chopped
1 medium egg

1 To make the filling, melt the butter in a medium skillet, then add the ground chicken or turkey and chopped herbs.

2 Add a little nutmeg, salt, and pepper to taste. Cook gently for 5–6 minutes, stirring frequently and breaking up any lumps in the meat with a wooden spoon.

3 Add the stock and mix well, then simmer gently, uncovered, for 15–20 minutes, or until the meat is cooked and quite dry.

4 Transfer the meat to a bowl with a slotted spoon and leave to cool. Add the grated Parmesan, mortadella, and egg to the meat and stir well to mix.

5 Sift the flour and a pinch of salt onto a clean counter and make a well in the center with your fist. Pour the eggs and oil into the well. Gradually mix in the eggs with your fingers. Knead the pasta until smooth, then wrap, and let rest for at least 30 minutes.

6 Using a pasta machine, roll out one-quarter of the pasta into two 18-inch lengths. With a 2-inch fluted ravioli or cookie cutter, stamp out 8–10 disks from one of the pasta strips.

7 Using a teaspoon, put a little mound of filling in the center of each disk, then brush a little water around the edge of the pasta filling. Fold the disk in half over the filling so that the edges do not quite meet. Press to seal.

8 Wrap each tortellini shape around your index finger and pinch the bottom corners together to seal securely.

9 Put the tortellini in a single layer on floured dishtowels, dust lightly with flour, and leave to dry while repeating the process with the remaining dough to make 64–80 tortellini altogether. If you have any stuffing left, reroll the pasta trimmings and make more tortellini.

10 Bring the beef stock to a boil in a large pan. Drop in the tortellini, then bring back to a boil, and boil for 4–5 minutes. Taste the stock and season with salt and pepper if necessary.

11 Pour the tortellini and stock into a warm, large soup tureen, sprinkle with a little grated Parmesan cheese, and serve immediately. Hand around more Parmesan separately.

Chicken Stellette Soup

2 Add the scallions and sliced mushrooms to the stock.

3 Slice the chicken thinly, then set aside.

4 Add the pasta to the pan, cover, and simmer for 7–8 minutes. Just before serving, add the chicken, wine, and parsley, and heat through for 2–3 minutes.

Tiny pasta stars—stellette—look attractive in soup, and add taste and texture. This low-fat soup with mushrooms, chicken, and wine is full of flavor.

INGREDIENTS

Serves 4–6

3³/4 cups chicken stock

1 bay leaf

4 scallions, sliced

3 cups white mushrooms, sliced

4 ounces boneless chicken
  breast portion, cooked
  and skinned

¹/2 cup soup pasta (stellette)

²/3 cup dry white wine

1 tablespoon chopped fresh parsley

salt and ground black pepper

1 Put the stock and bay leaf into a pan and bring to a boil.

Chicken Vermicelli Soup with Egg Shreds

This light soup can be put together in a matter of moments and is full of flavor.

INGREDIENTS

Serves 4–6

3 extra large eggs

2 tablespoons chopped fresh cilantro
  or parsley

6$\frac{1}{4}$ cups good chicken stock or
  canned consommé

1 cup dried vermicelli or angel hair pasta

4 ounces skinless, boneless cooked chicken
  breast portion, sliced

salt and ground black pepper

3 Roll up each omelet and slice thinly into shreds. Set aside.

4 Bring the stock or consommé to a boil and add the pasta, breaking it into short lengths. Cook for 3–5 minutes, or until the pasta is almost tender, then add the chicken, salt, and pepper. Heat through for 2–3 minutes, then stir in the egg shreds. Serve immediately.

1 First make the egg shreds. Whisk the eggs together in a small bowl and stir in the chopped cilantro or parsley.

2 Heat a small, nonstick skillet and pour in 2–3 tablespoons of the egg, swirling to cover the base evenly. Cook until set. Transfer to a cutting board. Repeat until all the mixture is used up.

Thai Chicken Soup with Ginger and Lime

A fragrant blend of lemongrass, ginger, and lime, with a hint of chile.

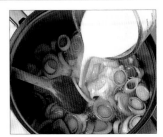

INGREDIENTS

Serves 4

1 teaspoon oil

1–2 fresh red chiles, seeded and chopped

2 garlic cloves, crushed

1 large leek, thinly sliced

2$^{1}/_{2}$ cups chicken stock

1$^{2}/_{3}$ cups coconut milk

1 pound skinless chicken, cut into pieces

2 tablespoons Thai fish sauce

1 lemongrass stalk, split

1-inch piece fresh ginger root, peeled and
    finely chopped

1 teaspoon sugar

$^{3}/_{4}$ cup frozen peas, thawed

3 tablespoons chopped cilantro

1 Heat the oil in a large pan and cook the chiles and garlic for about 2 minutes. Add the leek and cook for 2 minutes more.

2 Stir in the stock and coconut milk and bring to a boil.

3 Add the chicken, with the Thai fish sauce, lemongrass, ginger, and sugar.

4 Simmer, covered, for about 15 minutes, or until the chicken is tender, stirring occasionally. Add the peas and cook for about 3 minutes more. Remove the lemongrass and stir in the cilantro just before serving.

Thai Chicken Soup

Piquant Thai flavorings blended with coconut give this soup a terrific taste.

INGREDIENTS

Serves 4

1 tablespoon vegetable oil

1 garlic clove, finely chopped

2 skinless, boneless chicken
breast portions, about 6 ounces
each, chopped

$1/2$ teaspoon ground turmeric

$1/4$ teaspoon hot chili powder

$1^1/2$ cups coconut cream

$3^3/4$ cups hot chicken stock

2 tablespoons lemon or
lime juice

2 tablespoons crunchy peanut butter

1 cup thread egg noodles, broken into
small pieces

1 tablespoon scallions, finely chopped

1 tablespoon cilantro

salt and ground black black pepper

2 tablespoons dry unsweetened
shredded coconut and $1/2$ fresh red
chile, seeded and finely chopped,
to garnish

2 Stir the coconut cream into the
chicken stock in a pitcher until
well combined. Pour the mixture
onto the chicken and add the
lemon or lime juice, peanut butter,
and thread egg noodles.

3 Cover the pan and simmer for
about 15 minutes.

1 Heat the oil in a pan and cook
the garlic for 1 minute. Add the
chicken and spices and stir-fry for
3–4 minutes.

4 Add the scallions and fresh
cilantro, then season well,
and cook for 5 minutes more.
Meanwhile, place the shredded
coconut and chopped chile in
a small skillet and heat for
2–3 minutes, stirring frequently.

5 Ladle the soup into bowls,
sprinkle with the coconut and
chile, and serve.

Pot-cooked Chicken and Udon in Miso Soup

3 Heat the water and dashi-no-moto in a large pan. When it has come to a boil, add the chicken pieces, shiitake mushrooms, and abura-age and cook for 5 minutes. Remove the pan from the heat and add the scallions.

4 Put the mirin and miso paste into a small bowl. Scoop 2 tablespoons soup from the pan and mix this in well.

5 To cook the udon noodles, boil at least 9 cups water in a large pan. The water should not come higher than two-thirds of the depth of the pan. Cook the udon for 6 minutes and drain.

6 Put the udon in a large, flameproof clay pot or casserole. Mix the miso paste into the soup and check the taste. Add more miso if required. Ladle in enough soup to cover the udon, and arrange the rest of the soup ingredients on top of the udon.

Udon is a white wheat noodle, cooked here with a rich miso soup topped with eggs. Chicken is the main ingredient in this authentic Japanese dish.

INGREDIENTS

Serves 4

7 ounces skinless, boneless chicken
    breast portion
2 teaspoons sake
2 abura-age (see Cook's Tip)
3³/4 cups water mixed with 1¹/2 teaspoons
    dashi-no-moto (see Cook's Tip)
6 large fresh shiitake mushrooms, stems
    removed, quartered
4 scallions, trimmed and chopped into
    ¹/8-inch lengths
2 tablespoons mirin
about 3¹/2 ounces aka miso or hatcho miso
11 ounces dried udon noodles
4 eggs

1 Cut the chicken into bitesize pieces. Sprinkle with sake and marinate for 15 minutes.

2 Put the abura-age in a strainer and rinse with freshly boiled water to wash off the oil. Drain and cut each into four squares.

COOK'S TIP

Abura-age are pouches made from beancurd that have been deep-fried. Dashi-no-moto are freeze-dried granules for making dashi stock— traditionally used in Japanese cooking. All the ingredients for this recipe are available from Japanese supermarkets.

7 Put the soup on medium heat and break the eggs on top. When the soup bubbles, wait for 1 minute, then cover, and remove from the heat. Let stand for 2 minutes before serving in warm individual bowls.

Chicken Steamboat

This chicken dish is named after the utensil in which it is cooked—like a fondue pot, with a funnel and a moat. Electric steamboats or traditional fondue pots can be used instead.

INGREDIENTS

Serves 8

8 Chinese dried mushrooms, soaked for
    30 minutes in warm water to cover

6^1/4 cups chicken stock

2 teaspoons rice wine or medium-
    dry sherry

2 teaspoons sesame oil

8 ounces each lean pork and round steak,
    thinly sliced

1 skinless, boneless chicken breast portion,
    thickly sliced

2 chicken livers, trimmed and sliced

2 cups raw shrimp, peeled

1 pound white fish fillets, skinned
    and cubed

7 ounces fish balls (from Asian stores)

4 ounces fried beancurd, each
    piece halved

leafy greens, such as lettuce, Chinese
    cabbage, spinach leaves, and mizuna, cut
    into 6-inch lengths

8 ounces Chinese rice vermicelli

8 eggs

^{1}/2 bunch scallions, chopped

salt and ground white pepper

selection of sauces, including soy sauce
    with sesame seeds; soy sauce with
    crushed ginger; chili sauce; plum sauce,
    and hot mustard, to serve

1 Drain the mushrooms, reserving the soaking liquid. Cut off and discard the stems and slice the caps.

2 Pour the stock into a large pan, with the rice wine or sherry, sesame oil, and reserved mushroom liquid. Bring the mixture to a boil, then season with salt and white pepper. Reduce the heat and simmer gently.

3 Put the meat, fish, beancurd, greens, and mushrooms in bowls on the table. Soak the vermicelli in hot water for 5 minutes, drain, and place in eight soup bowls. Crack an egg for each diner into a small bowl. Put the sauces in bowls beside each diner.

4 Add the scallions to the stock, and bring to a boil. Pour the liquid into a lighted steamboat at the table. Each guest then lowers a few chosen morsels into the boiling stock, using chopsticks or fondue forks. After a minute or two, they are removed and eaten with the sauces.

5 When all the ingredients have been cooked, the stock will be concentrated and enriched. Add boiling water if necessary. Pour the hot soup into the soup bowls containing the soaked noodles and slide a whole egg into each, stirring until it cooks and forms threads.

Celebration Soup

This chicken brunch soup is traditionally served at new year in Japan. The ingredients can be bought from a Japanese supermarket.

INGREDIENTS

Serves 4

4 dried shiitake mushrooms
11 ounces chicken thighs, bones removed
    and reserved
11 ounces salmon fillet, skin on, scaled
2 tablespoons sake
2 ounces satoimo or Jerusalem artichokes
2 ounces daikon, peeled
2 ounces carrots, peeled
4 scallions, white part only, trimmed
4 mitsuba sprigs, root part removed
1 yuzu or lime
4 large raw jumbo shrimp, peeled, but with
    tails left on
2 tablespoons shoyu
8 canned gingko nuts (optional)
8 mochi slices
salt

1 First, make the soup stock. Soak the dried shiitake overnight in 4 cups cold water. Remove the shiitake and pour the water into a pan. Bring to a boil, add the chicken bones, then reduce the heat to medium. Skim frequently to remove the scum. After 20 minutes, reduce the heat to low. Simmer for 30 minutes, or until the liquid has reduced by a third. Strain the stock into another pan.

2 Chop the chicken and salmon into small cubes. Par-boil them both in boiling water with 1 tablespoon sake for 1 minute. Drain and wash off the scum.

3 Scrub the satoimo or Jerusalem artichokes, and peel thickly. Put in a pan and add water to cover. Add a pinch of salt and bring to a boil. Reduce the heat to medium, cook for 15 minutes, and drain. Rinse the satoimo (to remove the sticky juice) under running water. Wipe gently with paper towels. Cut the satoimo or artichokes, daikon, and carrots into ½-inch cubes.

4 Remove and discard the stems from the shiitake, and slice the caps thinly. Chop the scallions into 1-inch lengths.

5 Put the mitsuba sprigs into a strainer and pour hot water over them. Divide the leaf and stalk parts. Take a stalk and fold it into two, then tie it in the middle to make a bow. Make four bows.

6 Cut the yuzu or lime into four ⅛-inch thick round slices. Hollow out the inside to make rings of peel.

7 Add the remaining sake to the soup stock and bring to a boil. Add the daikon, carrots, and shiitake, then reduce the heat to medium, and cook for 15 minutes.

8 Put the shrimp, satoimo or artichokes, scallions, chicken, and salmon into the pan. Wait for 5 minutes, then add the shoyu. Reduce the heat to low and add the gingko nuts, if using.

9 Cut the mochi in half cross-wise. Toast under a medium preheated broiler. Turn every minute, or until both sides are golden and the pieces have started to swell like a balloon; this will take about 5 minutes.

10 Quickly place the toasted mochi in individual soup bowls and pour the hot soup over the top. Arrange a mitsuba leaf in the centre of each bowl, put a yuzu or lime ring on top, and lay a mitsuba bow across. Serve.

Galangal, Chicken, and Coconut Soup

This aromatic soup is intensely flavored with galangal, lemongrass, and kaffir lime leaves.

INGREDIENTS

Serves 4–6

4 lemongrass stalks, roots trimmed

3 1/2 cups canned coconut milk

2 cups chicken stock

1-inch piece of galangal, peeled and
    thinly sliced

10 black peppercorns, crushed

10 kaffir lime leaves, torn

11 ounces skinless, boneless chicken breast
    portions, cut into thin strips

1 2/3 cups mushrooms, halved

2 ounces baby corncobs, quartered

4 tablespoons lime juice

3 tablespoons Thai fish sauce

chopped chiles, scallions, and cilantro,
    to garnish

1 Cut off the lower 2 inches from each lemongrass stalk and chop the end finely. Bruise the remaining pieces of stalk. Bring the coconut milk and chicken stock to a boil in a large pan. Add the lemongrass, the galangal, peppercorns, and half the lime leaves, then lower the heat, and simmer gently for 10 minutes. Strain the liquid into a clean pan.

2 Return the soup to the heat, then add the chicken, mushrooms, and corn. Simmer for 5–7 minutes, or until the chicken is cooked.

3 Stir in the lime juice and Thai fish sauce, then add the remaining lime leaves. Serve the soup hot, garnished with chiles, scallions, and cilantro.

Mini Chicken Spring Rolls

Light phyllo pastry encloses a chicken and vegetable filling for these dainty rolls.

INGREDIENTS

Makes 20

1 green chile

$^1/_2$ cup vegetable oil

1 small onion, finely chopped

1 garlic clove, crushed

3 ounces cooked boneless chicken breast portion, skinned

1 small carrot, cut into fine batons

1 scallion, thinly sliced

1 small red bell pepper, seeded and cut into fine batons

$^1/_4$ cup bean sprouts

1 tablespoon sesame oil

4 sheets phyllo pastry, thawed if frozen

1 egg white, lightly beaten

fresh chives, to garnish (optional)

3 tablespoons light soy sauce, to serve

1 Carefully remove the seeds from the chile and chop finely, wearing latex gloves to protect your hands, if necessary.

2 Heat a wok or large skillet, then add 2 tablespoons of the vegetable oil. When hot, add the onion, garlic, and chile. Stir-fry for 1 minute.

3 Slice the chicken thinly, then add to the wok and stir-fry over high heat, stirring and tossing constantly until browned.

4 Add the carrot, scallion, and red bell pepper and stir-fry for 2 minutes. Add the bean sprouts, stir in the sesame oil, remove from the heat, and let cool.

COOK'S TIP

Always keep phyllo pastry sheets covered with a damp, clean cloth until needed, to prevent them from drying out.

5 Cut each sheet of phyllo into five short strips. Place a small amount of filling at one end of each strip, then fold in the long sides, and roll up the pastry. Seal and glaze the parcels with the egg white, then chill, uncovered, for 15 minutes before cooking.

6 Wipe out the wok with paper towels, heat it, and add the remaining vegetable oil. When the oil is hot, cook the rolls, in batches, until crisp and golden brown. Drain on paper towels. Garnish with chives, if using, and serve with light soy sauce for dipping.

Spicy Chicken Canapés

These tiny little cocktail sandwiches have a spicy filling, and are finished with different toppings. Use square bread so that you can cut out more rounds and have less wastage.

INGREDIENTS

Makes 18

3/4 cup finely chopped cooked chicken

2 scallions, finely chopped

2 tablespoons chopped red
    bell pepper

6 tablespoons curry mayonnaise

6 slices white bread

1 tablespoon paprika

1 tablespoon chopped fresh parsley

2 tablespoons chopped
    salted peanuts

1 Combine the chicken, scallions, bell pepper, and half the curry mayonnaise in a bowl.

2 Spread the mixture over three of the bread slices and sandwich with the remaining bread, pressing well together. Spread the remaining curry mayonnaise over the top and cut into 1¹/₂-inch rounds using a plain cookie cutter.

3 Dip into paprika, chopped parsley, or chopped nuts and arrange on a plate.

Chicken Cigars

Serve these small crispy rolls warm as canapés with drinks before dinner, as part of a party buffet table, or as a tempting first course with a crisp, colorful salad.

INGREDIENTS

Serves 4

10-ounce packet of phyllo pastry, thawed
  if frozen
3 tablespoons olive oil
fresh parsley, to garnish

For the filling

3 cups ground raw chicken
1 egg, beaten
1/2 teaspoon ground cinnamon
1/2 teaspoon ground ginger
2 tablespoons raisins
1 tablespoon olive oil
1 small onion, finely chopped
salt and ground black pepper

1 To make the filling, combine the chicken, egg, cinnamon, ginger, and raisins in a bowl. Season to taste. Heat the oil in a large skillet and cook the onion until tender. Let cool. Add the mixed filling ingredients.

2 Preheat the oven to 350°F. Once the phyllo pastry packet has been opened, keep the pastry covered at all times with a damp dishtowel. Work fast, as the pastry dries out very quickly when it is exposed to the air. Unravel the pastry and cut into 10 x 4in strips.

3 Take a strip, brush with a little oil and place a spoonful of filling 1/2 inch from the end.

4 Fold the sides inward and roll into a cigar shape. Place on a greased cookie sheet and brush with oil. Bake for 20–25 minutes, or until golden brown and crisp. Garnish with fresh parsley.

Chicken Goujons

Serve these crisp goujons and the herbed dip as a first course for eight people or as a filling main course for four. Delicious served with new baby potatoes and salad greens.

INGREDIENTS

Serves 8

4 skinless, boneless chicken
   breast portions
3 cups fresh bread crumbs
1 teaspoon ground coriander
2 teaspoons paprika
$^1/_2$ teaspoon ground cumin
3 tablespoons all-purpose flour
2 eggs, beaten
oil, for deep-frying
salt and ground black pepper
lemon slices, to garnish
sprigs of fresh cilantro,
   to garnish

For the dip

$1^1/_4$ cups strained plain yogurt
2 tablespoons lemon juice
4 tablespoons chopped fresh cilantro
4 tablespoons chopped fresh parsley

3 Combine the bread crumbs, spices, and seasoning. Toss the chicken into the flour, keeping the pieces separate.

5 Thoroughly mix all the ingredients for the dip together and season to taste. Cover and chill until required.

4 Dip the goujons into the egg, then coat in the bread crumbs.

6 Heat the oil in a heavy pan. It is ready for deep-frying when a piece of bread tossed into the oil sizzles on the surface. Cook the goujons, in batches, until golden and crisp. Drain on paper towels and keep warm in the oven until all the chicken has been fried. Garnish with lemon slices and sprigs of fresh cilantro and serve with the yogurt dip.

1 Divide the chicken breast portions into two natural fillets. Place them between two sheets of plastic wrap and, using a rolling pin, flatten each one to a thickness of $^1/_2$ inch.

2 Cut the chicken into diagonal 1-inch strips.

Chinese Chicken Wings

Choose these tasty chicken wings as a first course for an informal meal as they are best eaten with the fingers. Make sure you provide finger bowls and plenty of paper napkins.

INGREDIENTS

Serves 4

12 chicken wings

3 garlic cloves, crushed

$1^1/2$-inch piece of fresh ginger root, peeled
  and grated

juice of 1 large lemon

3 tablespoons soy sauce

3 tablespoons honey

$1/2$ teaspoon chili powder

$2/3$ cup chicken stock

salt and ground black pepper

lemon wedges, to garnish

1 Remove the wing tips and use to make the stock. Cut the wings into two pieces.

2 Combine all the remaining ingredients, except the stock, and pour the mixture over the chicken. Cover with plastic wrap and marinate overnight.

3 Preheat the oven to 425°F. Remove the wings from the marinade and arrange them in a single layer in a large roasting pan. Bake for 20–25 minutes, basting at least twice with the marinade during cooking.

4 Place the wings on a serving plate. Add the stock to the marinade in the roasting pan, and bring to a boil. Cook to a syrupy consistency and spoon a little over the wings. Serve garnished with lemon wedges.

Sesame Seed Chicken Bites

Stir-fry these crunchy bites in a wok, then serve them warm with the spicy sauce. A glass of chilled dry white wine is the perfect accompaniment.

INGREDIENTS

Makes 20

6 ounces skinless, boneless chicken
    breast portion
2 garlic cloves, crushed
1-inch piece of fresh ginger root,
    peeled and grated
1 egg white
1 teaspoon cornstarch
$1/4$ cup shelled pistachio nuts,
    coarsely chopped
4 tablespoons sesame seeds
2 tablespoons grapeseed oil
salt and ground black pepper

For the sauce
3 tablespoons hoi-sin sauce
1 tablespoon sweet chili sauce

For the garnish
fresh ginger root, peeled and shredded
pistachio nuts, coarsely chopped
fresh dill sprigs

1 Place the chicken, garlic, grated ginger, egg white, and cornstarch in a food processor or blender and process to a paste.

2 Add the pistachio nuts and season with salt and pepper.

3 Roll into 20 balls and coat with sesame seeds. Heat a wok and add the oil. When the oil is hot, stir-fry the chicken bites, in batches, turning regularly until golden. Drain on paper towels.

4 Make the sauce by combining the hoi-sin and chili sauces in a bowl. Garnish the bites with shredded ginger, pistachio nuts, and dill. Serve hot, with a dish of sauce for dipping.

Little Chicken Turnovers

These savory Russian turnovers are often served with soup or as a snack, but they also make a delicious and unusual first course.

INGREDIENTS

Makes 35

2 cups strong white bread flour

$1/2$ teaspoon salt

$1/2$ teaspoon superfine sugar

1 teaspoon rapid-rise dried yeast

2 tablespoons butter, softened

1 egg, beaten, plus extra for brushing

6 tablespoons warm milk

For the filling

1 small onion, finely chopped

$1^1/2$ cups ground chicken

1 tablespoon sunflower oil

5 tablespoons chicken stock

2 tablespoons chopped fresh parsley

pinch of freshly grated nutmeg

salt and ground black pepper

1 Sift the flour, salt, and sugar into a bowl. Stir in the yeast, then make a well in the center.

2 Add the butter, egg, and milk and mix to a soft dough. Turn onto a lightly floured counter and knead for 10 minutes, or until smooth and elastic.

3 Put the dough in a clean bowl, cover with plastic wrap, and leave in a warm place to rise for 1 hour, or until the dough has doubled in size.

4 Meanwhile, cook the onion and chicken in the oil for 10 minutes. Add the stock and simmer for 5 minutes. Stir in the parsley, nutmeg, salt, and pepper. Remove from the heat and let cool.

5 Preheat the oven to 425°F. Knead the dough, then roll out until about $1/8$ inch thick. Cut out 3-inch rounds.

6 Brush the edges with beaten egg. Put a little filling in the middle, then press the edges together. Leave to rise on oiled cookie sheets, covered with oiled plastic wrap, for 15 minutes.

7 Brush with a little more egg. Bake for 5 minutes, then for 10 minutes at 375°F, until well risen and golden brown.

Nutty Chicken Balls

Serve these tasty bites as a first
course with the lemon sauce, or
make them into smaller balls and
serve as canapés.

INGREDIENTS

Serves 4

12 ounces skinless, boneless chicken breast
portions

$1/2$ cup pistachio nuts, finely chopped

1 tablespoon lemon juice

2 eggs, beaten

all-purpose flour, for shaping

$3/4$ cup blanched chopped almonds

generous 1 cup dried bread crumbs

salt and ground black pepper

For the lemon sauce

$2/3$ cup chicken stock

1 cup cream cheese

1 tablespoon lemon juice

1 tablespoon chopped fresh parsley

1 tablespoon chopped fresh chives

1 Grind or chop the chicken
finely. Combine with salt and
freshly ground black pepper, the
pistachio nuts, lemon juice, and
half the beaten egg.

2 Shape into 16 small balls with
floured hands (use a spoon as
a guide, so that all the balls are
about the same size). Roll the balls
in the remaining beaten egg and
coat firstly with the almonds, and
then the dried bread crumbs,
pressing them on firmly. Chill until
ready to cook.

3 Preheat the oven to 375°F. Place
the balls on a greased cookie
sheet and bake for 15 minutes, or
until golden brown and crisp.

4 To make the lemon sauce,
gently heat the chicken stock
and cream cheese together in a pan,
whisking until smooth. Add the
lemon juice, parsley, and chives,
and season with salt and pepper.
Serve with the chicken balls.

Chicken Roulades

These tender chicken rolls enclosing a filling of pine nuts and spinach make a light lunch dish for two or a first course for four. They can be sliced and served cold with a salad.

INGREDIENTS

Makes 4

4 chicken thighs, boned and skinned

4 ounces chopped fresh or
frozen spinach

1 tablespoon butter

$^{1}/_{4}$ cup pine nuts

pinch of grated nutmeg

$^{1}/_{2}$ cup fresh white bread crumbs

4 strips fatty bacon

2 tablespoons olive oil

$^{2}/_{3}$ cup white wine or
chicken stock

2 teaspoons cornstarch

2 tablespoons light cream

1 tablespoon chopped fresh chives

salt and ground black pepper

1 Preheat the oven to 350°F. Place the chicken thighs between two sheets of plastic wrap and flatten with a rolling pin.

2 Put the spinach and butter into a pan. Heat gently until the spinach has thawed, if frozen, then increase the heat, and cook rapidly, stirring occasionally until all the moisture has evaporated. Add the pine nuts, seasoning, nutmeg, and fresh bread crumbs.

3 Divide the filling among the chicken pieces and roll up neatly. Wrap a strip of bacon around each piece and tie securely with fine string.

4 Heat the oil in a large skillet and brown the rolls all over. Lift out using a slotted spoon to drain off the oil and place in a shallow ovenproof dish.

5 Pour in the wine or chicken stock. Cover, and bake for 15–20 minutes, or until tender. Transfer the chicken to a serving plate and remove the string. Strain the cooking liquid into a pan.

6 Blend the cornstarch with a little cold water and add to the juices in the pan, along with the cream. Bring to a boil, stirring until thick. Adjust the seasoning and add the chives. Pour the sauce around the chicken and serve.

Drunken Chicken

As the chicken is marinated for several days, it is important to use a very fresh bird from a reputable supplier. Serve cold as part of an appetizer, or cut the meat into small, neat pieces and serve as a snack with cocktails before dinner.

INGREDIENTS

Serves 4–6

1 chicken, about 3 pounds

1/2-inch piece of fresh ginger root, peeled and thinly sliced

2 scallions, trimmed

7 1/2 cups water to cover

1 tablespoon salt

1 1/4 cups dry sherry

1–2 tablespoons brandy (optional)

scallions, shredded, and fresh herbs, to garnish

1 Rinse and dry the chicken inside and out. Place the ginger and scallions in the body cavity. Put the chicken in a large pan or flameproof casserole and just cover with water. Bring to the boil, skim, and cook for 15 minutes.

2 Turn off the heat, cover the pan or casserole tightly, and leave the chicken in the cooking liquid for 3–4 hours, by which time it will be cooked. Drain well. Pour 1 1/4 cups of the stock into a measuring cup. Freeze the remaining stock for future use.

3 Remove the skin from the chicken, and cut it into pieces. Divide each leg into a drumstick and thigh. Make two more portions from the wings and some of the breast. Finally, cut away the remainder of the breast pieces (still on the bone) and divide each breast into two even-size portions.

4 Arrange the chicken portions in a shallow dish. Rub salt into the chicken and cover the dish with plastic wrap. Leave in a cool place for several hours or overnight in the refrigerator.

5 Lift off any fat from the stock. Combine the sherry and brandy, if using, in a pitcher, add the stock, and pour the mixture over the chicken. Cover and leave in the refrigerator to marinate for 2 or 3 days, turning occasionally.

6 When ready to serve, cut the chicken through the bone into chunky pieces and arrange on a serving platter garnished with scallion shreds and herbs.

VARIATION

To serve as a cocktail snack, take the meat off the bones, cut it into bitesize pieces, then spear each piece on a toothpick.

Broiled Skewered Chicken

*This dish is actually a Japanese
snack as an accompaniment for
drinks. The broiled skewered chicken
is dipped in yakitori sauce and eaten
as finger food.*

INGREDIENTS

Serves 4

8 chicken thighs with skin, boned

8 large, thick scallions, trimmed

shichimi togarashi, sansho, or
   lemon wedges, to serve
   (see Cook's Tip)

For the sauce

4 tablespoons sake

5 tablespoons shoyu

1 tablespoon mirin

1 tablespoon superfine sugar

1 First, make the yakitori sauce. Combine all the ingredients in a small pan. Bring to a boil, then reduce the heat, and simmer gently for 10 minutes, or until the sauce has thickened.

2 Cut the chicken into 1-inch cubes. Cut the scallions into 1-inch long sticks.

3 To broil, preheat the broiler. Oil the wire rack and spread out the chicken cubes on it. Broil both sides of the chicken until the juices drip, then dip the pieces in the sauce, and put back on the rack. Broil for 30 seconds on each side, repeating the dipping and broiling process twice more.

4 Set the chicken aside and keep warm. Gently broil the scallions until soft and slightly brown outside. Do not dip them. Thread about four pieces of chicken and three scallion pieces onto each of eight bamboo skewers.

5 Arrange the skewers on a platter and serve sprinkled with shichimi togarashi, or sansho, or accompanied by lemon wedges.

COOK'S TIP

Shichimi togarashi is a blend
of flavorings and sansho is a
spice. They are both used as
condiments and are available
from Japanese supermarkets.

Broiled Chicken on Bamboo Skewers

These tasty chicken balls, known as tsukune, are a favorite family dish in Japan, as it is easy for children to eat them directly from the skewer. You can make the balls in advance up to the end of step 2, and they also freeze well.

INGREDIENTS

Serves 4

2³/₄ cups ground chicken

2 eggs

¹/₂ teaspoon salt

2 teaspoons all-purpose flour

2 teaspoons cornstarch

6 tablespoons dried bread crumbs

1-inch piece of fresh ginger root, grated

shichimi togarashi or sansho (optional),
    to serve

For the sauce

4 tablespoons sake

5 tablespoons shoyu

1 tablespoon mirin

1 tablespoon superfine sugar

¹/₂ teaspoon cornstarch blended with
    1 teaspoon water

1 Soak eight bamboo skewers in water for 30 minutes to prevent them from charring.

2 Put all the ingredients for the chicken balls, except the ginger, in a food processor and process. Wet your hands and scoop about a tablespoonful of the mixture into your palm. Shape it into a small ball. Make another 30–32 balls.

3 Squeeze the juice from the grated ginger into a small mixing bowl. Discard the pulp.

4 Add the ginger juice to a pan of boiling water. Add the chicken balls, and boil for about 7 minutes, or until the color of the meat changes and the balls float to the surface. Scoop out and drain on a plate covered with paper towels.

5 In a small pan, combine all the ingredients for the yakitori sauce, except for the cornstarch paste. Bring to a boil, then reduce the heat, and simmer for about 10 minutes, or until the sauce has slightly reduced. Add the cornstarch paste and stir until thick. Transfer to a small bowl.

6 Thread three to four balls onto each skewer. Cook under a medium broiler or on a barbecue, keeping the skewer handles away from the fire. Turn them frequently for a few minutes, or until the balls start to brown. Brush with sauce and return to the heat. Repeat the process twice. Serve, sprinkled with shichimi togarashi or sansho, if you like.

Chicken, Juniper, and Peppercorn Terrine

This is an ideal dish for entertaining, as it can be made several days in advance.

INGREDIENTS

Serves 10–12

8 ounces chicken livers, trimmed
1 pound ground chicken
1 pound ground pork
8 ounces cubetti pancetta
$^1/_2$ cup shelled pistachio nuts,
  coarsely chopped
1 teaspoon salt
$^1/_2$ teaspoon ground mace
2 garlic cloves, crushed
1 teaspoon drained green peppercorns
  in brine
1 teaspoon juniper berries
$^1/_2$ cup dry white wine
2 tablespoons gin
finely grated rind of 1 orange
8 large vacuum-packed grape leaves in
  brine, rinsed and drained
oil, for greasing
spiced kumquats, red bell pepper chutney,
  or chili jelly, to serve

1 Chop the livers finely. Put them in a bowl with the pork, ground chicken, pancetta, pistachio nuts, salt, mace, and garlic. Mix well.

2 Crush the peppercorns and juniper berries. Add to the mix. Stir in the wine, gin, and orange rind. Cover and chill overnight.

3 The next day, preheat the oven to 325°F.

4 Oil a 5-cup loaf pan. Line the tin with the grape leaves, so that the ends hang over the sides. Pack the mixture into the pan and fold the leaves over to enclose the filling. Brush lightly with oil.

5 Cover the terrine with its lid or with foil. Place it in a roasting pan and pour in boiling water to come halfway up the sides of the terrine. Bake for 1$^3/_4$ hours, checking the level of the water occasionally, so that the roasting pan does not dry out.

6 Let the terrine cool, then carefully pour off the surface juices. Cover with plastic wrap, then foil, and place weights on top. Chill overnight. Serve at room temperature with kumquats, chutney, or chili jelly.

Chicken and Pistachio Pâté

This simplified version of a classic French dish can be made using a whole boned bird, or chicken pieces. Serve it as a first course for a large gathering or for an elegant picnic or a cold buffet accompanied by a herb mayonnaise.

INGREDIENTS

Serves 20 as a first course, 10–12 as a main course

2 pounds boneless chicken meat

1 skinless, boneless chicken breast portion, about 6 ounces

$^1/_2$ cup fresh white bread crumbs

$^1/_2$ cup whipping cream

1 egg white

4 scallions, finely chopped

1 garlic clove, finely chopped

3 ounces cooked ham, cut into
    $^1/_2$-inch cubes

$^1/_2$ cup shelled pistachio nuts

3 tablespoons chopped fresh tarragon

pinch of freshly grated nutmeg

$^3/_4$ teaspoon salt

$1^1/_2$ teaspoons pepper

salad greens, to serve

1 Trim all the fat, tendons, and connective tissue from the chicken meat and cut into 2-inch cubes. Put in a food processor fitted with the metal blade and pulse to chop the meat to a smooth purée, in two or three batches (depending on capacity). Alternatively, pass the meat through the medium or fine blade of a grinder.

2 Preheat the oven to 350°F. Cut the chicken breast portion into $^1/_2$-inch cubes.

3 In a large bowl, soak the bread crumbs in the cream. Add the chicken, egg white, scallions, garlic, ham, pistachio nuts, tarragon, nutmeg, and seasoning. Using a wooden spoon, mix until thoroughly combined.

4 On a piece of foil about 18 inches long, brush oil on a 12-inch square in the center. Spoon the chicken onto the foil to form a log about 12 x 3$^1/_2$ inches. Bring together the long sides of the foil and fold over securely. Twist the ends and tie with string.

5 Transfer to an ovenproof dish and bake for 1$^1/_2$ hours. Let cool in the dish and chill until cold. Serve sliced with salad greens.

> ### COOK'S TIP
> ❧
> You could use turkey meat in place of some or all of the chicken.

Chicken, Bacon, and Walnut Terrine

Walnuts, warm spices, and Madeira give this chicken terrine a truly wonderful flavor.

INGREDIENTS

Serves 8–10

2 skinless, boneless chicken breast
    portions, skinned
1 large garlic clove, crushed
1/2 slice bread
1 egg
12 ounces bacon chops, ground
8 ounces chicken livers, finely chopped
1/4 cup chopped walnuts, toasted
2 tablespoons sweet sherry or Madeira
1/2 teaspoon ground allspice
1/2 teaspoon cayenne pepper
pinch each of ground nutmeg and cloves
8 long strips fatty bacon
salt and ground black pepper
Belgian endive leaves and fresh chives,
    to garnish

1 Cut the chicken breast portions into thin strips and season.

2 Mash the garlic, bread, and egg together in a bowl. Gradually work in the ground bacon—using your hands is really the easiest way—and then the finely chopped livers. Stir in the chopped walnuts, sweet sherry or Madeira, allspice, cayenne, nutmeg, cloves, and seasoning to taste.

3 Preheat the oven to 400°F. Stretch the bacon strips with a metal spatula or round-bladed knife and use to line a 1 1/2-pound loaf pan, then pack in half of the meat mixture.

4 Lay the chicken strips on the top and spread the rest of the mixture over them. Cover the loaf pan with lightly greased foil, seal well, and press down very firmly.

5 Place the terrine in a roasting pan half-full of hot water and bake for 1–1 1/2 hours, or until firm to the touch. Remove from the oven, place weights on the top, and let cool completely. Drain off any excess fat or liquid while the terrine is still warm.

6 When really cold, turn out the terrine, cut into thick slices, and serve immediately, garnished with a few Belgian endive leaves and fresh chives.

Chicken Liver and Marsala Pâté

2 Transfer the livers to a blender or food processor, using a slotted spoon, and add the Marsala and chopped sage.

3 Melt 10 tablespoons of the remaining butter in the skillet, stirring with a wooden spoon to loosen any sediment, then pour into the blender or processor, and process until smooth. Season well.

This is a really quick and simple pâté to make, yet it has a delicious and quite sophisticated flavor. It contains Marsala, a soft and pungent fortified wine from Sicily. If it is unavailable, use brandy or a medium-dry sherry.

INGREDIENTS

Serves 4

12 ounces chicken livers, thawed
    if frozen
1 cup butter, softened
2 garlic cloves, crushed
1 tablespoon Marsala
1 teaspoon chopped fresh sage
salt and ground black pepper
8 sage leaves, to garnish
thin, crisp toast, to serve

1 Rinse the chicken livers and pat dry with paper towels. Melt 2 tablespoons of the butter in a skillet, and cook the chicken livers with the garlic over medium heat, stirring frequently, for about 5 minutes, or until they are firm but still quite pink in the middle.

4 Spoon the pâté into four individual pots and smooth the surface. Melt the remaining butter in a separate pan and pour it over the pâtés. Garnish with sage leaves and chill until set. Serve with triangles of toast.

Chicken and Pork Terrine

This delicately flavored Ukrainian pâté can be served with salad as a first course or with warm, crusty bread for a light lunch.

INGREDIENTS

Serves 6–8

8 ounces fatty bacon

13 ounces skinless, boneless
   chicken portions

1 tablespoon lemon juice

2 cups lean ground pork

$^1/_2$ small onion, finely chopped

2 eggs, beaten

2 tablespoons chopped fresh parsley

1 teaspoon salt

1 teaspoon green peppercorns, crushed

fresh salad greens, radishes, and lemon
   wedges, to serve

1 Preheat the oven to 325°F. Put the bacon on a board and stretch it using the back of a knife so that it can be arranged in overlapping slices over the base and sides of a 2-pound loaf pan.

2 Cut 4 ounces of the chicken into 4-inch strips. Sprinkle with lemon juice. Put the rest of the chicken in a food processor or blender with the pork and the onion. Process until fairly smooth.

3 Add the eggs, parsley, salt, and peppercorns to the meat mixture and process again briefly. Spoon half the mixture into the loaf pan and then level the surface.

4 Arrange the chicken strips on top, then spoon in the remaining meat mixture and smooth the top. Tap the pan to knock out any pockets of air.

5 Cover with a piece of oiled foil and put in a roasting pan. Pour in enough hot water to come halfway up the sides of the loaf pan. Bake for about 45–50 minutes.

6 Let cool in the tin before turning out and chilling. Serve sliced, with salad greens, radishes, and wedges of lemon.

Chicken Liver Pâté with Garlic

This smooth, garlicky pâté is wickedly indulgent and absolutely delicious. It is ideal as a first course, with toast and pickled gherkins.

INGREDIENTS

Serves 6–8

1 cup sweet butter

14 ounces chicken livers, chopped

3–4 tablespoons Madeira

3 large shallots, chopped

2 large garlic cloves, finely chopped

1 teaspoon finely chopped
   fresh thyme

pinch of ground allspice

2 tablespoons heavy cream (optional)

salt and ground black pepper

small fresh bay leaves or fresh thyme
   sprigs, to garnish

1 Melt 6 tablespoons of the butter in a small pan over low heat, then bubble gently until it is clear. Pour off the clarified butter into a bowl.

2 Melt 3 tablespoons of the remaining butter in a skillet and cook the chicken livers for 4–5 minutes, or until browned.

> ### COOK'S TIP
> The flavor of the pâté deepens and matures on chilling, so it is best if you make it a day before it is required.

3 Add the Madeira and set it alight, then scrape the contents of the pan into a food processor or blender.

4 Melt 2 tablespoons butter in a pan and cook the shallots for 5 minutes. Add the herbs and allspice and cook for 2–3 minutes. Add to the livers with the butter and cream, if using, then process.

5 Add about 1½ teaspoons each of salt and pepper and more Madeira to taste. Scrape the pâté into a serving dish and place a few bay leaves or thyme sprigs on top.

6 Melt the clarified butter, if necessary, then pour it over the pâté. Cool and chill in the refrigerator for at least 4 hours or overnight.

Chicken Liver Mousse

This mousse makes an elegant yet surprisingly easy first course. The onion marmalade is a delicious accompaniment, along with Belgian endive or other bitter leaves.

INGREDIENTS

Serves 6–8

³/₄ cup butter, diced
1 small onion, finely chopped
1 garlic clove, finely chopped
1 pound chicken livers
¹/₂ teaspoon dried thyme
2–3 tablespoons brandy
salt and ground black pepper
salad, greens to serve

For the onion marmalade
2 tablespoons butter
1 pound red onions,
    thinly sliced
1 garlic clove, finely chopped
¹/₂ teaspoon dried thyme
2–3 tablespoons raspberry or red
    wine vinegar
1–2 tablespoons honey
¹/₄ cup golden raisins

1 Trim the chicken livers, removing any filaments or fat.

2 In a heavy skillet, melt 2 tablespoons of the butter over medium heat. Add the onion and cook for 5–7 minutes, or until soft and golden, then add the garlic and cook for 1 minute more.

COOK'S TIP

The mousse will keep for 3–4 days. If made ahead, cover and chill until ready to use. The onion marmalade can be made up to 2 days ahead and gently reheated over low heat or in the microwave until just warm.

3 Increase the heat and add the livers, thyme, and seasoning. Cook for 3–5 minutes, stirring frequently; the livers should remain pink inside. Add the brandy and cook for 1 minute more.

4 Transfer the livers to a food processor fitted with the metal blade. Pour in the cooking juices and process for 1 minute, or until smooth, scraping down the sides once. With the machine running, add the remaining butter, until it is fully incorporated.

5 Press the mousse mixture through a fine strainer with a wooden spoon or rubber spatula.

6 Line a 2-cup loaf pan with plastic wrap, smoothing out as many wrinkles as you possibly can. Pour the chicken liver mousse mixture into the lined pan. Cool, then cover, and chill in the refrigerator until firm.

7 To make the onion marmalade, heat the butter in a heavy skillet over medium-low heat, add the onions, and cook for 20 minutes, or until softened, stirring frequently. Stir in the garlic, thyme, vinegar, honey, and golden raisins and cook, covered, for 10–15 minutes, or until the onions are completely soft and pulpy, stirring occasionally. Spoon into a bowl and cool to room temperature.

8 To serve, dip the loaf pan into hot water for 5 seconds, wipe dry, and invert onto a board. Lift off the pan, peel off the plastic wrap, and smooth the surface with a knife. Serve sliced with a little of the onion marmalade and salad greens.

SALADS &
BARBECUES

Whatever the time of year, crisp, fresh salads are always a popular choice.
In this chapter warm salads feature. They combine cooked chicken with crisp
raw vegetables or salad greens. All kinds of delicious cold salads are included too—
perfect for hot summer days.
Summer is also the time for outdoor eating, and as well as fresh salads,
everyone enjoys a barbecue. There are plenty of mouthwatering chicken recipes
here, with a variety of exciting marinades and accompaniments,
to enable you to create the perfect outdoor meal.

Classic Chicken Salad with Green Beans

A piquant dressing makes this salad of chicken, young spinach, and green beans simply delicious.

INGREDIENTS

Serves 8

1 chicken, about 4 pounds

$1^1/4$ cups white wine and water, mixed

24 x $^1/4$-inch slices French bread

1 garlic clove, peeled

8 ounces green beans, cut into
  2-inch lengths

4 ounces fresh young spinach leaves,
  torn into small pieces

2 celery stalks, thinly sliced

2 sun-dried tomatoes, chopped

2 scallions, thinly sliced

fresh chives and parsley, to garnish

For the vinaigrette

2 tablespoons red wine vinegar

6 tablespoons olive oil

1 tablespoon whole-grain mustard

1 tablespoon honey

2 tablespoons chopped mixed
  fresh herbs

2 teaspoons finely chopped capers

salt and ground black pepper

2 Put all the ingredients for the vinaigrette into a screw-topped jar and shake vigorously. Adjust the seasoning to taste.

3 Toast the French bread until golden brown to make croutons. Rub with garlic.

4 Cook the green beans in boiling water until just tender. Drain and rinse under cold water.

5 Arrange the spinach on serving plates with the celery, green beans, sun-dried tomatoes, chicken, and scallions. Spoon the dressing over the salad, add the toasted croutons, and garnish with chives and parsley.

1 Preheat the oven to 375°F. Put the chicken, wine, and water into a large casserole. Roast for $1^1/2$ hours, until tender. Let cool in the cooking liquid. Remove the skin and bones and cut the flesh into small pieces.

Dijon Chicken Salad

Here is an attractive dish to serve for lunch with herb and garlic bread.

INGREDIENTS

Serves 4

4 skinless, boneless chicken
  breast portions
mixed salad greens, to serve

For the marinade

2 tablespoons Dijon mustard
3 garlic cloves, crushed
1 tablespoon grated onion
4 tablespoons white wine

For the mustard dressing

2 tablespoons tarragon wine vinegar
1 teaspoon Dijon mustard
1 teaspoon honey
6 tablespoons olive oil
salt and ground black pepper

1 Combine all the marinade ingredients in a shallow dish that is large enough to hold the chicken in a single layer.

2 Turn the chicken over in the marinade to coat it completely. Cover with plastic wrap and then chill in the refrigerator overnight.

3 Preheat the oven to 375°F. Transfer the chicken and the marinade into an ovenproof dish, cover with foil, and bake for about 35 minutes, or until tender. Remove the dish from the oven and let cool.

4 Put all the mustard dressing ingredients into a screw-topped jar, shake vigorously to emulsify, and adjust the seasoning. (The dressing can be made several days in advance and stored in the refrigerator.)

5 Slice the chicken thinly, fan out the slices, and arrange on a serving dish with the salad greens.

6 Spoon some of the mustard dressing over the plate, and serve immediately.

Swiss Cheese, Chicken, and Tongue Salad

The rich sweet flavors of this salad marry well with the peppery mesclun or arugula. A minted lemon dressing freshens the overall taste. Serve with new potatoes.

INGREDIENTS

Serves 4

2 skinless, boneless chicken
    breast portions
$1/2$ chicken bouillon cube
8 ounces sliced beef tongue or ham,
    $1/2$ inch thick
8 ounces Swiss cheese
1 lollo rosso lettuce
1 butterhead or Belgian endive lettuce
1 bunch mesclun or arugula
2 green-skinned apples, cored and sliced
3 celery stalks, sliced
4 tablespoons sesame seeds, toasted
salt, ground black pepper, and nutmeg

For the dressing
5 tablespoons peanut or
    sunflower oil
1 teaspoon sesame oil
3 tablespoons lemon juice
2 teaspoons chopped fresh mint
3 drops hot chili sauce

1 Place the chicken portions in a shallow pan, cover with $1^1/4$ cups water, add $1/2$ bouillon cube, and bring to a boil. Put the lid on the pan and simmer for 15 minutes. Drain, reserving the stock for another occasion, then cool the chicken under cold running water.

2 To make the dressing, measure the two oils, lemon juice, mint, and chili sauce into a screw-topped jar and shake. Cut the chicken, tongue or ham, and Swiss cheese into fine strips. Moisten with a little dressing and set aside.

3 Arrange the salad greens, apple, and celery on four large plates. Pile the chicken, tongue or ham, and cheese in the center, sprinkle with toasted sesame seeds, season to taste with salt, pepper, and freshly grated nutmeg, and serve, with the dressing.

Chicken and Avocado Mayonnaise

Creamy avocados complement chicken in this tasty light and summery salad. Serve with crisp nacho or tortilla chips for dipping.

INGREDIENTS

Serves 4

2 tablespoons mayonnaise

1 tablespoon ricotta cheese

2 garlic cloves, crushed

scant 1 cup chopped cooked chicken

1 large ripe, but firm, avocado, peeled and pitted

2 tablespoons lemon juice

salt and ground black pepper

nacho chips or tortilla chips, to serve

2 Chop the avocado and toss immediately in lemon juice.

3 Mix the avocado gently into the chicken mixture. Check the seasoning and chill until required.

4 Serve in small serving dishes with the nacho or tortilla chips as scoops, if you like.

1 Combine the mayonnaise, ricotta, garlic, and seasoning to taste, in a small bowl. Stir in the chopped chicken.

COOK'S TIP

This mixture makes a great, chunky filling for sandwiches, baps, or pita pockets. It can also be served as a main course salad, heaped onto a base of mixed salad greens.

Chicken and Fruit Salad

Refreshing cantaloupe melon makes this salad ideal for a warm summer's day. The chickens may be cooked the day before.

INGREDIENTS

Serves 8

4 tarragon or rosemary sprigs
2 chickens, about 4 pounds each
5 tablespoons softened butter
$^2/_3$ cup chicken stock
$^2/_3$ cup white wine
1 cup walnut pieces
1 small cantaloupe melon
lettuce leaves
1 pound seedless grapes or pitted cherries
salt and ground black pepper

For the dressing
2 tablespoons tarragon vinegar
$^1/_2$ cup light olive oil
2 tablespoons chopped mixed fresh herbs,
    such as parsley, mint and tarragon

1 Preheat the oven to 400°F. Put the herb sprigs inside the cavities of the chickens and season. Tie the chickens with string. Spread the chickens with 4 tablespoons of the softened butter, place in a roasting pan, and pour in the stock. Cover loosely with foil and roast for about 1$^1/_2$ hours, basting twice, until browned and the juices run clear. Remove the chickens from the roasting pan.

2 Add the wine to the roasting pan. Bring to a boil and cook until syrupy. Strain and let cool. Heat the remaining butter in a skillet and gently cook the walnuts until browned. Drain and cool. Scoop the melon into balls or cut into cubes. Cut the chickens into serving pieces.

3 To make the dressing, whisk the vinegar and oil together with a little salt and freshly ground black pepper. Remove all the fat from the chicken juices and add these to the dressing with the herbs.

4 Arrange the chicken pieces on a bed of lettuce, sprinkle over the grapes or pitted cherries, melon balls or cubes, and spoon over the herb dressing. Sprinkle with toasted walnuts.

Citrus Chicken Salad

Oranges and limes give a zest to this salad that makes a delicious change from rich food. It is a good choice for a post-Thanksgiving buffet, when cooked turkey can be used instead.

INGREDIENTS

Serves 6

$^1/_2$ cup extra virgin olive oil

6 skinless, boneless chicken
    breast portions

4 oranges

1 teaspoon Dijon mustard

3 teaspoons honey

$2^3/_4$ cups finely shredded
    white cabbage

11 ounces carrots, peeled and thinly sliced

2 scallions, thinly sliced

2 celery stalks, cut into batons

2 tablespoons chopped fresh tarragon

2 limes

salt and ground black pepper

1 Heat 2 tablespoons of the oil in a large, heavy skillet. Add the chicken portions and cook for 15–20 minutes, or until the chicken is cooked through and golden brown. (If your skillet is too small, cook the chicken in two or three batches.) Remove the chicken from the pan and let cool.

2 Cut a thin slice of peel and pith from each end of two of the oranges. Place cut side down on a plate and cut off the peel and pith. Cut out each segment, leaving the membrane behind. Set aside.

3 Grate the rind and squeeze the juice from one of the remaining oranges and place in a bowl. Stir in the mustard, 1 teaspoon of honey, 4 tablespoons of the oil, and seasoning. Mix in the cabbage, carrots, scallions, and celery.

VARIATION

For a creamy result, mayonnaise, crème fraîche, or sour cream can be used to dress the chicken.

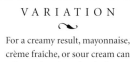

4 Meanwhile, squeeze the juice from the remaining orange and mix it with the remaining honey and oil, and the tarragon. Peel and segment the limes, as for the oranges, and lightly mix the segments into the dressing with the reserved orange segments and seasoning to taste.

5 Slice the cooked chicken portions and stir into the dressing. Spoon the vegetable salad onto plates and add the chicken mixture, then serve immediately.

Chicken and Broccoli Salad

Gorgonzola makes a tangy dressing that goes well with both chicken and broccoli. Serve for a lunch or supper dish, with crusty Italian bread.

INGREDIENTS

Serves 4

6 ounces broccoli flowerets, divided into
    small sprigs

2 cups farfalle

2 large skinless, boneless chicken breast
    portions, cooked

For the dressing

$3^1/2$ ounces Gorgonzola cheese

1 tablespoon white wine vinegar

4 tablespoons extra virgin olive oil

$1/2$–1 teaspoon finely chopped fresh sage,
    plus extra sage sprigs to garnish

salt and ground black pepper

1 Cook the broccoli flowerets in a large pan of salted, boiling water for 3 minutes. Remove with a slotted spoon and rinse under cold running water, then spread out on paper towels to drain and dry.

2 Add the pasta to the broccoli cooking water, then bring back to a boil, and cook according to the packet instructions. When cooked, drain the pasta into a colander, rinse thoroughly under cold running water until cold, then let drain and dry, shaking the colander occasionally.

3 Cut the chicken portions into bitesize pieces.

4 To make the dressing, put the cheese in a large bowl and mash with a fork, then whisk in the wine vinegar, followed by the oil and sage, and season with salt and pepper to taste.

5 Add the pasta, chicken, and broccoli. Toss well, then season to taste. Serve, garnished with sage.

Chicken and Pasta Salad

*This is a delicious way to use up
leftover cooked chicken.*

INGREDIENTS

Serves 4

2 cups tri-colored pasta twists
2 tablespoons pesto
1 tablespoon olive oil
1 beefsteak tomato
12 pitted black olives
1¹/2 cups cooked green beans
3 cups cubed cooked chicken
salt and ground black pepper
fresh basil, to garnish

1 Cook the pasta in plenty of
salted, boiling water until
al dente (about 12 minutes or
as directed on the packet).

2 Drain the pasta and rinse in
plenty of cold running water.
Put it into a bowl and stir in the
pesto and olive oil.

3 Plunge the tomato into boiling
water for about 30 seconds,
then refresh in cold water. Peel off
the skin.

4 Cut the tomato into small
cubes and add to the pasta with
the olives, seasoning, and green
beans cut into 1¹/2-inch lengths.
Add the cubed chicken. Toss gently
together and transfer to a serving
platter. Garnish with fresh basil.

Chicken and Mango Salad with Orange Rice

The combination of sweet and savory has always been popular. In this recipe, ripe mango and curried chicken mayonnaise top delicious citrus rice.

INGREDIENTS

Serves 4

1 tablespoon sunflower oil
1 onion, chopped
1 garlic clove, crushed
2 tablespoons red curry paste
2 teaspoons apricot jelly
2 tablespoons chicken stock
1 pound cooked chicken, cut into
    small pieces
$^2/_3$ cup plain yogurt
4–5 tablespoons mayonnaise
1 large mango, cut into $^1/_2$-inch dice
fresh flat leaf parsley sprigs, to garnish
poppadums, to serve

For the rice

scant 1 cup white long grain rice
$1^1/_2$ cups grated carrots
1 large orange, cut into segments
$^1/_3$ cup roasted sliced almonds

For the dressing

3 tablespoons olive oil
4 tablespoons sunflower oil
3 tablespoons lemon juice
1 garlic clove, crushed
1 tablespoon chopped mixed fresh herbs
    (tarragon, parsley, chives)
salt and ground black pepper

1 Heat the oil in a skillet and cook the onion and garlic for 3–4 minutes, or until soft.

2 Stir in the curry paste, cook for about 1 minute, then lower the heat, and stir in the apricot jelly and stock. Mix well, add the chopped chicken, and stir until the chicken is thoroughly coated in the paste. Spoon the mixture into a large bowl and let cool.

3 Meanwhile, boil the rice in plenty of lightly salted water until just tender. Drain, rinse under cold water, and drain again. When cool, stir into the grated carrots, and add the orange segments and sliced almonds.

4 Make the dressing by whisking all the ingredients together in a small bowl.

5 When the chicken mixture is cool, stir in the yogurt and mayonnaise, then add the mango, stirring it in carefully so as not to break the flesh. Chill for about 30 minutes.

6 To serve, pour the dressing into the rice salad and mix well. Spoon onto a platter and mound the cold curried chicken on top. Garnish with flat leaf parsley and serve with poppadums.

COOK'S TIP

A simple way of dicing a mango is to take two thick slices from either side of the large flat pit without peeling the fruit. Make criss-cross cuts in the flesh on each slice and then turn inside out. The cubes of flesh will stand proud of the skin and can be easily cut off.

Orange Chicken Salad

A colorful and very delicately flavored rice salad.

INGREDIENTS

Serves 4

3 large seedless oranges

scant 1 cup long grain rice

2 cups water

$^3/_4$ cup vinaigrette dressing, made with red wine vinegar and a mixture of olive and vegetable oils

2 teaspoons Dijon mustard

$^1/_2$ teaspoon superfine sugar

4 cups diced cooked chicken

3 tablespoons chopped fresh chives

$^3/_4$ cup roasted cashew nuts

salt and ground black pepper

cucumber slices, to garnish

1 Thinly peel 1 orange, taking only the colored part of the rind and leaving the white pith.

2 Combine the orange rind, rice, and water in a pan. Add a pinch of salt. Bring to a boil, then cover, and steam over very low heat for 15–18 minutes, or until the rice is tender and all the water has been absorbed.

3 To segment the oranges, using a sharp knife, cut a thin slice of peel from each end of the remaining oranges. Place cut side down on a plate and cut off the peel and pith in strips. Remove any remaining pith. Cut out each segment, leaving the membrane behind.

4 Add the orange juice to the vinaigrette dressing. Add the mustard and sugar and whisk to combine well. Taste and add more salt and pepper if needed.

5 When the rice is cooked, remove it from the heat and cool slightly, uncovered. Discard the orange rind.

6 Turn the rice into a bowl and add half of the dressing. Toss well and let cool completely.

7 Add the chicken, chives, cashew nuts, and orange segments to the rice with the remaining dressing. Toss gently. Serve at room temperature, garnished with cucumber slices.

Vinaigrette Dressing

A good vinaigrette can do more than dress a salad. It can also be used to baste meat, poultry, seafood, or vegetables during cooking, and it can be used as a flavoring and tenderizing marinade. The basic mixture of oil, vinegar, and seasoning lends itself to a number of variations.

Vinaigrette dressing will keep in the refrigerator, in a tightly sealed container, for several weeks. Add flavorings, especially fresh herbs, just before using.

INGREDIENTS

Makes just over $^3/_4$ cup

3 tablespoons wine vinegar

5 tablespoons vegetable oil

5 tablespoons extra virgin olive oil

salt and ground pepper

1 Put the vinegar, salt, and pepper in a bowl and whisk to dissolve the salt.

2 Gradually add the oil, stirring with the whisk.

Maryland Chicken Salad

Barbecue-cooked chicken, corn, bacon, and banana combine here in a sensational main-course salad. It's perfect served with baked potatoes.

INGREDIENTS

Serves 4

4 skinless, boneless chicken
  breast portions
oil, for brushing
8 ounces unsmoked bacon
4 corncobs
3 tablespoons melted butter
4 ripe bananas, peeled and halved
4 firm tomatoes, halved
1 escarole or butterhead lettuce
1 bunch watercress or arugula
salt and ground black pepper

For the dressing
5 tablespoons peanut oil
1 tablespoon white wine vinegar
2 teaspoons maple syrup
2 teaspoons mild mustard

1 Prepare a barbecue. Season the chicken, brush with oil, and cook for 15 minutes, turning once. Cook the bacon for 8–10 minutes, or until crisp.

2 Boil the corncobs for 20 minutes in a large pan of salted water, then brush with butter, and brown over the barbecue. Brush the bananas and tomatoes with butter too, if you like, and cook over the barbecue for 6–8 minutes.

3 To make the dressing, combine the oil, vinegar, maple syrup, and mustard with seasoning and 1 tablespoon water in a screw-topped jar and shake well.

4 Lightly toss the salad greens in the dressing.

5 Distribute the salad leaves among four large plates. Slice the chicken and arrange over the leaves with the bacon, banana, corn, and tomatoes.

Broiled Chicken Salad with Lavender

Lavender may seem like an odd salad ingredient, but its delightful scent has a natural affinity with sweet garlic, orange, and other wild herbs. Golden polenta makes this salad both filling and delicious.

INGREDIENTS

Serves 4

4 skinless, boneless chicken
   breast portions
3³/4 cups light chicken stock
1¹/2 cups fine polenta
¹/4 cup butter
1 pound young spinach
6 ounces corn salad
8 fresh lavender sprigs
8 small tomatoes, halved
salt and ground black pepper

For the marinade
6 fresh lavender flowers
2 teaspoons finely grated orange rind
2 garlic cloves, crushed
2 teaspoons honey
2 tablespoons olive oil
2 teaspoons chopped fresh thyme
2 teaspoons chopped fresh marjoram

1 To make the marinade, strip the lavender flowers from the stems and combine with the orange rind, garlic, honey, and salt to taste. Add the olive oil and herbs. Slash the chicken deeply, spread the mixture evenly over the chicken, and let marinate in a cool place for at least 20 minutes.

2 To cook the polenta, bring the chicken stock to a boil in a heavy pan. Add the polenta in a steady stream, stirring constantly until thick; this will take 2–3 minutes. Turn the cooked polenta out onto a 1-inch deep buttered tray and let cool.

3 Preheat the broiler. Broil the chicken, turning once, for about 15 minutes, until golden brown and cooked through.

4 Cut the polenta into 1-inch cubes with a wet knife. Heat the butter in a large skillet and cook the polenta until golden.

5 Divide the salad greens among four large plates. Slice each chicken portion and lay the slices on the salad. Place the polenta among the salad greens and garnish it with sprigs of lavender and tomatoes. Season to taste with salt and ground black pepper and serve immediately.

Warm Chicken Salad with Rice

Succulent cooked chicken pieces are combined with vegetables in a light chili dressing.

INGREDIENTS

Serves 6

2 ounces mixed salad greens

2 ounces baby spinach leaves

2 ounces mesclun or arugula

2 tablespoons chili sauce

2 tablespoons dry sherry

1 tablespoon light soy sauce

1 tablespoon tomato ketchup

2 teaspoons olive oil

8 shallots, finely chopped

1 garlic clove, crushed

12 ounces skinless, boneless chicken breast
portions, cut into thin strips

1 red bell pepper, seeded and sliced

6 ounces snow peas

4-ounce can baby corncobs, drained
and halved

10-ounce can brown rice

salt and ground black pepper

parsley sprig, to garnish

1 Arrange the mixed salad greens, tearing up any large ones, and the spinach leaves on a serving dish. Add the mesclun or arugula and toss to mix.

2 In a small bowl, combine the chili sauce, sherry, soy sauce, and tomato ketchup and set aside.

3 Heat the oil in a large, nonstick skillet or wok. Add the chopped shallots and garlic and stir-fry over medium heat for 1 minute.

4 Add the chicken and stir-fry for 3–4 minutes.

5 Add the bell pepper, snow peas, corncobs, and rice and stir-fry for 2–3 minutes.

6 Pour in the chili sauce mixture and stir-fry for 2–3 minutes, or until hot and bubbling. Season to taste. Spoon the chicken mixture over the salad greens, toss together to mix, and serve immediately, garnished with fresh parsley.

Warm Chicken Liver and Grapefruit Salad

There are times when warm salads are just right. Serve this delicious combination as either a first course or a light meal, with chunks of bread to dip into the dressing.

INGREDIENTS

Serves 4

4 ounces each fresh young spinach leaves, arugula, and lollo rosso lettuce

2 pink grapefruit

6 tablespoons sunflower oil

2 teaspoons sesame oil

2 teaspoons soy sauce

8 ounces chicken livers, chopped

salt and ground black pepper

1 Tear up all the salad greens. Combine in a large salad bowl.

2 Using a sharp knife, cut the peel and pith from each end of the grapefruit. Place cut side down on a plate and cut off all the peel and pith in strips. Cut out each segment, leaving the membrane behind. Reserve the juice. Add the segments to the salad greens.

3 To make the dressing, combine 4 tablespoons of the sunflower oil, the sesame oil, soy sauce, seasoning, and reserved grapefruit juice to taste.

4 Heat the remaining sunflower oil in a small pan and cook the chicken livers, stirring gently, until firm and lightly browned.

5 Tip the chicken livers and dressing over the salad and serve immediately.

> ### COOK'S TIP
> ∾
> Chicken or turkey livers are ideal for this recipe, and there's no need to leave them to thaw completely before cooking.

Chicken Liver, Bacon, and Tomato Salad

This salad is especially welcome during the fall months when the evenings are growing shorter and cooler. Crisp, bacon-flavored croutons make a wonderfully rich contrast to the fresh green leaves.

INGREDIENTS

Serves 4

8 ounces young spinach, stems removed

1 frisée lettuce

7 tablespoons peanut or
    sunflower oil

6 ounces unsmoked bacon, cut into
    thin strips

3 ounces day-old bread, crusts removed
    and cut into short lengths

1 pound chicken livers

4 ounces cherry tomatoes

salt and ground black pepper

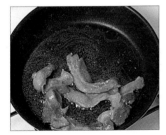

1 Place the salad greens in a salad bowl. Heat 4 tablespoons of the oil in a large skillet. Add the bacon and cook for 3–4 minutes, or until crisp and brown. Remove the bacon with a slotted spoon and drain on paper towels.

2 To make the croutons, cook the bread in the bacon-flavored oil, tossing until crisp and golden. Drain on paper towels.

3 Heat the remaining oil in the skillet, add the chicken livers, and cook briskly for 2–3 minutes. Turn out over the salad greens and add the bacon, croutons, and tomatoes. Season, toss, and serve.

Pan-fried Chicken Liver Salad

2 Heat 2 tablespoons of the oil with the butter. Add the livers, and toss over medium-high heat for 5 minutes, until browned. Remove from the heat.

3 Remove the livers from the pan, drain them on paper towels, then place on top of the spinach.

This Italian salad uses vin santo, a sweet dessert wine from Tuscany, but this is not essential – any dessert wine will do.

INGREDIENTS

Serves 4

3 ounces fresh baby spinach leaves

3 ounces lollo rosso leaves

5 tablespoons olive oil

1 tablespoon butter

8 ounces chicken livers, trimmed and thinly sliced

3 tablespoons vin santo

2–3 ounces fresh Parmesan cheese, shaved into curls

salt and ground black pepper

1 Wash and dry the spinach and lollo rosso. Tear the leaves into a large bowl, season to taste, and toss gently to mix.

4 Return the pan to medium heat, add the remaining oil, and the vin santo, and stir until sizzling. Pour the hot dressing over the spinach and livers and toss to coat. Put the salad in a serving bowl and sprinkle over the Parmesan shavings. Serve immediately.

Warm Chicken Salad with Hazelnut Dressing

This salad combines pan-fried chicken and spinach with a light and tasty nutty dressing.

INGREDIENTS

Serves 4

3 tablespoons olive oil

2 tablespoons hazelnut oil

1 tablespoon white wine vinegar

1 garlic clove, crushed

1 tablespoon chopped fresh
    mixed herbs

8 ounces baby spinach leaves

9 ounces cherry tomatoes, halved

1 bunch scallions, chopped

2 skinless, boneless chicken breast
    portions, cut into thin strips

salt and ground black pepper

1 First make the dressing. Place 2 tablespoons of the olive oil, the hazelnut oil, vinegar, garlic, and chopped herbs in a small bowl or pitcher and whisk together until thoroughly mixed. Set aside.

2 Trim any long stalks from the spinach leaves, then place in a large serving bowl with the tomatoes and scallions, and toss together to mix.

3 Heat the remaining olive oil in a skillet, add the chicken, and cook over high heat for about 7–10 minutes, or until cooked through and lightly browned.

4 Arrange the chicken pieces over the salad, give the dressing a quick whisk to blend, then drizzle it over the salad, and gently toss all the ingredients to mix. Season to taste and serve immediately.

Warm Chicken and Mushroom Salad

This salad needs to be served warm to make the most of the wonderfully aromatic sesame and coriander flavorings. It makes a simple first course for a dinner party or a delicious light lunch dish.

INGREDIENTS

Serves 6

4 medium skinless, boneless chicken
    breast portions
8 ounces snow peas
2 heads decorative lettuce such as lollo
    rosso or oak leaf
3 carrots, peeled and cut into
    small batons
2¹/2 cups white mushrooms, sliced
6 strips of bacon, fried and chopped
1 tablespoon chopped fresh
    cilantro leaves, to garnish

For the dressing
¹/2 cup lemon juice
2 tablespoons whole-grain mustard
1 cup olive oil
4 tablespoons sesame oil
1 teaspoon coriander seeds, crushed

1 Combine all the dressing
ingredients in a bowl. Place the
chicken portions in a shallow dish
and pour in half the dressing. Chill
overnight, and store the remaining
dressing in the refrigerator.

2 Cook the snow peas for
2 minutes in boiling water, then
cool under running cold water to
stop them cooking any further.
Tear the lettuces into small pieces
and mix the snow peas, carrots,
mushrooms, and bacon together.
Arrange all these in individual
serving dishes.

3 Broil the chicken portions until
cooked through, then slice
them on the diagonal into quite
thin pieces. Divide among the
bowls of salad, and add some
dressing to each dish. Combine
quickly and sprinkle some fresh
cilantro over each bowl.

Wild Rice and Chicken Salad

Once you have cooked the wild rice, this is a very simple salad to make.

INGREDIENTS

Serves 4

1 cup wild rice, boiled and cooled (see Cook's Tip)

2 celery stalks, thinly sliced

2 ounces scallions, chopped

1²/₃ cups small white mushrooms, quartered

3³/₄ cups diced cooked chicken meat

¹/₂ cup vinaigrette dressing

1 teaspoon fresh thyme leaves

2 pears, peeled, halved, and cored

¹/₄ cup walnut pieces, toasted

1 Combine the cooled cooked wild rice with the celery, scallions, mushrooms, and chicken in a bowl.

2 Add the dressing and thyme; toss well together.

3 Thinly slice the pear halves lengthwise without cutting through the stalk end, and spread the slices into a fan. Divide the salad among four plates. Garnish each with a fanned pear half and the toasted walnuts.

COOK'S TIP

To boil wild rice, add the rice to a large pan of salted, boiling water (about four parts water to one part rice). Bring back to a gentle boil and cook for 45–50 minutes, or until the rice is tender but still firm and has begun to split open. Drain well. Alternatively, put the rice in a pan with the measured quantity of salted water. Bring to a boil, cover, and simmer over very low heat for 45–50 minutes, or until tender. Cook uncovered for the last 5 minutes to evaporate any excess water.

Spicy Chicken Salad

Marinated chicken mixed with pasta and crisp vegetables makes a superb salad. Start preparations the night before if you can.

INGREDIENTS

Serves 6

1 teaspoon ground cumin seeds
1 teaspoon ground paprika
1 teaspoon ground turmeric
1–2 garlic cloves, crushed
3–4 tablespoons lime juice
4 skinless, boneless chicken
    breast portions
8 ounces rigatoni
1 red bell pepper, seeded and chopped
2 celery stalks, thinly sliced
1 shallot or small onion,
    finely chopped
1/4 cup stuffed green olives, halved
2 tablespoons honey
1 tablespoon whole-grain mustard
salt and ground black pepper
mixed salad greens, to serve

1 Combine the cumin, paprika, turmeric, garlic, seasoning, and 2 tablespoons of the lime juice in a bowl. Rub this mixture over the chicken portions. Lay the chicken in a shallow dish, cover with plastic wrap, and leave in a cool place for about 3 hours or overnight.

2 Preheat the oven to 400°F. Put the chicken in a single layer on a rack over a roasting pan and bake for 20 minutes. Alternatively, cook under a preheated broiler for 8–10 minutes on each side.

3 Cook the rigatoni in a large pan of lightly salted boiling water for 8–10 minutes, or until *al dente*. Drain and rinse under cold water. Let drain thoroughly.

4 Put the red bell pepper, celery, shallot or onion, and olives into a large bowl with the pasta.

5 Combine the honey, mustard, and the remaining lime juice to taste in a bowl and pour it over the pasta. Toss to coat.

6 Cut the chicken in bitesize pieces. Arrange the mixed salad greens on a serving dish, spoon the pasta mixture into the center, and top with the spicy chicken pieces.

Warm Stir-fried Chicken Salad

Ginger and fresh tarragon give this salad a deliciously unusual flavor. Arrange the salad greens on four individual plates, so the hot stir-fry can be served straight from the wok, to make sure that the lettuce remains crisp and the chicken warm.

INGREDIENTS

Serves 4

1 tablespoon fresh tarragon
2 skinless, boneless chicken breast
    portions, about 8 ounces each
2-inch piece of fresh ginger root, peeled
    and finely chopped
3 tablespoons light soy sauce
1 tablespoon sugar
1 tablespoon sunflower oil
1 head Chinese cabbage
$^1/_2$ frisée lettuce, torn into bitesize pieces
1 cup unsalted cashew nuts
2 large carrots, peeled and cut into
    fine strips
salt and ground black pepper

1 Chop the fresh tarragon. Cut the chicken into fine strips and place in a bowl.

2 To make the marinade, combine the tarragon, ginger, soy sauce, sugar, and seasoning in a bowl.

3 Pour the marinade over the chicken strips and leave to marinate for 2–4 hours.

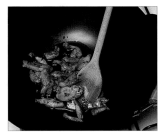

4 Drain the chicken from the marinade, reserving the liquid. Heat a wok or large skillet, then add the oil. When the oil is hot, stir-fry the chicken for 3 minutes, then add the reserved marinade, and bubble for 2–3 minutes.

5 Slice the Chinese cabbage and arrange on a plate with the frisée. Toss the cashew nuts and carrot strips together with the chicken and sauce, pile on top of the bed of lettuce, and serve the salad immediately.

Thai Chicken Salad

This delicious salad originates from Chiang Mai, a city in the northeast of Thailand. The city is culturally very close to Laos and famous for its flavorful chicken salad.

INGREDIENTS

Serves 4–6

1 pound ground chicken
1 lemongrass stalk, root trimmed
3 kaffir lime leaves, finely chopped
4 fresh red chiles, seeded
    and chopped
4 tablespoons lime juice
2 tablespoons Thai fish sauce
1 tablespoon roasted ground rice (see
    Cook's Tip)
2 scallions, chopped
2 tablespoons fresh cilantro leaves
thinly sliced kaffir lime leaves, mixed
    salad greens, and fresh mint sprigs,
    to garnish

1 Heat a large, nonstick skillet. Add the ground chicken and moisten with a little water. Stir constantly over medium heat for 7–10 minutes, or until the chicken is cooked. Meanwhile, cut off the lower 2 inches of the lemongrass stalk and chop finely.

2 Transfer the chicken to a bowl and add the lemongrass, lime leaves, chiles, lime juice, Thai fish sauce, ground rice, scallions, and cilantro. Mix thoroughly.

3 Spoon the chicken into a salad bowl. Sprinkle sliced kaffir lime leaves over the top and garnish with salad leaves and mint.

COOK'S TIP

Use glutinous rice for the roasted ground rice. Dry-roast the rice in a skillet until golden brown. Remove and grind to a powder, using a mortar and pestle. When cold, store it in a glass jar in a cool and dry place.

Chicken, Vegetable, and Chile Salad

Crunchy fresh vegetables, chiles, and gherkins give this salad plenty of flavor.

INGREDIENTS

Serves 4

8 ounces Chinese cabbage

2 carrots, cut in batons

$^1/_2$ cucumber, cut in batons

2 red chiles, seeded and cut into strips

1 small onion, sliced into fine rings

4 pickled gherkins, sliced, plus
  3 tablespoons of the liquid

$^1/_2$ cup peanuts, lightly ground

8 ounces cooked chicken, skinned and
  thinly sliced

1 garlic clove, crushed

1 teaspoon granulated sugar

2 tablespoons white vinegar

salt

1 Finely slice the Chinese cabbage and set aside with the carrots. Spread out the cucumber batons on a board and sprinkle with salt. Set aside for 15 minutes.

2 Combine the chiles and onion in a bowl. Add the gherkins and peanuts, and stir.

3 Tip the salted cucumber into a colander, rinse well, and drain thoroughly. Using a wooden spatula, press out as much liquid from the cucumber as possible, then pat dry with paper towels.

4 Put the cucumber into a salad bowl and add the Chinese cabbage and carrot batons. Toss to mix, then add the chile mixture and slices of cooked chicken.

5 Make a dressing by whisking the gherkin liquid with the garlic, sugar, and vinegar in a small bowl or pitcher. Pour the dressing over the salad, toss lightly, and serve immediately.

Hot and Sour Chicken Salad

Chicken is marinated in a delicious combination of spices, stir-fried, and then served on a bed of vegetables.

INGREDIENTS

Serves 4–6

2 skinless, boneless chicken
   breast portions
$^1/_2$-inch piece of fresh ginger root, peeled
1 red chile, seeded and finely chopped
1 garlic clove, crushed
1 tablespoon crunchy peanut butter
2 tablespoons chopped cilantro
1 teaspoon sugar
$^1/_2$ teaspoon salt
1 tablespoon rice or white wine vinegar
4 tablespoons vegetable oil
2 teaspoons Thai fish sauce (optional)
1 head Chinese cabbage
$^1/_2$ cup bean sprouts
2 medium carrots, cut into thin sticks
1 red onion, cut into fine rings
2 large gherkins, sliced

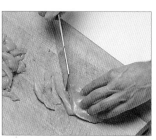

1 Slice the chicken thinly, place in a shallow bowl, and set aside. Chop the ginger and grind it in a mortar and pestle with the chile and garlic. Add the peanut butter, cilantro, sugar, and salt.

2 Add the vinegar, 2 tablespoons of the oil, and the Thai fish sauce, if using. Combine well. Cover the chicken with the spice mixture and let marinate for at least 2–3 hours.

3 Shred the Chinese cabbage coarsely and arrange with the bean sprouts, carrot sticks, onion rings, and sliced gherkins on a serving platter.

4 Heat the remaining oil in a wok or skillet. Add the chicken slices and cook over medium heat, tossing the meat occasionally, for 10–12 minutes, until golden brown and cooked through. Serve arranged on the salad.

Curried Chicken Salad

Serve this flavorful salad for lunch or
a midweek family supper.

2 Cook the pasta in a large pan of
lightly salted boiling water for
8–10 minutes, or until *al dente.*
Drain and rinse thoroughly.

3 To make the sauce, combine the
yogurt, curry powder, garlic,
green chile, and chopped cilantro
in a bowl. Stir in the strips of
chicken and leave to stand for
about 30 minutes.

INGREDIENTS

Serves 4

2 skinless, boneless chicken breast
    portions, cooked

6 ounces green beans

12 ounces multi-colored penne

4 firm ripe tomatoes, peeled, seeded, and
    cut in strips

salt and ground black pepper

cilantro leaves, to garnish

For the sauce

²/3 cup low-fat plain yogurt

1 teaspoon mild curry powder

1 garlic clove, crushed

1 green chile, seeded and finely chopped

2 tablespoons chopped fresh cilantro

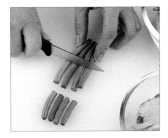

1 Cut the chicken in strips. Cut
the green beans into 1-inch
lengths and cook in boiling water
for 5 minutes. Drain and rinse
under cold water.

4 Transfer the pasta to a glass
bowl, add the beans and
tomatoes and toss together. Spoon
the chicken and sauce over them.
Garnish with cilantro leaves.

Coronation Chicken

A summer favorite—serve with a mixture of crisp salad greens.

INGREDIENTS

Serves 8

$^1/_2$ lemon

1 chicken, about 5 pounds

1 onion, quartered

1 carrot, quartered

large bouquet garni

8 black peppercorns, crushed

salt

mesclun or parsley sprigs,
  to garnish

For the sauce

1 small onion, chopped

1 tablespoon butter

1 tablespoon curry paste

1 tablespoon tomato paste

$^1/_2$ cup red wine

bay leaf

juice of $^1/_2$ lemon, or more to taste

2–3 teaspoons apricot jelly

$1^1/_4$ cups mayonnaise

$^1/_2$ cup whipping cream

salt and ground black pepper

1 Put the lemon half in the chicken cavity, then place the chicken in a pan that fits tightly. Add the vegetables, bouquet garni, peppercorns, and salt.

2 Add sufficient water to come two-thirds of the way up the chicken, bring to a boil, then cover, and cook gently for $1^1/_2$ hours, or until the juices run clear.

3 Transfer the chicken to a large bowl, pour the cooking liquid over it, and let cool. Skin, bone, then chop the chicken flesh.

4 To make the sauce, cook the onion in the butter until soft. Add the curry paste, tomato paste, wine, bay leaf, and lemon juice, then cook for 10 minutes. Add the apricot jelly, then strain, and cool.

5 Beat the sauce into the mayonnaise. Whip the cream, fold into the mayonnaise mixture. Add seasoning, then stir in the chicken, and garnish with mesclun or parsley sprigs.

Chinese-style Chicken Salad

Shredded chicken is served with a tasty peanut sauce.

INGREDIENTS

Serves 4

4 boneless chicken breast portions, about
    6 ounces each

4 tablespoons dark soy sauce

pinch of Chinese five-spice powder

a good squeeze of lemon juice

$1/2$ cucumber, peeled and cut
    into batons

1 teaspoon salt

3 tablespoons sunflower oil

2 tablespoons sesame oil

1 tablespoon sesame seeds

2 tablespoons dry sherry

2 carrots, cut into batons

8 scallions, shredded

$3/4$ cup bean sprouts

For the sauce

4 tablespoons crunchy peanut butter

2 teaspoons lemon juice

2 teaspoons sesame oil

$1/4$ teaspoon hot chili powder

1 scallion, finely chopped

1 Put the chicken breast portions into a large pan and just cover with water. Add 1 tablespoon of the soy sauce, the Chinese five-spice powder, and lemon juice. Cover and bring to a boil, then simmer for about 20 minutes.

2 Place the cucumber batons in a colander, sprinkle with the salt, and cover with a weighted plate. Let drain for 30 minutes.

3 Heat the sunflower and sesame oils in a large skillet or wok. Add the sesame seeds, cook for 30 seconds, and then stir in the remaining soy sauce and the sherry. Add the carrots and stir-fry over medium heat for 2–3 minutes. Remove and reserve.

4 Remove the chicken from the pan and leave until cool enough to handle. Discard the skins and hit the chicken lightly with a rolling pin to loosen the fibers. Slice in strips and reserve.

5 Rinse the cucumber well, pat dry with paper towels, and place in a bowl. Add the scallions, bean sprouts, cooked carrots, pan juices, and shredded chicken, and mix together. Transfer to a shallow dish. Cover and chill for about 1 hour, turning the mixture in the juices once or twice.

6 To make the sauce, cream the peanut butter with the lemon juice, sesame oil, and chili powder, adding a little hot water to form a paste, then stir in the scallion. Arrange the chicken mixture on a serving dish and serve with the peanut butter sauce.

Mediterranean Chicken Skewers

Pickled onions and vegetable-wrapped chunks of chicken provide an interesting contrast of flavors in these delicious kebabs.

INGREDIENTS

Serves 4

6 tablespoons olive oil

3 tablespoons fresh lemon juice

1 garlic clove, finely chopped

2 tablespoons chopped fresh basil

2 medium zucchini

1 long thin eggplant

11 ounces skinless, boneless chicken breast
    portions, cut into 2-inch cubes

12–16 pickled onions

1 red or yellow bell pepper, cut into
    2-inch squares

salt and ground black pepper

1 Soak four wooden skewers in water for 30 minutes. Combine the oil, lemon juice, garlic, and basil in a small bowl. Season with salt and pepper.

2 Slice the zucchini and eggplant lengthwise into strips ¼ inch thick. Cut them crosswise about two-thirds of the way along their length. Discard the shorter length. Wrap half the chicken pieces with the zucchini slices, and the other half with the eggplant slices.

3 Thread alternating pieces of chicken, onions, and bell pepper onto the skewers. Lay them on a platter, and sprinkle with the flavored oil. Let marinate for at least 30 minutes. Prepare a barbecue, if using.

4 Cook the skewers on the barbecue or under a preheated broiler for about 10 minutes, or until the vegetables are tender and the chicken is cooked through, turning the skewers occasionally. Serve hot.

Chicken Liver Kebabs

2 Wrap the prunes around the cherry tomatoes. Prepare a barbecue, if using.

3 Thread the bacon-wrapped livers onto metal skewers with the prunes, tomatoes, and mushrooms. Brush with oil. Cover the tomatoes and prunes with a strip of foil to protect them while cooking. Cook on the barbecue or under a hot broiler for about 5 minutes on each side.

These tasty kebabs may be grilled outdoors and served with salads and baked potatoes or broiled indoors and served with rice and broccoli.

INGREDIENTS

Serves 4

4 ounces fatty bacon strips

12 ounces chicken livers

12 large ready-to-eat prunes

12 cherry tomatoes

8 white mushrooms

2 tablespoons olive oil

1 Using a sharp knife or kitchen scissors, cut each strip of bacon into two, wrap a piece around each chicken liver, and secure in position with wooden toothpicks.

4 Remove and discard the toothpicks and serve the kebabs immediately.

Sweet and Sour Chicken Kebabs

This marinade contains sugar and will burn very easily, so cook the kebabs slowly, turning frequently. Serve with harlequin rice.

INGREDIENTS

Serves 4

2 skinless, boneless chicken
   breast portions
8 pearl onions or 2 medium onions
4 fatty bacon strips
3 firm bananas
1 red bell pepper, seeded
   and sliced

For the marinade

2 tablespoons soft brown sugar
1 tablespoon Worcestershire sauce
2 tablespoons lemon juice
salt and ground black pepper

For the harlequin rice

2 tablespoons olive oil
2 cups cooked rice
1 cup cooked peas
1 small red bell pepper, seeded and diced

1 Combine all the marinade ingredients. Cut each chicken portion into four pieces, add to the marinade, cover, and marinate for at least 4 hours or, preferably, overnight in the refrigerator.

2 Peel the onions, blanch them in boiling water for 5 minutes, and drain. If using medium onions, quarter them after blanching. Prepare a barbecue, if using.

3 Cut each strip of bacon in half. Peel the bananas and cut each into three pieces. Wrap a strip of bacon around each of eight pieces of banana.

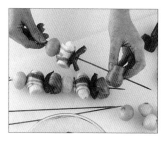

4 Thread onto four metal skewers with the chicken pieces, onions, and bell pepper slices. Brush with the marinade.

5 Cook on low heat on the barbecue or under a preheated broiler for 15 minutes, turning and basting frequently with the marinade. Keep warm while you prepare the rice.

6 Heat the oil in a skillet and add the rice, peas, and diced bell pepper. Stir until heated through and serve with the kebabs.

Chicken with Pineapple

This chicken has a delicate tang and is very tender. The pineapple not only tenderizes the chicken but also gives it a slight sweetness.

INGREDIENTS

Serves 6

8-ounce can pineapple chunks
1 teaspoon ground cumin
1 teaspoon ground coriander
$1/2$ teaspoon crushed garlic
1 teaspoon chili powder
1 teaspoon salt
2 tablespoons plain yogurt
1 tablespoon chopped fresh cilantro
orange food coloring (optional)
10 ounces chicken, skinned
    and boned
$1/2$ red bell pepper
$1/2$ yellow or green bell pepper
1 large onion
6 cherry tomatoes
1 tablespoon vegetable oil

1 Drain the pineapple juice into a bowl. Reserve eight large chunks of pineapple and squeeze the juice from the remaining chunks into the bowl and set aside. You should have about $1/2$ cup pineapple juice.

2 In a large mixing bowl, blend together the cumin, ground coriander, garlic, chili powder, salt, yogurt, fresh cilantro, and a few drops of food coloring, if using. Pour in the reserved pineapple juice and mix together.

3 Cut the chicken into bitesize cubes, add to the mixing bowl with the yogurt and spice mixture, and leave to marinate for about 1–$1^1/2$ hours.

4 If using wooden skewers, soak six in water for 30 minutes. Cut the bell peppers and onion into bitesize chunks.

5 Prepare a barbecue, if using. Arrange the chicken pieces, bell peppers, onion, tomatoes, and reserved pineapple chunks alternately on the skewers.

6 Baste the kebabs with the oil. Cook on the barbecue or under a preheated broiler for about 15 minutes, turning and basting the chicken pieces with the marinade regularly.

7 Once the chicken pieces are cooked, remove them from the barbecue or broiler and serve either with salad or plain boiled rice.

COOK'S TIP

If possible, use a mixture of chicken breast and thigh meat for this recipe.

Citrus Kebabs

A blend of fresh mint, cumin, and citrus fruits makes these kebabs really flavorful. Preparation time is quick, but allow at least 2 hours marinating time for the flavors to develop. Perfect served on a bed of lettuce leaves and garnished with fresh mint and orange and lemon slices.

INGREDIENTS

Serves 4

4 skinless, boneless chicken
   breast portions
fresh mint sprigs, to garnish
orange, lemon or lime slices, to garnish

For the marinade
finely grated rind and juice of ½ orange
finely grated rind and juice of ½ small
   lemon or lime
2 tablespoons olive oil
2 tablespoons honey
2 tablespoons chopped fresh mint
¼ teaspoon ground cumin
salt and ground black pepper

1 Cut the chicken portions into 1-inch cubes.

2 Combine all the marinade ingredients in a glass or ceramic bowl, add the chicken cubes, and leave to marinate for at least 2 hours. Prepare a barbecue, or preheat the broiler.

3 Thread the chicken pieces onto four metal skewers and cook for 15 minutes, basting with the marinade and turning frequently, until cooked through. Serve garnished with extra mint and citrus slices.

Caribbean Chicken Kebabs

These kebabs have a rich, Caribbean flavor and the marinade keeps them moist without the need for oil. Serve them with a colorful salad and rice.

INGREDIENTS

Serves 4

1¹/4 pounds skinless, boneless chicken
    breast portions
finely grated rind of 1 lime
2 tablespoons lime juice
1 tablespoon rum or sherry
1 tablespoon brown sugar
1 teaspoon ground cinnamon
2 mangoes, peeled, pitted,
    and cubed
rice and salad, to serve

2 Prepare a barbecue, if using. Save the marinade and thread the chicken onto the skewers, alternating with the mango cubes.

3 Cook the skewers on a barbecue or under a preheated broiler for 8–10 minutes, turning occasionally and basting with the reserved marinade, until the chicken is golden brown and cooked through. Serve immediately with rice and salad.

1 If using wooden skewers, soak four in water for 30 minutes. Cut the chicken portions into bitesize chunks and place in a bowl with the grated lime rind and juice, rum or sherry, sugar, and ground cinnamon. Toss well, cover, and marinate for 1 hour.

COOK'S TIP

The rum or sherry adds a lovely rich flavor, but it is optional so can be omitted if you prefer to make the dish more economical.

Turkey Sosaties with a Curried Apricot Sauce

This is a South African way of cooking poultry in a delicious sweet-and-sour spiced sauce.

INGREDIENTS

Serves 4

1 tablespoon oil
1 onion, finely chopped
1 garlic clove, crushed
2 bay leaves
juice of 1 lemon
2 tablespoons curry powder
4 tablespoons apricot jelly
4 tablespoons apple juice
salt
1¹/₂ pounds turkey breast fillet
4 tablespoons crème fraîche

1 Heat the oil in a pan. Add the onion, garlic, and bay leaves and cook over low heat for about 10 minutes, or until the onions are soft. Add the lemon juice, curry powder, apricot jelly, and apple juice, with salt to taste. Cook gently for 5 minutes. Let cool.

2 Cut the turkey into ³/₄-inch cubes and add to the marinade. Mix well, cover, and leave in a cool place to marinate for at least 2 hours or chill overnight.

3 Prepare a barbecue or preheat the broiler. Thread the turkey onto four metal skewers, letting the marinade run back into the bowl. Cook the sosaties for about 6–8 minutes, turning several times, until done.

4 Meanwhile, transfer the marinade to a pan and simmer for 2 minutes. Stir in the crème fraîche and serve with the sosaties.

Spicy Indonesian Chicken Satay

This spicy marinade quickly gives an exotic flavor to tender chicken. The satays can be cooked on a barbecue or under the broiler.

INGREDIENTS

Serves 4

4 skinless, boneless chicken breast
    portions, about 6 ounces each
2 tablespoons deep-fried onion slices

For the sambal kecap
1 fresh red chile, seeded and
    finely chopped
2 garlic cloves, crushed
4 tablespoons dark soy sauce
4 teaspoons lemon juice or
    1–1¹/₂ tablespoons tamarind juice
2 tablespoons hot water

1 Soak eight wooden skewers in water for 30 minutes.

2 To make the sambal kecap, combine the chile, garlic, soy sauce, lemon or tamarind juice, and hot water in a bowl. Let stand for 30 minutes.

3 Cut the chicken portions into 1-inch cubes and place in a bowl with the sambal kecap. Mix thoroughly. Cover and leave in a cool place to marinate for 1 hour.

4 Tip the chicken and marinade into a strainer placed over a pan and let drain for a few minutes. Set the strainer aside.

5 Add 2 tablespoons hot water to the marinade and bring to a boil. Lower the heat and simmer for 2 minutes, then pour the mixture into a bowl, and let cool. When completely cold, add the deep-fried onions.

6 Prepare a barbecue or preheat the broiler. Thread the skewers with the chicken and cook for about 10 minutes, turning frequently, until the chicken is golden brown and cooked through. Serve immediately with the sambal kecap as a dip.

Satay Chicken Skewers

A spicy peanut mixture makes a perfect marinade for chicken kebabs. Let the chicken marinate in the mixture overnight to enable the flavors to penetrate thoroughly.

INGREDIENTS

Serves 4

4 skinless, boneless chicken
   breast portions
lemon slices, to garnish
lettuce leaves and scallions, to serve

For the satay marinade
$^1/_2$ cup crunchy peanut butter
1 small onion, chopped
1 garlic clove, crushed
2 tablespoons chutney
4 tablespoons olive oil
1 teaspoon light soy sauce
2 tablespoons lemon juice
$^1/_4$ teaspoon chili powder or
   cayenne pepper

1 Put all the satay ingredients into a food processor or blender and process until smooth. Spoon into a large dish.

2 Cut the chicken breast portions into 1-inch cubes. Add to the satay mixture and stir well to coat all over. Cover the dish with plastic wrap and chill for at least 4 hours or, better still, overnight. Soak four wooden skewers in water for 30 minutes.

3 Prepare a barbecue or preheat the broiler. Thread the chicken pieces onto the skewers.

4 Cook for 10 minutes, brushing occasionally with the marinade, until done. Serve with lettuce, scallions, and lemon.

Japanese Chicken Kebabs

These "Yakitori" kebabs are ideal for barbecues. Make extra sauce if you like, to serve with the kebabs.

INGREDIENTS

Serves 4

6 boneless chicken thighs

bunch of scallions

shichimi (seven-flavor spice) or paprika, to serve (optional)

For the yakitori sauce

$2/3$ cup Japanese soy sauce

$3/4$ cup sugar

$1^1/2$ tablespoons sake or dry white wine

1 tablespoon all-purpose flour

1 Soak 12 bamboo skewers in water for 30 minutes.

4 Cut the scallions into $1^1/4$-inch pieces. Prepare a barbecue or preheat the broiler.

5 Thread the chicken and scallions alternately onto the skewers. Cook on the barbecue or broil, brushing generously several times with the yakitori sauce. Cook the skewers for about 5–10 minutes, or until the chicken is tender and cooked through but still moist.

6 Serve immediately with a little extra yakitori sauce.

2 To make the sauce, stir the soy sauce, sugar, and sake or wine into the flour in a pan. Bring to a boil, stirring. Lower the heat and simmer for 10 minutes, or until reduced by a third. Set aside.

3 Cut each chicken thigh into bitesize pieces and set aside.

Chicken Wings Teriyaki-style

This simple, Japanese glaze can be used with any cut of chicken. Chicken wings cooked this way are very tasty.

1 Place the garlic, soy sauce, sherry, honey, ginger, and sesame oil in a large bowl and beat with a fork, to mix evenly.

INGREDIENTS

Serves 4

1 garlic clove, crushed

3 tablespoons soy sauce

2 tablespoons dry sherry

2 teaspoons honey

2 teaspoons grated fresh ginger root

1 teaspoon sesame oil

12 chicken wings

1 tablespoon sesame seeds, toasted

salad greens, to serve

COOK'S TIP

Toasting the sesame seeds lightly helps to bring out their flavor. To do this, either put them in a heavy pan over medium heat and stir until golden, or sprinkle on a cookie sheet and cook under a medium broiler, until golden.

2 Add the chicken wings and toss thoroughly, to coat in the marinade. Cover and marinate in the refrigerator for about 30 minutes or longer if possible.

3 Cook the wings on a fairly hot barbecue for 20–25 minutes, turning occasionally and brushing with the remaining marinade.

4 Sprinkle with sesame seeds and serve with crisp salad greens.

Blackened Cajun Chicken and Corn

Food coated in a mix of hot Cajun spices will char and blacken slightly when cooked on the barbecue, giving it a delicious smoky flavor.

Serves 4

8 chicken portions, such as drumsticks, thighs, or wings
2 corncobs
2 teaspoons garlic salt
2 teaspoons ground black pepper
1 1/2 teaspoons ground cumin
1 1/2 teaspoons paprika
1 teaspoon cayenne pepper
3 tablespoons butter, melted
chopped parsley, to garnish

1 Cut any excess fat from the chicken, but leave the skin on. Slash the deepest parts with a knife, to let the flavors penetrate.

2 Pull the husks and silks off the corncobs and cut them into thick slices.

3 Prepare a barbecue. Combine the garlic salt, pepper, cumin, paprika, and cayenne. Brush the chicken and corn with melted butter and sprinkle the spice mixture over them. Toss well to coat evenly.

4 Cook the chicken pieces over medium-hot coals for about 25 minutes, turning occasionally, until tender. Add the corn after 15 minutes, and cook, turning often, until golden brown. Serve garnished with chopped parsley.

Barbecue-cooked Jerk Chicken

Jerk refers to the blend of herb and spice seasoning rubbed into meat before it is roasted over charcoal sprinkled with pimiento berries. In Jamaica, jerk seasoning was originally used only for pork, but jerked chicken is equally good.

INGREDIENTS

Serves 4

8 chicken pieces

salad greens, to serve

For the marinade

1 teaspoon ground allspice

1 teaspoon ground cinnamon

1 teaspoon dried thyme

$1/4$ teaspoon freshly grated nutmeg

2 teaspoons raw sugar

2 garlic cloves, crushed

1 tablespoon finely chopped onion

1 tablespoon chopped scallion

1 tablespoon vinegar

2 tablespoons oil, plus extra for brushing

1 tablespoon lime juice

1 hot chile, chopped

salt and ground black pepper

1 Combine all the marinade ingredients in a small bowl. Using a fork, mash them together well to form a thick paste.

2 Lay the chicken pieces on a plate or board and make several lengthwise slits in the flesh. Rub the seasoning all over the chicken and into the slits.

3 Place the chicken in a dish, cover with plastic wrap, and marinate in the refrigerator. Prepare a barbecue, if using. Shake off any excess seasoning from the chicken. Brush with oil. Place on a barbecue rack or on a cookie sheet if broiling.

4 Cook over the barbecue coals for 30 minutes, turning often, or under a preheated broiler for 45 minutes, turning often, until done. Serve hot with salad greens.

COOK'S TIP
〜

The flavor is best if you marinate the chicken overnight.

Chicken Fillets in Spices and Coconut

A medley of spices blended with coconut makes a fabulous marinade for grilled chicken fillets that are perfect served with nan bread. The chicken can be prepared in advance, so this dish is great for entertaining.

INGREDIENTS

Serves 4

3 garlic cloves, chopped

2 scallions, chopped

1 fresh green chile, chopped

2-inch piece of fresh ginger root, peeled
   and chopped

1 teaspoon fennel seeds

$1/2$ teaspoon black peppercorns

seeds from 4 cardamom pods

2 tablespoons ground coriander

1 teaspoon ground cumin

1 teaspoon ground star anise

1 teaspoon ground nutmeg

$1/2$ teaspoon ground cloves

$1/2$ teaspoon ground turmeric

$1^1/4$ cups coconut cream

4 large skinless, boneless chicken
   breast portions

onion rings and cilantro sprigs,
   to garnish

1 Place the garlic, scallions, chile, ginger, fennel seeds, peppercorns, cardamom seeds, coriander, cumin, star anise, nutmeg, cloves, and turmeric in a blender or food processor. Add the coconut cream and process to a smooth paste.

2 Make several diagonal cuts across the chicken portions. Arrange them in one layer in a shallow dish. Spoon half the coconut mixture over them and toss well to coat the chicken portions evenly. Cover the dish with plastic wrap and marinate in the refrigerator for at least 30 minutes or overnight.

3 Prepare a barbecue. Cook the chicken over medium heat for 12–15 minutes, turning once, until well browned and thoroughly cooked. Heat the remaining coconut mixture gently in a small pan, until it is boiling. Serve the sauce with the chicken, garnished with onion rings and sprigs of fresh cilantro.

Spiced Chicken

Almost every street-corner stall in Israel seems to sell barbecue-cooked chicken. In this recipe, the Egyptian-inspired marinade is strongly scented with cumin and cinnamon.

INGREDIENTS

Serves 4

5 garlic cloves, chopped
2 tablespoons ground cumin
1¹/₂ teaspoons ground cinnamon
1 teaspoon paprika
juice of 1 lemon
2 tablespoons olive oil
1 chicken, about 3 pounds, cut into
   8 portions
 salt and ground black pepper
fresh cilantro, to garnish
warm pita bread, salad, and lemon
   wedges, to serve

1 Combine the garlic, cumin, cinnamon, paprika, lemon juice, oil, salt, and pepper in a bowl. Add the chicken and turn to coat thoroughly. Marinate for at least 1 hour or cover and place in the refrigerator overnight.

2 Prepare a barbecue. After about 40 minutes it will be ready for cooking.

3 Cook the dark meat on the rack for 10 minutes, turning once, until done. Remove and keep warm.

4 Place the remaining chicken on the rack and cook for 7–10 minutes, turning occasionally, until golden brown and cooked through. Garnish with cilantro and serve immediately, with pita bread, salad, and lemon wedges.

Spiced Grilled Cornish Hens

The cumin and coriander coating on the Cornish hens keeps them moist during cooking as well as giving them a delicious flavor.

INGREDIENTS

Serves 4

2 garlic cloves, coarsely chopped
1 teaspoon ground cumin
1 teaspoon ground coriander
pinch of cayenne pepper
$^1/_2$ small onion, chopped
4 tablespoons olive oil
$^1/_2$ teaspoon salt
2 Cornish hens
lemon wedges,
    to garnish

1 Combine the garlic, cumin, coriander, cayenne pepper, onion, olive oil, and salt in a blender or food processor. Process to make a paste that will spread smoothly.

2 Cut the Cornish hens in half lengthwise. Place them skin side up in a shallow dish and spread with the spice paste. Cover and marinate in a cool place for about 2 hours.

3 Prepare a barbecue or preheat the broiler. Cook the Cornish hens for 15–20 minutes, turning frequently, until cooked and lightly charred on the outside. Serve immediately, garnished with lemon wedges.

VARIATION
Chicken portions and quail can also be cooked in this way.

Cornish Hens with Lime and Chili

The Cornish hens in this recipe are flattened out—butterflied—so that they will cook evenly and quickly. The breast is stuffed with chili and sun-dried tomato butter, which keeps them moist and tastes great.

INGREDIENTS

Serves 4

4 Cornish hens, about 1 pound each
3 tablespoons butter
2 tablespoons sun-dried tomato paste
finely grated rind of 1 lime
2 teaspoons chili sauce
juice of $1/2$ lime
flat leaf parsley sprigs,
    to garnish
lime wedges, to serve

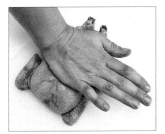

1 Place each Cornish hen on a board, breast side up, and press down firmly with your hand, to break the breastbone.

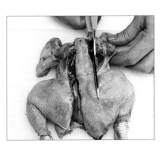

2 Turn the Cornish hen over and, with poultry shears or strong kitchen scissors, cut down either side of the backbone and remove it.

3 Turn the Cornish hen breast side up and flatten it neatly. Lift the breast skin carefully and gently ease your fingertips underneath, to loosen it from the flesh.

4 Combine the butter, tomato paste, lime rind, and chili sauce. Spread about three-quarters of the mixture under the skin of each Cornish hen, smoothing it evenly.

COOK'S TIP
∿
If you wish to serve half a Cornish hen per portion, you may find it easier simply to cut the birds in half lengthwise. Use poultry shears or a large sharp knife to cut through the breastbone and backbone.

5 To hold the Cornish hens flat during cooking, thread two skewers through each bird, crossing at the center. Each skewer should pass through a wing and then out through a drumstick on the other side.

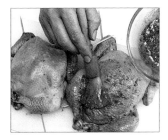

6 Prepare a barbecue. Mix the reserved paste with the lime juice and brush it over the skin of the Cornish hens. Cook over medium-hot coals, turning occasionally, for 25–30 minutes, or until the juices run clear when the thickest part of the leg is pierced. Garnish with flat leaf parsley and serve with lime wedges.

Chicken with Pica de Gallo Salsa

This dish originates from Mexico. Its hot, fruity flavors are associated with the Tex-Mex style of cooking.

INGREDIENTS

Serves 4

4 skinless, boneless chicken
   breast portions
pinch of celery salt and cayenne
   pepper combined
2 tablespoons vegetable oil
corn chips, to serve

For the salsa

10 ounces watermelon
6 ounces cantaloupe melon
1 small red onion
1–2 green chiles
2 tablespoons lime juice
4 tablespoons chopped fresh cilantro
pinch of salt

COOK'S TIP

When handling chiles you may prefer to wear latex gloves.

1 To make the salsa, remove the rind and as many seeds as you can from the melons. Finely dice the flesh and put it into a bowl.

2 Finely chop the onion, split the chiles (discarding the seeds which contain most of the heat), and chop. Take care when handling cut chiles. Mix with the melon.

3 Add the lime juice and cilantro, and season with salt. Turn the salsa into a small bowl.

4 Prepare a barbecue or preheat a broiler. Slash the chicken breast portions deeply to speed up the cooking time.

5 Season the chicken with celery salt and cayenne, brush with oil, and cook for about 15 minutes, turning once, until cooked through.

6 Serve the chicken on a plate, with the salsa and corn chips.

Butterflied Cornish Hens

*These little birds are delicious
steeped in a scallion and herb sauce.*

INGREDIENTS

Serves 4

4 Cornish hens, about 1 pound each

olive oil

salt and ground black pepper

red bell pepper strips and parsley sprigs,
     to garnish

For the sauce

2 tablespoons dry sherry

2 tablespoons lemon juice

2 tablespoons olive oil

2 ounces scallions, chopped

1 garlic clove, finely chopped

4 tablespoons chopped mixed fresh herbs,
     such as tarragon, parsley, thyme,
     marjoram, lemon balm

1 Place each Cornish hen breast down on a board and split it along the back. Open out the bird and turn it over, so that the breast side is uppermost. Press the bird as flat as possible, then thread two metal skewers through it, across the breast and thigh, to keep it flat.

2 Prepare a barbecue or preheat the broiler.

3 Season the butterflied birds, then brush them with a little olive oil. Set them on the barbecue 6 inches above the coals or on the rack in the broiling pan, about 4 inches from the heat.

4 Cook for 20–25 minutes, or until tender. Turn and brush with more oil halfway through the cooking time.

5 Meanwhile, to make the sauce, whisk together the sherry, lemon juice, olive oil, scallions, and garlic. Season to taste.

6 When the Cornish hens are done, transfer them to a deep serving platter. Whisk the herbs into the sauce, then spoon it over the birds. Cover tightly with another platter or with foil and let rest for 15 minutes before serving, garnished with the red bell pepper strips and parsley.

LIGHT BITES
& LUNCHES

Tender chicken is the perfect ingredient for a light snack or lunch, and there are so
many different ways it can be enjoyed. In this chapter there are recipes from a
variety of different countries that will give you inspiration for midday eating.
They range from light bundles of vegetables and chicken, wraps made with lettuce
or lotus leaves, filled pita and nan bread pockets to pizzas, light risottos, and
stir-fries, and so much more. You will never lack ideas for a lunchtime dish,
whether you are cooking for a family or entertaining friends.

Chicken and Pasta Omelet

Vegetables, pasta, and chicken make a tasty and substantial omelet. It is an ideal dish to make using leftovers.

INGREDIENTS

Serves 4–6

2 tablespoons olive oil

1 large onion, chopped

2 large garlic cloves, crushed

4 ounces bacon, chopped

2 ounces cold cooked chicken, chopped

4 ounces leftover, lightly cooked vegetables

1 cup cooked pasta or rice

4 eggs

2 tablespoons chopped, mixed fresh
herbs, such as parsley, chives,
marjoram, or tarragon, or
2 teaspoons dried

about 1 teaspoon Worcestershire sauce,
to taste

1 tablespoon grated sharp Cheddar cheese

salt and ground black pepper

1 Heat the oil in a large skillet with a flameproof handle or cover the handle with foil. Cook the onion, garlic, and bacon until all the fat has run out of the bacon.

2 Add the chopped chicken, vegetables, and pasta or rice. Beat the eggs, herbs, and Worcestershire sauce together with seasoning. Pour into the skillet, stir lightly, then leave the mixture undisturbed to cook gently for about 5 minutes.

3 When just beginning to set, sprinkle with the cheese and place under a preheated broiler until just firm and golden.

COOK'S TIP

This is surprisingly good cold, and is perfect for taking on picnics or using for packed lunches.

Chicken and Rice Omelet

In Japan, these rice omelets are a favorite with children, who usually top them with a liberal helping of tomato ketchup.

INGREDIENTS

Serves 4

1 skinless, boneless chicken thigh, about
    4 ounces, cubed

8 teaspoons butter

1 small onion, chopped

$1/2$ carrot, diced

2 shiitake mushrooms, stems removed
    and chopped

1 tablespoon finely chopped fresh parsley

2 cups cooked long grain
    white rice

2 tablespoons tomato ketchup,
    plus extra to serve

6 eggs, lightly beaten

4 tablespoons milk

1 teaspoon salt, plus extra to season

freshly ground black pepper

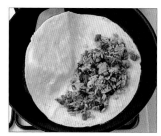

3 Beat the eggs with the milk in a bowl. Stir in the measured salt, and add pepper. Melt 1 teaspoon of the remaining butter in an omelet pan. Pour in a quarter of the egg mixture and stir it briefly with a fork, then let it set for 1 minute. Top with a quarter of the rice mixture.

4 Fold the omelet over the rice and slide it to the edge of the pan to shape it into a curve. Slide it onto a warmed plate, cover with paper towels, and press neatly into a rectangular shape. Keep hot while cooking three more omelets from the remaining ingredients. Serve immediately, with tomato ketchup.

1 Season the chicken. Melt 2 teaspoons butter in a skillet. Cook the onion for 1 minute, then add the chicken, and cook until golden. Add the mushrooms and carrot, stir-fry until soft, then add the parsley. Set aside. Wipe the skillet with paper towels.

2 Melt 2 teaspoons butter in the skillet, add the rice, and stir well. Add the cooked ingredients, ketchup, and black pepper. Stir well, adding salt to taste. Keep the mixture warm.

Chicken Crêpes

Use leftover cooked chicken and store-bought crêpes to make this quick and appetizing lunch.

INGREDIENTS

Serves 4

8 ounces cooked, boned chicken

2 tablespoons butter

1 small onion, finely chopped

scant 1 cup mushrooms, finely chopped

2 tablespoons all-purpose flour

$^2/3$ cup chicken stock or milk

1 tablespoon chopped fresh parsley

8 small or 4 large cooked crêpes

oil, for brushing

2 tablespoons grated cheese

salt and ground black pepper

3 Add the flour and then the stock or milk, stirring constantly. Boil to thicken and simmer for 2 minutes. Season with salt and black pepper.

4 Add the chicken cubes and chopped fresh parsley.

1 Remove the skin from the chicken and cut into cubes.

2 Heat the butter in a pan and cook the onion gently until tender. Add the mushrooms. Cook, covered, for 3–4 minutes more.

5 Divide the filling equally among the crêpes, roll them up, and arrange in a greased ovenproof dish. Preheat the broiler.

6 Brush the crêpes with a little oil and sprinkle with cheese. Broil until browned. Serve hot.

Chicken Crêpe Packets

Chicken and apple might seem an unlikely combination, but make a delicious filling for these quick and easy crêpes. Crisp snow peas and a fruity cranberry sauce make an ideal accompaniment.

INGREDIENTS

Serves 4

1 cup all-purpose flour
pinch of salt
1 egg, beaten
1¹/4 cups milk
oil, for frying

For the filling
2 tablespoons oil
4 cups ground chicken
2 tablespoons chopped fresh chives
2 green eating apples, cored
   and diced
¹/4 cup all-purpose flour
³/4 cup chicken stock
salt and ground black pepper

For the sauce
4 tablespoons cranberry sauce
¹/4 cup chicken stock
1 tablespoon honey
2 tablespoons cornstarch

1 To make the filling, heat the oil in a large pan and cook the chicken for 5 minutes. Add the chives and apples and then the flour. Stir in the stock and seasoning. Cook for 20 minutes.

2 To make the crêpes, sift the flour into a bowl together with a pinch of salt. Make a well in the center and drop in the egg. Beat it in gradually with the milk to form a smooth batter. Heat the oil in a 6-inch omelet pan. Pour off the oil and add one-quarter of the crêpe mixture. Tilt the pan to cover the base with the mixture and cook for 2–3 minutes. Turn the crêpe over and cook for 2 minutes more. Stack the crêpes on top of one another, interleaved with waxed paper or baking parchment, and keep warm.

3 To make the sauce, put the cranberry sauce, stock, and honey into a pan. Heat gently until melted. Blend the cornstarch with 4 teaspoons cold water to make a smooth paste, stir it in, and bring to a boil. Cook, stirring constantly, until clear.

4 Place each crêpe on a warmed individual serving plate, spoon the filling into the center, and fold it over around the filling. Spoon the cranberry sauce onto the plates and serve immediately.

Chicken and Vegetable Bundles

This popular and delicious dim sum is extremely easy to prepare and makes an ideal light lunch.

INGREDIENTS

Serves 4

4 skinless, boneless chicken thighs

1 teaspoon cornstarch

2 teaspoons dry sherry

2 tablespoons light soy sauce

$1/2$ teaspoon salt

large pinch of ground white pepper

4 fresh shiitake mushrooms

1 small carrot

1 small zucchini

$1/2$ cup sliced, drained, canned
   bamboo shoots

1 leek, trimmed

$1/4$ teaspoon sesame oil

2 Add the cornstarch, sherry, and half the soy sauce to the bowl. Season and mix well. Cover and marinate for 10 minutes.

3 Remove and discard the mushroom stalks, then cut each mushroom cap in half (or in slices if very large). Cut the carrot and zucchini into eight batons, each about 2 inches long, then mix the mushroom halves and bamboo shoots together.

4 Bring a pan of water to a boil. Add the leek and blanch until soft. Drain thoroughly, then slit the leek down its length. Separate each layer to give eight long strips.

5 Divide the marinated chicken into eight portions. Do the same with the vegetables. Wrap a strip of leek around a portion of chicken and vegetables to make eight neat bundles. Have ready a pan with about 2 inches boiling water and a steamer or a heatproof plate that will fit inside it on a metal trivet.

6 Place the chicken and vegetable bundles in the steamer or on the plate. Place in the pan, cover, and steam over high heat for 12–15 minutes, or until the filling is cooked. Meanwhile, combine the remaining soy sauce and sesame oil and use as a sauce for the bundles.

1 Remove any fat from the chicken thighs and cut each lengthwise into eight strips. Place the strips in a bowl.

Indonesian-style Satay Chicken

Coconut, peanuts, fresh ginger, and chili sauce are the key ingredients for this popular Southeast Asian dish. The spicy chicken is delicious served with rice and a fresh salad of mixed green leaves.

INGREDIENTS

Serves 4

$^1/_2$ cup raw peanuts

3 tablespoons vegetable oil

1 small onion, finely chopped

1-inch piece of fresh ginger root, peeled
    and finely chopped

1 garlic clove, crushed

$1^1/_2$ pounds skinless, boneless chicken
    thighs, cut into cubes

1 tablespoon chili sauce

$^1/_4$ cup crunchy peanut butter

1 teaspoon soft dark brown sugar

$^2/_3$ cup coconut cream

$^1/_4$ teaspoon salt

1 Soak four wooden skewers in water for 30 minutes to prevent them from charring. Shell and rub the skins from the peanuts, then soak them for 1 minute in a bowl with just enough water to cover them. Drain the peanuts and carefully cut them into fine slivers with a sharp knife.

2 Heat a large wok or skillet and add 1 teaspoon of the oil. When the oil is hot, stir-fry the peanuts for 1 minute. Remove them with a slotted spoon and drain well on paper towels.

3 Add the remaining oil to the wok or skillet. When the oil is hot, add the onion, ginger, and garlic. Stir-fry for 2–3 minutes, or until softened but not browned. Remove and drain on paper towels.

4 Add the chicken and stir-fry for 3–4 minutes, or until crisp on all sides and cooked through.

5 Thread onto the pre-soaked bamboo skewers and keep warm in a low oven.

6 Add the chili sauce, peanut butter, and cooked onion, ginger, and garlic mixture to the wok or skillet and cook for 2 minutes. Stir in the sugar, coconut cream, and salt and simmer for 3 minutes more.

7 Serve the skewered chicken hot, with a dash of the hot dipping sauce sprinkled with the peanuts.

Chicken Lettuce Wraps

Known as Sang Choy in Hong Kong, this is a popular assemble-it-yourself treat. The filling—an imaginative blend of textures and flavors—is served with crisp lettuce leaves, which are used as wraps.

INGREDIENTS

Serves 6

2 boneless chicken breast portions, total
weight about 12 ounces

4 dried Chinese mushrooms, soaked for
30 minutes in warm water to cover

2 tablespoons vegetable oil

2 garlic cloves, crushed

6 drained canned water chestnuts,
thinly sliced

2 tablespoons light soy sauce

1 teaspoon Sichuan peppercorns, dry-fried
and crushed

4 scallions, finely chopped

1 teaspoon sesame oil

vegetable oil, for deep-frying

2 ounces cellophane noodles

salt and ground black pepper (optional)

1 crisp lettuce, divided into leaves, and
4 tablespoons hoi-sin sauce, to serve

1 Remove the skin from the chicken and set aside. Chop the chicken into thin strips. Drain the mushrooms, discard the stems, and slice the caps finely. Set aside.

2 Heat the oil in a wok or large skillet. Add the garlic, then add the chicken, and stir-fry until the pieces are cooked through and no longer pink.

3 Add the mushrooms, water chestnuts, soy sauce, and peppercorns. Toss for 2–3 minutes, then season, if needed. Stir in half the scallions, then the sesame oil. Remove from the heat. Set aside.

4 Heat the oil to 375°F. Test by dropping a cube of bread into it: it should brown in 60 seconds. Cut the chicken skin into strips, deep-fry until crisp, and drain. Add the noodles to the oil and deep-fry until crisp. Transfer to a plate lined with paper towels.

5 Crush the noodles and put them in a serving dish. Top with the chicken skin, chicken mixture, and the remaining scallions. Arrange the lettuce leaves on a large platter.

6 Toss the chicken and noodles to mix. Each diner can take one or two lettuce leaves, spread the inside with hoi-sin sauce, and add a spoonful of filling, turning in the sides of the leaves and rolling them into a packet. The wraps are eaten held in the hand.

Sticky Chicken and Rice Packets

Glutinous rice gives the filling a wonderful texture in this deliciously unusual dish from China.

INGREDIENTS

Serves 4

2^1/4 cups glutinous rice

4 teaspoons vegetable oil

1 tablespoon dark soy sauce

^{1}/4 teaspoon five-spice powder

1 tablespoon dry sherry

4 skinless, boneless chicken thighs, each
cut into 4 pieces

8 dried Chinese mushrooms, soaked in hot
water until soft

1 ounce dried shrimp, soaked in hot water
until soft

^{1}/2 cup sliced, drained, canned
bamboo shoots

1^1/4 cups chicken stock

2 teaspoons cornstarch

1 tablespoon cold water

4 lotus leaves, soaked in warm water
until soft

salt and ground white pepper

1 Rinse the glutinous rice until the water runs clear, then let soak in water for 2 hours. Drain and stir in 1 teaspoon of the oil and ^{1}/2 teaspoon salt. Line a large steamer with a piece of clean cheesecloth. Transfer the rice into this. Cover and steam over boiling water for 45 minutes, stirring the rice from time to time and adding more boiling water if needed.

2 Combine the soy sauce, five-spice powder, and sherry. Put the chicken pieces in a bowl, add the marinade, stir to coat, then cover, and leave to marinate for 20 minutes.

3 Drain the Chinese mushrooms, cut out, and discard the stems, then chop the caps coarsely. Drain the dried shrimp. Heat the remaining oil in a nonstick skillet or wok. Stir-fry the chicken for 2 minutes, then add the chopped mushroom caps, shrimp, bamboo shoots, and stock. Simmer for 10 minutes.

4 Mix the cornstarch to a paste with the cold water. Add the mixture to the wok or skillet and cook, stirring constantly, until the sauce has thickened. Add salt and white pepper to taste. Lift the cooked rice out of the steamer and let it cool slightly.

5 With lightly dampened hands, divide the rice into four equal portions. Put half of one portion in the center of a lotus leaf. Spread it into a round and place a quarter of the chicken mixture on top. Cover with the remaining half portion of rice. Fold the leaf around the filling to make a neat rectangular packet. Make three more packets in the same way.

6 Prepare a steamer. Put the rice packets, seam side down, into the steamer. Cover and steam over high heat for about 30 minutes. Serve on individual heated plates.

COOK'S TIP

The packets can be made several days in advance and resteamed before serving. If you do this, allow an extra 20 minutes' cooking time to make sure that the filling is hot.

Turkey Rolls with Gazpacho Sauce

This Spanish-style recipe uses turkey steaks wrapped around chorizo sausages and cooked on a barbecue. Served with the gazpacho sauce this makes an unusual and tasty meal.

INGREDIENTS

Serves 4

4 turkey breast steaks

1 tablespoon red pesto or
    tomato paste

4 chorizo sausages

For the sauce

1 green bell pepper, seeded and chopped

1 red bell pepper, seeded and chopped

3-inch piece cucumber

1 medium tomato

1 garlic clove

3 tablespoons olive oil

1 tablespoon red wine vinegar

salt and ground black pepper

1 To make the gazpacho sauce, place the green and red bell peppers, cucumber, tomato, garlic, 2 tablespoons of the oil, and the vinegar in a food processor and process until almost smooth. Season to taste and set aside.

2 If the turkey breast steaks are quite thick, place them between two sheets of plastic wrap and beat them with the side of a rolling pin, to flatten them.

3 Spread the pesto or tomato paste over the turkey and then place a chorizo on each piece, and roll up firmly.

4 Prepare a barbecue. Slice the rolls thickly and thread them onto metal skewers. Grill on a medium-hot barbecue for 10–12 minutes, turning once, until cooked through; serve with the gazpacho sauce.

Chicken with Herb and Ricotta Stuffing

These little chicken drumsticks are full of flavor and the stuffing and bacon help to keep them moist and tender.

INGREDIENTS

Serves 4

4 tablespoons ricotta cheese

1 garlic clove, crushed

3 tablespoons mixed chopped
    fresh herbs, such as chives, flat leaf
    parsley, and mint

2 tablespoons fresh brown bread crumbs

8 chicken drumsticks

8 strips smoked fatty bacon

1 teaspoon whole-grain mustard

1 tablespoon sunflower oil

salt and ground black pepper

1 Combine the ricotta, garlic, herbs, and bread crumbs. Season with salt and pepper.

2 Carefully loosen the skin from each drumstick and spoon a little of the herb stuffing under each, smoothing the skin back over firmly.

3 Wrap a bacon strip around the wide end of each drumstick, to hold the skin in place over the stuffing.

4 Combine the mustard and oil and brush them over the chicken. Prepare a barbecue. Cook over medium-hot coals for about 25 minutes, turning occasionally, until the juices run clear and not pink when the flesh is pierced.

Stuffed Chicken Wings

These tasty stuffed wings are excellent served for lunch or hot or cold at a buffet. They can be prepared and frozen in advance.

INGREDIENTS

Makes 12
12 large chicken wings

For the filling
1 teaspoon cornstarch
$^1/_4$ teaspoon salt
$^1/_2$ teaspoon fresh thyme
pinch of ground black pepper

For the coating
$3^1/_4$ cups dried bread crumbs
2 tablespoons sesame seeds
2 eggs, beaten
oil, for deep-frying

1 Remove the wing tips and discard or use them for making stock. Skin the second joint sections, removing the two small bones, and grind the meat for the filling.

2 Mix the ground meat with the filling ingredients.

3 Holding the large end of the bone on the third section of the wing and using a sharp knife, cut the skin and flesh away from the bone, scraping down, and pulling the meat over the small end forming a pocket. Repeat this process with the remaining wing sections.

4 Fill the tiny pockets with the filling. Combine the dried bread crumbs and the sesame seeds. Place the bread crumb mixture and the beaten egg in separate dishes.

5 Brush the meat with beaten egg and roll in bread crumbs to cover. Chill and repeat to give a second layer, forming a thick coating. Chill until ready to fry.

6 Preheat the oven to 350°F. Heat 2 inches of oil in a heavy pan until hot but not smoking or the bread crumbs will burn. Gently fry two or three wings at a time until golden brown. Remove and drain on paper towels. Complete the cooking in the preheated oven for 15–20 minutes, or until tender and cooked through.

Turkey Patties

Turkey makes deliciously light patties, which are ideal for summer meals. You could use chicken if you prefer. Serve the patties in split and toasted rolls or pieces of crusty bread, with chutney, salad greens, and chunky fries.

INGREDIENTS

Serves 6

1¹/₂ pounds ground turkey

1 small red onion, finely chopped

grated rind and juice of 1 lime

small handful of fresh thyme leaves

1–2 tablespoons olive oil

salt and ground black pepper

1 Combine the turkey, onion, lime rind and juice, thyme, and seasoning. Cover and chill for up to 4 hours to allow the flavors to develop, then divide the mixture into six equal portions, and shape into round patties.

2 Preheat a griddle. Brush the patties with oil, then place them on the griddle, and cook for 10–12 minutes. Turn the patties over, brush with more oil, and cook for 10–12 minutes on the second side, or until cooked through.

Crispy Turkey Balls

Turkey meat makes a good base for these spicy, Eastern-inspired balls that are great for a light lunch. Chicken can be used instead of the turkey if you prefer.

INGREDIENTS

Serves 4–6

4 thin slices of white bread,
    crusts removed

1 teaspoon olive oil

8 ounces skinless, boneless turkey meat,
    coarsely chopped

1/3 cup drained, canned
    water chestnuts

2 fresh red chiles, seeded and
    coarsely chopped

1 egg white

1/4 cup fresh cilantro leaves

1 teaspoon cornstarch

1/2 teaspoon salt

1/4 teaspoon ground white pepper

2 tablespoons light soy sauce

1 teaspoon superfine sugar

2 tablespoons rice vinegar

1/2 teaspoon chili oil

shredded red chiles and fresh cilantro
    sprigs, to garnish

1 Preheat the oven to 250°F. Brush the bread slices lightly with olive oil and cut them into 1/4-inch cubes. Spread them out on a cookie sheet and bake for about 15 minutes, or until dry and crisp.

2 Meanwhile, combine the turkey meat, water chestnuts, and chiles in a food processor. Process to a coarse paste.

3 Add the egg white, cilantro leaves, cornstarch, salt, and pepper. Pour in half the soy sauce and process for about 30 seconds. Scrape into a bowl, cover, and leave in a cool place for 20 minutes.

4 Remove the toasted bread cubes from the oven and set them aside. Raise the oven temperature to 400°F. With dampened hands, divide the turkey mixture into 12 portions and form into balls.

5 Coarsely crush the toasted bread cubes, then transfer to a plate. Roll each ball, in turn, over the toasted crumbs until coated. Place on a cookie sheet and bake for about 20 minutes, or until the coating is brown and the turkey filling has cooked through.

6 In a small bowl, combine the remaining soy sauce, superfine sugar, rice vinegar, and chili oil. Serve this sauce with the turkey balls, garnished with shredded chiles and cilantro sprigs.

Mexican Chicken Panuchos

These Mexican tortillas are time consuming, but well worth the effort. Start preparations the day before, as the onion relish needs time to develop the flavors fully.

INGREDIENTS

Serves 6

1 cup dried pinto beans, soaked overnight in water
1 onion, halved
5 garlic cloves, peeled
1 cup masa harina
$1/2$ cup warm water
2 skinless, boneless chicken breast portions
1 teaspoon dried oregano
$1/2$ cup chopped fresh cilantro
2 hard-cooked eggs, sliced
oil, for shallow frying
salt and ground black pepper

For the onion relish

2 red Fresno chiles
1 teaspoon allspice berries
$1/2$ teaspoon black peppercorns
1 teaspoon dried oregano
2 garlic cloves, peeled
2 white onions, halved and thinly sliced
$1/2$ cup white wine vinegar
scant 1 cup cider vinegar
salt

1 To make the onion relish, dry-fry the chiles on a griddle until the skins scorch. Seal them in a plastic bag and set aside for 20 minutes. Place the allspice, black peppercorns, and oregano in a food processor or blender and process until coarsely ground. Alternatively, use a mortar and pestle.

2 Dry-roast the garlic in a heavy skillet until golden. Crush, then put in a bowl with the onions. Peel off the skins from the chiles. Slit them and scrape out the seeds. Chop the chiles.

3 Add the ground spices and chiles to the onion mixture. Mix in the vinegars and add salt to taste. Chill for at least 1 day before use.

4 Drain and rinse the pinto beans, then place in a large pan with $3^3/4$ cups water. Add the onion and the whole garlic cloves. Bring to a boil and simmer for $1^1/2$ hours, or until tender.

5 To make the tortillas, combine the masa harina and a pinch of salt in a large bowl. Add the warm water, a little at a time, to make a dough. Knead on a lightly floured counter for 3–4 minutes, or until smooth, then wrap the dough ball in plastic wrap and leave to rest for 1 hour.

6 Put the chicken in a pan, add the oregano, and pour in water to cover. Bring to a boil, lower the heat, and simmer for 10 minutes, or until cooked. Remove from the pan, discard the water, and let the chicken cool a little. Shred chicken into small pieces. Set aside.

COOK'S TIP
〜

Masa harina is a type of heavy white flour used extensively in Mexican cooking.

---

7 Divide the dough into 12 small pieces and roll into balls. Open a tortilla press and line both sides with plastic cut from a sandwich bag. Put a dough ball on the press and flatten it into a $2^1/2$-inch round. Alternatively, roll out the dough using a rolling pin. Use the remaining dough balls to make more tortillas in the same way.

8 Mash the beans and liquid to a smooth paste. Stir in the cilantro and salt to taste.

9 Cook each tortilla in a hot skillet for 15–20 seconds on each side. After a further 15 seconds on one side remove and wrap in a clean dishtowel.

10 Cut a slit in each tortilla, about $1/2$ inch deep around the rim. Put a spoonful of the bean paste and a slice of hard-cooked egg in each slit.

11 Heat the oil for shallow frying in a large skillet. Cook the tortilla pockets until they are crisp and golden brown on all sides, turning at least once during cooking. Drain them on paper towels and place on six individual serving plates. Top with a little of the shredded chicken and some onion relish. Season to taste and serve immediately.

Chicken Fajitas

Fajitas are warmed soft tortillas, filled and folded like an envelope. They are traditional Mexican fast food, delicious and easy to prepare, and a family favorite.

INGREDIENTS

Serves 4

generous 1/2 cup white long
    grain rice
3 tablespoons wild rice
1 tablespoon olive oil
1 tablespoon sunflower oil
1 onion, cut into thin wedges
4 skinless, boneless chicken breast
    portions, cut into thin strips
1 red bell pepper, seeded and finely sliced
1 teaspoon ground cumin
generous pinch of cayenne pepper
1/2 teaspoon ground turmeric
3/4 cup bottled strained tomatoes
1/2–3/4 cup chicken stock
12 small or 8 large wheat tortillas, and
    warmed sour cream, to serve

For the salsa
1 shallot, coarsely chopped
1 small garlic clove
1/2 –1 fresh green chile, seeded and
    coarsely chopped
small bunch of fresh parsley
5 tomatoes
2 teaspoons olive oil
1 tablespoon lemon juice
2 tablespoons tomato juice
salt and ground black pepper

For the guacamole
1 large ripe avocado
2 scallions, chopped
1–2 tablespoons fresh lime or
    lemon juice
generous pinch of cayenne pepper
1 tablespoon chopped fresh cilantro

1 Cook the long grain and wild rice separately, following the instructions on the packets. Drain and set aside.

2 To make the salsa, finely chop the shallot, garlic, chile, and parsley in a blender or food processor. Spoon into a bowl. Plunge the tomatoes into boiling water for 30 seconds, then refresh in cold water. Peel off the skins, remove the seeds, and chop the flesh. Stir in the chopped tomatoes, olive oil, lemon juice, and tomato juice. Season to taste with salt and pepper. Cover with plastic wrap and chill.

3 To make the guacamole, scoop the avocado flesh into a bowl. Mash it lightly with the scallions, citrus juice, cayenne pepper, fresh cilantro, and seasoning, so that small pieces still remain. Cover the surface closely with plastic wrap and chill.

4 Heat the olive and sunflower oils in a skillet and cook the onion wedges for 4–5 minutes, or until softened. Add the chicken strips and bell pepper slices and cook until evenly browned.

5 Stir in the cumin, cayenne, and turmeric. Cook, stirring, for about 1 minute, then stir in the bottled tomatoes and stock. Bring to a boil, then lower the heat, and simmer gently for 5–6 minutes, or until the chicken is cooked through. Season to taste.

6 Stir both types of rice into the chicken and cook for 1–2 minutes, or until the rice is warmed through.

7 Spoon a little of the chicken and rice mixture onto each warmed tortilla. Top with salsa, guacamole, and sour cream and roll up. Alternatively, let everyone assemble their own fajitas at the table.

Chicken Flautas

Crisp, fried corn tortillas with a chicken and cheese filling make a delicious light meal, especially when served with a spicy tomato salsa. The secret of success is to make sure that the oil is sufficiently hot to prevent the flutes from absorbing too much of it.

INGREDIENTS

Makes 12

2 skinless, boneless chicken
    breast portions
1 tablespoon vegetable oil
1 onion, finely chopped
2 garlic cloves, crushed
3 1/2 ounces feta cheese, crumbled
12 corn tortillas, freshly made or a few
    days old
oil, for frying
salt and ground black pepper

For the salsa

3 tomatoes
juice of 1/2 lime
small bunch of fresh cilantro, chopped
1/2 small onion, finely chopped
3 fresh Fresno chiles or similar fresh green
    chiles, seeded and chopped

1 To make the salsa, plunge the tomatoes into boiling water for 30 seconds, then refresh in cold water. Peel off the skins, remove the seeds, and chop the flesh. Combine the chopped tomatoes, lime juice, cilantro, onion, and chiles in a bowl. Season with salt to taste and set aside.

2 Put the chicken portions in a large pan, add water to cover, and bring to a boil. Lower the heat and simmer for 15–20 minutes, or until the chicken is cooked. Remove the chicken from the pan and let it cool a little. Using two forks, shred the chicken into small pieces. Set it aside.

3 Heat the oil in a skillet, add the onion and garlic, and cook over low heat for about 5 minutes, or until the onion has softened but not colored. Add the shredded chicken, with salt and pepper to taste. Mix well, remove from the heat, and stir in the feta cheese.

4 So that they can be rolled, soften the tortillas by steaming three or four at a time on a plate over boiling water for a few moments until they are pliable. Alternatively, wrap them in microwave-safe wrap and then heat them in a microwave oven on full power for about 30 seconds.

5 Place a spoonful of the chicken on one tortilla. Roll it tightly around the filling to make a neat cylinder. Secure with a toothpick. Cover with plastic wrap to prevent the tortilla from drying out. Repeat with the remaining tortillas and chicken.

6 Heat 1 inch oil in a skillet until a small cube of day-old bread, added to the oil, rises to the top and bubbles at the edges. Remove the toothpicks. Add the rolls to the skillet, a few at a time.

7 Cook the rolls for 2–3 minutes, turning frequently. Drain and serve immediately with the salsa.

COOK'S TIP

You might find it easier to keep the toothpicks in place until after the rolls have been cooked, in which case remove them before serving.

Smoked Chicken Pizzas

Mozzarella, yellow bell peppers, and smoked chicken complement each other perfectly and make a really delicious topping for these individual pizzas.

INGREDIENTS

Serves 4

4 small pizza bases, about
    5 inches diameter
3 tablespoons olive oil
4 tablespoons sun-dried tomato paste
2 yellow bell peppers, seeded and cut into
    thin strips
6 ounces sliced smoked chicken
    or turkey, chopped
5 ounces mozzarella cheese, cubed
2 tablespoons chopped fresh basil
salt and ground black pepper

1 Preheat the oven to 425°F. Place the pizza bases well apart on two greased cookie sheets.

2 Brush the pizza bases with 1 tablespoon of the oil, then brush generously with tomato paste.

3 Stir-fry the bell peppers in half the remaining oil for 3–4 minutes.

4 Arrange the chicken and bell peppers on top of the sun-dried tomato paste.

5 Sprinkle the mozzarella and basil on top. Season to taste with salt and black pepper.

6 Drizzle with the remaining oil and bake in the oven for 15–20 minutes, or until crisp and golden. Serve immediately.

Chicken and Avocado Pita Pizzas

Pita bread is used here to make quick and easy bases for tasty pizzas with a heavenly topping. Use round pita bread if you can.

INGREDIENTS

Serves 4

10 ounces Cheddar or Jack cheese
8 plum tomatoes, quartered
3–4 tablespoons olive oil
1 large ripe avocado
8 round pita breads
6–7 slices cooked chicken, chopped
1 onion, thinly sliced
2 tablespoons chopped
   fresh cilantro
salt and ground black pepper

1 Preheat the oven to 450°F. Grate the cheese and set aside.

4 Peel and pit the avocado. Cut into 16 thin slices.

5 Brush the edges of the pita breads with oil. Arrange the breads on two cookie sheets.

6 Spread each pita bread with mashed tomato, covering it almost to the edges.

7 Top each pita bread with four avocado slices. Sprinkle with the chicken, then add a few onion slices. Season to taste. Sprinkle the grated cheese on top.

8 Bake until the cheese begins to melt, about 15–20 minutes. Sprinkle with the cilantro and serve hot.

2 Place the tomatoes in an ovenproof dish. Drizzle 1 tablespoon of the oil over them and season to taste. Bake for 30 minutes; do not stir.

3 Remove the dish from the oven and mash the tomatoes with a fork, removing the skins as you mash. Set aside.

Chicken and Shiitake Mushroom Pizza

The addition of shiitake mushrooms adds an earthy flavor to this colorful pizza, while fresh red chile gives a hint of spiciness.

INGREDIENTS

Serves 3–4

3 tablespoons olive oil

12 ounces skinless, boneless chicken breast
   portions, cut into thin strips

1 bunch scallions, sliced

1 fresh red chile, seeded and chopped

1 red bell pepper, seeded and cut into
   thin strips

generous 1 cup fresh shiitake mushrooms,
   wiped and sliced

3–4 tablespoons chopped
   fresh cilantro

1 pizza base, about
   10–12 inches diameter

1 tablespoon chili oil

5 ounces mozzarella cheese

salt and ground black pepper

1 Preheat the oven to 425°F. Heat 2 tablespoons of the olive oil in a wok or large skillet. Add the chicken, scallions, chile, bell pepper, and mushrooms. Stir-fry over high heat for 2–3 minutes, or until the chicken is firm but still slightly pink within. Season with salt and pepper.

2 Pour off any excess oil, then set the chicken mixture aside until cool.

3 Stir the fresh cilantro into the chicken mixture. Brush the pizza base with the chili oil.

4 Spoon the chicken mixture over the base and drizzle with the remaining olive oil. Grate the cheese and sprinkle on top. Bake for 15–20 minutes, or until crisp and golden. Serve immediately.

COOK'S TIP

To make a basic pizza base, sift 1 1/2 cups strong white bread flour and 1/4 teaspoon salt into a mixing bowl. Stir in 1 teaspoon rapid-rise dried yeast. Make a well in the center of the dry ingredients and pour in 1/2–2/3 cup lukewarm water and 1 tablespoon olive oil. Mix well. Knead the dough on a lightly floured counter for 10 minutes until smooth and elastic. Place in a greased bowl and cover with plastic wrap. Leave in a warm place to rise for about 1 hour, or until doubled in size. Punch down the dough. Turn onto a lightly floured counter, and knead again for 2–3 minutes. Roll out as required and place on a greased cookie sheet or pizza pan. Push up the edge of the dough all around to make a small rim.

Chicken Pita Breads with Red Coleslaw

Pita breads are convenient for simple snacks and packed lunches, and it's easy to pack them with lots of fresh, healthy ingredients.

INGREDIENTS

Serves 4

¼ red cabbage

1 small red onion, thinly sliced

2 radishes, thinly sliced

1 red apple, peeled, cored, and grated

1 tablespoon lemon juice

3 tablespoons cream cheese

1 skinless, boneless chicken breast portion, cooked, about 6 ounces

4 large or 8 small pita breads

salt and ground black pepper

chopped fresh parsley, to garnish

1 Remove the tough central core from the cabbage leaves, then finely shred the leaves using a large sharp knife. Place the shredded cabbage in a bowl and stir in the onion, radishes, apple, and lemon juice.

COOK'S TIP

⌒

If the filled pita breads need to be made more than an hour in advance, line them with crisp lettuce leaves before adding the filling.

---

2 Stir the cream cheese into the shredded cabbage mixture and season to taste with salt and pepper. Thinly slice the cooked chicken portion and stir into the shredded cabbage mixture until well coated.

3 Sprinkle the pita breads with a little water, then warm them under a hot broiler. Split them along one edge using a round-bladed knife. Share the filling equally among the pita breads, then garnish with chopped fresh parsley.

Chicken and Chorizo Tacos

A lightly spiced filling tastes great in taco shells topped with lettuce, tomatoes, and cheese. This quick dish is sure to be a success with all the family.

INGREDIENTS

Serves 4

8 ounces Cheddar or Jack cheese
1 tablespoon vegetable oil
4 cups ground chicken
1 teaspoon salt
1 teaspoon ground cumin
12 taco shells
3 ounces chorizo sausage, ground
3 scallions, chopped
2 tomatoes, chopped
$^{1}/_{2}$ head of lettuce, shredded
tomato salsa, to serve

1 Preheat the oven to 350°F. Grate the cheese and set aside.

2 Heat the oil in a nonstick skillet. Add the chicken, salt, and cumin and cook over medium heat for 5–8 minutes, or until the chicken is cooked through. Stir frequently to prevent any large lumps from forming.

3 Meanwhile, arrange the taco shells in one layer on a large cookie sheet and heat in the oven for about 10 minutes, or according to the directions on the packet.

4 Add the chorizo and scallions to the chicken and stir to mix. Cook until just warmed through, stirring occasionally.

5 To assemble each taco, place 1–2 spoonfuls of the chicken mixture in the base of a warmed taco shell. Top with a generous sprinkling of chopped tomato, shredded lettuce, and cheese.

6 Serve immediately, with tomato salsa to accompany.

Gingered Chicken Noodles

A blend of ginger, spices, and coconut milk flavors this delicious dish, which is made in minutes. For a real Eastern touch, add a little Thai fish sauce, just before serving.

INGREDIENTS

Serves 4

12 ounces skinless, boneless chicken
    breast portions

8 ounces zucchini

10 ounces eggplant

2 tablespoons oil

2-inch piece of fresh ginger root, peeled
    and finely chopped

6 scallions, sliced

2 teaspoons Thai green curry paste

1²/₃ cups coconut milk

2 cups chicken stock

4 ounces medium egg noodles

3 tablespoons chopped fresh cilantro

1 tablespoon lemon juice

salt and ground black pepper

chopped fresh cilantro, to garnish

3 Add a little more oil to the pan, if necessary, and cook the ginger and scallions for 3 minutes. Add the zucchini and cook for 2–3 minutes, or until beginning to turn golden. Stir in the curry paste and cook for 1 minute.

4 Add the coconut milk, stock, eggplant, and chicken and simmer for 10 minutes. Add the noodles and cook for 5 minutes. Stir in the cilantro and lemon juice and adjust the seasoning. Serve garnished with cilantro.

1 Cut the chicken into bitesize pieces. Halve the zucchini lengthwise and coarsely chop them. Cut the eggplant into similarly sized pieces.

2 Heat the oil in a large pan and cook the chicken until golden. Remove with a slotted spoon and drain on paper towels.

Five Ingredients Rice

The Japanese have invented many ways to enjoy rice. Here, chicken and vegetables are cooked with short grain rice making a healthy lunch dish called Kayaku-gohan. Serve with a clear soup and tangy pickles.

INGREDIENTS

Serves 4

1½ cups Japanese short
   grain rice
3¹/2 ounces carrot, peeled
¹/2 teaspoon lemon juice
3¹/2 ounces gobo or canned
   bamboo shoots
8 ounces oyster mushrooms
8 mitsuba sprigs, root part removed
1¹/2 teaspoons dashi-no-moto
   (dashi stock granules) dissolved in
   1¹/2 cups water
5-ounce skinless, boneless chicken breast
   portion, cut into ³/4-inch dice
2 tablespoons shoyu
2 tablespoons sake
1¹/2 tablespoons mirin
pinch of salt

1 Put the rice in a strainer and wash under cold running water until the water runs clear. Let drain for 30 minutes.

2 Cut the carrot into rounds, then cut the disks into flowers.

3 Fill a bowl with cold water and add the lemon juice. Peel the gobo and then slice with a knife as if you were sharpening a pencil into the bowl. Leave for about 15 minutes, then drain. If using canned bamboo shoots, slice into thin batons.

4 Tear the oyster mushrooms into thin strips. Chop the mitsuba sprigs into ³/4-inch long pieces. Put them in a strainer and pour freshly boiled water over them to wilt them. Let drain. Set aside.

5 Heat the water and dashi-no-moto in a pan. Add the carrots and gobo or bamboo shoots. Bring to a boil and add the chicken. Remove any scum that rises to the surface, and add the shoyu, sake, mirin, and salt.

6 Add the rice and mushrooms and cover with a lid. Bring to a boil for 5 minutes, then reduce the heat, and simmer for 10 minutes. Remove from the heat without lifting the lid and leave to stand for 15 minutes. Add the mitsuba and serve immediately.

COOK'S TIP

Although gobo, or burdock, is a poisonous plant, the Japanese have always eaten it, but it must be cooked. It contains iron and acidic elements that are harmful if eaten raw, but after soaking in alkaline water and cooking for a short time, gobo is no longer poisonous. Mitsuba, or Japanese parsley, and gobo are available from Japanese supermarkets.

Adobo of Chicken and Pork

Four ingredients are essential in an adobo, one of the best-loved recipes from the Philippine Islands: vinegar, garlic, peppercorns, and bay leaves. It is great served with plantain chips.

INGREDIENTS

Serves 4

1 chicken, about 3 pounds, or
    4 chicken quarters
12 ounces pork leg steaks (with fat)
2 teaspoons sugar
4 tablespoons sunflower oil
5 tablespoons wine vinegar
4 plump garlic cloves, crushed
$^{1}/_{2}$ teaspoon black peppercorns,
    lightly crushed
1 tablespoon light soy sauce
4 bay leaves
$^{1}/_{2}$ teaspoon annatto seeds, soaked in
    2 tablespoons boiling water, or
      $^{1}/_{2}$ teaspoon ground turmeric
salt

For the plantain chips
vegetable oil, for deep-frying
1–2 large plantains and/or 1 sweet potato

1 Wipe the chicken and cut into eight even-size pieces, or halve the chicken quarters, if using. Cut the pork into neat pieces. Spread out the meat on a board, sprinkle lightly with sugar, and set aside.

2 Heat the oil in a wok or large pan and cook the chicken and pork pieces, in batches if necessary, until they are golden on both sides.

3 Add the wine vinegar, garlic, peppercorns, soy sauce, and bay leaves and stir well.

4 Strain the annatto seed liquid and stir it into the pan or stir in the turmeric. Add salt to taste. Bring to a boil, cover, lower the heat, and simmer gently for 30–35 minutes. Remove the lid and simmer for 10 minutes more.

5 Cook the plantain chips. Heat the oil. Test by dropping a cube of day-old bread into the hot oil, it should brown in 35 seconds. Peel and slice the plantains and/or sweet potato. Deep-fry them, in batches, until cooked but not brown. Drain.

6 To serve, reheat the oil and fry the plantains for a few seconds. Drain. Spoon the chicken and pork adobo into a serving dish and serve with the chips.

> ### COOK'S TIP
> Sprinkling the chicken and pork lightly with sugar turns the skin beautifully brown when cooked.

Fennel Stuffed with Chicken

Fennel not only tastes delicious but it also divides into neat boat shapes, which are ideal for stuffing.

INGREDIENTS

Serves 4

2 large fennel bulbs

3 eggs

2 tablespoons olive oil

1 onion, chopped, or 1 tablespoon dried onion

2 skinless, boneless chicken breast portions

2¹/₂ cups chopped oyster mushrooms

4 tablespoons all-purpose flour or cornstarch

1¹/₄ cups home-made or canned chicken broth, boiling

1 teaspoon Dijon mustard

2 tablespoons sherry

salt and ground black pepper

fresh parsley sprigs, to garnish

boiled rice, to serve

1 Preheat the oven to 375°F. Trim the base of the fennel and pull each bulb apart into four pieces. Reserve the central part and boil the outer pieces of fennel in lightly salted water for 3–4 minutes. Drain and let cool. Boil the eggs for 10 minutes. Allow to cool, peel, and set aside.

2 Finely chop the central part of the fennel. Cook gently in oil with the onion for 3–4 minutes.

3 Cut the chicken into pieces and add to the skillet with the mushrooms. Cook over medium heat for 6 minutes, stirring. Add the flour or cornstarch and remove from the heat.

4 Gradually add the chicken broth, making sure the thickener is completely absorbed. Return to the heat and simmer until thickened, stirring constantly. Chop one of the eggs into the chicken mixture, and add the mustard, sherry, and seasoning to taste.

5 Arrange the fennel in an ovenproof dish. Spoon the filling into each one, cover with foil, and bake for 20–25 minutes. Quarter the remaining eggs. Serve the fennel on a bed of rice, garnished with eggs and parsley.

COOK'S TIP

If you find the fennel difficult to cut, cook it before trying to cut it. It will be much easier to deal with once it is cooked.

Pan-fried Chicken with Pesto

Warm pesto accompanying pan-fried chicken makes a deliciously quick meal. Serve with pasta or rice noodles and braised vegetables.

INGREDIENTS

Serves 4

1 tablespoon olive oil

4 skinless, boneless chicken
    breast portions

fresh basil leaves, to garnish

pasta or noodles and braised baby carrots
    and celery, to serve

For the pesto

6 tablespoons olive oil

$^1/_2$ cup pine nuts

$^2/_3$ cup freshly grated Parmesan cheese

1 cup fresh basil leaves

$^1/_4$ cup fresh parsley

2 garlic cloves, crushed

salt and ground black pepper

1 Heat the olive oil in a skillet or large pan. Add the chicken portions and cook gently for 15–20 minutes, turning several times, until they are tender, lightly browned, and thoroughly cooked.

2 To make the pesto, place the olive oil, pine nuts, Parmesan cheese, basil leaves, parsley, garlic, and salt and pepper in a blender or food processor and process until smooth and well mixed.

3 Remove the chicken from the pan, cover, and keep hot. Reduce the heat slightly, then add the pesto to the pan, and cook gently, stirring constantly, for a few minutes, or until the pesto has warmed through.

4 Pour the warm pesto over the chicken, then garnish with basil leaves, and serve with pasta or noodles and braised baby carrots and celery.

Mediterranean Chicken

Chicken with a cheese filling served with fresh Mediterranean vegetables makes a perfect lunch-party dish, served simply with olive ciabatta or crusty bread.

INGREDIENTS

Serves 4

4 chicken breast portions, about
   1^1/$_2$ pounds total weight
1 cup soft cheese with garlic
   and herbs
1 pound zucchini
2 red bell peppers, seeded
1 pound plum tomatoes
4 celery stalks
2 tablespoons olive oil
10 ounces onions, coarsely chopped
3 garlic cloves, crushed
8 sun-dried tomatoes, coarsely chopped
1 teaspoon dried oregano
2 tablespoons balsamic vinegar
1 teaspoon paprika
salt and ground black pepper
olive ciabatta or crusty bread, to serve

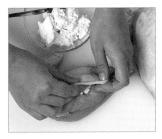

1 Preheat the oven to 375°F. Loosen the skin of each chicken portion, without removing it, to make a pocket. Divide the cheese into four and push one quarter underneath the skin of each chicken portion in an even layer.

2 Cut the zucchini and bell peppers into similarly sized chunky pieces. Quarter the tomatoes and slice the celery stalks.

3 Heat 2 tablespoons of the oil in a large, shallow flameproof casserole. Cook the onions and garlic for 4 minutes, or until soft and golden, stirring frequently.

4 Add the zucchini, bell peppers, and celery and cook for 5 minutes more.

5 Stir in the tomatoes, sun-dried tomatoes, oregano, and balsamic vinegar. Season well.

6 Place the chicken on top, drizzle with a little more olive oil, and season with salt and the paprika. Bake in the oven for 35–40 minutes, or until the chicken is golden and cooked through. Serve with plenty of olive ciabatta or crusty bread.

Lemon Chicken with Guacamole Sauce

The avocado sauce makes an unusual accompaniment to the griddled chicken.

INGREDIENTS

Serves 4

juice of 2 lemons

3 tablespoons olive oil

2 garlic cloves, crushed

4 chicken breast portions, about
    7 ounces each

2 beefsteak tomatoes, cored and
    cut in half

salt and ground black pepper

chopped fresh cilantro, to garnish

For the sauce

1 ripe avocado

$^1/_4$ cup sour cream

3 tablespoons fresh lemon juice

$^1/_2$ teaspoon salt

$^1/_4$ cup water

1 Combine the lemon juice, oil, garlic, $^1/_2$ teaspoon salt, and a little pepper in a bowl. Stir to mix.

2 Arrange the chicken portions, in one layer, in a shallow glass or ceramic dish. Pour the lemon mixture over them and turn to coat evenly. Cover and marinate for at least 1 hour at room temperature, or chill overnight.

3 To make the sauce, cut the avocado in half, remove the pit, and scoop the flesh into a food processor or blender.

4 Add the sour cream, lemon juice, and salt and process until smooth. Add the water and process just to blend. If necessary, add more water to thin the sauce. Transfer to a bowl, taste, and adjust the seasoning, if necessary. Set aside.

5 Preheat the broiler and heat a ridged griddle. Remove the chicken from the marinade and pat dry with paper towels.

6 When the griddle is hot, add the chicken portions and cook, turning frequently, until they are cooked through, about 10 minutes.

7 Meanwhile, arrange the tomato halves, cut sides up, on a cookie sheet and season lightly with salt and pepper. Broil until hot and bubbling, about 5 minutes.

8 Place a chicken portion, tomato half, and a spoonful of avocado sauce on each individual plate. Sprinkle with cilantro and serve.

VARIATION

To cook on a barbecue, light the barbecue, and when the coals are glowing red and covered with gray ash, spread them in a single layer. Set an oiled rack about 5 inches above the coals and cook the chicken portions until lightly charred and cooked through, about 15–20 minutes, basting with extra olive oil.

MIDWEEK MEALS

Weekday meals should be as exciting and adventurous as the meals we prepare at the weekends, but we don't always have a great deal of preparation time. This chapter has a collection of chicken recipes that will cater for all occasions: from tasty fast-food recipes to tried and trusted everyday classics. Thankfully, many aspects of the preparation, such as marinating, can be done in advance, which is ideal for busy people. So dip into this chapter and sample some of the enticing recipes for midweek meals.

Broiled Chicken

The flavor of this dish, known in Indonesia as Ayam Bakur, will be more intense if the chicken is marinated overnight. Celery leaves make a pretty and tasty garnish, if you have any.

INGREDIENTS

Serves 4

3–3¹/₂-pound chicken

4 garlic cloves, crushed

2 lemongrass stems, lower 2 inches sliced

1 teaspoon ground turmeric

2 cups water

3–4 bay leaves

3 tablespoons each dark and light
    soy sauce

¹/₄ cup butter or margarine

salt

boiled rice, to serve

1 Cut the chicken into four or eight portions. Slash the fleshy part of each portion twice and set aside.

2 Grind the garlic, sliced lemongrass, turmeric, and salt together into a paste in a food processor or with a mortar and pestle. Rub the paste into the chicken pieces and leave for at least 30 minutes or overnight. Wear latex gloves for this, as the turmeric will stain heavily, or wash your hands immediately afterward, if you prefer.

3 Transfer the chicken to a wok and pour in the water. Add the bay leaves and bring to a boil. Cover and cook gently for 30 minutes, adding a little more water, if necessary, and stirring from time to time.

4 Add the two soy sauces to the wok together with the butter or margarine. Cook until the chicken is well coated and the sauce has reduced and thickened.

5 Transfer the chicken to a preheated broiler or an oven preheated to 400°F. Cook for 10–15 minutes more, turning the pieces often so that they become golden brown all over. Baste with the remaining sauce during cooking. Serve with boiled rice.

Chicken Kiev

Cut through the crispy-coated chicken to reveal a creamy filling.

INGREDIENTS

Serves 4

4 large skinless, boneless chicken
   breast portions
1 tablespoon lemon juice
$^1/_2$ cup ricotta cheese
1 garlic clove, crushed
2 tablespoons chopped fresh parsley
$^1/_4$ teaspoon freshly grated nutmeg
2 tablespoons all-purpose flour
pinch of cayenne pepper
$^1/_4$ teaspoon salt
2 cups fresh white bread crumbs
2 egg whites, lightly beaten
creamed potatoes, green beans, and
   broiled tomatoes, to serve

1 Place the chicken portions between two sheets of plastic wrap and gently beat with a rolling pin until flattened. Sprinkle with the lemon juice.

2 Combine the ricotta cheese, garlic, 1 tablespoon of the chopped parsley, and the nutmeg. Shape into four 2-inch long rolls.

3 Put one portion of the cheese and herb mixture in the center of each chicken portion and fold the meat over, tucking in the edges to enclose the filling completely.

4 Secure the chicken with toothpicks pushed through the center of each. Combine the flour, cayenne pepper, and salt, and use to dust the chicken.

5 Combine the bread crumbs and remaining parsley. Dip the chicken into the egg, then coat with bread crumbs. Preheat the oven to 400°F. Chill the chicken for 30 minutes, then dip into the egg and bread crumbs again.

6 Put the chicken on a nonstick cookie sheet. Bake in the preheated oven for 25 minutes, or until the coating is golden brown and the chicken completely cooked. Remove the toothpicks and serve with creamed potatoes, green beans, and broiled tomatoes.

Hunter's Chicken

*Porcini and portabello mushrooms
give this traditional Italian chicken
dish a marvelously rich flavor. Serve
with creamed potatoes or polenta to
soak up the lovely sauce.*

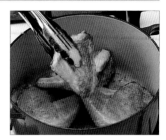

INGREDIENTS

Serves 4

1 cup dried porcini mushrooms

2 tablespoons olive oil

1 tablespoon butter

4 chicken portions, skinned

1 large onion, thinly sliced

14-ounce can chopped tomatoes

²/₃ cup red wine

1 garlic clove, crushed

leaves from 1 rosemary sprig,
   finely chopped

1¹/₂ cups portabello mushrooms,
   thinly sliced

salt and ground black pepper

rosemary sprigs, to garnish

creamed potato or polenta,
   to serve (optional)

1 Put the porcini in a bowl, add
1 cup warm water, and soak for
20–30 minutes. Remove the porcini
from the liquid and squeeze. Strain
the liquid and reserve. Chop the
porcini finely.

> ### VARIATION
> ❧
> Substitute strips of green bell
> pepper for the fresh mushrooms,
> if you like.

2 Heat the oil and butter in a
large, flameproof casserole until
foaming. Add the chicken. Cook
over medium heat for 5 minutes, or
until golden. Remove and drain on
paper towels.

3 Add the onion and chopped
mushrooms. Cook gently,
stirring frequently, for 3 minutes,
or until the onion has softened but
not browned. Stir in the tomatoes,
wine, and reserved mushroom
soaking liquid, then add the garlic
and rosemary, and season with
salt and pepper to taste. Bring to a
boil, stirring constantly.

4 Return the chicken to the pan
and coat with the sauce. Cover
and simmer gently for 30 minutes.

5 Add the fresh mushrooms and
mix into the sauce. Continue
simmering gently for 10 minutes,
or until the chicken is tender. Taste
for seasoning. Serve hot with
creamed potato or polenta, if you
like. Garnish with rosemary.

Turkey with Marsala Cream Sauce

Marsala makes a very rich and tasty sauce. The addition of lemon juice gives it a sharp edge, which helps to offset the richness.

INGREDIENTS

Serves 6

6 turkey breast steaks

3 tablespoons all-purpose flour

2 tablespoons olive oil

2 tablespoons butter

4 tablespoons lemon juice

$^3/_4$ cup dry Marsala

$^3/_4$ cup heavy cream

salt and ground black pepper

lemon wedges and chopped fresh parsley,
    to garnish

snow peas and green beans,
    to serve

1 Put each turkey steak between two sheets of plastic wrap and pound with a rolling pin to flatten and stretch. Cut each in half or into quarters, cutting away and discarding any sinew.

2 Put the flour in a shallow bowl. Season well and coat the meat.

VARIATION

Skinless, boneless chicken breast portions can be used instead of the turkey, and ¼ cup mascarpone cheese instead of the heavy cream, if you like.

3 Heat the oil and butter in a deep, heavy skillet until sizzling. Add as many pieces of turkey as the pan will hold and cook over medium heat for about 3 minutes on each side until crisp and tender. Transfer to a warmed serving dish and keep hot. Repeat with the remaining turkey.

4 Lower the heat. Combine the lemon juice and Marsala, add to the skillet, and raise the heat. Bring to a boil, stirring in the sediment, then add the cream. Simmer, stirring, until the sauce is reduced and glossy. Season to taste. Spoon the sauce over the turkey, garnish with the lemon wedges and parsley and serve immediately with the snow peas and green beans.

Chicken with Orange and Mustard Sauce

The beauty of this recipe is its simplicity; the chicken continues to cook in its own juices while you prepare the sauce.

INGREDIENTS

Serves 4

2 large oranges

4 skinless, boneless chicken
  breast portions

1 teaspoon sunflower oil

salt and ground black pepper

new potatoes and sliced zucchini tossed in
  parsley, to serve

For the sauce

2 teaspoons cornstarch

$^2/_3$ cup plain yogurt

1 teaspoon Dijon mustard

1 Using a sharp knife, cut a slice of peel and pith from each end of the oranges, then cut off all the peel and pith in strips, reserving the juice. Remove any remaining pith. Cut out each segment, leaving the membrane behind. Squeeze the remaining juice from the membrane.

2 Season the chicken with salt and freshly ground black pepper. Heat the oil in a nonstick skillet and cook the chicken portions for 5 minutes on each side. Take out of the skillet and wrap in foil; the meat will continue to cook for a while.

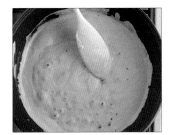

3 To make the sauce, blend together the cornstarch with the juice from the oranges. Add the yogurt and mustard. Put into the skillet and gradually bring to a boil. Simmer for 1 minute.

4 Add the orange segments to the sauce and heat gently. Unwrap the chicken, check that it is cooked through, and add any excess juices to the sauce. Slice the portions on the diagonal and serve with the sauce, new potatoes, and sliced zucchini tossed in parsley.

Chicken with Yellow Bell Pepper Sauce

Fillets of chicken are filled with garlic cheese and accompanied by a yellow bell pepper sauce. Serve with fresh tagliatelle for a tasty supper.

INGREDIENTS

Serves 4

2 tablespoons olive oil

2 large yellow bell peppers, seeded
and chopped

1 small onion, chopped

1 tablespoon freshly squeezed orange juice

$1^1/4$ cups chicken stock

4 skinless, boneless chicken
breast portions

scant $^1/2$ cup garlic cream cheese

12 fresh basil leaves

2 tablespoons butter

salt and black pepper

1 To make the yellow bell pepper sauce, heat half the olive oil in a pan and gently cook the bell peppers and onion until beginning to soften. Add the orange juice and stock and cook until very soft.

VARIATION
Turkey breast fillets could be used in place of the chicken, if you prefer.

2 Meanwhile, lay the chicken portions out flat and beat them out lightly.

3 Spread the chicken portions with the garlic cream cheese. Chop half the basil and sprinkle it on top, then roll up the chicken portions, tucking in the ends like an envelope, and secure neatly with half a toothpick.

4 Heat the remaining oil and the butter in a skillet and cook the rolls for 7–8 minutes, turning frequently, until cooked through.

5 Meanwhile, press the bell pepper mixture through a strainer, or blend until smooth, then strain back into the pan. Season to taste and warm through. Serve with the chicken, garnished with the remaining basil leaves.

Chicken with Tarragon Cream

The anise-like flavor of tarragon has a particular affinity with chicken, especially in creamy sauces. Serve seasonal vegetables and boiled red Wehani rice with the chicken.

INGREDIENTS

Serves 4

2 tablespoons light olive oil

4 skinless chicken breast portions, about 9 ounces each

3 shallots, finely chopped

2 garlic cloves, finely chopped

1 1/2 cups wild mushrooms (such as chanterelles or ceps) or shiitake mushrooms, halved

2/3 cup dry white wine

1 1/4 cups heavy cream

1/4 cup chopped mixed fresh tarragon and flat leaf parsley

salt and ground black pepper

sprigs of fresh tarragon and flat leaf parsley, to garnish

1 Heat the olive oil in a skillet and add the chicken, skin side down. Cook for 10 minutes, turning the chicken until it is a golden brown color on both sides.

2 Reduce the heat and cook the chicken for 10 minutes more, turning occasionally. Remove from the skillet and set aside.

3 Add the shallots and garlic to the skillet and cook gently, stirring, until the shallots are softened but not browned.

4 Increase the heat, add the mushrooms, and stir-fry for 2 minutes. Replace the chicken, then pour in the wine. Simmer for 5–10 minutes, or until most of the wine has evaporated and the chicken is cooked through.

5 Gently stir in the cream. Simmer for 10 minutes, or until the sauce has thickened. Stir the herbs into the sauce and season to taste. Arrange the chicken on warm plates and spoon the sauce over it. Garnish with tarragon and parsley.

Spinach-stuffed Chicken Portions

Large chicken breast portions are filled with an herbed spinach mixture, then topped with butter and baked until tender.

INGREDIENTS

Serves 6

4 ounces mealy potatoes, diced

4 ounces spinach leaves, finely chopped

1 egg, beaten

2 tablespoons chopped fresh cilantro

4 large boneless or part-boned chicken breast portions

1/4 cup butter

salt and ground black pepper

fried mushrooms, to serve

For the sauce

14-ounce can chopped tomatoes

1 garlic clove, crushed

2/3 cup hot chicken stock

2 tablespoons chopped fresh cilantro

1 Preheat the oven to 350°F. Boil the potatoes in a large pan of salted, boiling water for about 15 minutes, or until tender. Drain and place them in a large bowl and coarsely mash with a fork.

2 Stir the spinach into the potato with the egg and cilantro. Season to taste.

3 Cut almost all the way through the chicken portions and open out to form a pocket in each. Spoon the filling into the center and fold the chicken back over again. Secure with wooden toothpicks and place in a roasting pan.

4 Dot with butter and cover with foil. Bake for 25 minutes. Remove the foil and cook for 10 minutes more.

5 To make the sauce, heat the tomatoes, garlic, and stock in a pan. Boil rapidly for 10 minutes. Season and stir in the cilantro. Remove the chicken from the oven and serve with the sauce and fried mushrooms.

COOK'S TIP

Young spinach leaves are sweet and are ideal for this dish.

Chicken Spirals

2 Spread each chicken portion with tomato paste, then top with a few basil leaves, a little crushed garlic, and seasoning.

3 Roll up firmly around the filling and secure with a toothpick. Brush with milk and sprinkle with flour to coat lightly.

4 Place the spirals on a foil-lined broiling pan. Cook under a preheated broiler for about 15–20 minutes, turning them occasionally, until thoroughly cooked. Serve hot, sliced, with a spoonful or two of bottled tomatoes or fresh tomato sauce and accompanied with pasta sprinkled with fresh basil.

These little spirals look impressive, but they're very simple to make, and a good way to pep up plain chicken.

INGREDIENTS

Serves 4

4 skinless, boneless chicken breast
   portions, about 3^1/$_2$ ounces each
4 teaspoons tomato paste
^{1}/$_2$ cup large basil leaves, plus extra
   to garnish
1 garlic clove, crushed
1 tablespoon skim milk
2 tablespoons whole-wheat flour
salt and ground black pepper
bottled strained tomatoes or fresh tomato
   sauce and pasta, to serve

1 Place the chicken portions on a board. If too thick to roll easily, flatten them slightly by beating gently with a rolling pin or meat mallet.

COOK'S TIP

When flattening the chicken breasts with a rolling pin, place them between two sheets of plastic wrap.

Chicken and Beef Roulé

A relatively simple dish to prepare,
this recipe uses ground beef as a
filling. It is rolled in chicken which is
spread with a creamy garlic cheese
that just melts in the mouth.

INGREDIENTS

Serves 4

4 skinless, boneless chicken breast
    portions, about 4 ounces each
1 cup ground beef
2 tablespoons chopped fresh chives
1 cup garlic cream cheese
2 tablespoons honey
salt and ground black pepper
green beans and mushrooms,
    to serve

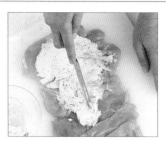

3 Place the chicken on a board
  and spread evenly with the
cream cheese.

4 Top with the ground beef
  mixture, spreading it over the
chicken evenly.

5 Roll up the chicken tightly to
  form a sausage shape.

6 Brush with honey and place in
  a roasting pan. Cook for 1 hour
in the preheated oven. Remove
from the pan and slice thinly. Serve
with freshly cooked vegetables.

1 Preheat the oven to 375°F.
  Place the chicken breast
portions, side by side, between
two pieces of plastic wrap. Beat
lightly with a meat mallet until
they are about 1/2 inch thick and
joined together.

2 Place the ground beef in a large
  pan. Cook for 3 minutes, add
the fresh chives, and season. Cool.

Chicken with White Wine and Garlic

If you like a lot of garlic, use up to six cloves in this delicious recipe.

INGREDIENTS

Serves 4

3¹/₂-pound chicken, cut into portions

1 onion, sliced

3–6 garlic cloves, crushed

1 teaspoon dried thyme

2 cups dry white wine

1 cup pitted green olives (16–18)

1 bay leaf

1 tablespoon lemon juice

1–2 tablespoons butter

salt and ground black pepper

1 Heat a deep skillet. Add the chicken pieces, skin side down, and cook over medium heat for about 10 minutes, or until browned. Turn and brown the other side, 5–8 minutes more.

2 Transfer the chicken pieces to a plate and set aside.

3 Drain the excess fat from the skillet, leaving about 1 tablespoon. Add the sliced onion and ¹/₂ teaspoon salt and cook for about 5 minutes, or until just soft. Add garlic to taste and thyme, and cook for 1 minute more.

4 Add the wine and stir, scraping up any sediment that clings to the pan. Bring to a boil and boil for 1 minute. Stir in the olives.

5 Return the chicken pieces to the pan. Add the bay leaf and season lightly with pepper. Lower the heat, cover the pan, and simmer until the chicken is cooked through, about 20–30 minutes.

6 Transfer the chicken pieces to a warm plate. Stir the lemon juice into the sauce. Whisk in the butter to thicken the sauce slightly. Spoon it over the chicken and serve.

Chicken Meat Loaf

Serve this herbed chicken loaf either hot or cold with steamed vegetables or a crisp salad.

INGREDIENTS

Serves 4

1 tablespoon olive oil

1 onion, chopped

1 green bell pepper, seeded and chopped

1 garlic clove, crushed

4 cups ground chicken

1 cup fresh bread crumbs

1 egg, beaten

¹/₂ cup pine nuts

12 sun-dried tomatoes in oil, drained
   and chopped

¹/₃ cup milk

2 teaspoons chopped fresh rosemary, or
   ¹/₂ teaspoon dried

1 teaspoon ground fennel seeds

¹/₂ teaspoon dried oregano

¹/₂ teaspoon salt

1 Preheat the oven to 375°F. Heat the oil in a skillet. Add the onion, green bell pepper, and garlic and cook over low heat, stirring frequently, until just softened, about 8–10 minutes. Remove from the heat and let cool.

2 Place the chicken in a large bowl. Add the onion mixture and the remaining ingredients and mix thoroughly together.

3 Transfer to an 8¹/₄ × 4¹/₂in loaf pan, packing the mixture down firmly. Bake for about 1 hour, or until golden brown and cooked through. Serve the meat loaf hot or cold in slices.

Chicken Pastitsio

A traditional Greek pastitsio is a rich dish made with beef, but this lighter lower-fat version with chicken is just as tasty.

INGREDIENTS

Serves 4–6

4 cups lean ground chicken
1 large onion, finely chopped
4 tablespoons tomato paste
1 cup red wine or stock
1 teaspoon ground cinnamon
2³/4 cups macaroni
1¹/4 cups milk
2 tablespoons sunflower margarine
¹/4 cup all-purpose flour
1 teaspoon freshly
   grated nutmeg
2 tomatoes, sliced
4 tablespoons whole-wheat
   bread crumbs
salt and ground black pepper
salad greens, to serve

1 Preheat the oven to 425°F. Cook the ground chicken and onion in a nonstick pan without adding any fat, stirring until lightly browned all over.

2 Stir in the tomato paste, red wine or stock, and cinnamon. Season, then cover and simmer for 5 minutes, stirring from time to time. Remove from the heat.

3 Cook the macaroni in plenty of salted, boiling water until just tender, then drain.

4 Layer the macaroni with the meat mixture in a wide ovenproof dish.

5 Place the milk, margarine, and flour in a pan and whisk over medium heat until thickened and smooth. Add the nutmeg, and season to taste.

6 Pour the sauce evenly over the pasta and meat layers. Arrange the tomato slices on top and sprinkle lines of whole-wheat bread crumbs over the surface.

7 Bake for 30–35 minutes, or until golden brown and bubbling. Serve hot with fresh salad greens.

Minty Yogurt Chicken

Chicken is marinated with yogurt, mint, lemon, and honey and then broiled.

INGREDIENTS

Serves 4

8 chicken thigh portions, skinned
1 tablespoon honey
2 tablespoons lime or lemon juice
2 tablespoons plain yogurt
4 tablespoons chopped fresh mint
salt and ground black pepper
new potatoes and a tomato salad, to serve

1 Slash the chicken flesh at regular intervals with a sharp knife. Place in a bowl.

2 Combine the honey, lime or lemon juice, yogurt, seasoning, and half the mint.

3 Spoon the marinade over the chicken and let marinate for 30 minutes. Line the broiler pan with foil and cook the chicken under a preheated medium broiler until thoroughly cooked and golden brown, turning the chicken occasionally during cooking.

4 Sprinkle with the remaining mint and serve with the potatoes and tomato salad.

Tarragon Chicken

The classic French version of this dish uses a whole chicken, but boneless breast portions are quick to cook and look elegant. The combination of dried and fresh tarragon makes a wonderfully aromatic sauce.

INGREDIENTS

Serves 4

4 skinless, boneless chicken breast
   portions, about 5–6 ounces each
$1/2$ cup dry white wine
$1^1/4$ cups chicken stock
1 tablespoon dried tarragon
1 garlic clove, finely chopped
$3/4$ cup whipping cream
1 tablespoon chopped fresh tarragon
salt and ground black pepper
fresh tarragon sprigs, to garnish

1 Season the chicken portions lightly with salt and pepper and put them in a pan just large enough to hold them in one layer. Pour in the wine and stock, adding more stock to cover, if necessary, then add the dried tarragon and the garlic. Bring the stock just to a simmer over medium heat and cook gently for 8–10 minutes, or until the juices run clear when the chicken is pierced with a knife.

2 With a slotted spoon, transfer the chicken to a plate and cover to keep warm. Strain the cooking liquid into a small pan, skim off any fat, and boil to reduce by two-thirds.

3 Add the cream and boil to reduce by half. Stir in the fresh tarragon and adjust the seasoning. Slice the chicken portions, spoon a little sauce over them and garnish with tarragon sprigs.

COOK'S TIP

Tarragon is traditionally paired with chicken, but you could use chopped fresh basil or parsley instead.

Chicken with Grapes

When grapes are used in a French dish, it is often called "Véronique" or sometimes "à la vigneronne"—in the style of the grape grower. Here they are cooked with chicken in a creamy sauce.

INGREDIENTS

Serves 4

4 skinless, boneless chicken
   breast portions, about
   7 ounces each
2 tablespoons butter
1 large or 2 small shallots, chopped
$1/2$ cup dry white wine
1 cup chicken stock
$1/2$ cup whipping cream
5 ounces seedless green grapes
   (about 30)
salt and ground black pepper
fresh parsley, to garnish

1 Season the chicken portions. Melt half the butter in a skillet over medium-high heat and cook the chicken for 4–5 minutes on each side until cooked through.

2 Transfer the chicken to a plate and cover to keep warm. Add the remaining butter and cook the shallots until just softened, stirring frequently. Add the wine, bring to a boil, and boil to reduce by half, then add the stock, and continue boiling to reduce by half again.

3 Add the cream to the sauce, bring back to a boil, and add any juices from the chicken. Add the grapes and cook gently for 5 minutes. Slice the chicken portions and serve with the sauce, garnished with parsley.

Stuffed Chicken in Bacon Coats

Nothing could be simpler for a midweek supper than these chicken breast portions stuffed with a cream cheese and chive filling. They are beautifully moist when cooked in their bacon wrapping. Serve baked potatoes and crisp salad greens as accompaniments.

INGREDIENTS

Serves 4

4 skinless, boneless chicken breast
   portions, about 6 ounces each
$^{1}/_{2}$ cup cream cheese
1 tablespoon chopped fresh chives
8 unsmoked bacon strips
1 tablespoon olive oil
ground black pepper

1 Preheat the oven to 400°F. Using a sharp knife, make a horizontal slit from the side into each chicken portion.

2 Beat together the cream cheese and chives. Divide into four portions and, using a teaspoon, fill each slit with some of the cream cheese. Push the sides of the slit together to keep the filling in.

3 Wrap each portion in two strips of bacon and place in an ovenproof dish. Drizzle the oil over the chicken and bake for about 25–30 minutes, brushing occasionally with the oil, until cooked through. Season with black pepper and serve immediately.

Southern Fried Chicken

This is a low-fat interpretation of the original deep-fried dish popularized by Colonel Sanders in the 1950s, which is now an international fast-food favorite. Serve with potato wedges to complete the meal.

INGREDIENTS

Serves 4

1 tablespoon paprika
2 tablespoons all-purpose flour
4 skinless, boneless chicken breast
   portions, about 6 ounces each
2 tablespoons sunflower oil
$^{2}/_{3}$ cup sour cream
1 tablespoon chopped fresh chives
salt and ground black pepper

For the corn cakes

7 ounces corn kernels
4 cups mashed potato, cooled
2 tablespoons butter

1 Combine the paprika and flour on a plate. Coat the chicken portions in the seasoned flour.

2 Heat the sunflower oil in a large, heavy skillet and add the floured chicken portions. Cook over high heat until a golden brown color on both sides. Reduce the heat and continue cooking for 20 minutes more, turning once or twice, until the chicken is cooked right through.

3 Meanwhile, make the corn cakes. Stir the corn kernels into the cooled mashed potato and season to taste. Using lightly floured hands, shape the mixture into 12 even-size round cakes, each about 2 inches in diameter.

4 When the chicken is cooked, remove from the skillet and keep hot. Melt the butter in the skillet and cook the corn cakes for 3 minutes on each side, or until golden and heated through.

5 Meanwhile, combine the sour cream and chopped chives in a small bowl to make a dip. Transfer the corn cakes from the skillet to serving plates and top with the chicken. Serve immediately, offering the sour cream with chives on the side.

Chicken in Herb Crusts

Mustard gives the chicken a piquant flavor in this quick-to-prepare dish. Serve with new potatoes and salad.

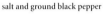

INGREDIENTS

Serves 4

4 skinless, boneless chicken
   breast portions
1 tablespoon Dijon mustard
1 cup fresh bread crumbs
2 tablespoons chopped fresh parsley
1 tablespoon mixed dried herbs
2 tablespoons butter, melted
salt and ground black pepper

1 Preheat the oven to 350°F. Place the chicken in a greased ovenproof dish. Spread with the mustard and season.

2 Mix the bread crumbs and herbs together thoroughly.

3 Press the bread crumb mixture onto the chicken to coat. Spoon the melted butter over the top. Bake uncovered for 20 minutes, or until crisp and cooked through.

COOK'S TIP

The chicken portions can be brushed with melted butter instead of mustard before being coated in the bread crumb mixture, if you like.

Oat-crusted Chicken with Sage

Chicken thighs and drumsticks are coated with a crisp oat and sage mixture that is simply delicious.

INGREDIENTS

Serves 4

3 tablespoons skim milk

2 teaspoons hot mustard

$^1/_2$ cup rolled oats

3 tablespoons chopped fresh
   sage leaves

8 chicken thighs or drumsticks, skinned

$^1/_2$ cup low-fat plain yogurt

1 teaspoon whole-grain mustard

salt and ground black pepper

fresh sage leaves, to garnish

1 Preheat the oven to 400°F. Combine the milk and hot mustard in a small bowl.

2 Mix the oats with 2 tablespoons of the sage and the seasoning on a plate. Brush the chicken with the milk and press into the oats.

COOK'S TIP

If fresh sage is not available, choose another fresh herb, such as thyme or parsley, rather than a dried alternative.

3 Place the chicken on a cookie sheet and bake for about 40 minutes, or until the juices run clear, not pink, when pierced through the thickest part.

4 Combine the low-fat yogurt, whole-grain mustard, the remaining sage, and seasoning, then serve with the chicken. Garnish the chicken with fresh sage and serve hot or cold.

Oven "Fried" Chicken

4 Sprinkle a little water onto the chicken pieces, and coat again lightly with the seasoned flour.

5 Beat the egg with the water in a shallow dish. Stir in the herbs. Dip the chicken pieces into the egg mixture, turning them over to coat them thoroughly.

6 Combine the bread crumbs and grated Parmesan cheese on a plate. Roll the chicken pieces in the crumbs, patting with your fingers to help them to adhere.

7 Place the chicken pieces in the prepared dish, arranging them in a single layer. Bake until thoroughly cooked and golden brown, 20–30 minutes. To check that they are cooked, prick with a fork; the juices that run out should be clear, not pink. Serve hot, with lemon wedges.

This healthy chicken dish is baked until crisp in the oven.

INGREDIENTS

Serves 4

4 large chicken pieces
$^1/_2$ cup all-purpose flour
$^1/_2$ teaspoon salt
$^1/_4$ teaspoon pepper
1 egg
2 tablespoons water
2 tablespoons chopped mixed
   fresh herbs, such as parsley, basil,
   and thyme
1 cup dry bread crumbs
$^1/_3$ cup freshly grated Parmesan cheese
lemon wedges, to serve

1 Preheat the oven to 400°F. Grease an ovenproof dish.

2 Rinse the chicken in cold water. Pat dry with paper towels.

3 Combine the flour, salt, and pepper on a plate and stir with a fork to mix. Coat the chicken pieces on all sides with the flour and shake off the excess.

Pan-fried Honey Chicken Drumsticks

Tender chicken drumsticks are marinated in honey, lemon, and soy sauce, and then quickly fried. They are sure to be popular with all the family.

INGREDIENTS

Serves 4

scant $^1/_2$ cup honey

juice of 1 lemon

2 tablespoons soy sauce

1 tablespoon sesame seeds

$^1/_2$ teaspoon fresh or dried thyme leaves

12 chicken drumsticks

$^1/_2$ teaspoon salt

$^1/_2$ teaspoon pepper

$^3/_4$ cup all-purpose flour

3 tablespoons butter or margarine

3 tablespoons vegetable oil

$^1/_2$ cup white wine

$^1/_2$ cup chicken stock

fresh parsley sprigs, to garnish

1 In a large bowl, combine the honey, lemon juice, soy sauce, sesame seeds, and thyme. Add the chicken drumsticks and mix to coat them well. Leave to marinate in a cool place for 2 hours or more, turning occasionally.

2 Mix the salt, pepper, and flour in a shallow bowl. Drain the drumsticks, reserving the marinade. Roll them in the seasoned flour to coat all over.

3 Heat the butter or margarine with the oil in a large skillet. When hot and sizzling, add the drumsticks. Brown them on all sides. Reduce the heat to medium–low and cook until the chicken is tender, 12–15 minutes.

4 Test the drumsticks with a fork; the juices should be clear. Remove the drumsticks to a serving platter and keep hot.

5 Pour off most of the fat from the skillet. Add the wine, stock, and reserved marinade and stir well to mix in the cooking juices on the base of the skillet. Bring to a boil and simmer until reduced by half. Check and adjust the seasoning, then spoon the sauce over the drumsticks, and serve garnished with parsley.

Blackened Chicken

Cumin, cayenne, and paprika give the coating for these chicken portions a lovely warm piquancy. For the best flavor, cook them until they begin to blacken.

INGREDIENTS

Serves 6

6 medium skinless, boneless chicken
   breast portions
6 tablespoons butter or margarine
1 teaspoon garlic paste
4 tablespoons finely grated onion
1 teaspoon cayenne pepper
2 teaspoons sweet paprika
1¹/₂ teaspoons salt
¹/₂ teaspoon white pepper
1 teaspoon black pepper
¹/₄ teaspoon ground cumin
1 teaspoon dried thyme leaves
bell peppers and salad greens, to serve

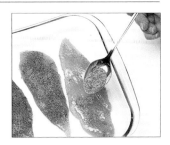

1 Slice each chicken portion in half horizontally. Flatten each slightly with the heel of the hand.

2 Melt the butter or margarine in a small pan together with the garlic paste.

3 Combine all the remaining ingredients in a shallow bowl and stir well. Brush the chicken pieces on both sides with melted butter or margarine, then sprinkle evenly with the seasoned mixture.

4 Heat a large, heavy skillet over high heat until a drop of water sprinkled on the surface sizzles. This will take 5–8 minutes.

5 Drizzle 1 teaspoon of melted butter on each chicken piece. Place them in the skillet in a single layer, two or three at a time. Cook until the underside begins to blacken, 2–3 minutes. Turn over and cook for 2–3 minutes more, until cooked through. Serve hot accompanied by salad.

Chicken with Tomato-corn Salsa

This hot tomato salsa is good with any broiled or grilled meats.

INGREDIENTS

Serves 4

4 skinless, boneless chicken breast
    portions, about 6 ounces each
2 tablespoons fresh lemon juice
2 tablespoons olive oil
2 teaspoons ground cumin
2 teaspoons dried oregano
1 tablespoon coarse black pepper
salt

For the salsa

1 fresh hot green chile
1 pound tomatoes, seeded and chopped
1 1/2 cups corn, freshly cooked or
    thawed frozen
3 scallions, chopped
1 tablespoon chopped fresh parsley
2 tablespoons chopped
    fresh cilantro
2 tablespoons fresh lemon juice
3 tablespoons olive oil
1 teaspoon salt

1 With a meat mallet, pound the chicken breast portions between two sheets of plastic wrap until thin.

2 In a shallow dish, combine the lemon juice, oil, cumin, oregano, and pepper.

3 Add the chicken and turn to coat. Cover and leave to stand for at least 2 hours, or chill overnight in the refrigerator.

4 To make the salsa, char the chile skin either over a gas flame or under the broiler. Leave to cool for 5 minutes. Wearing latex gloves, carefully rub off the charred skin. For a less hot flavor, discard the seeds.

5 Chop the chile finely and place in a bowl. Add the remaining salsa ingredients and mix well.

6 Remove the chicken from the marinade. Season lightly.

7 Heat a ridged griddle. Add the chicken portions and cook until browned, about 3 minutes. Turn and cook for 3–4 minutes more. Serve with the chile salsa.

Chicken, Carrot, and Leek Packets

These intriguing packets may sound a bit awkward for every day, but the solution is to make them ahead of time and freeze them—ready to cook gently from frozen.

INGREDIENTS

Serves 4

4 skinless, boneless chicken
  breast portions
2 small leeks, sliced
2 carrots, grated
4 pitted black olives, chopped
1 garlic clove, crushed
1–2 tablespoons olive oil
8 anchovy fillets
salt and ground black pepper
black olives and herb sprigs, to garnish

1 Preheat the oven to 400°F.
  Season the chicken well with
salt and pepper.

2 Divide the leeks equally among
  four sheets of greased baking
parchment, about 9 inches square.
Place a piece of chicken on top of
each one.

3 Mix the carrots, olives, garlic,
  and oil together. Season lightly
and place on top of the chicken
portions. Top each with two of the
anchovy fillets, then carefully wrap
up each packet, making sure the
paper folds are underneath and the
carrot mixture on top.

4 Bake for 20 minutes and serve
  hot, in the paper, garnished
with black olives and herb sprigs.

Chicken in a Tomato Coat

Roasted chicken with a coating of tomato sauce and fresh tomatoes makes a tasty meal served with rice.

INGREDIENTS

Serves 4–6

1 chicken, about 3–4$^{1}/_{2}$ pounds
1 small onion
pat of butter
5 tablespoons ready-made tomato sauce
2 tablespoons chopped, mixed fresh
  herbs, such as parsley, tarragon,
  sage, basil, and marjoram, or
  2 teaspoons dried
$^{2}/_{3}$ cup dry white wine
2–3 small tomatoes, sliced
olive oil
a little cornstarch (optional)
salt and ground black pepper

1 Preheat the oven to 375°F.
  Place the chicken in a roasting
pan. Put the onion, the pat of
butter and some seasoning inside
the chicken.

2 Spread most of the tomato
  sauce over the chicken and
sprinkle with half the herbs and
some seasoning. Pour the wine
into the roasting pan.

3 Cover with foil, then roast for
  1$^{1}/_{2}$ hours, basting occasionally.
Remove the foil. Spread the
chicken with the remaining sauce
and the sliced tomatoes and drizzle
with oil. Continue cooking for
20–30 minutes more, or until
cooked through.

4 Sprinkle the remaining herbs
  over the chicken, then carve.
Cook the sauce with the cornstarch
until thickened if you like.

Chicken with Lemon and Herbs

The herbs for this recipe can be varied according to what is available; for example, parsley or thyme could be used instead of tarragon and fennel. Serve accompanied by sautéed potatoes for a quick and satisfying meal.

INGREDIENTS

Serves 2

$1/4$ cup butter

2 scallions, white part only, finely chopped

1 tablespoon chopped fresh tarragon

1 tablespoon chopped fresh fennel

juice of 1 lemon

4 chicken thighs

salt and ground black pepper

lemon slices and herb sprigs,
   to garnish

1 Preheat the broiler to medium. In a small pan, melt the butter, then add the scallions, herbs, and lemon juice, and season with a little salt and pepper.

2 Brush the chicken generously with the herb mixture, then broil for 10–12 minutes, basting frequently with the herb mixture.

3 Turn the chicken over, baste again, then cook for about 10 minutes more, or until the juices run clear.

4 Serve garnished with lemon and herbs.

Chicken with Red Cabbage

Chestnuts and red cabbage make a colorful winter dish.

INGREDIENTS

Serves 4

$1/4$ cup butter

4 large chicken portions, halved

1 onion, chopped

$1 1/4$ pounds red cabbage, finely shredded

4 juniper berries, crushed

12 cooked peeled chestnuts

$1/2$ cup full-bodied red wine

salt and ground black pepper

1 Heat the butter in a heavy, flameproof casserole and lightly brown the chicken pieces. Transfer to a plate.

2 Add the onion and cook until soft and light golden brown. Stir in the cabbage and juniper berries, season, and cook over medium heat for 6–7 minutes, stirring once or twice.

3 Stir the chestnuts into the casserole, then tuck the chicken pieces under the cabbage so that they are on the bottom of the casserole. Pour in the red wine.

4 Cover and cook gently for about 40 minutes, or until the chicken juices run clear and the cabbage is very tender. Check the seasoning and serve.

Two-way Chicken with Vegetables

This tender, slow-cooked chicken makes a tasty family supper, with the stock and remaining vegetables providing a nourishing soup for a second meal.

INGREDIENTS

Serves 6

1 chicken, about 3 pounds

2 onions, quartered

3 carrots, thickly sliced

2 celery stalks, chopped

1 parsnip or turnip, thickly sliced

$^1/_2$ cup white mushrooms,
   coarsely chopped

1–2 fresh thyme sprigs or 1 teaspoon
   dried thyme

4 bay leaves

large bunch of fresh parsley

1 cup whole-wheat pasta shapes

salt and ground black pepper

new potatoes or pasta,
   snow peas or green beans, and
   bread, to serve

1 Trim the chicken of any extra fat. Put it in a flameproof casserole and add the vegetables and herbs. Pour in enough water to cover and add salt and pepper. Bring to a boil over medium heat, skimming off any scum. When the water boils, lower the heat, and simmer for 2–3 hours.

2 Carve the chicken neatly, discarding the skin and bones, but returning any small pieces to the pan. Serve the chicken with some of the vegetables from the pan, plus new potatoes or pasta and snow peas or green beans.

3 For the soup, remove any large pieces of parsley and thyme from the pan, let the remaining mixture cool, then chill it overnight. Next day, lift off the fat that has solidified on the surface. Reheat the soup gently.

4 When the soup comes to a boil, add the pasta shapes, with salt, if required, and cook for 10–12 minutes, or until the pasta is tender. Adjust the seasoning and garnish with parsley. Serve with whole-wheat bread.

Chicken Baked with Lima Beans and Garlic

This simple one-pot meal combines chicken with leeks, fennel, and garlic-flavored lima beans.

INGREDIENTS

Serves 6

2 leeks

1 small fennel bulb

4 garlic cloves, peeled

2 x 14-ounce cans lima beans, drained

2 large handfuls of fresh
  parsley, chopped

1¹/₄ cups dry white wine

1¹/₄ cups vegetable stock

1 chicken, about 3 pounds

salt and ground black pepper

parsley sprigs, to garnish

cooked green vegetables, to serve

1 Preheat the oven to 350°F. Slit the leeks, wash out any grit, then slice them thickly. Cut the fennel into quarters, remove the core, and chop the flesh coarsely.

2 Combine the leeks, fennel, whole garlic cloves, lima beans, and parsley in a bowl. Season to taste with salt and pepper, then spread out the mixture on the bottom of a heavy, flameproof casserole that is large enough to hold the chicken. Pour in the white wine and vegetable stock.

3 Place the chicken on top and season lightly with salt and pepper. Bring to a boil, cover the casserole, and transfer it to the oven. Bake for 1–1¹/₂ hours, or until the chicken is cooked and so tender that it falls off the bone. Garnish with parsley and serve with green vegetables.

Chicken Börek

This is a rich pastry packet with a savory filling. Serve at room temperature with a refreshing minty yogurt sauce.

INGREDIENTS

Serves 4

$^1/_2$ cup couscous
3 tablespoons olive oil
1 onion, chopped
$1^2/_3$ cups mushrooms
1 garlic clove, crushed
scant 1 cup diced cooked chicken
2 tablespoons walnuts, chopped
2 tablespoons raisins
4 tablespoons chopped
    fresh parsley
1 teaspoon chopped fresh thyme
2 eggs, hard-cooked and peeled
salt and ground black pepper

For the pastry
$3^1/_2$ cups self-rising flour, plus extra
    for dusting
1 teaspoon salt
1 egg, plus extra for glazing
$^2/_3$ cup plain yogurt
$^2/_3$ cup olive oil
grated rind of $^1/_2$ lemon

For the sauce
scant 1 cup plain yogurt
3 tablespoons chopped fresh mint
$^1/_2$ teaspoon superfine sugar
$^1/_4$ teaspoon cayenne pepper
$^1/_4$ teaspoon celery salt
a little milk or water, if necessary

1 Preheat the oven to 375°F. Place the couscous in a bowl, just cover with boiling water, and soak for 10 minutes, or until all the liquid is absorbed.

2 Heat the oil in a pan and soften the onion. Add the mushrooms and garlic, and cook until the juices begin to run. Increase the heat to boil off the juices.

3 Transfer the mushroom and onion mixture to a mixing bowl, add the chicken, walnuts, raisins, parsley, thyme, and couscous, and stir well. Chop the eggs and stir them into the mixture with seasoning to taste.

4 To make the pastry, sift the flour and salt into a bowl. Make a well in the center, add the egg, yogurt, olive oil, and lemon rind, and mix together with a round-bladed knife.

5 Turn out onto a floured counter and roll into a 12-inch round. Pile the filling into the center and bring the edges over to enclose it. Turn upside down onto a cookie sheet and press out flat with your hand. Glaze with beaten egg and bake for 25 minutes.

6 Meanwhile, make the sauce. Blend together all the ingredients, adding milk or water if the mixture is too thick. Spoon a little sauce over each serving.

Chicken with Serrano Ham

This modern Spanish dish is light and very easy to make. It looks fabulous, too.

INGREDIENTS

Serves 4

4 skinless, boneless chicken
    breast portions
4 slices Serrano ham
6 tablespoons butter
2 tablespoons chopped capers
2 tablespoons fresh thyme leaves
1 large lemon, cut lengthwise
    into 8 slices
a few small fresh thyme sprigs
salt and ground black pepper
boiled new potatoes and steamed broccoli
    or snow peas, to serve

1 Preheat the oven to 400°F. Wrap each chicken portion in plastic wrap and beat gently with with the side of a rolling pin until slightly flattened. Arrange the portions in a large, shallow ovenproof dish, then top each with a slice of Serrano ham.

2 Beat the butter with the capers, thyme, and seasoning until well mixed. Divide the butter into quarters and shape each into a neat portion, then place on each ham-topped chicken portion. Arrange 2 lemon slices on the butter and sprinkle with small thyme sprigs. Bake for 25 minutes, or until the chicken is cooked through.

3 Transfer the chicken to a warmed serving platter and spoon the buttery juices over the top. Serve immediately, with boiled new potatoes and steamed broccoli or snow peas. Discard the lemon slices before serving, if you like.

Chicken Fillets with Olives

This quick and tasty dish makes a good light main course.

INGREDIENTS

Serves 4

6 tablespoons olive oil

1 garlic clove, peeled and
   lightly crushed

1 dried chile, lightly crushed

1 1/4 pounds skinless, boneless chicken
   breast portions, cut into 1/4-inch slices

1/2 cup dry white wine

4 tomatoes, peeled and seeded,
   cut into thin strips

about 24 black olives

6–8 fresh basil leaves, torn into pieces

salt and ground black pepper

1 Heat 4 tablespoons of the olive oil in a large skillet. Add the garlic and crushed dried chile, and cook over low heat until the garlic is golden.

2 Raise the heat to medium and add the remaining oil. Place the chicken slices in the skillet, and brown them lightly on both sides for about 2 minutes. Season with salt and pepper. Remove the chicken to a heated dish.

3 Discard the garlic and chile. Add the wine, tomato strips, and olives. Cook over medium heat for 3–4 minutes, scraping up any meat residue from the base of the skillet.

4 Return the chicken to the skillet. Sprinkle with the torn basil. Heat through for 30 seconds, then serve immediately.

Chicken with Herbs and Lentils

Lentils and herbs are baked with chicken to give it a lovely full flavor. Topped with garlic butter it makes a robust dish.

Serves 4

4-ounce piece of thick bacon or pork side, rind removed, chopped

1 large onion, sliced

2 cups well-flavored chicken stock

1 bay leaf

2 sprigs each fresh parsley, marjoram, and thyme

1 cup green or brown lentils

4 chicken portions

salt and ground black pepper

2–4 tablespoons garlic butter (see Cook's Tip)

1 Cook the bacon or pork gently in a large, heavy, flameproof casserole until all the fat runs out and the meat begins to brown. Add the onion and cook for about 2 minutes.

2 Stir in the chicken stock, bay leaf, herb stalks and some of the leafy parts (reserve some herb sprigs for garnish), lentils, and seasoning. Preheat the oven to 375°F.

3 Cook the chicken portions in a skillet to brown the skin before placing on top of the lentils. Sprinkle with seasoning and some of the herbs.

4 Cover the casserole and cook in the oven for about 40 minutes, until cooked through. Serve with a spoonful of garlic butter on each portion, and a few herb sprigs.

COOK'S TIP

To make garlic butter, blend ½ cup softened butter with 4 crushed garlic cloves. Form into a roll and chill. Slice into rounds. Garlic butter freezes well.

Thai Chicken and Vegetable Stir-fry

Lemongrass and ginger give this speedy stir fry a delicious fragrance. You can make the dish a little hotter by adding more fresh root ginger, if you like.

INGREDIENTS

Serves 4

1 lemongrass stalk or the rind of
 $^1/_2$ lemon

$^1/_2$-inch piece of fresh ginger root

1 large garlic clove

2 tablespoons sunflower oil

10 ounces lean chicken, thinly sliced

$^1/_2$ red bell pepper, seeded
 and sliced

$^1/_2$ green bell pepper, seeded
 and sliced

4 scallions, chopped

2 medium carrots, cut into batons

4 ounces fine green beans

2 tablespoons oyster sauce

pinch of sugar

salt and ground black pepper

$^1/_4$ cup salted peanuts, lightly crushed, and
 fresh cilantro leaves, to garnish

cooked rice, to serve

1 Thinly slice the lemongrass or lemon rind. Peel and chop the ginger and garlic. Heat the oil in a skillet over high heat. Add the lemongrass or lemon rind, ginger, and garlic, and stir-fry for 30 seconds, or until brown.

2 Add the chicken and stir-fry for 2 minutes. Then add the vegetables and stir-fry for 4–5 minutes, or until the chicken is cooked and the vegetables are almost cooked.

3 Finally, stir in the oyster sauce, sugar, and seasoning to taste and stir-fry for another minute to mix and blend well. Serve immediately, sprinkled with the peanuts and cilantro leaves and accompanied by cooked rice.

Chicken Stroganov

This chicken version of the classic Russian dish—usually made with beef tenderloin—is perfect served with rice mixed with vegetables.

INGREDIENTS

Serves 4

4 large skinless, boneless chicken
   breast portions
3 tablespoons olive oil
1 large onion, thinly sliced
3 cups mushrooms, sliced
1¼ cups sour cream
salt and ground black pepper
1 tablespoon chopped fresh parsley,
   to garnish

4 Add the mushrooms and cook until golden brown. Remove and keep warm.

5 Increase the heat, add the remaining oil, and cook the chicken very quickly, in small batches, for 3–4 minutes, until lightly colored and cooked through. Remove to a dish and keep warm.

6 Return all the chicken, onions, and mushrooms to the skillet and season with salt and black pepper. Stir in the sour cream and bring to a boil. Sprinkle with fresh parsley and serve immediately.

1 Divide each chicken portion into two natural fillets, place between two sheets of plastic wrap, and flatten each to a thickness of ½ inch with a rolling pin.

2 Cut into 1-inch strips diagonally across the fillets.

3 Heat 2 tablespoons of the oil in a skillet and cook the onion slowly until soft but not colored.

Chicken with Honey and Grapefruit

Chicken breast portions cook very quickly and are ideal for suppers on-the-run—but be careful not to overcook them. You could substitute boneless turkey steaks or duck breast fillets for the chicken, if you prefer.

INGREDIENTS

Serves 4

4 skinless chicken breast portions

3–4 tablespoons honey

1 pink grapefruit, peeled and
    cut into 12 segments

salt and ground black pepper

noodles and salad greens, to serve

1 Make three quite deep, diagonal slits in the chicken flesh using a large sharp knife.

2 Brush the chicken all over with some of the honey and sprinkle well with seasoning.

3 Put the chicken in a flameproof dish, uncut side uppermost, and place under a preheated broiler for 2–3 minutes.

4 Turn the chicken over and place the grapefruit segments in the slits. Brush with more honey and cook for 5 minutes more, or until tender and cooked through. If necessary, reduce the heat so that the honey glaze does not burn. Serve immediately with noodles and salad greens.

Crispy Chicken with Garlic Rice

Chicken wings cooked until they are really tender have a surprising amount of meat on them, and make a very economical supper for a crowd of youngsters. Provide lots of paper towels, napkins, and finger bowls for the sticky fingers.

INGREDIENTS

Serves 4

1 large onion, chopped

2 garlic cloves, crushed

2 tablespoons sunflower oil

scant 1 cup basmati rice

$1^{1}/_{2}$ cups hot chicken stock

2 teaspoons finely grated lemon rind

2 tablespoons chopped mixed herbs

8 or 12 chicken wings

$^{1}/_{2}$ cup all-purpose flour

salt and ground black pepper

fresh tomato sauce and vegetables,
    to serve

1 Preheat the oven to 400°F. Cook the onion and garlic in the oil in a large, flameproof casserole until golden. Stir in the rice and toss until all the grains are well coated in oil.

2 Stir in the stock, lemon rind, and herbs and bring to a boil. Cover and cook in the middle of the oven for 40–50 minutes. Stir once or twice during cooking.

3 Meanwhile, wipe dry the chicken wings. Season the flour and use to coat the chicken portions.

4 Put the chicken wings in a small roasting pan and cook in the top of the oven for 30–40 minutes, turning once, until crisp and cooked through.

5 Serve the rice and chicken wings with a fresh tomato sauce and a selection of vegetables.

Chicken and Bean Risotto

2 Stir in the chicken, kidney beans, corn, and golden raisins. Cook, stirring, for 20 minutes more, or until almost all the liquid has been absorbed.

3 Meanwhile, cook the broccoli in boiling water for 5 minutes, then drain thoroughly.

4 Stir in the broccoli and chopped herbs, season to taste, and serve immediately.

Nutty-flavored brown rice tastes good mixed with kidney beans, corn, and broccoli in this tasty risotto.

INGREDIENTS

Serves 4–6

1 onion, chopped

2 garlic cloves, crushed

1 red chile, seeded and finely chopped

2^{1}/$_{4}$ cups mushrooms, sliced

2 celery stalks, chopped

generous 1 cup long grain
    brown rice

scant 2 cups chicken or vegetable stock

^{2}/$_{3}$ cup white wine

8 ounces skinless, boneless chicken
    breast portion, diced

14-ounce can red kidney
    beans, drained

7-ounce can corn kernels

^{2}/$_{3}$ cup golden raisins

6 ounces small broccoli flowerets

2–3 tablespoons chopped fresh
    mixed herbs

salt and ground black pepper

1 Put the onion, garlic, chile, mushrooms, celery, rice, stock, and wine in a pan. Cover, bring to a boil, and simmer for 15 minutes.

COOK'S TIP

Use 1 teaspoon hot chili powder in place of the fresh chile, if you like.

Stir-fried Chicken with Snow Peas

This dish is easy to prepare, but remember to marinate the chicken the night before.

INGREDIENTS

Serves 4

2 tablespoons sesame oil

6 tablespoons lemon juice

1 garlic clove, crushed

$1/2$-inch piece of fresh ginger root, peeled and grated

1 teaspoon honey

1 pound skinless, boneless chicken breast portions, cut into strips

4 ounces snow peas, trimmed

2 tablespoons peanut oil

$1/2$ cup cashew nuts

6 scallions, cut into strips

8-ounce can water chestnuts, drained and thinly sliced

salt

saffron rice, to serve

1 Combine the sesame oil, lemon juice, garlic, ginger, and honey in a shallow nonmetallic dish. Add the chicken and mix well. Cover with plastic wrap and marinate in the refrigerator overnight.

2 Blanch the snow peas in lightly salted, boiling water for 1 minute. Drain and refresh under cold running water.

3 Drain the chicken strips and reserve the marinade. Heat the peanut oil in a wok or large skillet, add the cashew nuts, and stir-fry for about 1–2 minutes, or until golden brown. Remove the cashew nuts from the wok or skillet using a slotted spoon and set aside.

4 Add the chicken and stir-fry for 3–4 minutes, or until golden brown. Add the scallions, snow peas, water chestnuts, and the reserved marinade. Cook for a few minutes, until the chicken is cooked through and the sauce is bubbling and hot. Stir in the cashew nuts and serve with saffron rice.

Spicy Chicken Stir-fry

The chicken is marinated in an aromatic blend of spices and then stir-fried with crisp vegetables. If you find it too spicy, serve with a spoonful of sour cream or yogurt. This dish is just as delicious hot or cold.

INGREDIENTS

Serves 4

$^1/_2$ teaspoon ground turmeric
$^1/_2$ teaspoon ground ginger
1 teaspoon each salt and ground
   black pepper
2 teaspoons ground cumin
1 tablespoon ground coriander
1 tablespoon superfine sugar
1 pound skinless, boneless chicken
   breast portions
1 bunch scallions
4 celery stalks
2 red bell peppers
1 yellow bell pepper
6 ounces zucchini
$1^1/_2$ cups snow peas or sugar snap peas
about 3 tablespoons sunflower oil
1 tablespoon lime juice
1 tablespoon honey

1 Combine the turmeric, ginger, salt, pepper, cumin, coriander, and sugar in a bowl until thoroughly mixed.

2 Cut the chicken into bitesize strips. Add to the spice mixture and stir to coat the chicken pieces thoroughly. Set aside.

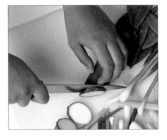

3 Prepare the vegetables. Cut the scallions, celery, and bell peppers into 2-inch long, thin strips. Cut the zucchini at a slight angle into thin rounds and trim the snow peas or sugar snap peas.

4 Heat 2 tablespoons of the oil in a large skillet or wok. Stir-fry the chicken, in batches, until cooked through and golden brown, adding a little more oil if necessary. Remove from the skillet and keep warm.

5 Add a little more oil to the skillet and cook the onions, celery, bell peppers, and zucchini over medium heat for about 8–10 minutes, or until beginning to soften and turn golden. Add the snow peas or sugar snap peas and cook for 2 minutes more.

6 Return the chicken to the skillet, with the lime juice and honey. Cook for 2 minutes. Adjust the seasoning and serve.

Stir-fried Turkey, Broccoli, and Mushrooms

This is a really easy, tasty dish, which works well with chicken too.

INGREDIENTS

Serves 4

4 ounces broccoli flowerets

4 scallions

1 teaspoon cornstarch

3 tablespoons oyster sauce

1 tablespoon dark soy sauce

$1/2$ cup chicken stock

2 teaspoons lemon juice

3 tablespoons peanut oil

1 pound turkey steaks, cut into strips
about $1/4$ x 2 inches

1 small onion, chopped

2 garlic cloves, crushed

2 teaspoons grated fresh ginger root

$1^1/2$ cups fresh shiitake
mushrooms, sliced

3 ounces baby corn, halved lengthwise

1 tablespoon sesame oil

salt and ground black pepper

egg noodles, to serve

1 Divide the broccoli flowerets into smaller sprigs and cut the stalks into thin diagonal slices.

2 Finely chop the white parts of the scallions and slice the green parts into thin shreds.

3 In a bowl, blend together the cornstarch, oyster sauce, soy sauce, stock, and lemon juice. Set aside.

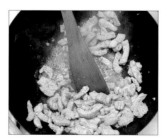

4 Heat a wok until it is hot, add 2 tablespoons of the peanut oil and swirl it around. Add the turkey strips and stir-fry for about 2 minutes, or until golden and crisp at the edges, and cooked through. Remove the turkey with a slotted spoon and keep it warm.

5 Add the remaining peanut oil to the wok and stir-fry the chopped onion, garlic, and ginger over medium heat for about 1 minute. Increase the heat to high, add the broccoli, mushrooms, and corn, and stir-fry for 2 minutes.

6 Return the turkey to the wok, then add the cornstarch mixture with the chopped scallions and seasoning. Cook, stirring, for about 1 minute, or until the sauce has thickened. Stir in the sesame oil. Serve immediately on a bed of egg noodles with the finely shredded scallion sprinkled on top.

Tequila Chicken

In Mexico, tequila is a popular drink, and here it is combined with sherry, apples, plaintains, and raisins to give a most unusual sweet-and-sour flavor to chicken. Serve with rice or flour tortillas to mop up the sauce, if you like.

INGREDIENTS

Serves 4

1 cup raisins
$^{1}/_{2}$ cup sherry
1 cup all-purpose flour
$^{1}/_{2}$ teaspoon salt
$^{1}/_{2}$ teaspoon ground black pepper
3 tablespoons vegetable oil
8 skinless chicken thighs
1 onion, halved and thinly sliced
3 garlic cloves, crushed
2 tart eating apples, peeled, cored,
    and diced
1 cup sliced almonds
1 ripe plantain, peeled and sliced
1$^{1}/_{2}$ cups chicken stock
1 cup tequila
fresh herbs, chopped, to garnish (optional)

1 Put the raisins in a bowl and pour in the sherry. Set aside to plump up. Season the flour with the salt and pepper and spread it out on a large, flat dish or soup plate. Heat 2 tablespoons of the oil in a large skillet. Dip each chicken thigh in turn in the seasoned flour, then cook in the hot oil until browned, turning occasionally. Drain on paper towels.

2 Heat the remaining oil. Add the onions and garlic and cook for 2–3 minutes.

3 Add the diced apples to the onion mixture with the almonds and plantain slices. Cook, stirring occasionally, for 3–4 minutes, then add the raisins with any remaining sherry. Add the chicken to the skillet.

4 Pour the stock and tequila over the chicken mixture. Cover the skillet with a lid and cook for 15 minutes, then take off the lid, and cook for 10 minutes more, or until the sauce has reduced by about half.

5 Check that the chicken thighs are cooked by lifting one out of the skillet and piercing it in the thickest part with a sharp knife or skewer. Any juices that come out should be clear. If necessary, cook the chicken for a little longer before serving, sprinkled with chopped fresh herbs, if you like.

Chicken with Mixed Vegetables

*This delectable dish is a riot of color
with a variety of contrasting textures
and tastes.*

INGREDIENTS

Serves 4

12 ounces skinless, boneless chicken
    breast portions
4 teaspoons vegetable oil
1¼ cups chicken stock
¾ cup drained, canned straw mushrooms
½ cup drained, canned bamboo
    shoots, sliced
⅓ cup drained, canned water
    chestnuts, sliced
1 small carrot, sliced
½ cup snow peas
1 tablespoon dry sherry
1 tablespoon oyster sauce
1 teaspoon superfine sugar
1 teaspoon cornstarch
1 tablespoon cold water
salt and ground white pepper

3 Heat the remaining oil in a
nonstick skillet or wok, add all
the vegetables, and stir-fry for
2 minutes. Stir in the sherry, oyster
sauce, superfine sugar, and reserved
stock. Add the chicken to the pan
and cook for 2 minutes.

4 Mix the cornstarch to a paste
with the water. Add the mixture
to the pan and cook, stirring, until
the sauce thickens slightly. Season
to taste with salt and pepper and
serve immediately.

1 Put the chicken in a shallow
bowl. Add 1 teaspoon of the oil,
¼ teaspoon salt, and a pinch of
pepper. Cover and set aside for
10 minutes in a cool place.

2 Bring the stock to a boil in a
pan. Add the chicken and cook
for 12 minutes, or until tender
and cooked through. Drain and
slice, reserving 5 tablespoons of
the stock.

Tandoori Chicken Kebabs

This dish originates from the plains of the Punjab at the foot of the Himalayas, where food is traditionally cooked in clay ovens known as tandoors—hence the name.

INGREDIENTS

Serves 4

4 skinless, boneless chicken breast
   portions, about 6 ounces each
1 tablespoon lemon juice
3 tablespoons tandoori paste
3 tablespoons plain yogurt
1 garlic clove, crushed
2 tablespoons chopped fresh cilantro
1 small onion, cut into wedges and
   separated into layers
a little oil, for brushing
salt and ground black pepper
fresh cilantro sprigs, to garnish
pilau rice and nan bread,
   to serve

1 Chop the chicken portions into 1-inch cubes, place in a bowl, and add the lemon juice, tandoori paste, yogurt, garlic, cilantro, and seasoning. Cover and leave to marinate in the refrigerator for at least 2–3 hours. Soak four wooden skewers in water for 30 minutes.

2 Preheat the broiler. Thread alternate pieces of chicken and onion onto the skewers.

3 Brush the onion with a little oil, lay the kebabs on a broiler rack, and cook under high heat for about 10–12 minutes, turning once, until cooked through. Garnish the kebabs with fresh cilantro and serve immediately with pilau rice and nan bread.

Chinese Chicken with Cashew Nuts

Marinated chicken is quickly cooked with cashew nuts, scallions, and egg noodles in this tasty stir-fried dish.

INGREDIENTS

Serves 4

4 skinless, boneless chicken breast
   portions, about 6 ounces each, sliced
   into strips
3 garlic cloves, crushed
4 tablespoons soy sauce
2 tablespoons cornstarch
8 ounces dried egg noodles
3 tablespoons peanut or
   sunflower oil
1 tablespoon sesame oil
1 cup roasted cashew nuts
6 scallions, cut into 2-inch pieces and
   halved lengthwise
scallion curls and a little chopped red
   chile, to garnish

4 Add the cashew nuts and scallions to the skillet and stir-fry for 2–3 minutes.

1 Mix the chicken, garlic, soy sauce, and cornstarch in a bowl. Cover and chill for 30 minutes.

2 Bring a pan of water to a boil and add the noodles. Turn off the heat and let stand for 5 minutes. Drain well and reserve.

3 Heat the oils in a large skillet and add the chicken and marinade. Stir-fry for 3–4 minutes, or until golden brown and done.

5 Add the drained noodles and stir-fry for 2 minutes more. Serve immediately, garnished with the scallion curls and chopped red chile.

Lemon Chicken Stir-fry

This mouthwatering dish is cooked in minutes. As with all stir-fries, it is essential to prepare all the ingredients before you begin so that they are ready to cook.

Serves 4

4 skinless, boneless chicken
    breast portions
1 tablespoon light soy sauce
5 tablespoons cornstarch
1 bunch of scallions
1 lemon
1 garlic clove, crushed
1 tablespoon superfine sugar
2 tablespoons sherry
about ²/3 cup chicken stock
4 tablespoons olive oil
salt and ground black pepper

1 Divide the chicken portions into two natural fillets. Place each between two sheets of plastic wrap and flatten to ¹/4 inch thick with a rolling pin.

2 Cut into 1-inch strips across the grain of the fillets. Put in a bowl with the soy sauce and toss to coat. Sprinkle on 4 tablespoons of the cornstarch and toss.

3 Cut the scallions diagonally into ¹/2-inch pieces. With a swivel vegetable peeler, remove the lemon rind in thin strips and cut into fine shreds. Alternatively, grate finely. Squeeze the lemon and reserve the juice. Blend the remaining cornstarch into a paste with a little water.

4 Heat the oil in a wok or large skillet and cook the chicken very quickly, in small batches, for 3–4 minutes, or until golden and cooked through. Remove to a dish and keep warm.

5 Add the scallions and garlic to the wok or skillet and cook for 2 minutes.

6 Add the sugar, sherry, stock, lemon juice, and cornstarch mixture, with the chicken, and bring to a boil, stirring until thickened. Add more sherry or stock if necessary, and stir until the chicken is evenly covered with sauce. Season and reheat for about 2 minutes.

Chicken with Lemon Sauce

Succulent chicken with a refreshing lemony sauce is a sure winner.

Serves 4

4 small skinless, boneless chicken
    breast portions
1 teaspoon sesame oil
1 tablespoon dry sherry
1 egg white, lightly beaten
2 tablespoons cornstarch
1 tablespoon vegetable oil
salt and ground white pepper
chopped cilantro leaves, scallions, and
    lemon wedges, to garnish

For the sauce

3 tablespoons fresh lemon juice
2 tablespoons sweetened lime juice
3 tablespoons superfine sugar
2 teaspoons cornstarch
6 tablespoons cold water

1 Place the chicken in a shallow bowl. Mix the sesame oil with the sherry and add $1/2$ teaspoon salt and $1/4$ teaspoon pepper. Pour it over the chicken, cover with plastic wrap, and marinate for 15 minutes.

2 Combine the egg white and cornstarch. Add the mixture to the chicken and turn to coat thoroughly. Heat the vegetable oil in a nonstick skillet or wok and cook the chicken portions for about 15 minutes, or until the fillets are cooked through and golden brown on both sides.

3 Meanwhile, make the sauce. Combine all the ingredients in a small pan. Add $1/4$ teaspoon salt. Bring to a boil over low heat, stirring constantly until the sauce is smooth and has thickened slightly.

4 Cut the chicken into pieces and arrange on a warm serving plate. Pour the sauce over the chicken, garnish with the cilantro leaves, scallions, and lemon wedges and serve immediately.

Chili Chicken Couscous

Couscous makes a good base for chicken, garbanzos, and vegetables, spiced up with a kick of chile.

INGREDIENTS

Serves 4

3/4 cup couscous

4 cups boiling water

1 teaspoon olive oil

14 ounces chicken without
   skin and bone, diced

1 yellow bell pepper, seeded and sliced

2 large zucchini, thickly sliced

1 small green chile, thinly sliced,
   or 1 teaspoon chili sauce

1 large tomato, diced

15-ounce can garbanzo beans, drained

salt and ground black pepper

fresh cilantro or parsley sprigs
   to garnish

1 Place the couscous in a large bowl and pour in the boiling water. Cover and let stand for 30 minutes.

2 Heat the oil in a large, nonstick pan and stir-fry the chicken quickly to seal, then reduce the heat to low.

3 Stir in the bell pepper, zucchini, and chile or sauce and cook for about 10 minutes, or until the vegetables are softened.

4 Stir in the tomato and garbanzo beans, then add the couscous. Adjust the seasoning and stir over medium heat until hot. Serve garnished with sprigs of fresh cilantro or parsley.

Chicken with Beans and Eggplant

Sliced eggplant layered with beans and chicken, and then topped with yogurt, makes a hearty evening meal.

INGREDIENTS

Serves 4

1 medium eggplant, thinly sliced

1 tablespoon olive oil, for brushing

1 pound skinless, boneless chicken breast
   portions, diced

1 medium onion, chopped

14-ounce can chopped tomatoes

15-ounce can red kidney beans, drained
   and rinsed

1 tablespoon paprika

1 tablespoon chopped fresh thyme,
   or 1 teaspoon dried

1 teaspoon chili sauce

1 1/2 cups strained plain yogurt

1/2 teaspoon freshly
   grated nutmeg

salt and ground black pepper

1 Arrange the eggplant in a colander and sprinkle with salt. Leave the eggplant for 30 minutes, then rinse, and pat dry on paper towels.

2 Preheat the oven to 375°F. Brush a nonstick pan with oil and cook the eggplant, in batches, turning once, until golden. Brush with more oil as necessary.

3 Remove the eggplant, add the chicken and onion to the pan, and cook until lightly browned. Stir in the tomatoes, beans, paprika, thyme, chili sauce, and seasoning. In a bowl, combine the yogurt and grated nutmeg.

4 Layer the chicken and eggplant in an ovenproof dish, finishing with eggplant. Spread the yogurt evenly over the top and bake for 50–60 minutes, or until golden.

Chicken with Prosciutto and Cheese

In this Italian dish, chicken is filled with prosciutto and basil and topped with a slice of Fontina cheese before it is baked. The result is absolutely wonderful.

INGREDIENTS

Serves 4

2 thin slices of prosciutto

4 part-boned chicken breast
 portions, skinned

4 fresh basil sprigs

2 tablespoons olive oil

1 tablespoon butter

$1/2$ cup dry white wine

2 thin slices of Fontina cheese

salt and ground black pepper

young salad greens, to serve

1 Preheat the oven to 400°F. Lightly oil an ovenproof dish.

2 Cut the prosciutto slices in half crosswise. Open out a slit in the center of each chicken portion, and fill each cavity with half a ham slice and a basil sprig.

COOK'S TIP

Instead of Fontina cheese you could use a Swiss mountain cheese, such as Gruyère or Emmenthal. Ask for the cheese to be sliced thinly at the delicatessen counter.

3 Heat the oil and butter in a wide, heavy skillet until foaming. Cook the chicken portions over medium heat for 1–2 minutes on each side until they change color. Transfer to the prepared dish. Add the wine to the pan juices, stir until sizzling, then pour them over the chicken and season to taste.

4 Top each chicken portion with a half slice of Fontina. Bake for 20 minutes, or until the chicken is cooked through. Serve hot, with young salad greens.

Deviled Chicken

Chicken is marinated in lemon rind, garlic, and chiles before it is quickly cooked. It can be prepared in advance, and makes a useful and quick midweek meal.

INGREDIENTS

Serves 4

$1/2$ cup olive oil

finely grated rind and juice of
 1 large lemon

2 garlic cloves, finely chopped

2 teaspoons finely chopped or crumbled
 dried red chiles

12 skinless, boneless chicken thighs, each
 cut into 3 or 4 pieces

salt and ground black pepper

flat leaf parsley leaves, to garnish

lemon wedges, to serve

1 Make a marinade by combining the oil, lemon rind and juice, garlic, and chiles in a large, shallow glass or china dish. Add salt and pepper to taste. Whisk well, then add the chicken pieces, turning to coat with the marinade. Cover and marinate in the refrigerator for at least 4 hours, or overnight.

2 When ready to cook, prepare the barbecue or preheat the broiler and thread the chicken pieces onto eight oiled metal skewers. Cook for 6–8 minutes, turning frequently, until cooked through. Garnish with parsley leaves and serve hot, with lemon wedges for squeezing.

Chicken and Mushroom Layers

A delicious and moist combination of chicken, vegetables, and gravy in a simple, one-dish meal topped with crunchy slices of potato.

INGREDIENTS

Serves 4–6

1 tablespoon olive oil

4 large, skinless, boneless chicken breast
    portions, cut into chunks

1 leek, finely sliced into rings

$1/4$ cup butter

$1/4$ cup all-purpose flour

2 cups milk

1 teaspoon whole-
    grain mustard

1 carrot, very finely diced

3 cups white mushrooms

2 pounds potatoes, thinly sliced

salt and ground black pepper

1 Preheat the oven to 350°F. Heat the oil in a large pan.

2 Add the chunks of chicken and cook, stirring frequently, for about 5 minutes, or until browned all over. Add the leek and cook for 5 minutes more.

3 Add half the butter to the pan and let it melt. Sprinkle the flour over the mixture and stir in the milk. Cook over low heat until thickened, then stir in the mustard.

4 Add the diced carrot with the mushrooms. Season to taste.

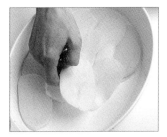

5 Line the base of a 7½-cup ovenproof dish with potato slices. Spoon one-third of the chicken mixture over them. Cover with another layer of potatoes. Repeat layering, finishing with a layer of potatoes. Dot with the remaining butter.

6 Bake for 1½ hours, covering with foil after 30 minutes' cooking time. Serve hot.

COOK'S TIP

The liquid from the mushrooms keeps the chicken moist and the potatoes help to mop up any excess juices.

Chicken with Potato Dumplings

Poached chicken in a creamy sauce topped with light herb and potato dumplings makes a delicately flavored yet hearty meal.

INGREDIENTS

Serves 6

1 onion, chopped

1 1/4 cups vegetable stock

1/2 cup white wine

4 large, skinless, boneless chicken
 breast portions

1 1/4 cups light cream

1 tablespoon chopped fresh tarragon

salt and ground black pepper

For the dumplings

1 1/2 cups chilled, grated shortening

1 cup self-rising flour

2 tablespoons chopped mixed
 fresh herbs

8 ounces potatoes, boiled
 and mashed

1/4 cup water

1 Place the onion, stock, and wine in a deep pan. Add the chicken, cover and simmer gently for 20 minutes.

2 Remove the chicken from the stock, cut into chunks, and reserve. Strain the stock and discard the onion. Reduce the stock by one-third over high heat. Stir in the cream and tarragon and simmer until just thickened. Stir in the chicken and season with salt and ground black pepper.

3 Spoon the mixture into a 3 3/4-cup ovenproof dish.

COOK'S TIP

Do not reduce the sauce too much before it is cooked in the oven as the dumplings absorb quite a lot of the liquid.

4 Preheat the oven to 375°F. For the dumplings, combine the shortening, flour and herbs, add salt and pepper, then stir in the potatoes and water to make a soft dough. Divide into six and shape into balls with lightly floured hands. Place the dumplings on top of the chicken mixture and bake uncovered for 30 minutes.

Chicken Koftas in Tomato Sauce

Meatballs in a tomato sauce make an ideal supper. Serve with pasta and grated cheese, if you like.

INGREDIENTS

Serves 4

1 chicken, about 1$^1/_2$ pounds

1 onion, grated

1 garlic clove, crushed

1 tablespoon chopped fresh parsley

$^1/_2$ teaspoon ground cumin

$^1/_2$ teaspoon ground coriander

1 egg, beaten

seasoned flour, for rolling

$^1/_4$ cup olive oil

salt and ground black pepper

chopped fresh parsley, to garnish

For the sauce

1 tablespoon butter

2 tablespoons all-purpose flour

1 cup chicken stock

14-ounce can chopped tomatoes, with
 the juice

1 teaspoon superfine sugar

$^1/_4$ teaspoon dried mixed herbs

1 Remove any skin and bone from the chicken and grind or chop finely.

2 Put into a bowl together with the onion, garlic, parsley, spices, seasoning, and beaten egg.

3 Mix together thoroughly and shape into 24 × 1$^1/_2$-inch balls. Roll lightly in seasoned flour.

4 Heat the oil in a skillet and brown the balls in small batches (this keeps the oil temperature hot and prevents the flour from becoming soggy). Remove and drain on paper towels. There is no need to cook the balls any further at this stage as they will cook in the tomato sauce. Preheat the oven to 350°F.

5 To make the tomato sauce, melt the butter in a large pan. Add the flour, and then blend in the stock and tomatoes along with their juice. Add the superfine sugar and mixed herbs. Bring to a boil, then cover, and simmer gently for 10–15 minutes.

6 Place the browned chicken balls into a shallow ovenproof dish and pour the tomato sauce over them. Cover with foil and bake for 30–40 minutes. Adjust the seasoning to taste and sprinkle with parsley.

Chicken and Tomato Hotchpotch

*Here is another chicken meatball
recipe, this time with a delicious
tomato and rice sauce.*

INGREDIENTS

Serves 4

1 ounce white bread, crust removed

2 tablespoons milk

1 garlic clove, crushed

$^1/_2$ teaspoon caraway seeds

2 cups ground chicken

1 egg white

1$^1/_2$ cups chicken stock

14-ounce can plum tomatoes

1 tablespoon tomato paste

$^1/_2$ cup easy-cook rice

salt and ground black pepper

1 tablespoon chopped fresh basil,
    to garnish

carrot and zucchini ribbons,
    to serve

4 Put the chicken stock, plum
tomatoes, and tomato paste
into a large, heavy pan and bring
to a boil.

5 Add the rice, stir, and cook
briskly for about 5 minutes.
Turn the heat down to a simmer.

6 Meanwhile, shape the chicken
mixture into 16 small balls.
Carefully drop them into the
tomato stock, and simmer for 8–10
minutes more, or until the chicken
balls and rice are cooked. Garnish
with the basil, and serve with
carrot and zucchini ribbons.

1 Cut the bread into small cubes
and put into a mixing bowl.
Sprinkle the milk over them and
let soak for 5 minutes.

2 Add the garlic clove, caraway
seeds, chicken, salt, and freshly
ground black pepper to the bread.
Mix together well.

3 Whisk the egg white until stiff,
then fold, half at a time, into
the chicken mixture. Chill for
10 minutes in the refrigerator.

Chicken and Chanterelle Roll

Delicate chanterelle mushrooms are combined with chicken, Dijon mustard, and thyme to make a flavorful filling for this traditional-style savory pastry roll. It's perfect for a cold evening.

INGREDIENTS

Serves 4

1 medium onion, chopped
1 celery stalk, sliced
2 teaspoons chopped fresh thyme
2 tablespoons vegetable oil
2 skinless, boneless chicken
    breast portions
4 ounces fresh chanterelle
    mushrooms, trimmed and sliced,
    or $1/4$ cup dried, soaked in warm
    water for 20 minutes
$1/3$ cup all-purpose flour
$1 1/4$ cups chicken stock, boiling
1 teaspoon Dijon mustard
2 teaspoons wine vinegar
salt and ground black pepper

For the dough
3 cups self-rising flour
$1/2$ teaspoon salt
10 tablespoons chilled sweet
    butter, diced
5 tablespoons cold water

1 Cook the onion, celery, and thyme gently in the oil without coloring. Cut the chicken into bitesize pieces, add to the pan with the mushrooms, and cook briefly. Stir in the flour, then remove from the heat.

2 Stir in the stock. Return to the heat, simmer, stirring, to thicken, then add the mustard, vinegar, and seasoning. Set aside to cool.

3 Sift the flour and salt into a bowl. Add the butter, then rub together until it resembles bread crumbs. Add the water and mix.

4 Roll out on a floured counter into a rectangle 10 x 12 inches. Dampen a piece of cheesecloth about twice as big as the dough. Place the dough on the cheesecloth. Spread the chicken filling over the dough and roll up from the short end using the cheesecloth to help. Enclose in cheesecloth and tie each end with string.

5 Lower the roll into a pan of boiling water, cover, and simmer for $1 1/2$ hours. Lift out, untie the string, and turn onto a serving platter. Slice and serve.

Turkey Scallops with Capers

Thin slices of turkey are marinated, then coated in bread crumbs, and cooked very quickly. Lemon and capers add a piquancy that goes perfectly with the scallops.

INGREDIENTS

Serves 2

4 thin turkey breast scallops (about
   3 ounces each)
1 large unwaxed lemon
$^1/_2$ teaspoon chopped fresh sage
4–5 tablespoons extra virgin olive oil
$^3/_4$ cup fine dry bread crumbs
1 tablespoon capers, rinsed and drained
salt and ground black pepper
sage leaves and lemon wedges, to garnish

1 Place the turkey scallops between two sheets of baking parchment or plastic wrap and either pound with the flat side of a meat mallet or roll with a rolling pin to flatten to a thickness of about $^1/_4$ inch.

2 With a vegetable peeler, remove four pieces of lemon rind. Cut them into thin julienne strips, cover with plastic wrap, and set aside. Grate the remainder of the lemon rind and squeeze the lemon. Put the grated rind in a large, shallow dish and add the sage, salt, and pepper. Stir in 1 tablespoon of the lemon juice, reserving the rest, and about 1 tablespoon of the olive oil, then add the turkey, turn to coat, and marinate for 30 minutes.

3 Place the bread crumbs in another shallow dish and dip the scallops into the crumbs, coating them on both sides. In a heavy skillet heat 2 tablespoons of the olive oil over high heat, add the scallops, and cook for 2–3 minutes, turning once, until golden and cooked through. Transfer the scallops to two warmed serving plates and keep warm.

4 Wipe out the skillet, add the remaining oil, the lemon julienne, and the capers, and heat through, stirring constantly. Spoon a little sauce over the turkey and garnish with sage leaves and lemon.

Turkey Croquettes

3 Meanwhile, to make the sauce, heat the oil in a skillet and cook the onion for 5 minutes, or until softened. Add the tomatoes and tomato paste, stir, and simmer for 10 minutes. Stir in the parsley, season with salt and pepper, and keep the sauce warm until needed.

4 Remove the potato mixture from the refrigerator and divide it into eight pieces. Shape each piece into a sausage shape, and dip in the remaining beaten egg, and then in the bread crumbs.

5 Heat the vegetable oil in a pan or deep-fryer to 330°F. Test by dropping a cube of day-old bread into the hot oil: it should sink, rise to the surface, and sizzle in 10 seconds. Deep-fry the croquettes for 5 minutes, or until golden and crisp. Serve with the sauce.

A crisp patty of smoked turkey, mixed with mashed potato and scallions, and rolled in bread crumbs, makes a tasty midweek supper served with a delightfully tangy tomato sauce.

INGREDIENTS

Serves 4

1 pound potatoes, diced

3 eggs

2 tablespoons milk

6 ounces smoked turkey strips,
   finely chopped

2 scallions, thinly sliced

2 cups fresh white bread crumbs

vegetable oil, for deep-frying

salt and ground black pepper

For the sauce

1 tablespoon olive oil

1 onion, finely chopped

14-ounce can tomatoes, drained

2 tablespoons tomato paste

1 tablespoon chopped fresh parsley

1 Boil the potatoes for about 20 minutes, or until tender. Drain and return to the pan over low heat to make sure all the excess water evaporates.

2 Mash the potatoes with 2 eggs and the milk. Season well with salt and pepper. Stir in the turkey and scallions. Chill for 1 hour.

Turkey or Chicken Schnitzel

A schnitzel is a pounded-flat, crisp-coated, fried steak of turkey, chicken, or veal. It makes an ideal quick supper as it cooks very rapidly.

INGREDIENTS

Serves 4

4 turkey or chicken breast fillets (about
    6 ounces each), skinned

juice of 1 lemon

2 garlic cloves, chopped

all-purpose flour, for dusting

1–2 eggs

1 tablespoon water

1/4 cup matzo meal

a mixture of vegetable and olive oil, for
    shallow frying

salt, ground black pepper, and paprika

lemon wedges and a selection of
    vegetables, to serve

1 Place each piece of meat between two sheets of baking parchment and pound with the end of a rolling pin until it is about half its original thickness.

2 In a bowl, combine the lemon juice, garlic, salt, and pepper. Coat the meat in it, then leave to marinate.

3 Meanwhile, arrange three wide plates or shallow dishes in a row. Fill one plate or dish with flour, beat the egg and water together in another, and combine the matzo meal, salt, pepper, and paprika on the third.

4 Working quickly, dip each fillet into the flour, then the egg, then the matzo meal. Pat everything in well, then arrange the crumbed fillets on a plate, and chill for at least 30 minutes, and up to 2 hours.

5 In a large, heavy skillet, heat the oil to 375°F or until a cube of day-old bread dropped into the oil turns golden brown in 30–60 seconds. Carefully add the crumbed fillets (in batches if necessary) and cook until golden brown and cooked through, turning once. Remove and drain on paper towels. Serve immediately with lemon wedges and vegetables.

PASTRIES
& PIES

Versatile chicken makes a delicious filling for pastries or pies.
In this chapter is a collection of inspiring recipes from around the world
using a wide selection of flavorings in as many varied ways as possible.
For example, dainty phyllo pastry tartlets contain the delicate combination
of smoked chicken and peach mayonnaise, and chicken combined with
cheese and leeks is enclosed in an attractively braided jalousie.
You are sure to find the perfect pastry dish for every occasion.

Turkey and Cranberry Bundles

After the traditional Christmas or Thanksgiving meal, it is easy to end up with lots of turkey leftovers. These delicious phyllo-pastry packets are a marvelous way of using up the small pieces of cooked turkey.

INGREDIENTS

Serves 6

1 pound cooked turkey, cut into chunks

1 cup diced Brie

2 tablespoons cranberry sauce

2 tablespoons chopped fresh parsley

9 sheets phyllo pastry, 18 x 11 inches each, thawed if frozen

1/4 cup butter, melted

salt and ground black pepper

salad greens, to serve

1 Preheat the oven to 400°F. Combine the turkey, diced Brie, cranberry sauce, and chopped parsley in a large bowl. Season with salt and pepper.

2 Cut the phyllo sheets in half widthwise to make 18 squares.

3 Layer three pieces of pastry together, brushing each with a little melted butter so that they stick together. Keep the unused pastry covered with a clean, damp dishtowel to prevent drying. Repeat with the remaining phyllo squares to give six pieces.

4 Divide the turkey mixture among the pastry, making neat piles on each piece. Gather up the pastry to enclose the filling in neat bundles. Place on a cookie sheet, brush with melted butter, and bake for 20 minutes, until the pastry is crisp and golden. Serve hot or warm with salad greens.

VARIATION

To make Chicken and Stilton Bundles, use cooked chicken in place of the turkey and white Stilton instead of Brie. Replace the cranberry sauce with mango chutney.

Tunisian Chicken Packets

You can make these little packets into any shape you like, but the most important thing is to encase the egg white before it starts to run out.

INGREDIENTS

Serves 6

3 tablespoons butter, melted

1 small red onion, finely chopped

5 ounces chicken or turkey breast
 fillet, ground

1 large garlic clove, crushed

juice of $^1/_2$ lemon

2 tablespoons chopped fresh parsley

12 sheets of phyllo pastry, each about
 6 x 10 inches, thawed if frozen

6 small eggs, such as bantam, rock hen, or
 guinea fowl

oil, for deep-frying

salt and ground black pepper

1 Melt half the butter in a pan and cook the onion for about 3 minutes, or until softened. Add the meat, garlic, lemon juice, parsley, and seasoning, and cook, stirring, for 2–3 minutes, or until the meat is just cooked. Set aside to cool.

2 Place one sheet of pastry lengthwise on the counter and brush with melted butter; top with a second sheet. Keep the unused pastry covered with a clean, damp dishtowel. Brush the edges with butter and place one-sixth of the mixture close to the bottom corner of the pastry. Flatten the filling, making a hollow in it.

3 Crack an egg into the hollow and be ready to fold up the pastry immediately so that the egg white does not run out. Lift the right-hand corner and fold it over the filling and seal quickly, then fold the bottom left corner straight up, and then fold the bottom left corner up to the right edge, forming a triangle.

4 Use the remaining phyllo pastry sheets and filling to make another five packets, then heat the oil in a skillet until a cube of day-old bread turns golden in about 1½ minutes. Cook the pastries, two or three at a time, until golden. Lift them out of the pan with a slotted spoon and drain on paper towels. Serve hot or cold.

Smoked Chicken with Peach Mayonnaise

2 Place a round of pastry in each pan and brush with a little butter. Add another round of pastry, brush each again with butter, then add a third round of pastry.

3 Bake the tartlets for 5 minutes, or until the pastry is golden brown. Leave in the pans for a few moments before transferring to a wire rack to cool.

4 Place the peaches in a bowl and pour in boiling water to cover. Leave to stand for 30–60 seconds (the riper the peaches, the quicker their skins loosen). Use a slotted spoon to remove each peach from the water. Slit the skin with the point of a knife, then slip it off the fruit. Remove the pits and chop the flesh.

5 Mix the chicken, mayonnaise, lime rind and juice, peaches, and seasoning. Chill this chicken mixture for at least 30 minutes, or up to 12 hours. When ready to serve, spoon the chicken mixture into the phyllo tartlets and garnish with tarragon sprigs, lime slices, and salad greens.

These are attractive and, because smoked chicken is sold ready cooked, they require the minimum of culinary effort. The filling can be prepared a day in advance and chilled, but do not fill the pastry cases until you are ready to serve them or they will become soggy.

INGREDIENTS

Makes 12

2 tablespoons butter, melted

3 sheets phyllo pastry, each 18 x 11 inches, thawed if frozen

2 ripe peaches

2 skinless, boneless smoked chicken breast portions, thinly sliced

$^2/_3$ cup mayonnaise

grated rind of 1 lime

2 tablespoons lime juice

salt and ground black pepper

fresh tarragon sprigs, lime slices, and salad greens, to garnish

1 Preheat the oven to 400°F. Brush 12 small individual muffin pans with a little of the melted butter. Using a cookie cutter, cut each sheet of phyllo pastry into 12 equal rounds large enough to line the pans, with the edges standing up above the tops of the pans. Keep the unused pastry covered with a clean, damp dishtowel to prevent it from drying out.

> ### COOK'S TIP
> If you are peeling a large number of peaches, blanch them in batches to avoid soaking some for too long. If left to cool for more than a few minutes, the skin is more difficult to peel off.

Old-fashioned Chicken Pie

The chicken can be roasted and the sauce prepared a day in advance. Leave to cool completely before covering with pastry and baking. Make into four individual pies if you prefer but bake for 10 minutes less.

INGREDIENTS

Serves 4

1 chicken, about $3^1/_2$ pounds

1 onion, quartered

1 fresh tarragon or rosemary sprig

2 tablespoons butter

$1^1/_2$ cups white mushrooms

2 tablespoons all-purpose flour

$1^1/_4$ cups chicken stock

4 ounces cooked ham, diced

2 tablespoons chopped fresh parsley

1 pound ready-made puff or flaky pastry, thawed if frozen

1 beaten egg, to glaze

salt and ground black pepper

1 Preheat the oven to 400°F. Put the chicken into a casserole together with the quartered onion and the tarragon or rosemary. Add $1^1/_4$ cups water and season. Cover and roast for about $1^1/_4$ hours, or until the chicken is cooked through.

2 Remove the chicken and strain the liquid into a measuring cup. Cool and remove any fat that settles on the surface. Make up to $1^1/_4$ cups with water and reserve for the sauce.

3 Remove the chicken from the bones and cut into large cubes. Melt the butter in a pan, add the mushrooms, and cook for about 2–3 minutes. Sprinkle in the flour and gradually blend in the stock.

4 Bring to a boil, season to taste, and add the ham, chicken, and parsley. Turn into a large pie pan and let cool.

5 Roll out the pastry on a lightly floured counter to 2 inches larger than the pie pan. Cut a narrow strip of pastry to place around the edge of the pan. Dampen with a little water and stick to the rim of the pan. Brush the strip with beaten egg.

6 Lay the pastry loosely over the pie, taking care not to stretch it. Press firmly onto the rim. Using a sharp knife, trim away the excess pastry and knock up around the sides to encourage the pastry to rise. Crimp the edge neatly and cut a hole in the center of the pie. This lets steam escape during cooking. Decorate with pastry leaves, and chill until ready to bake.

7 Brush the pastry with beaten egg (taking care not to glaze over the sides of the pastry). Bake for 35–45 minutes, or until well risen and nicely browned all over.

Chicken en Croute

Chicken layered with herbs and stuffing and wrapped in light puff pastry makes an impressive dish.

INGREDIENTS

Serves 8

1-pound packet puff pastry, thawed if frozen

4 large, skinless, boneless chicken
    breast portions

1 beaten egg, to glaze

For the stuffing

1 cup thinly sliced leeks

$^1/_3$ cup chopped fatty bacon

2 tablespoons butter

2 cups fresh white bread crumbs

2 tablespoons chopped fresh herbs, such as
    parsley, thyme, marjoram, and chives

grated rind of 1 large orange

orange juice or chicken stock, if necessary

1 egg, beaten

salt and ground black pepper

1 To make the stuffing, cook the sliced leeks and bacon in the butter until soft. Put the bread crumbs into a bowl with the mixed herbs and plenty of seasoning. Add the leeks, bacon, and butter with the grated orange rind, and bind together with the beaten egg. If the mixture is too dry and crumbly, you can stir in a little orange juice or chicken stock to bring it to a moist consistency.

2 Roll out the pastry to a large rectangle about 12 × 16 inches. Trim the edges and reserve for decorating the top.

3 Place the chicken portions between two pieces of plastic wrap and flatten to a thickness of about $^1/_4$ inch with a rolling pin. Spread a third of the leek stuffing over the center of the pastry. Lay two chicken portions side by side on top of the stuffing. Cover them with another third of the stuffing, then repeat with the remaining chicken portions and the remainder of the stuffing.

4 Make a cut diagonally from each corner of the pastry to the chicken. Brush the pastry with beaten egg.

5 Bring up the sides and overlap them slightly. Trim away any excess pastry before folding the ends over like a packet. Turn over onto a greased cookie sheet, so that the joins are underneath. Shape neatly and trim any excess pastry.

6 With a sharp knife, lightly criss-cross the pastry into a diamond pattern. Brush with beaten egg and cut leaves from the trimmings to decorate the top. Bake at 400°F for 50–60 minutes, or until well risen and golden brown on top.

Chicken Packets with Herb Butter

Buttery chicken is coated in herbs and wrapped in crisp phyllo pastry.

INGREDIENTS

Serves 4

4 skinless, boneless chicken
    breast portions
10 tablespoons butter, softened
6 tablespoons chopped mixed fresh herbs,
    such as thyme, parsley, oregano,
    and rosemary
1 teaspoon lemon juice
5 large sheets phyllo pastry, thawed if
    frozen
1 egg, beaten
2 tablespoons freshly grated
    Parmesan cheese
salt and ground black pepper

1 Season the chicken portions and cook in 2 tablespoons of the butter to seal and brown lightly. Let cool.

2 Preheat the oven to 375°F. Lightly grease a cookie sheet. Put the remaining butter, the herbs, lemon juice, and seasoning in a food processor and process until smooth. Melt half the herb butter.

3 Take one sheet of phyllo pastry and brush it lightly with melted herb butter. Cover the rest of the pastry with a clean, damp dishtowel. Fold the pastry sheet in half and brush again with butter. Place a chicken portion about 1 inch from the top end.

4 Dot the chicken with a quarter of the remaining herb butter. Fold in the sides of the pastry, then roll up to enclose it completely. Place seam side down on the prepared cookie sheet. Repeat with the other chicken portions.

5 Brush the phyllo packets with beaten egg to glaze. Cut the remaining sheet of phyllo pastry into strips, then crumple, and arrange on top. Brush the packets once again with the egg glaze, then sprinkle with grated Parmesan cheese. Bake for about 35–40 minutes, until golden brown. Serve hot.

Chicken and Apricot Phyllo Pie

The filling for this pie has a Middle Eastern flavor—chicken combined with apricots, bulgur wheat, nuts, herbs, and spices.

INGREDIENTS

Serves 6

$^1/_2$ cup bulgur wheat

6 tablespoons butter

1 onion, chopped

4 cups ground chicken

$^1/_4$ cup dried apricots,
    finely chopped

$^1/_4$ cup blanched almonds, chopped

1 teaspoon ground cinnamon

$^1/_2$ teaspoon ground allspice

$^1/_4$ cup strained plain yogurt

1 tablespoon chopped fresh chives

2 tablespoons chopped
    fresh parsley

6 large sheets phyllo pastry, thawed
    if frozen

salt and ground black pepper

chives, to garnish

1 Preheat the oven to 400°F. Put the bulgur wheat in a bowl with $^1/_2$ cup boiling water. Soak for 5–10 minutes, or until the water is absorbed.

2 Heat 2 tablespoons of the butter in a pan until melted, add the onion and chicken, and cook over low heat, stirring occasionally, until pale golden.

3 Stir in the apricots, almonds, and bulgur wheat and cook for 2 minutes more.

4 Remove the pan from the heat and stir in the cinnamon, allspice, yogurt, chives, and parsley. Season with salt and pepper.

5 Melt the remaining butter. Unroll the phyllo pastry and cut into 10-inch rounds. Keep the pastry rounds covered with a clean, damp dishtowel to prevent drying.

6 Line a 9-inch loose-based quiche pan with three of the pastry rounds, brushing each one with butter as you layer them. Spoon in the chicken mixture and cover with three more pastry rounds, brushed with melted butter as before.

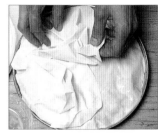

7 Crumple the remaining rounds and place them on top of the pie, then brush over any remaining melted butter. Bake the pie for about 30 minutes, or until the pastry is golden brown and crisp. Serve the pie hot or cold, cut in wedges and garnished with chives.

Chicken and Stilton Pies

These individual chicken and Stilton pies are wrapped in a crisp shortcrust pastry and shaped into turnovers. They are great for lunch, served hot or cold.

INGREDIENTS

Makes 4

3 cups self-rising flour

$^1/_2$ teaspoon salt

6 tablespoons white cooking fat

6 tablespoons butter

4–5 tablespoons cold water

beaten egg, to glaze

For the filling

1 pound chicken thighs, boned
 and skinned

$^1/_4$ cup chopped walnuts

1 ounce scallions, sliced

2 ounces Stilton, crumbled

$^1/_4$ cup finely chopped celery

$^1/_2$ teaspoon dried thyme

salt and ground black pepper

1 Preheat the oven to 400°F. Combine the flour and salt in a bowl. Rub in the white cooking fat and butter with your fingers until the mixture resembles fine bread crumbs. Using a knife to cut and stir, mix in the cold water to form a stiff, pliable dough.

2 Turn out onto a counter and knead lightly until smooth. Divide into four and roll out each piece to a thickness of $^1/_4$ inch. Cut into an 8-inch round.

3 Remove any fat from the chicken thighs and cut into small cubes. Mix with the chopped walnuts, scallions, Stilton, celery, thyme, and seasoning and divide the filling equally among the four pastry rounds.

4 Brush the edge of the pastry with beaten egg and fold over, pinching and crimping the edges together well. Place on a greased cookie sheet and bake in the oven for about 45 minutes, or until golden brown.

Chicken, Cheese, and Leek Jalousie

A jalousie is a family-size lattice pastry roll with a mild, creamy filling. Ready-made puff pastry and cooked chicken make this a good choice for informal entertaining.

INGREDIENTS

Serves 6

1 chicken, about 3¹/₂ pounds, roasted

2 large leeks, thinly sliced

2 garlic cloves, crushed

3 tablespoons butter

1²/₃ cups white mushrooms, sliced

scant 1 cup low-fat cream cheese

grated rind of 1 small lemon

3 tablespoons chopped
    fresh parsley

2 x 9-ounce blocks puff pastry,
    thawed if frozen

1 egg, beaten

salt and ground black pepper

fresh herbs, to garnish

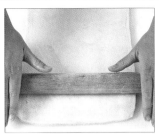

3 Stack the blocks of pastry on top of each other and roll out on a lightly floured counter to a large rectangle, measuring about 14 x 10 inches. Drape the pastry over a rolling pin and lift it onto a nonstick cookie sheet.

5 Brush the edges of the pastry with the beaten egg. Draw the pastry strips over each other in alternate crosses to "braid" the pastry. Seal the top and bottom edges.

1 Strip the meat from the chicken, discarding the skin and bones. Chop or shred the meat and set it aside.

2 Cook the leeks and garlic in the butter for 10 minutes. Stir in the mushrooms and cook for 5 minutes. Leave until cold, then stir in the cream cheese, lemon rind, parsley, chicken, and salt and pepper.

4 Spoon the filling onto the pastry, leaving a generous margin at the top and bottom, and 4 inches on each side. Cut the pastry diagonally upward at ³/₄-inch intervals at the sides of the filling.

6 Glaze the jalousie with beaten egg, then leave it to rest while you preheat the oven to 400°F. Bake for 15 minutes, then lower the oven temperature to 375°F, and bake for 15 minutes more, or until the pastry is golden brown in color and crisp.

7 Let the jalousie stand for about 10 minutes before sliding it onto a board or platter to serve. Garnish with fresh herbs.

> ### VARIATION
> Try a creamy blue cheese, such as Dolcelatte, for this jalousie.

Greek Chicken Pie

3 Preheat the oven to 375°F. Have a damp dishtowel ready to keep the phyllo pastry covered at all times. You will need to work fast, as the pastry dries out very quickly when exposed to air. Unravel the pastry and cut the whole batch into a 12-inch square.

4 Taking half the phyllo sheets (cover the remainder with the dishtowel), lightly brush one sheet with a little olive oil, and lay it on a well-greased 5²/₃-cup ovenproof dish.

5 Sprinkle with a few almonds. Repeat with the other phyllo sheets, overlapping them into the dish. Spoon in the filling and cover the pie in the same way with the rest of the overlapping pastry.

6 Fold in the edges and mark a diamond pattern on the surface with a sharp knife. Brush with milk and sprinkle on any remaining almonds. Bake for 20–30 minutes, or until golden.

This is based on a traditional recipe. Serve with a Greek salad of onions, feta cheese, tomatoes, and cucumber.

INGREDIENTS

Serves 4

10 ounces phyllo pastry, thawed if frozen
2 tablespoons olive oil
¹/₂ cup chopped toasted almonds
2 tablespoons milk

For the filling
1 tablespoon olive oil
1 medium onion, finely chopped
1 garlic clove, crushed
1 pound cooked chicken, boned
2 ounces feta cheese, crumbled
2 eggs, beaten
1 tablespoon chopped fresh parsley
1 tablespoon chopped fresh cilantro
1 tablespoon chopped fresh mint
salt and ground black pepper

1 To make the filling, heat the oil in a large skillet and cook the chopped onion over low heat until tender. Add the crushed garlic and cook for 2 minutes more. Transfer to a bowl.

2 Remove the skin from the chicken and discard, and grind or chop the flesh finely with a knife. Add to the onion with all the rest of the filling ingredients. Mix thoroughly and season with salt and black pepper.

Chicken and Ham Pie

This substantial double-crust pie is suitable for a cold buffet, picnics, or any packed meals.

INGREDIENTS

Serves 8

14 ounces ready-made unsweetened
    shortcrust pastry, thawed if frozen
1³/4 pounds skinless, boneless chicken
    breast portions
12 ounces uncooked smoked or
    cured ham
¹/4 cup heavy cream
6 scallions, finely chopped
1 tablespoon chopped fresh tarragon
2 teaspoons chopped fresh thyme
grated rind and juice of ¹/2 large lemon
1 teaspoon freshly ground mace
beaten egg or milk, to glaze
salt and ground black pepper

1 Preheat the oven to 375°F. Roll out one-third of the pastry and use it to line an 8-inch pie pan 1¹/2 inches deep. Place the pan on a cookie sheet.

2 Grind 4 ounces of the chicken with the ham, then mix with the cream, scallions, herbs, lemon rind, 1 tablespoon of the lemon juice, and seasoning to make a soft mixture; add a little more cream if necessary.

3 Cut the remaining chicken into ¹/2-inch pieces and mix with the remaining lemon juice, the mace, and seasoning.

4 Make a layer of one-third of the ham mixture in the pie shell, cover evenly with half the chopped chicken, then add another layer of one-third of the ham mixture. Add all the remaining chicken, followed by the remaining ham mixture.

5 Dampen the edges of the pie shell. Roll out the remaining two-thirds of the pastry to make a lid for the pie.

6 Use the trimmings to make a lattice decoration. Make a small hole in the center of the pie, brush the top with beaten egg or milk, then bake for about 20 minutes. Reduce the oven temperature to 325°F and bake for 1–1¹/4 hours more; cover the top with foil if the pastry becomes too brown. Transfer the pie to a wire rack and let cool.

Chicken, Leek, and Parsley Pie

The flavors of chicken and leek complement each other wonderfully.

INGREDIENTS

Serves 4–6

3 part-boned chicken breast portions

flavoring ingredients, such as bouquet
    garni, black peppercorns, onion,
    and carrot

$^1/_4$ cup butter

2 leeks, thinly sliced

$^1/_2$ cup grated Cheddar or
    Jack cheese

$^1/_3$ cup freshly grated
    Parmesan cheese

3 tablespoons chopped
    fresh parsley

2 tablespoons whole-grain mustard

1 teaspoon cornstarch

$1^1/_4$ cups heavy cream

beaten egg, to glaze

salt and ground black pepper

mixed salad greens, to serve

For the pastry

$2^1/_2$ cups all-purpose flour

pinch of salt

scant 1 cup butter, diced

2 egg yolks

1 To make the pastry, first sift the flour and salt. Blend together the butter and egg yolks in a food processor or bowl until creamy. Add the flour and process or mix until the mixture is just coming together. Add about 1 tablespoon cold water and process or mix for a few seconds more. Turn out onto a lightly floured counter and knead lightly. Wrap in plastic wrap and chill for about 1 hour.

2 Meanwhile, poach the chicken portions in water to cover, with the flavoring ingredients added. Simmer until tender and cooked through. Let cool in the liquid.

3 Preheat the oven to 400°F. Divide the pastry into two pieces, one slightly larger than the other. Roll out the larger piece on a lightly floured counter and use to line a 7 × 11-inch ovenproof dish. Prick the base all over with a fork and bake for 15 minutes. Leave to cool.

4 Lift the cooled chicken from the poaching liquid and discard the skins and bones. Cut the chicken flesh into strips, then set aside.

5 Melt the butter in a skillet and cook the sliced leeks over low heat, stirring occasionally, until soft.

6 Stir in the Cheddar or Jack, Parmesan, and chopped parsley. Spread half the leek mixture evenly over the cooked pie shell, leaving a border all the way around.

7 Cover the leek mixture with the chicken strips, then top with the remaining leek mixture. Combine the whole-grain mustard, cornstarch, and heavy cream in a small bowl. Add seasoning to taste. Pour the mixture over the chicken and leek filling.

8 Moisten the edges of the cooked pie shell. Roll out the remaining pastry into a rectangle and use to cover the pie. Brush the lid of the pie with beaten egg, and bake in the preheated oven for 30–40 minutes, or until the pie is golden and crisp. Serve hot, cut into generous square portions, with mixed salad greens on the side.

Chicken, Leek, and Mixed Herb Pie

A crisp pastry, made with fresh herbs, tops a tarragon-flavored chicken and leek sauce to make this tempting savory pie a highly popular choice.

INGREDIENTS

Serves 4

1¹/₂ cups all-purpose flour

pinch of salt

7 tablespoons butter

1 tablespoon chopped fresh
   mixed herbs

3 leeks, sliced

3 tablespoons cornstarch

1²/₃ cups low-fat milk

1–2 tablespoons chopped
   fresh tarragon

12 ounces skinless, boneless chicken breast
   portions, cooked and diced

7-ounce can corn kernels, drained

salt and ground black pepper

fresh herbs and salt flakes, to garnish

1 To make the pastry, place the flour and salt in a bowl and lightly rub in 6 tablespoons of the butter until the mixture resembles bread crumbs. Stir in the mixed herbs and add a little cold water to make a smooth, firm dough. Wrap the pastry in a plastic bag and chill for 30 minutes.

2 Preheat the oven to 375°F. Steam the leeks for about 10 minutes, or until they are just tender. Drain thoroughly and keep warm.

> ### VARIATION
> ∽
> Use half milk and half chicken or vegetable stock, if you like.

3 Meanwhile, blend the cornstarch with 5 tablespoons of the milk. Heat the remaining milk in a pan until it is just beginning to boil, then pour it onto the cornstarch, stirring constantly. Return the mixture to the pan and bring to a boil, stirring constantly. Simmer for 2 minutes, stirring, until thickened.

4 Add the remaining butter to the pan with the tarragon, leeks, chicken, and corn. Season to taste and mix together well.

5 Spoon the chicken into a 5-cup pie pan and place on a cookie sheet. Roll out the pastry slightly larger than the pie pan. Lay it over the pan and press to seal. Trim, decorate the top with the trimmings, if you like, and make a slit in the center.

6 Bake for 35–40 minutes, or until the pastry is golden brown. Serve immediately, sprinkled with herbs and salt.

Chicken and Game Pie

Game and chicken make a rich filling for a pie, which is delicious flavored with ginger and sherry. It makes a hearty and substantial dish for fall meals.

Serves 4

1 pound boneless chicken and game meat
   (plus the carcasses and bones)

1 small onion, halved

2 bay leaves

2 carrots, halved

a few black peppercorns

1 tablespoon oil

3 ounces fatty bacon pieces, rinded
   and chopped

1 tablespoon all-purpose flour

3 tablespoons sweet sherry or Madeira

2 teaspoons ground ginger

grated rind and juice of $1/2$ orange

12 ounces ready-made puff pastry,
   thawed if frozen

beaten egg or milk, to glaze

salt and ground black pepper

1 Place the carcasses and bones in a pan, with any giblets and half the onion, the bay leaves, carrots, and black peppercorns. Cover with water and bring to a boil. Simmer until reduced to about $1^1/4$ cups, then strain the stock, ready to use.

2 Cut the chicken and game meat into even-size pieces. Chop, then cook the remaining onion in the oil until softened. Then add the bacon and meat, and cook quickly to seal. Sprinkle in the flour and stir until beginning to brown. Gradually add the stock, stirring as it thickens, then add the sherry or Madeira, ginger, orange rind and juice, and seasoning. Simmer for 20 minutes.

3 Transfer to a $3^3/4$-cup pie pan and leave to cool slightly. Use a pie funnel to help hold up the pastry.

4 Preheat the oven to 425°F. Roll out the pastry to 1 inch larger than the dish. Cut off a $1/2$-inch strip all around. Dampen the rim of the pan and press on the strip of pastry. Dampen again and then lift the pastry carefully over the pie, sealing the edges well at the rim. Trim off the excess pastry, and use to decorate the top. Brush the pie with egg or milk.

5 Bake for 15 minutes, then reduce the oven temperature to 375°F, for 25–30 minutes more.

Chicken and Mushroom Pie

Dried and fresh mushrooms give this pie a rich flavor.

INGREDIENTS

Serves 6

$^1/_4$ cup dried porcini mushrooms
$^1/_4$ cup butter
2 tablespoons all-purpose flour
1 cup chicken stock, warmed
$^1/_4$ cup whipping cream
   or milk
1 onion, coarsely chopped
2 carrots, sliced
2 celery stalks, coarsely chopped
1 cup mushrooms, quartered
1 pound cooked chicken
   meat, cubed
$^1/_2$ cup shelled fresh or
   frozen peas
beaten egg, to glaze
salt and ground black pepper

For the crust
2 cups all-purpose flour
$^1/_4$ teaspoon salt
$^1/_2$ cup cold butter, cut in pieces
$^1/_4$ cup white cooking fat
6–8 tablespoons ice water

1 To make the crust, sift the flour and salt into a bowl. Cut in the butter and white cooking fat until the mixture resembles fine bread crumbs. Sprinkle with 6 tablespoons ice water and mix until the dough holds together. Add a little more water, if necessary, 1 tablespoon at a time.

2 Gather the dough into a ball and then flatten it into a disk. Wrap in baking parchment and chill in the refrigerator for at least 30 minutes.

3 Place the porcini mushrooms in a small bowl. Add just enough hot water to cover and soak for about 30 minutes, until softened and reconstituted. Lift out of the water with a slotted spoon to leave any grit behind, and drain. Discard the soaking water.

4 Preheat the oven to 375°F. Melt 2 tablespoons of the butter in a heavy pan. Whisk in the flour and cook until bubbling, whisking constantly. Add the warm stock and cook over medium heat, whisking, until the mixture boils. Cook for 2–3 minutes more. Whisk in the cream or milk. Season with salt and pepper. Put to one side.

5 Heat the remaining butter in a large, nonstick skillet until foamy. Add the onion and carrots and cook until softened, about 5 minutes. Add the celery and fresh mushrooms and cook for about 5 minutes more. Stir in the cubed chicken, peas, and drained porcini mushrooms, mixing well.

6 Add the chicken mixture to the sauce and stir. Taste for seasoning. Transfer to a 10-cup ovenproof dish.

7 Roll out the dough to about $^1/_8$-inch thickness. Cut out a piece about 1 inch larger all around than the dish. Carefully lay the dough over the filling. Make a decorative crimped edge with your fingers and thumbs.

8 Cut several vents in the top crust to let steam escape. Brush with the egg to glaze.

9 Press together the dough trimmings, then roll out again. Cut into strips and lay them over the top crust. Glaze again. If you like, roll small balls of dough and set them in the "windows" in the lattice.

10 Bake until the top crust is browned, about 30 minutes. Serve the pie hot.

Chicken Charter Pie

Rich heavy cream is used in the filling for this chicken pie, which originated in Cornwall, England.

INGREDIENTS

Serves 4

¹/4 cup butter

4 chicken legs

1 onion, finely chopped

²/3 cup milk

²/3 cup sour cream

4 scallions, quartered

³/4 cup fresh parsley, finely chopped

8 ounces ready-made puff pastry,
    thawed if frozen

2 eggs, beaten, plus extra to glaze

¹/2 cup heavy cream

salt and ground black pepper

1 Melt the butter in a heavy, shallow pan, then brown the chicken legs. Transfer them onto a plate.

2 Add the chopped onion to the pan and cook until softened. Stir the milk, sour cream, scallions, parsley, and seasoning into the pan, bring to a boil, then simmer for a couple of minutes.

3 Return the chicken to the pan with any juices, then cover tightly and cook very gently for about 30 minutes. Transfer the chicken and sauce mixture to a 5-cup pie pan and leave to cool.

4 Roll out the pastry until about 2³/4 inches larger all around than the top of the pie pan. Leave the pastry to relax while the chicken is cooling.

5 Preheat the oven to 425°F. Cut off a narrow strip around the edge of the pastry, then place this strip on the edge of the pie pan. Moisten the strip, then cover the dish with the pastry. Press the edges together to seal.

6 Make a hole in the center of the pastry and insert a small funnel of foil. Brush the pastry with egg, then bake for 15–20 minutes, until golden brown.

7 Reduce the oven temperature to 350°F. Combine the cream and eggs, then pour into the pie through the funnel. Shake the pie to distribute the cream, then return it to the oven for 5–10 minutes. Remove from the oven and leave in a warm place for 5–10 minutes before serving.

English Farmhouse Flan

The lattice pastry topping makes this flan look extra special.

INGREDIENTS

Serves 4

2 cups whole-wheat flour

$^1/_4$ cup butter, cubed

$^1/_4$ cup white cooking fat

1 teaspoon caraway seeds

1 tablespoon oil

1 onion, chopped

1 garlic clove, crushed

8 ounces cooked chicken, chopped

3 ounces watercress or arugula
    leaves, chopped

grated rind of $^1/_2$ small lemon

2 eggs, lightly beaten

$^3/_4$ cup heavy cream

3 tablespoons plain yogurt

a good pinch of freshly grated nutmeg

3 tablespoons grated Caerphilly or
    Cheddar cheese

beaten egg, to glaze

salt and ground black pepper

1 Place the flour in a bowl with a pinch of salt. Add the butter and white cooking fat and rub into the flour with your fingertips until the mixture resembles bread crumbs. (Alternatively, you can use a blender or food processor for this.)

2 Stir in the caraway seeds and 3 tablespoons ice water and mix to a firm dough. Knead lightly on a floured counter until smooth.

3 Roll out the pastry and use to line a 7 × 11-inch loose-based quiche pan. Reserve the trimmings. Prick the base all over with a fork and chill for 20 minutes. Place a cookie sheet in the oven and preheat to 400°F.

4 Heat the oil in a skillet and cook the onions and garlic for 5–8 minutes, or until just softened. Remove from the heat and leave to cool.

5 Line the pastry shell with baking parchment and fill with baking beans. Bake for 10 minutes, then remove the parchment and beans and cook for 5 minutes.

6 Combine the onions, garlic, chicken, watercress or arugula, and lemon rind. Spoon into the pie shell. Beat the eggs, cream, yogurt, nutmeg, cheese, and seasoning and pour over the filling.

7 Roll out the pastry trimmings and cut out $^1/_2$-inch strips. Brush with egg, then lay in a lattice over the flan. Press the ends onto the pastry edge. Bake for 35 minutes.

St George's Chicken Pot Pie

The St George's mushroom, so named because it emerges near to St George's Day, April 23, combines well with chicken in this traditional English pot pie, but other wild mushrooms will also taste excellent.

INGREDIENTS

Serves 4

4 tablespoons vegetable oil
1 medium onion, chopped
1 celery stalk, sliced
1 small carrot, peeled and cut into
   julienne strips
3 skinless, boneless chicken
   breast portions
1 pound St George's mushrooms
6 tablespoons all-purpose flour
$2^{1}/_{4}$ cups chicken
   stock, boiling
2 teaspoons Dijon mustard
2 tablespoons medium sherry
2 teaspoons wine vinegar
salt and ground black pepper

For the topping
$2^{1}/_{2}$ cups self-rising flour
pinch of celery salt
pinch of cayenne pepper
$^{1}/_{2}$ cup firm sweet butter, diced
$^{1}/_{2}$ cup grated Cheddar or
   Jack cheese
$^{2}/_{3}$ cup cold water
beaten egg, to glaze (optional)

VARIATIONS
∾

• A mixture of bay boletus, saffron milk-caps, parasol mushroom, yellow russula, oyster or closed portabello mushrooms would work well in this recipe.
• This recipe can easily be made as an ordinary pie by replacing the pot pie topping with a layer of flaky or puff pastry.

1 Preheat the oven to 400°F. Heat the oil in a large, heavy pan, add the onion, celery and carrot and cook over low heat, stirring occasionally, without coloring, to soften. Cut the chicken portions into bitesize pieces, add to the vegetables, and cook briefly. Add the mushrooms, cook until the juices run, then stir in the flour.

2 Remove the pan from the heat and stir in the stock gradually so that the flour is completely blended in. Return the pan to the heat, and simmer gently to thicken, stirring constantly. Add the mustard, sherry, vinegar, and seasoning. Cover and keep warm.

3 To make the topping, sift the flour, celery salt, and cayenne pepper into a bowl or a food processor fitted with a metal blade. Add the butter and half of the cheese, then either rub the mixture together with your fingers or process until it resembles bread crumbs. Add the water and combine without overmixing.

4 Turn out onto a floured board, form into a round, and flatten to about a $^{1}/_{2}$-inch thickness. Cut out as many 2-inch shapes as you can, using a cookie cutter.

5 Transfer the chicken mixture to a 5-cup pie pan, then overlap the topping rounds around the edge. Brush with beaten egg, if using, sprinkle over the remaining cheese and bake in the oven for 25–30 minutes, or until the topping is well risen and golden.

Turkey and Cranberry Pie

Fresh cranberries add a tart layer to this meaty pie, but cranberry sauce can be used if fresh are not available. The pie freezes well.

Serves 8

1 pound bulk pork sausage

4 cups lean ground pork

1 tablespoon ground coriander

1 tablespoon dried mixed herbs

finely grated rind of
   2 large oranges

2 teaspoons grated fresh ginger root or
   $^{1}/_{2}$ teaspoon ground ginger

2 teaspoons salt

1 pound turkey breast
   fillets, skinned

1 cup fresh cranberries

ground black pepper

beaten egg, to glaze

$1^{1}/_{4}$ cups aspic jelly, made according
   to the instructions on
   the packet

For the pastry

4 cups all-purpose flour

1 teaspoon salt

10 tablespoons white cooking fat

$^{2}/_{3}$ cup milk and water mixed

1 Preheat the oven to 350°F. Place a cookie sheet in the oven to preheat. In a bowl, combine the bulk pork sausage, ground pork, coriander, herbs, orange rind, ginger, and salt. Season with black pepper to taste.

2 To make the pastry, sift the flour into a large bowl with the salt. Heat the white cooking fat in a small pan with the milk and water until just beginning to boil. Remove the pan from the heat and let the mixture cool slightly.

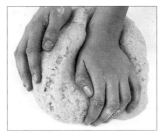

3 Quickly stir the liquid into the flour until a very stiff dough is formed. Place on a clean counter and knead until smooth. Cut off one-third of the dough for the lid, wrap in plastic wrap and keep in a warm place.

4 Roll out the large piece of dough on a floured counter and use to line the base and sides of a greased 8-inch loose-based, springform cake pan. Work with the dough while it is still warm, as it will break if it becomes too cold.

5 Thinly slice the turkey breast fillets. Put them between two pieces of plastic wrap and flatten with a rolling pin to a thickness of $^{1}/_{8}$ inch. Spoon half the pork mixture into the pan, pressing it well into the edges. Cover it with half the turkey slices and then the cranberries, followed by the remaining turkey, and finally the rest of the pork mixture.

6 Roll out the remaining dough and use to cover the filling. Trim off any excess and seal the edges with a little beaten egg. Make a steam hole in the center of the lid and decorate the top by cutting pastry trimmings into leaf shapes. Brush with some beaten egg and bake for 2 hours. Cover the pie with foil if the top gets too brown.

7 Place the pie on a wire rack to cool. When cold, use a funnel to fill the pie with liquid aspic jelly. Leave the jelly to set for a few hours or overnight, before unmolding the pie to serve it.

Spiced Chicken and Egg Phyllo Pie

This recipe is based on one of the most elaborate and intriguing dishes in Moroccan cuisine—bisteeya— where, traditionally, pastry is interleaved with layers of meat and spices. In this version layers of spicy meat, herbed egg, and almonds are enclosed in phyllo pastry.

INGREDIENTS

Serves 4

2 tablespoons sunflower oil, plus extra
    for brushing

2 tablespoons butter

3 chicken quarters, preferably with
    breasts attached

1 1/2 Bermuda onions, very finely chopped

generous pinch of ground ginger

generous pinch of saffron threads

2 teaspoons ground cinnamon, plus extra
    for dusting

1/3 cup sliced almonds

1 large bunch of fresh cilantro,
    finely chopped

1 large bunch of fresh parsley, chopped

3 eggs, beaten

6 ounces phyllo pastry,
    thawed if frozen

1–2 teaspoons confectioners' sugar, plus
    extra for dusting (optional)

salt and ground black pepper

1 Heat the oil and butter in a large pan, add the chicken pieces, and cook, stirring frequently, until browned. Add the onions, ginger, saffron, 1/2 teaspoon of the cinnamon and 1 1/4 cups water. Season well. Bring to a boil and then lower the heat, cover, and simmer very gently for 45–55 minutes.

2 When the chicken is cooked but still tender, transfer it to a plate. Dry-fry the almonds until golden, and set aside.

3 As soon as the cooked chicken is cool enough to handle, remove the skin and bones and cut the flesh into neat, bitesize pieces.

4 Stir the cilantro and parsley into the pan and simmer the sauce until well reduced and thickened. Add the beaten eggs and cook over very gentle heat, stirring constantly, until the eggs are just lightly scrambled.

5 Preheat the oven to 350°F. Oil a shallow 10-inch round ovenproof dish. Place 1–2 sheets of phyllo pastry in an even layer over the base and sides of the dish, so that it is completely covered and the edges of the pastry sheets hang over the sides. Lightly brush the pastry with a little oil and make two more layers of phyllo, brushing with oil between the layers. Keep the unused pastry covered with a clean, damp dishtowel to prevent drying.

6 Place the chicken in the pastry shell, then spoon the egg and herb mixture on top. Level the surface with the back of a spoon.

7 Place a layer of phyllo on top of the filling (you may need to use more than one sheet of pastry) and sprinkle with the dry-fried almonds. Lightly sprinkle with the remaining cinnamon and the confectioners' sugar, if using.

8 Fold the edges of the phyllo over the almonds and then make four more layers of phyllo (using one or two sheets per layer, depending on size), brushing each layer with a little oil. Tuck the phyllo edges down the side of the pie and brush the top layer with oil.

9 Bake the pie for 40–45 minutes, or until it is golden brown. Dust the top of the pie with confectioners' sugar and cinnamon, creating a geometric design by using a paper template if you like. Serve the pie immediately.

Rich Game Raised Pie

Terrific for stylish picnics or just as smart for a more formal special occasion, this pie looks spectacular when baked in a fluted raised pie mold.

INGREDIENTS

Serves 10

2 tablespoons butter
1 onion, finely chopped
2 garlic cloves, finely chopped
2 pounds mixed boneless game meat,
    such as skinless pheasant
    and/or squab breast, venison,
    and rabbit, diced
2 tablespoons chopped mixed
    fresh herbs
1 egg, beaten
salt and ground black pepper

For the pâté
$1/4$ cup butter
2 garlic cloves, finely chopped
1 pound chicken livers, trimmed
    and chopped
4 tablespoons brandy
1 teaspoon ground mace

For the pastry
6 cups strong white bread flour
1 teaspoon salt
$1/2$ cup milk
6 tablespoons water
$1/2$ cup white cooking fat, diced
$1/2$ cup butter, diced

For the jelly
$1^1/4$ cups game or
    beef consommé
$1/2$ teaspoon powdered gelatin

1 Melt the butter in a small pan, then add the onion and garlic, and cook gently until softened but not colored. Transfer the onion and garlic to a bowl and add the diced game meat and the chopped mixed herbs. Mix well. Season, cover, and chill.

2 To make the pâté, melt the butter in a pan, add the garlic and chicken livers, and cook over medium heat, stirring frequently, until just browned. Remove the pan from the heat and stir in the brandy and ground mace. Process the mixture in a blender or food processor until smooth, then set aside, and let cool.

3 To make the pastry, sift the flour and salt into a bowl and make a well in the center. Put the milk, water, white cooking fat, and butter into a pan and heat gently until melted, then bring to a boil. Pour the hot liquid into the well in the flour and beat until smooth. Cover and let cool slightly.

4 Preheat the oven to 400°F. When the pastry is cool enough to handle, roll out two-thirds of it and use to line a 9-inch raised pie mold. Spoon in half the game mixture and press it down evenly. Add the pâté and then top with the remaining game.

5 Roll out the remaining pastry to form a lid. Brush the edge of the pastry case with a little water and cover with the pastry lid. Trim off the excess pastry from around the edge. Pinch the edges together to seal in the filling. Make two holes in the center of the lid and brush the lid with beaten egg. Use the pastry trimmings to make small leaves to decorate the pie. Brush the leaves with a little beaten egg.

6 Bake the pie for 20 minutes, then cover with foil and cook for 10 minutes more. Reduce the oven temperature to 300°F. Lightly glaze the pie again with beaten egg and cook for $1^1/2$ hours more, keeping the top covered loosely with foil.

7 Remove the pie from the oven and leave it to stand for 15 minutes to cool slightly. Meanwhile, increase the oven temperature to 400°F. Stand the mold on a cookie sheet and remove the sides. Quickly glaze the sides of the pie with beaten egg and cover the top with foil. Cook the pie for a final 15 minutes to brown the sides. Leave the pie to cool completely, then chill overnight.

8 Next day, make the jelly. Heat the game or beef consommé in a small pan until just beginning to bubble, whisk in the gelatin until dissolved, and let cool until just setting. Using a small funnel, carefully pour the jellied consommé into the holes in the pie. Chill until set. This pie will keep in the refrigerator for up to 3 days.

Chicken Bouche

A spectacular centerpiece, this light pastry shell contains a delicious chicken and mushroom filling with a hint of fruit. Ideal served with freshly cooked vegetables.

INGREDIENTS

Serves 4

1 pound ready-made puff pastry, thawed
    if frozen
beaten egg, to glaze

For the filling
1 tablespoon oil
4 cups ground chicken
$1/4$ cup all-purpose flour
$2/3$ cup milk
$2/3$ cup chicken stock
4 scallions, chopped
$1/4$ cup red currants
scant 1 cup white mushrooms, sliced
1 tablespoon chopped
    fresh tarragon
salt and ground black pepper

1 Preheat the oven to 400°F. Roll half the pastry out on a lightly floured counter to a 10-inch oval. Roll out the remainder to an oval of the same size and cut out a smaller 8-inch oval in the center.

2 Brush the edge of the first pastry shape with the beaten egg and place the smaller oval and the edge strip on top. Place on a dampened cookie sheet and bake for 30 minutes.

3 For the filling, heat the oil in a large pan. Cook the ground chicken for 5 minutes. Add the flour and cook for 1 minute more. Stir in the milk and stock and bring to a boil.

4 Add the scallions, red currants and mushrooms. Cook for 20 minutes.

5 Stir in the fresh tarragon and season to taste.

6 Place the pastry bouche on a serving plate, remove the oval center, and spoon in the filling. Place the oval lid on top. Serve with freshly cooked vegetables.

VARIATION

Use unsweetened shortcrust pastry for this dish and cook as a traditional chicken pie.

Curried Chicken and Apricot Pie

This pie is unusually sweet–sour and very moreish. Use boneless turkey instead of chicken, if you like. Serve with steamed vegetables.

Serves 6

2 tablespoons sunflower oil

1 large onion, chopped

1 pound chicken, boned and
  coarsely chopped

1 tablespoon curry paste or powder

2 tablespoons apricot or
  peach chutney

1/2 cup dried apricots, halved

4 ounces cooked carrots, sliced

1 teaspoon mixed dried herbs

4 tablespoons crème fraîche

12 ounces ready-made unsweetened
  shortcrust pastry, thawed if frozen

beaten egg or milk, to glaze

salt and ground black pepper

3 Roll out the pastry to 1 inch wider than the pie dish. Cut a strip of pastry from the edge. Dampen the rim of the pan, press on the strip, then brush with water, and place the sheet of pastry on top. Press to seal.

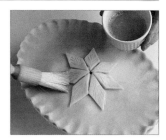

4 Preheat the oven to 375°F. Trim off any excess pastry and use to make an attractive pattern on the top if you like. Brush all over with beaten egg or milk to glaze and bake for 40 minutes, or until crisp and golden.

1 Heat the oil in a large pan and cook the onion and chicken until just coloring. Add the curry paste or powder and cook for 2 minutes more.

2 Add the chutney, apricots, carrots, herbs, and crème fraîche to the pan with seasoning. Mix well and then transfer to a deep 3³/4–5-cup pie dish.

ROASTS
& SPECIAL
OCCASIONS

When we are celebrating or entertaining or simply getting together with family and friends there are times when a roast is the first and only choice of dish we wish to serve. There's something very welcoming and celebratory about the delicious smell of roasting chicken as it wafts from the kitchen. In this chapter you will find many variations on the theme, using stuffings, sauces, and accompaniments that are truly mouthwatering. The chapter also includes exciting recipes for special meals using chicken in different ways, so you are sure to find the right dish for any occasion.

Traditional Roast Chicken

Serve this favorite Sunday roast with bacon rolls, chipolata sausages, gravy, and stuffing balls.

INGREDIENTS

Serves 4

1 chicken, about 4 pounds
4 fatty bacon strips
2 tablespoons butter
salt and ground black pepper

For the stuffing

2 tablespoons butter, melted
$1/4$ cup pitted prunes, chopped
$1/2$ cup chopped walnuts
1 cup fresh bread crumbs
1 egg, beaten
1 tablespoon chopped fresh parsley
1 tablespoon chopped fresh chives
2 tablespoons sherry or port

For the gravy

2 tablespoons all-purpose flour
$1^1/4$ cups chicken stock

1 Preheat the oven to 375°F. Combine all the stuffing ingredients in a bowl and season well with salt and pepper.

2 Stuff the neck end of the chicken quite loosely, allowing room for the bread crumbs to swell during cooking. (Any remaining stuffing can be shaped into balls and fried to accompany the roast.)

3 Tuck the neck skin under the bird to secure the stuffing and hold in place with the wing tips.

4 Place in a roasting pan and cover the breast with the bacon strips. Spread the bird with the remaining butter, cover loosely with foil, and roast for about $1^1/2$ hours, or until the juices run clear when the thickest part of the leg is pierced. Baste with the juices in the roasting pan three or four times during cooking.

5 Remove any trussing string, transfer to a serving plate, cover with foil, and let stand while making the gravy. (This standing time lets the flesh relax and makes carving easier.)

6 Spoon off the fat from the juices in the pan. Blend in the flour and cook gently until golden brown. Add the stock and bring to a boil, stirring until thickened. Adjust the seasoning and strain into a sauceboat to serve.

Roast Chicken with Celery Root

*Celery root has a more intense flavor
than celery and makes a rich and
unusual stuffing for chicken.*

INGREDIENTS

Serves 4

1 chicken, about 3^{1}/$_{2}$ pounds
1 tablespoon butter

For the stuffing
1 pound celery root, chopped
2 tablespoons butter
3 slices bacon, chopped
1 onion, finely chopped
leaves from 1 thyme
   sprig, chopped
leaves from 1 small tarragon
   sprig, chopped
2 tablespoons chopped fresh parsley
1^{1}/$_{2}$ cups fresh brown bread crumbs
dash of Worcestershire sauce
1 egg, beaten
salt and ground black pepper

1 To make the stuffing, cook the
celery root in boiling water
until tender. Drain well and then
chop finely.

2 Heat the butter in a pan, then
gently cook the bacon and
onion until the onion is soft. Stir
the celery root and herbs into the
pan and cook, stirring occasionally,
for 2–3 minutes. Meanwhile,
preheat the oven to 400°F.

3 Remove the pan from the
heat and stir in the fresh
bread crumbs, Worcestershire
sauce, seasoning, and sufficient
egg to bind the mixture.

4 Place the stuffing in the neck
end of the chicken. Season
the skin, then rub with the
remaining butter. Tuck the neck
end under the bird to secure the
stuffing. Roast the chicken, basting
occasionally with the juices, for
1^{1}/$_{4}$–1^{1}/$_{2}$ hours, or until the juices
run clear when the thickest part of
the leg is pierced. Let rest for
10 minutes before carving.

Chicken with Wild Mushrooms and Garlic

3 Pour the stock, wine, and lemon juice into the roasting pan. Sprinkle in the parsley and season well. Place the chicken in the oven and cook for 1¹/₂–1³/₄ hours, or until cooked through, basting occasionally to prevent drying out.

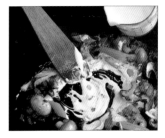

4 Remove the chicken from the roasting pan and keep warm. Put the pan on the stovetop and stir in the sour cream over low heat, adding a little extra stock or water if necessary to make the juices into a thick pouring sauce.

Wild mushrooms surround chicken while it roasts and are then mixed with cream to make a rich accompanying sauce.

INGREDIENTS

Serves 4

3 tablespoons olive or vegetable oil

1 chicken, about 3 pounds

1 large onion, finely chopped

3 celery stalks, chopped

2 garlic cloves, crushed

4 cups fresh wild mushrooms, sliced if large

1 teaspoon chopped fresh thyme

1 cup chicken stock

1 cup dry white wine

juice of 1 lemon

2 tablespoons chopped fresh parsley

¹/₂ cup sour cream

salt and ground black pepper

flat leaf parsley sprigs, to garnish

green beans, to serve

1 Preheat the oven to 375°F. Heat the oil in a roasting pan on the stovetop and brown the chicken all over.

2 Add the onion and cook for about 2 minutes. Add the celery, garlic, mushrooms, and thyme and cook for 3 minutes.

5 Arrange the chicken on a plate, surrounded by the mushrooms. Garnish with the parsley sprigs and serve the chicken with the sauce and fresh green beans.

COOK'S TIP

Always clean wild mushrooms well to remove any grit.

Chicken with Forty Cloves of Garlic

This dish does not have to be exact, so do not worry if you have 35 or even 50 cloves of garlic—the important thing is that there should be lots. The smell that emanates from the oven as the chicken and garlic cook is indescribably delicious.

INGREDIENTS

Serves 4–5

5–6 whole heads of garlic
1 tablespoon butter
3 tablespoons olive oil
1 chicken, about 4–4^1/$_2$ pounds
1^1/$_4$ cups all-purpose flour, plus
    1 teaspoon
5 tablespoons white port, Pineau de
    Charentes, or other white, fortified wine
2–3 fresh tarragon or rosemary sprigs
2 tablespoons crème fraîche (optional)
few drops of lemon juice (optional)
salt and ground black pepper

1 Separate 3 of the heads of garlic into cloves and peel them. Remove the first layer of papery skin from the remaining heads of garlic and cut off the tops to expose the cloves. Preheat the oven to 350°F.

2 Gently heat the butter and 1 tablespoon of the olive oil in a flameproof casserole. Add the chicken and cook over medium heat, turning frequently, for 10–15 minutes, or until it is browned all over.

3 Sprinkle in 1 teaspoon flour and cook for 1 minute. Add the port or wine. Tuck in the whole heads of garlic and the cloves with the herb sprigs. Pour over the remaining oil and season to taste.

4 Mix the main batch of flour with water to make a dough. Roll it into a sausage and press it around the rim of the casserole. Press on the lid, folding the dough up and over it to create a tight seal. Cook in the oven for 1^1/$_2$ hours.

5 To serve, lift off the lid to break the seal and transfer the chicken and whole garlic to a serving platter and keep warm.

6 Discard the herb sprigs, then place the casserole on the stovetop and whisk to combine the garlic cloves with the juices. Add the crème fraîche, if using, and lemon juice to taste. Process the sauce in a food processor or blender. Serve the garlic paste with the chicken.

Roast Chicken with Gravy and Bread Sauce

This is a traditional dish that makes a perfect family meal. Roast potatoes and seasonal green vegetables, such as Brussels sprouts stir-fried with chestnuts, are delicious accompaniments.

INGREDIENTS

Serves 4

$1/4$ cup butter
1 onion, chopped
$1^1/2$ cups fresh white
    bread crumbs
grated rind of 1 lemon
2 tablespoons chopped
    fresh parsley
2 tablespoons chopped
    fresh tarragon
1 egg yolk
1 chicken, about $3^1/4$ pounds
6 ounces fatty bacon strips
salt and ground black pepper

For the sauce

1 onion, studded with 6 cloves
1 bay leaf
$1^1/4$ cups milk
$2/3$ cup light cream
2 cups fresh white bread crumbs
$1^1/2$ teaspoons butter

For the gravy

2 teaspoons all-purpose flour
$1^1/4$ cups well-flavored chicken stock
dash of Madeira or sherry

1 Preheat the oven to 400°F. Melt half the butter in a pan, add the onion and cook over low heat for about 5 minutes, or until softened but not colored.

2 Remove the pan from the heat and add the bread crumbs, lemon rind, parsley, and half the chopped tarragon. Season with salt and pepper, then mix in the egg yolk to bind the ingredients into a moist stuffing.

3 Fill the neck end of the chicken with stuffing, then truss the chicken neatly, and weigh it. To calculate the cooking time, allow 20 minutes per pound, plus 20 minutes.

4 Put the chicken in a roasting pan and season it well. Beat together the remaining butter and tarragon, then smear over the bird.

5 Arrange the bacon strips over the top of the chicken (this helps stop the light breast meat from drying out) and roast for the calculated time. Baste the bird every 30 minutes during cooking and cover with buttered foil if the bacon begins to overbrown.

6 To make the bread sauce, put the clove-studded onion, bay leaf, and milk in a small pan and bring gradually to a boil. Remove from the heat and leave the milk to stand for at least 30 minutes so that it absorbs the flavors.

7 Strain the milk into a clean pan, discard the onion and bay leaf, and add the cream and bread crumbs. Bring to a boil, stirring constantly, then reduce the heat, and simmer for 5 minutes. Keep it warm while you make the gravy and carve the chicken, then stir in the butter and season to taste.

8 Transfer the chicken to a warmed serving dish, cover tightly with foil, and leave to stand for 10 minutes.

9 To make the gravy, pour off all but 1 tablespoon fat from the roasting pan. Place the pan over medium heat and stir in the flour. Cook the flour, stirring, for about 1 minute, or until golden brown, then gradually stir in the stock and Madeira or sherry. Bring to a boil, stirring constantly, then simmer, stirring, for about 3 minutes, or until thickened. Season to taste and strain into a warm sauceboat.

10 Carve the chicken and serve it with the stuffing, gravy, and hot bread sauce.

VARIATION

Cocktail sausages that have been wrapped in thin bacon strips make a delicious accompaniment to roast chicken. Roast them alongside the chicken for the final 25–30 minutes' cooking time.

Roast Chicken with Grapes and Ginger

This dish, with its blend of spices and sweet fruit, is inspired by Moroccan cuisine. Serve with couscous, mixed with a handful of cooked garbanzos.

INGREDIENTS

Serves 4

1 chicken, about 2¹/₄–3¹/₂ pounds
4–4¹/₂ ounces fresh ginger root, grated
6–8 garlic cloves, coarsely chopped
juice of 1 lemon
2 tablespoons olive oil
2–3 large pinches of ground cinnamon
1¹/₄ pounds seeded red and
   green grapes
1¹/₄ pounds seedless green grapes
5–7 shallots, chopped
about 1 cup chicken stock
salt and ground black pepper

1 Rub the chicken with half of the ginger, the garlic, half of the lemon juice, the olive oil, cinnamon, salt, and lots of pepper. Leave to marinate.

2 Meanwhile, cut the red and green seeded grapes in half, remove the seeds, and set aside. Add the whole green seedless grapes to the halved ones.

3 Preheat the oven to 350°F. Heat a heavy skillet or flameproof casserole until hot.

4 Remove the chicken from the marinade, add to the pan, and cook until browned on all sides. (There should be enough oil on the chicken to brown it but, if not, add a little extra.)

5 Put some of the shallots into the chicken cavity with the garlic and ginger from the marinade and as many of the red and green grapes as will fit inside. Roast for 40–60 minutes, or until cooked through.

6 Remove the chicken from the pan and keep warm. Pour off any oil from the pan, reserving any sediment. Add the remaining shallots to the pan and cook for about 5 minutes, or until softened.

7 Add half the remaining red and green grapes, the remaining ginger, the stock, and any juices from the roast chicken and cook over medium-high heat until the grapes have reduced to a thick sauce. Season with salt, ground black pepper, and the remaining lemon juice to taste.

8 Serve the chicken on a warmed serving dish, surrounded by the sauce and the reserved grapes.

VARIATIONS

• This dish works with duck in place of the chicken. Marinate and roast as above, adding 1–2 tablespoons honey to the pan sauce as it cooks.

• Use chicken breast portions, with the skin, instead of a whole chicken. Pan-fry the chicken portions, rather than roasting them.

COOK'S TIP

Seeded Italia or muscat grapes have a delicious, sweet fragrance and are perfect for using in this recipe.

Roast Turkey Flavored with Mushrooms

Explore some of the unusual wild mushrooms available to boost the flavor and succulence of roast turkey for a special occasion.

INGREDIENTS

Serves 6–8

1 turkey, about 10 pounds
butter, for basting and to finish gravy
watercress or arugula, to garnish

For the stuffing
$^1/_4$ cup sweet butter
1 medium onion, chopped
8 ounces wild mushrooms, such as chanterelle, ceps, bay boletus, chicken of the woods, saffron milk-caps, Caesar's mushrooms, and hedgehog fungus, trimmed and chopped
$1^1/_2$ cups fresh white bread crumbs
4 ounces pork sausages, skinned
1 small fresh truffle, sliced (optional)
5 drops truffle oil (optional)
salt and ground black pepper

For the gravy
5 tablespoons medium sherry
$1^2/_3$ cups chicken stock
$^1/_4$ cup dried ceps, soaked and drained
4 teaspoons cornstarch
1 teaspoon Dijon mustard
$^1/_2$ teaspoon wine vinegar
salt and ground black pepper

COOK'S TIP
~
Other sizes of turkey can be cooked this way—allow $1^1/_2$ pounds of turkey per person, weigh it after stuffing, and roast for 20 minutes per pound, plus 20 minutes.

1 Preheat the oven to 425°F. To make the stuffing, melt the butter in a pan, add the onion, and cook over a low heat without coloring. Add the mushrooms and stir until their juices begin to flow. Transfer to a bowl, add the bread crumbs, skinned sausages, and the truffle and truffle oil, if using, to the pan, season with salt and pepper, and stir well to combine.

2 Spoon the stuffing into the neck cavity of the turkey and enclose, fastening the skin on the underside with a skewer.

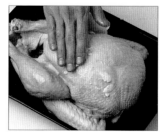

3 Rub the skin of the turkey with butter, place in a large roasting pan uncovered, and roast in the oven for 50 minutes. Lower the temperature to 350°F and cook for $2^1/_2$ hours more, or until cooked through and tender.

4 To make the gravy, transfer the turkey to a carving board, cover loosely with foil, and keep warm. Spoon off the fat from the roasting pan and discard. Heat the remaining liquid until reduced to a sediment. Add the sherry and stir briskly with a flat wooden spoon to loosen the sediment. Stir in the chicken stock and ceps.

5 Blend the cornstarch and mustard in a cup with 2 teaspoons water and the wine vinegar. Stir into the juices in the roasting pan and simmer, stirring, to thicken. Season, then stir in a pat of butter.

6 Garnish the turkey with watercress or arugula. Transfer the gravy into a warmed gravy boat and serve separately.

Chicken Stuffed with Forest Mushrooms

Add the wild aroma of woodland mushrooms to a good-quality chicken to make a fantastic feast of flavor and succulence. Serve with roast potatoes and braised carrots, if you like.

INGREDIENTS

Serves 4

2 tablespoons sweet butter, plus extra for
    basting and to finish sauce

1 shallot, chopped

8 ounces wild mushrooms, such as
    chanterelles, ceps, bay boletus, oyster,
    chicken of the woods, saffron milk-
    caps, and hedgehog fungus, trimmed
    and chopped

3/4 cup fresh white bread crumbs

2 egg yolks

1 chicken, about 4 pounds

1/2 celery stalk, chopped

1/2 small carrot, chopped

3 ounces potato, peeled
    and chopped

scant 1 cup chicken stock,
    plus extra if required

2 teaspoons wine vinegar

salt and ground black pepper

parsley sprigs, to garnish

1 Preheat the oven to 425°F. Melt the butter in a pan and gently cook the shallot without letting it color. Add about half of the chopped mushrooms and cook for 2–3 minutes, or until the moisture appears. Remove from the heat, stir in the bread crumbs, seasoning, and egg yolks, to bind.

COOK'S TIP

If fresh mushrooms are not available, replace with 1/4 cup of the dried equivalent and soak in warm water for 20 minutes before using.

2 Spoon the stuffing into the neck of the chicken, enclose, and fasten the skin on the underside with a skewer.

3 Rub the chicken with some extra butter and season well. Put the celery, carrot, potato, and remaining mushrooms in a roasting pan. Place the chicken on top of the vegetables, add the stock, and roast in the oven for 1 1/4 hours, until cooked through.

4 Transfer the chicken to a serving platter, then process the vegetables and mushrooms in a blender or food processor. Pour the mixture back into the pan and heat gently, adjusting the consistency with chicken stock if necessary. Taste and adjust the seasoning, then add the vinegar and a pat of butter and stir briskly. Pour the sauce into a serving pitcher and garnish the chicken with sprigs of fresh parsley.

Roast Chicken with Lemon and Herbs

A well-flavored chicken is essential for this simple recipe – use a corn-fed bird, if possible.

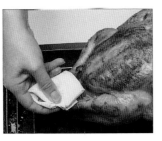

INGREDIENTS

Serves 4

1 chicken, about 3 pounds

1 lemon, halved

small bunch of thyme sprigs

1 bay leaf

1 tablespoon butter, softened

4–6 tablespoons chicken stock
or water

salt and ground black pepper

1 Preheat the oven to 400°F. Season the chicken inside and out with salt and pepper.

2 Squeeze the juice of one lemon half and then place the juice, the squeezed lemon half, the thyme, and the bay leaf in the chicken cavity. Tie the legs with string and rub the breast with butter.

3 Place the chicken on a rack in a roasting pan. Squeeze over the juice of the other lemon half. Roast the chicken for 1 hour, basting two or three times, until the juices run clear when the thickest part of the thigh is pierced.

4 Pour the juices from the cavity into the roasting pan and transfer the chicken to a carving board. Cover loosely with foil and let stand for about 10–15 minutes before carving.

5 Skim off the fat from the cooking juices. Add the stock or water and boil over medium heat, stirring and scraping the base of the pan, until slightly reduced. Strain and serve with the chicken.

Chicken in a Salt Crust

Cooking food in a casing of salt gives a deliciously moist, tender result that, surprisingly, is not too salty. The technique is used in Italy and France for chicken and whole fish.

INGREDIENTS

Serves 6

1 chicken, about 4 pounds

about 5 pounds coarse sea salt

For the garlic paste

1 pound onions, quartered

2 large heads of garlic

$^1/_2$ cup olive oil

salt and ground black pepper

For the tomatoes and bell peppers

1 pound plum tomatoes

3 red bell peppers, seeded and quartered

1 red chile, seeded and finely chopped

6 tablespoons olive oil

flat leaf parsley, to garnish

1 Preheat the oven to 425°F. Choose a deep ovenproof dish into which the whole chicken will fit snugly. Line the dish with a double thickness of heavy foil, allowing plenty of excess foil to overhang the top edge of the dish.

2 Truss the chicken tightly so that any salt cannot fall into the cavity. Sprinkle a thin layer of salt in the foil-lined dish, then place the chicken on top.

3 Pour the remaining salt all around and over the chicken until it is completely encased. Sprinkle the top with a little water.

4 Cover tightly with the foil and bake on the lower oven shelf for 1³/4 hours. Meanwhile, put the onions in a small pan. Break up the heads of garlic, but leave the skins on. Add to the pan with the olive oil and seasoning.

COOK'S TIP

Take the salt-crusted chicken to the table garnished with plenty of fresh mixed herbs. Once you've scraped away the salt, transfer the chicken to a clean plate to carve it.

---

5 Cover and cook over the lowest possible heat for about 1 hour or until the garlic is completely soft.

6 Plunge the tomatoes into boiling water for 30 seconds, then refresh in cold water. Peel off the skins and quarter. Put the red bell peppers, tomatoes, and chile in a shallow ovenproof dish and sprinkle with the oil. Bake on the shelf above the chicken for 45 minutes, or until the bell peppers are slightly charred.

7 Squeeze the garlic out of the skins. Process the onions, garlic, and pan juices in a blender or food processor until smooth. Return the paste to the clean pan.

8 To serve the chicken, open out the foil and ease it out of the dish. Place on a large serving platter. Transfer the bell pepper mixture to a serving dish and garnish with parsley. Reheat the garlic paste. Crack open the salt crust on the chicken, check that it is cooked, and brush away the salt before carving and serving with the garlic paste and bell pepper mixture.

Chicken Véronique

These broiling chickens are delicious with steamed green beans. Garnish with extra fresh tarragon, if you like.

INGREDIENTS

Serves 4

2 fresh tarragon or thyme sprigs

2 broiling chickens

2 tablespoons butter

4 tablespoons white wine

grated rind and juice of $1/2$ lemon

1 tablespoon olive oil

1 tablespoon all-purpose flour

$2/3$ cup chicken stock

4 ounces small seedless green grapes

salt and ground black pepper

chopped fresh parsley, to garnish

1 Preheat the oven to 350°F. Put the herbs inside the cavity of each broiling chicken and tie into a neat shape.

2 Heat the butter in a flameproof casserole, brown the chickens lightly all over and add the wine. Season, cover, and cook in the oven for 20–30 minutes, or until cooked through.

3 Remove the chickens from the casserole and cut in half with a pair of kitchen scissors, removing the backbones and small ribcage bones. Arrange in a shallow flameproof dish that will slide under the broiler. Sprinkle with lemon juice and brush with oil. Broil until lightly browned. Remove and keep warm.

4 Mix the flour into the butter and wine in the casserole, and blend in the stock. Bring to a boil, season to taste, and add the lemon rind and grapes, then simmer, stirring constantly, for 2–3 minutes. Spoon the sauce over the chickens, sprinkle with chopped parsley and serve immediately.

Butterflied Cornish Hens

Tender Cornish hens are delicious when butterflied—opened out and flattened—and broiled simply with butter and herbs. Serve with boiled new potatoes and salad.

INGREDIENTS

Serves 4

4 Cornish hens

¹/₄ cup butter, melted

1 tablespoon lemon juice

1 tablespoon chopped mixed fresh herbs, such as rosemary and parsley, plus extra to garnish

salt and ground black pepper

lemon slices, to garnish

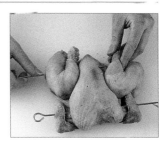

1 Remove any trussing strings and, using kitchen scissors, cut down on each side of the backbone and remove it. Lay the Cornish hens flat and flatten with the help of a rolling pin or mallet.

2 Thread the legs and wings on to skewers to keep the Cornish hens flat while they are cooking.

3 Brush both sides with melted butter and season with salt and pepper to taste. Sprinkle with lemon juice and herbs.

4 Preheat the broiler to medium heat and cook skin side first for 6 minutes, or until golden brown. Turn over, brush with butter and broil for 6–8 minutes more, or until cooked. Garnish with more chopped herbs and lemon slices.

Pot-roast Chicken with Sausage Stuffing

Roasting in a casserole makes these chickens moist, tender, and succulent.

INGREDIENTS

Serves 6

2 chickens, about 2^1/$_2$ pounds each

2 tablespoons vegetable oil

1^1/$_2$ cups chicken stock or half wine and
    half stock

1 bay leaf

salt and ground black pepper

For the stuffing

1 pound bulk pork sausage

1 small onion, chopped

1–2 garlic cloves, finely chopped

1 teaspoon hot paprika

^{1}/$_2$ teaspoon dried chile (optional)

^{1}/$_2$ teaspoon dried thyme

^{1}/$_4$ teaspoon ground allspice

^{3}/$_4$ cup coarse fresh
    bread crumbs

1 egg, beaten

1 Preheat the oven to 350°F. First, make the stuffing.

2 Put the bulk pork sausage, onion, and garlic in a heavy skillet and cook over medium heat until the pork sausage is lightly browned and crumbly, stirring and turning so that it cooks evenly. Remove the skillet from the heat and mix in the remaining stuffing ingredients, then season with salt and pepper to taste.

3 Divide the stuffing between the chickens, packing it into the body cavities (or, if you prefer, stuff the neck end and bake the leftover stuffing in a separate dish). Truss the birds.

4 Heat the oil in a flameproof casserole just big enough to hold the chickens. Brown the birds all over.

5 Add the stock, bay leaf, and seasoning. Cover and bring to a boil, then transfer to the oven. Pot roast for 1^1/$_4$ hours, or until the juices run clear when the thickest part of the bird is pierced.

6 Untruss the chickens and spoon the stuffing onto a serving platter. Serve with the strained cooking liquid.

VARIATION

This recipe works equally well
with guinea fowl.

French-style Pot-roast Cornish Hens

An incredibly simple dish to make that looks and tastes extra special.

Serves 4

1 tablespoon olive oil
1 onion, sliced
1 large garlic clove, sliced
scant $^{1}/_{2}$ cup diced lightly
   smoked bacon
2 Cornish hens (just under 1 pound each)
2 tablespoons melted butter
2 baby celery hearts, each cut into 4
8 baby carrots
2 small zucchini, cut into chunks
8 small new potatoes
$2^{1}/_{2}$ cups chicken stock
$^{2}/_{3}$ cup dry white wine
1 bay leaf
2 fresh thyme sprigs
2 fresh rosemary sprigs
1 tablespoon butter, softened
1 tablespoon all-purpose flour
salt and ground black pepper
fresh herbs, to garnish

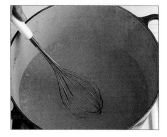

1 Preheat the oven to 375°F. Heat the olive oil in a large, flameproof casserole and add the onion, garlic, and bacon. Cook for 5–6 minutes, or until the onions have softened.

2 Brush the Cornish hens with a little of the melted butter and season well. Place on top of the onion mixture.

3 Arrange the vegetables around the Cornish hens. Add the stock, wine, and herbs. Cover and bake for 20 minutes, then remove the lid, and brush the birds with the remaining melted butter. Bake for 25–30 minutes more.

4 Transfer the Cornish hens to a serving plate and cut each in half. Remove the vegetables with a slotted spoon and arrange them around the birds. Cover with foil.

5 Discard the herbs from the pan juices. In a bowl, combine the softened butter and flour to form a paste. Bring the liquid in the pan to a boil and then gradually whisk in teaspoonfuls of the paste until thickened. Season the sauce and serve with the Cornish hens and vegetables, garnished with fresh herbs.

Crispy Spring Chickens

Small young chickens can be roasted in the oven fairly quickly and are delicious with a honey and sherry glaze. Serve either hot or cold.

INGREDIENTS

Serves 4

2 chickens, each 2 pounds
salt and ground black pepper

For the glaze

2 tablespoons honey
2 tablespoons sherry
1 tablespoon vinegar

1 Preheat the oven to 350°F. Truss the birds. Place on a wire rack over the sink. Pour boiling water over them to plump the flesh, and pat dry.

2 Combine the honey, sherry, and vinegar, and brush over the birds. Season well.

3 Put the rack into a roasting pan and roast the birds for 45–55 minutes, or until the juices run clear when the thickest part of the leg is pierced. Baste well during cooking with the honey glaze until crisp and golden brown.

Chicken with Mediterranean Vegetables

This is a delicious French alternative to a traditional roast chicken. Use a corn-fed bird, if available. This recipe also works very well with guinea fowl.

INGREDIENTS

Serves 4

1 chicken, about 4 pounds

2/3 cup extra virgin olive oil

1/2 lemon

few sprigs of fresh thyme

1 pound small new potatoes

1 eggplant, cut into
   1 inch cubes

1 red bell pepper, seeded
   and quartered

1 fennel bulb, trimmed and quartered

8 large garlic cloves, unpeeled

coarse salt and ground black pepper

1 Preheat the oven to 400°F. Rub the chicken all over with oil.

2 Season the chicken with pepper. Place the lemon half in the cavity of the bird, with a sprig or two of fresh thyme. Place the chicken, breast side down, in a large roasting pan. Roast for about 30 minutes.

3 Remove the chicken from the oven and season with salt. Turn right side up, and baste with the juices. Surround the bird with the potatoes, roll them in the pan juices, and return the roasting pan to the oven to continue roasting.

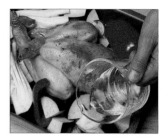

4 After 30 minutes, add the eggplant, bell pepper, fennel, and garlic cloves to the pan. Drizzle in the remaining oil, and season with salt and pepper. Add any remaining thyme to the vegetables. Return to the oven, and cook for 30–50 minutes more, basting and turning the vegetables occasionally.

5 To find out if the chicken is cooked, push the tip of a sharp knife between the thigh and breast. If the juices run clear, it is cooked. The vegetables should be tender and just beginning to brown. Place the vegetables in a warmed serving dish, cut the chicken into portions, and lay it on top. Skim the fat from the juices and serve in a gravy boat.

Roast Chicken with Comté Cheese

As it melts easily to a creamy, glossy texture with a good flavor, Comté cheese is excellent for cooking. It goes extremely well with chicken and a mushroom and vegetable sauce.

INGREDIENTS

Serves 6

6 tablespoons butter

2 tablespoons sunflower oil

1 chicken, about 4 pounds

3 carrots, sliced in rings

2 leeks, sliced

2 celery stalks, sliced

4 cups chicken stock
   or water

1¼ cups dry white wine

4 fresh thyme sprigs

3⅔ cups white mushrooms, halved

2 tablespoons all-purpose flour

⅔ cup crème fraîche or
   heavy cream

1 egg yolk

2 tablespoons fresh lemon juice

freshly grated nutmeg

1 cup grated Comté or other
   Swiss cheese

salt and ground black pepper

1 Heat a third of the butter with the oil in a large, flameproof casserole. Add the chicken and turn it in the fat until it is golden brown. Remove and set aside.

2 Add the vegetables to the casserole. Cook gently for 5 minutes, then place the bird on top. Pour in the stock or water and the wine, with 1 sprig of thyme. Season well, bring to a boil, then lower the heat, and cover the casserole. Simmer very gently for about 1 hour or until the chicken is cooked through.

3 Meanwhile, melt half the remaining butter in a small pan and stir-fry the mushrooms for 2–3 minutes. Do not let them soften or they will give up their liquid. Lift them out with a slotted spoon and set them aside. Mix the last of the butter with the flour to make a paste. Set aside too.

4 Preheat the oven to 425°F. Put the cream in a pitcher and stir in the egg yolk and lemon juice, with nutmeg to taste.

5 Transfer the cooked chicken to a shallow, heatproof dish and cover with tented aluminum foil. Remove the sprig of thyme from the casserole and discard it.

6 Return the casserole to the heat and boil rapidly until the liquid has reduced by half, then process the stock and vegetables together in a blender or food processor. Scrape the purée back into the casserole, return to a gentle simmer, and gradually whisk in the butter-and-flour paste until the sauce has thickened and is smooth. Remove from the heat again and slowly whisk in the cream mixture.

7 Surround the chicken with the mushrooms. Press half the cheese onto the chicken breast, trickle the sauce over it, and sprinkle with the rest of the cheese. Bake for about 15 minutes, or until the cheese is golden brown. Garnish with the remaining thyme sprigs and serve.

Moroccan Spiced Roast Chicken with Harissa

The spices and fruit in this stuffing give the chicken an unusual flavor. The piquant harissa sauce makes a perfect accompaniment.

INGREDIENTS

Serves 4–5

1 chicken, about 3½ pounds

2–4 tablespoons garlic and spice
   aromatic oil

a few bay leaves

2 teaspoons honey

2 teaspoons tomato paste

4 tablespoons lemon juice

²/3 cup chicken stock

¹/2–1 teaspoon harissa

salt and ground black pepper

For the stuffing

2 tablespoons butter

1 onion, chopped

1 garlic clove, crushed

1¹/2 teaspoons ground cinnamon

¹/2 teaspoon ground cumin

1¹/3 cups dried fruit, soaked for several
   hours (see Cook's Tip)

¹/4 cup blanched almonds,
   finely chopped

1 To make the stuffing, melt the butter in a pan. Add the onion and garlic and cook gently for 5 minutes, or until soft. Add the ground cinnamon and cumin and cook, stirring, for 2 minutes.

2 Drain the dried fruit, chop it coarsely, and add to the stuffing with the almonds. Season and cook for 2 minutes more. Tip into a bowl and let cool.

3 Preheat the oven to 400°F. Stuff the neck of the chicken with the fruit stuffing, reserving any excess. Brush the garlic and spice oil all over the chicken. Place the chicken in a roasting pan, tuck in the bay leaves, and roast for 1–1¹/4 hours, basting occasionally with the pan juices, until cooked.

4 Remove the chicken. Pour off any excess fat from the roasting pan. Stir the honey, tomato paste, lemon juice, stock, and harissa into the juices. Season. Bring to a boil, lower the heat, and simmer for 2 minutes, stirring. Meanwhile, reheat any excess stuffing. Carve the chicken, and serve with the sauce and the stuffing.

COOK'S TIP

The stuffing can be made with mixed dried fruit or a single variety, such as apricots, instead.

Sherry-braised Guinea Fowl

Complement guinea fowl with the rich taste and aroma of sherry and wild mushrooms to make a special roast.

INGREDIENTS

Serves 4

2 young guinea fowl, tied

$^1/_4$ cup sweet butter

5 tablespoons dry sherry

2 medium onions, sliced

1 small carrot, peeled and chopped

$^1/_2$ celery stalk, chopped

scant 2 cups chicken
    stock, boiling

1 thyme sprig

1 bay leaf

8 ounces assorted wild mushrooms,
    such as saffron milk-caps, chanterelles,
    oyster, St George's, parasol, and
    portabello, trimmed and sliced

1 tablespoon lemon juice

salt and ground black pepper

1 Preheat the oven to 375°F. Season the guinea fowl.

2 Melt half of the butter in a large, flameproof casserole, add the birds and turn until evenly browned all over.

3 Transfer the guinea fowl to a shallow dish, heat the sediment in the pan, pour in the sherry, and bring to a boil, stirring to deglaze the pan. Pour this liquid over the birds and set aside.

4 Wipe the casserole clean, then melt the remaining butter. Add the onions, carrots, and celery. Place the birds on top, cover, and cook in the oven for 40 minutes.

5 Add the stock, thyme, and bay leaf. Tie the mushrooms in a 12-inch square of cheesecloth. Place in the casserole, cover, and return to the oven for 40 minutes more, until cooked through and tender.

6 Transfer the birds to a platter, remove the thyme and bay leaf, and set the mushrooms in the bag aside. Process the braising liquid in a blender or food processor and pour back into the casserole. Add the mushrooms from the bag to the sauce. Season and add lemon juice to taste. Heat until simmering and serve poured over the guinea fowl or pour into a sauceboat.

COOK'S TIP

If fresh wild mushrooms are unavailable, replace with $^1/_2$ cup dried saffron milk-caps or ceps, with 3 ounces cultivated oyster or portabello mushrooms.

Glazed Cornish Hens

Golden Cornish hens make an impressive main course and they are also very easy to prepare. A simple mushroom risotto and refreshing side salad are good accompaniments.

INGREDIENTS

Serves 4

1/4 cup butter

2 teaspoons apple pie spice

2 tablespoons honey

grated rind and juice of 2 clementines

4 Cornish hens, about 1 pound each

1 onion, finely chopped

1 garlic clove, chopped

1 tablespoon all-purpose flour

1/4 cup Marsala

1 1/4 cups chicken stock

small bunch of fresh cilantro,
   to garnish

1 Preheat the oven to 425°F. Heat the butter, apple pie spice, honey, and clementine rind and juice until the butter has melted, stirring to mix well. Remove from the heat.

2 Place the Cornish hens in a roasting pan, brush with the glaze, then roast for 40 minutes. Brush with any remaining glaze and baste occasionally with the pan juices during cooking. Transfer the birds to a platter, cover, and stand for 10 minutes.

3 Skim off all but 1 tablespoon of the fat from the roasting pan. Add the onion and garlic to the juices in the pan and cook on the stovetop until beginning to brown. Stir in the flour, then gradually pour in the Marsala, followed by the stock, whisking constantly. Bring to a boil and simmer, stirring, for 3 minutes to make a smooth, rich gravy.

4 Garnish the Cornish hens with cilantro and serve with the gravy.

Butterflied Cornish Hens with Shallots

While they don't exactly look like butterflies, the word does describe how these Cornish hens are split and opened out. This makes the birds easy to fry or broil evenly and this recipe also works well if you want to cook them on the barbecue.

INGREDIENTS

Serves 2

2 Cornish hens, about
   1 pound each

1 shallot, finely chopped

2 garlic cloves, crushed

3 tablespoons chopped mixed fresh
   herbs, such as flat leaf parsley, sage,
   rosemary, and thyme

6 tablespoons butter, softened

salt and ground black pepper

1 To butterfly a Cornish hen, place it breast side down on a cutting board and split it along the back. Open out the bird and turn it over, so that the breast side is uppermost. Press the bird as flat as possible, then thread two metal skewers through it, across the breast and thigh, to keep it flat. Repeat with the second hen and place the skewered birds on a large broiling pan.

2 Add the chopped shallot, crushed garlic, and chopped mixed herbs to the butter with plenty of seasoning, and then beat well. Dot the butter over the butterflied Cornish hens.

3 Preheat the broiler to high and cook the Cornish hens for 30 minutes, turning them over halfway through. Turn again and baste with the cooking juices, then cook for 5–7 minutes more on each side, until cooked through.

Chicken in White Wine

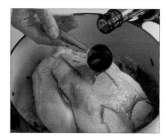

2 Add the chicken to the dish and pour in the sweet sherry or mead. Cook, covered, over very low heat for 15 minutes.

3 Add the mushrooms and wine. Cook, covered, for 1 hour. Baste the chicken with the liquid and cook, uncovered, for 30 minutes more, or until the chicken is done and most of the liquid has evaporated.

In Hungary, this chicken recipe is made with Badacsonyi wine, which has a distinctive bouquet, although any dry white wine will work.

INGREDIENTS

Serves 4

1/4 cup butter

4 scallions, chopped

3/4 cup diced rindless smoked bacon

2 bay leaves

1 fresh tarragon sprig

1 chicken, about 3 pounds

4 tablespoons sweet sherry
or mead

1 2/3 cups white mushrooms, sliced

1 1/4 cups Badacsonyi or dry
white wine

salt and ground black pepper

fresh tarragon and bay leaves,
to garnish

steamed rice, to serve

1 Heat the butter in a flameproof casserole and cook the scallions for 1 minute. Add the bacon, bay leaves, and the tarragon leaves. Cook for 1 minute more.

COOK'S TIP

Traditionally, this recipe was made with marc, a type of brandy.

4 Place the chicken, vegetables, and bacon in a serving dish and garnish with tarragon and bay leaves. Skim the cooking liquid, season, and pour into a sauceboat. Serve with rice.

Cornish Hens with Raisin and Nut Stuffing

Port-soaked raisins, walnuts, and mushrooms make an unusual and very tasty stuffing for Cornish hens. Serve with tomatoes and salad greens for a summer supper.

INGREDIENTS

Serves 4

4 Cornish hens

For the stuffing

1 cup port

$^1/_3$ cup raisins

1 tablespoon walnut oil

generous 1 cup mushrooms, ground

1 large celery stalk, ground

1 small onion, chopped

1 cup fresh bread crumbs

$^1/_2$ cup chopped walnuts

1 tablespoon each chopped fresh basil and
    parsley, or 2 tablespoons chopped
    fresh parsley

$^1/_2$ teaspoon dried thyme

6 tablespoons butter, melted

salt and ground black pepper

1 Preheat the oven to 350°F. Place the raisins in a small bowl, add the port, and set aside to soak and plump up for about 20 minutes.

2 Meanwhile, heat the oil in a nonstick pan. Add the mushrooms, celery, onion, and $^1/_4$ teaspoon salt and cook over low heat, stirring occasionally, until softened, about 8–10 minutes. Leave to cool.

3 Drain the raisins, reserving the port. Combine the raisins, bread crumbs, walnuts, basil, parsley, and thyme in a bowl. Stir in the onion mixture and $^1/_4$ cup of the butter. Add $^1/_2$ teaspoon salt and pepper to taste.

4 Fill the cavity of each Cornish hen with the stuffing. Do not pack down. Tie the legs together with kitchen string, to enclose the stuffing securely.

5 Brush the Cornish hens with the remaining butter and place in an ovenproof dish just large enough to hold the birds. Pour the reserved port over them.

6 Roast, basting occasionally, for about 1 hour. Test by piercing the thigh with a skewer; the juices should run clear. Serve immediately with some of the juices.

Cornish Hens with Grapes in Vermouth

Cornish hens with an elegant sauce of vermouth, grapes, and cream make a truly special dish, perfect for entertaining.

INGREDIENTS

Serves 4

1/4 cup butter, softened

4 Cornish hens, about
　1 pound each

2 shallots, chopped

4 tablespoons chopped fresh parsley

8 ounces white grapes, preferably muscat,
　halved and seeded

2/3 cup white vermouth

1 teaspoon cornstarch

4 tablespoons heavy cream

2 tablespoons pine nuts, toasted

salt and ground black pepper

watercress sprigs or arugula,
　to garnish

1 Preheat the oven to 400°F. Season the Cornish hens.

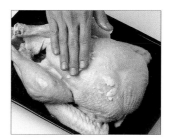

2 Spread the softened butter all over the Cornish hens and put a hazelnut-size piece in the cavity of each bird.

3 Combine the shallots and parsley and place a quarter of the mixture inside each bird. Put the hens in a roasting pan and roast for 40–50 minutes, or until the juices run clear when the thickest part of the leg is pierced. Transfer the Cornish hens to a warm serving dish, cover, and keep warm.

4 Skim off most of the fat from the roasting pan, then add the grapes and vermouth. Place the pan directly over low heat for a few minutes to warm and slightly soften the grapes.

5 Remove the grapes with a slotted spoon, and sprinkle them around the Cornish hens. Keep covered. Stir the cornstarch into the cream, then add to the pan juices. Cook gently for a few minutes, stirring, until the sauce has thickened. Adjust the seasoning. Pour the sauce around the Cornish hens. Sprinkle with the toasted pine nuts and garnish with watercress sprigs or arugula.

Cornish Hens Waldorf

Walnuts, apples, and rice add flavor and crunch to this roast. Serve with salad greens or vegetables.

INGREDIENTS

Serves 6

6 Cornish hens, each about 1¼ pounds

3–4 tablespoons butter, melted

salt and ground black pepper

For the stuffing

2 tablespoons butter

1 onion, finely chopped

2¾ cups cooked rice

2 celery stalks, finely chopped

2 red apples, cored and finely diced

½ cup chopped walnuts

5 tablespoons sweet sherry or
   apple juice

2 tablespoons lemon juice

1 Preheat the oven to 350°F. To make the stuffing, melt the butter in a small skillet and cook the onion, stirring occasionally, until soft. Tip the onion and butter into a bowl and add the remaining stuffing ingredients. Season with salt and pepper and mix well.

2 Divide the stuffing among the Cornish hens, stuffing the body cavities. Truss the birds and arrange in a roasting pan. Sprinkle with salt and pepper and drizzle the melted butter over them.

3 Roast for about 1¼–1½ hours, until the juices run clear when the thickest part of the leg is pierced.

Chicken Roll

This decorative roll can be prepared and cooked the day before use and will freeze well too. Bring to room temperature about an hour before serving.

INGREDIENTS

Serves 8

1 chicken, about 4^1/$_2$ pounds

For the stuffing

1 medium onion, finely chopped

^{1}/$_4$ cup butter, melted

2 cups lean ground pork

4 ounces fatty bacon, chopped

1 tablespoon chopped
  fresh parsley

2 teaspoons chopped fresh thyme

2 cups fresh white bread crumbs

2 tablespoons sherry

1 extra large egg, beaten

^{1}/$_4$ cup shelled pistachio nuts

^{1}/$_4$ cup pitted black olives
  (about 12)

salt and ground black pepper

1 To make the stuffing, cook the chopped onion gently in 2 tablespoons of the butter until soft. Turn into a bowl and let cool. Add the remaining ingredients, mix thoroughly, and season with salt and black pepper.

2 To bone the chicken, use a small, sharp knife to remove the wing tips. Turn the chicken onto its breast and cut a line down the backbone.

3 Cut the meat away from the carcass, scraping the bones clean. Carefully cut through the sinew around the leg and wing joints and scrape down the bones to free them. Remove the carcass, taking care not to cut through the skin along the breastbone.

4 To stuff the chicken, lay it flat, skin side down, and flatten as much as possible. Shape the stuffing down the center of the chicken and fold in the sides.

5 Preheat the oven to 350°F. Sew the meat neatly together, using a needle and dark thread. Tie into a roll with fine string.

6 Put the roll, join underneath, on a rack in a roasting pan and brush with the remaining butter. Cook, uncovered, for about 1^1/$_4$ hours. Baste with the juices during cooking. Let cool. Remove the string and thread. Wrap in aluminum foil and chill until needed.

Peanut Chicken in Pineapple Boats

Pineapple half-shells make delightful serving containers for a creamy, spiced chicken salad. It makes an impressive-looking dish to serve at a dinner party.

INGREDIENTS

Serves 4

2 small ripe pineapples
8 ounces cooked skinless, boneless chicken
    breast portions, cut into bitesize pieces
2 celery stalks, diced
2 ounces scallions, chopped
8 ounces seedless green grapes
$1/3$ cup salted peanuts,
    coarsely chopped

For the dressing
$1/3$ cup smooth peanut butter
$1/2$ cup mayonnaise
2 tablespoons cream or milk
1 garlic clove, finely chopped
1 teaspoon mild curry powder
1 tablespoon apricot jelly
salt and ground black pepper

1 Cut the pineapples in half lengthwise. Remove the flesh so that the shells remain intact. Cut the flesh into bitesize pieces.

2 Combine the pineapple flesh, chicken, celery, scallions, and grapes in a bowl.

3 Put all the dressing ingredients into another bowl and mix with a wooden spoon or whisk until evenly blended. Season with salt and pepper. (The dressing will be thick, until thinned by the juices from the pineapple.)

4 Add the dressing to the pineapple and chicken mix. Fold together gently but thoroughly.

5 Divide the chicken salad among the pineapple shells. Sprinkle the peanuts over the top before serving.

Turkey with Salted Pastry

This unusual Croatian recipe is ideal for a special occasion. The topping—pieces of crisp, salt-topped dough—helps soak up the juices.

INGREDIENTS

Serves 10–12

1 turkey, about 7 pounds

2 garlic cloves, halved

4 ounces smoked bacon, finely chopped

2 tablespoons chopped fresh rosemary

$^{1}/_{2}$ cup olive oil

1 cup dry white wine

fresh rosemary sprigs, to garnish

broiled bacon, to serve

For the salted pastry topping

3 cups all-purpose flour, sifted

$^{1}/_{2}-^{2}/_{3}$ cup warm water

2 tablespoons oil

coarse salt

1 Preheat the oven to 400°F. Dry the turkey well inside and out using paper towels. Rub the turkey all over with the halved garlic.

2 Toss the bacon and chopped rosemary together in a bowl and use to stuff the turkey neck flap. Secure the skin underneath with a toothpick. Brush with the olive oil.

3 Place the turkey in a roasting pan and cover loosely with aluminum foil. Cook for 45–50 minutes. Remove the foil and reduce the oven temperature to 325°F.

4 Baste the turkey, then pour the wine over it. Cook for 1 hour, basting occasionally. Reduce the temperature to 300°F, and cook for 45 minutes more, basting, until cooked through.

5 To make the pastry mix the flour with a little salt, the water, and oil to make a soft, pliable dough. Divide equally into four.

6 Knead well, then roll out the dough on a lightly floured counter into large rounds. Sprinkle with salt. Bake for 25 minutes. Crush into pieces about 4 inches long. Add the pastry to the pan with the turkey for the last 6–8 minutes of cooking time. Garnish with rosemary and serve with broiled bacon.

Baked Parmesan Chicken

Layers of chicken, tomato sauce, and Italian cheeses make an absolutely mouthwatering combination. The tomato sauce may be made the day before and let cool.

INGREDIENTS

Serves 4

4 skinless, boneless chicken
    breast portions
4 tablespoons all-purpose flour
4 tablespoons olive oil
8 ounces mozzarella cheese, sliced
4 tablespoons freshly grated
    Parmesan cheese
2 tablespoons fresh bread crumbs
salt and ground black pepper

For the sauce

1 tablespoon olive oil
1 onion, finely chopped
1 celery stalk, finely chopped
1 red bell pepper, seeded and diced
1 garlic clove, crushed
14-ounce can chopped tomatoes
$^2/_3$ cup chicken stock
1 tablespoon tomato paste
2 teaspoons superfine sugar
1 tablespoon chopped fresh basil
1 tablespoon chopped fresh parsley

2 Add the tomatoes with their can juice, the stock, tomato paste, sugar, and herbs. Season to taste and bring to a boil. Simmer for 30 minutes to make a thick sauce, stirring occasionally.

3 Divide each chicken portion into two natural fillets. Place between sheets of plastic wrap and flatten to a thickness of $^1/_4$ inch with a rolling pin.

4 Season the flour. Toss the chicken portions in the flour to coat, shaking to remove the excess.

5 Preheat the oven to 350°F. Heat the remaining oil in a large skillet and cook the chicken portions quickly, in batches, for 3–4 minutes, or until colored. Remove and keep warm while cooking the rest of the chicken.

6 To assemble, layer the chicken pieces in a large ovenproof dish with most of the cheeses and the thick tomato sauce, finishing with a layer of cheese and bread crumbs on top. Bake uncovered for 20–30 minutes, or until the chicken is cooked and the top is golden.

1 To make the tomato sauce, heat 1 tablespoon olive oil in a skillet and gently cook the onion, celery, bell pepper, and crushed garlic in the oil until tender.

Chicken Tonnato

This low-fat version of the Italian dish "vitello tonnato" is made with chicken instead of veal and garnished with strips of bell pepper instead of the traditional anchovy fillets.

INGREDIENTS

Serves 4

1 pound skinless, boneless chicken
    breast portions
1 small onion, sliced
1 bay leaf
4 black peppercorns
$1^{1}/2$ cups chicken stock
7-ounce can tuna in brine, drained
5 tablespoons low-fat mayonnaise
2 tablespoons lemon juice
pinch of salt
2 red bell peppers, seeded and thinly sliced
about 25 capers, drained

1 Put the chicken portions in a single layer in a large, heavy pan. Add the onion, bay leaf, peppercorns, and stock. Bring to a boil and reduce the heat. Cover and simmer for about 12 minutes, or until tender.

2 Turn off the heat and let the chicken cool in the stock, then remove with a slotted spoon. Slice the chicken thickly and arrange on a serving plate.

3 Boil the stock until reduced to about 5 tablespoons. Strain through a fine strainer and cool.

4 Put the tuna, mayonnaise, lemon juice, 3 tablespoons of the reduced stock, and salt into a blender or food processor and process until smooth.

5 Stir in enough of the remaining stock to make a thick, creamy sauce. Spoon the sauce over the chicken.

6 Arrange the strips of red bell pepper in a lattice pattern over the chicken. Put a caper in the center of each diamond shape. Chill in the refrigerator for 1 hour before serving. This dish is great served with fresh mixed salad and lemon wedges.

Stuffed Chicken Fillets with Cream Sauce

Chicken portions filled with a leek and lime-flavored stuffing and served in a cream sauce make an unusual and sophisticated supper.

INGREDIENTS

Serves 4

4 large, skinless, boneless chicken
    breast portions
$1/4$ cup butter
3 large leeks, white and pale green
    parts only, thinly sliced
1 teaspoon grated lime rind
1 cup chicken stock or half stock and half
    dry white wine
$1/2$ cup whipping or heavy cream
1 tablespoon lime juice
salt and ground black pepper
slices of lime, twisted, to garnish

1 Cut horizontally into the thickest part of each chicken portion to make a deep, wide pocket. Take care not to cut all the way through. Set the chicken portions aside.

2 Melt half the butter in a large, heavy skillet over low heat. Add the leeks and lime rind and cook, stirring occasionally, for about 15–20 minutes, or until the leeks are very soft but not colored.

3 Turn the leeks into a bowl and season to taste with salt and pepper. Let cool. Wash and dry the skillet.

4 Divide the leeks among the chicken portions, and use them to fill the pockets. Secure the openings with wooden toothpicks.

5 Melt the remaining butter in the skillet over medium-high heat. Add the chicken and brown lightly on both sides.

6 Add the stock and bring to a boil. Cover and simmer for 10 minutes, or until the chicken is cooked through. Turn the chicken portions over about halfway through the cooking.

7 With a slotted spoon, remove the chicken from the pan and keep warm. Boil the cooking liquid until it is reduced by half.

8 Stir the cream into the cooking liquid and boil until reduced by about half again. Stir in the lime juice and season to taste.

9 Remove the toothpicks from the chicken portions. Cut each portion on the diagonal into $1/2$-inch slices, pour the sauce over them, and serve immediately, garnished with lime.

VARIATION
〜

For onion-stuffed chicken portions, use 2 sweet onions, halved and thinly sliced, instead of the leeks.

Chicken Cordon Bleu

This is a rich dish, popular with cheese lovers. Serve simply with green beans and tiny baked potatoes, cut and filled with cream cheese.

INGREDIENTS

Serves 4

4 skinless, boneless chicken
    breast portions
4 slices cooked lean ham
4 tablespoons grated Gruyère or
    Emmenthal cheese
2 tablespoons olive oil
1³/4 cups white mushrooms, sliced
4 tablespoons white wine
salt and ground black pepper
watercress or arugula, to garnish

1 Place the chicken between two pieces of plastic wrap and flatten to a thickness of ¹/4 inch with a rolling pin. Place the chicken on the board, outer side down, and lay a slice of ham on each. Divide the cheese among the chicken and season with a little salt and freshly ground pepper.

2 Fold the chicken portions in half and secure with wooden toothpicks, making a large "stitch" to hold the pieces together.

3 Heat the oil in a large skillet and brown the chicken packets on all sides. Remove to a dish and keep warm.

4 Add the mushrooms to the skillet and cook until lightly browned. Replace the chicken and pour in the wine. Cover and cook gently for 15–20 minutes, or until cooked through. Remove the toothpicks. Arrange the chicken and mushrooms on a serving dish, garnish with watercress or arugula, and serve immediately.

Crunchy Stuffed Chicken

These tasty chicken fillets with a pine nut stuffing can be prepared in advance, kept chilled, and cooked just before serving.

INGREDIENTS

Serves 4

4 skinless, boneless chicken
   breast portions
2 tablespoons butter
1 garlic clove, crushed
1 tablespoon Dijon mustard

For the stuffing
1 tablespoon butter
1 bunch of scallions, sliced
3 tablespoons fresh bread crumbs
2 tablespoons pine nuts
1 egg yolk
1 tablespoon chopped fresh parsley
salt and ground black pepper
4 tablespoons grated cheese

For the topping
2 bacon strips, finely chopped
1 cup fresh bread crumbs
1 tablespoon freshly grated Parmesan
1 tablespoon chopped fresh parsley

1 Preheat the oven to 400°F. To make the stuffing, heat 1 tablespoon butter in a skillet and cook the scallions until softened. Remove from the heat and let cool.

2 Add the remaining ingredients and mix thoroughly.

3 To make the topping, cook the chopped bacon until crisp, drain, and add to the bread crumbs, Parmesan cheese, and fresh parsley.

4 Carefully cut a deep pocket in each of the chicken breast portions, using a sharp knife.

5 Divide the stuffing into four and use to fill the pockets. Place in a buttered ovenproof dish.

6 Melt the remaining butter, mix it with the crushed garlic and mustard, and brush liberally over the chicken. Press on the topping and bake uncovered for about 30–40 minutes, or until tender and cooked through.

Roast Chicken with Fennel

If you can get wild fennel, it will add character to this dish. Cultivated fennel bulb works just as well.

INGREDIENTS

Serves 4–5

$3^1/2$-pound roasting chicken

1 onion, quartered

$^1/2$ cup olive oil

2 medium fennel bulbs

1 garlic clove, peeled

pinch of freshly grated nutmeg

3–4 thin slices pancetta or bacon

$^1/2$ cup dry white wine

salt and ground black pepper

1 Preheat the oven to 350°F. Sprinkle the chicken cavity with salt and pepper. Place the onion quarters in the cavity. Rub the chicken with about 3 tablespoons of the olive oil, then place it in a roasting pan.

2 Cut the green fronds from the tops of the fennel bulbs. Chop the fronds together with the garlic. Place in a small bowl and mix with the nutmeg and seasoning.

3 Sprinkle the fennel mixture over the chicken, pressing it onto the oiled skin. Cover the breast with the slices of pancetta or bacon. Sprinkle with 2 tablespoons of the oil. Place in the oven and roast for 30 minutes.

4 Meanwhile, boil or steam the fennel bulbs until barely tender. Remove from the heat and cut into quarters or sixths lengthwise. After the chicken has been cooking for 30 minutes, remove the pan from the oven. Baste the chicken with any oils in the pan.

5 Arrange the fennel pieces around the chicken. Sprinkle the fennel with the remaining oil. Pour about half the wine over the chicken and return to the oven.

6 After 30 minutes more, baste the chicken again. Pour in the remaining wine. Cook for 15–20 minutes, or until the juices run clear when the thickest part of the leg is pierced. Serve the chicken surrounded by the fennel.

Chicken with Ham and Cheese

This tasty combination comes from Italy, where it is also prepared with veal.

INGREDIENTS

Serves 4

4 small, skinless, boneless chicken
    breast portions

flour seasoned with salt and freshly
    ground black pepper, for dredging

$^1/4$ cup butter

3–4 leaves fresh sage

4 thin slices prosciutto crudo,
    or cooked ham, cut in half

$^2/3$ cup freshly grated Parmesan cheese

1 Cut each chicken portion in half lengthwise to make two flat fillets of approximately the same thickness. Dredge the chicken with the seasoned flour, and shake off the excess.

2 Preheat the broiler. Heat the butter in a large, heavy skillet and add the sage leaves. Add the chicken, in one layer, and cook over low to medium heat until cooked through and golden brown on both sides, turning as necessary. This will take about 15 minutes.

3 Remove the chicken from the heat, and arrange on a flame-proof serving dish or broiling pan. Place one piece of ham on each chicken portion and top with the grated Parmesan cheese. Broil for 3–4 minutes, or until the cheese has melted. Serve immediately.

Chicken with Shallots, Garlic, and Fennel

This dish is guaranteed to be popular with garlic lovers. The fennel adds a deliciously unusual anise flavor.

INGREDIENTS

Serves 4

1 chicken, about 3^1/$_2$ – 4 pounds, cut into
   8 pieces, or 8 chicken pieces

9 ounces shallots, peeled

1 head garlic, separated into cloves
   and peeled

4 tablespoons extra virgin olive oil

3 tablespoons tarragon vinegar

3 tablespoons white wine or
   vermouth (optional)

1 teaspoon fennel seeds, crushed

2 bulbs fennel, cut into wedges, feathery
   tops reserved

^{2}/$_3$ cup heavy cream

1 teaspoon red currant jelly

1 tablespoon tarragon mustard

superfine sugar (optional)

2 tablespoons chopped fresh flat
   leaf parsley

salt and ground black pepper

1 Place the chicken pieces, shallots, and all but one of the garlic cloves in a flameproof dish or roasting pan. Add the oil, vinegar, wine or vermouth, if using, and fennel seeds. Season with pepper, then set aside to marinate for 2–3 hours.

2 Preheat the oven to 375°F. Add the fennel to the chicken, season with salt, and stir to mix.

3 Cook the chicken in the oven for 50–60 minutes, stirring once or twice. The chicken juices should run clear when the thick thigh meat is pierced.

4 Transfer the chicken and vegetables to a serving dish and keep them warm. Skim off some of the fat and bring the cooking juices to a boil, then pour in the cream. Stir, scraping up all the residue from the base of the pan. Whisk in the red currant jelly, followed by the mustard. Check the seasoning, adding a little sugar if you like.

5 Chop the remaining garlic with the feathery fennel tops and combine with the parsley. Pour the sauce over the chicken and sprinkle the chopped garlic and herb mixture over the top. Serve immediately.

Chicken with Spiced Figs

The Catalans have various recipes for fruit with meat. This is quite an unusual one, but it uses one of the fruits most strongly associated with the Mediterranean—the fig.

INGREDIENTS

Serves 4

3/4 cup sugar

1/2 cup white wine vinegar

1 lemon slice

1 cinnamon stick

1 pound fresh figs

1/2 cup medium sweet white wine

pared rind of 1/2 lemon

1 chicken, about 31/2 pounds, cut into 8 pieces

2 ounces lardons, or thick, fatty bacon cut into strips

1 tablespoon olive oil

1/4 cup chicken stock

salt and ground black pepper

salad greens, to serve

1 Put the sugar, vinegar, lemon slice, and cinnamon stick in a pan with 1/2 cup water. Bring to a boil, then simmer for 5 minutes. Add the figs, cover, and simmer for 10 minutes. Remove from the heat and leave, covered, for 3 hours.

2 Preheat the oven to 350°F. Drain the figs, and place in a bowl. Add the wine and lemon rind. Season the chicken. In a large skillet, cook the lardons or bacon strips until the fat melts. Transfer to an ovenproof dish, leaving any fat in the skillet. Add the oil to the skillet and brown the chicken pieces all over.

3 Drain the figs, adding the wine to the skillet with the chicken. Boil until the sauce has reduced and is syrupy. Transfer the contents of the skillet to the ovenproof dish and cook, uncovered, in the oven for about 20 minutes, until cooked. Add the figs and stock, cover, and return to the oven for 10 minutes more. Serve with salad greens.

Seville Chicken

Oranges and almonds are favorite ingredients in southern Spain, especially around Seville, where the orange and almond trees are a familiar and wonderful sight.

INGREDIENTS

Serves 4

1 orange

8 chicken thighs

all-purpose flour, seasoned with salt
   and pepper

3 tablespoons olive oil

1 large Bermuda onion,
   coarsely chopped

2 garlic cloves, crushed

1 red bell pepper, seeded and sliced

1 yellow bell pepper, seeded
   and sliced

4 ounces chorizo sausage, sliced

$1/2$ cup sliced almonds

generous 1 cup brown basmati rice

$2^1/2$ cups chicken stock

14-ounce can chopped tomatoes

$3/4$ cup white wine

generous pinch of dried thyme

salt and ground black pepper

fresh thyme sprigs, to garnish

1 Pare a thin strip of rind from the orange and set it aside. Using a sharp knife, cut a slice of rind and pith from each end of the orange. Place cut side down on a plate and cut off the peel and pith in strips. Cut out each segment, leaving the membrane behind. Dust the chicken thighs with seasoned flour.

2 Heat the oil in a large skillet and cook the chicken pieces on both sides until nicely brown. Transfer to a plate. Add the onion and garlic to the skillet and cook for 4–5 minutes, or until the onion begins to brown. Add the bell peppers and cook, stirring occasionally, until slightly softened.

3 Add the chorizo, stir-fry for a few minutes, then sprinkle in the almonds and rice. Cook, stirring, for 1–2 minutes.

4 Pour in the chicken stock, tomatoes, and wine and add the orange rind strip and thyme. Season well. Bring to simmering point, stirring, then return the chicken pieces to the skillet.

5 Cover tightly and cook over very low heat for 1–1¼ hours, or until the rice is tender and the chicken is cooked through. Just before serving, add the orange segments and cook briefly to heat through. Garnish with fresh thyme and serve immediately.

COOK'S TIP
～
Cooking times for this dish will depend largely on the heat. If the rice seems to be drying out too fast, add a little more stock or wine and reduce the heat. If, after about 40 minutes, the rice is still barely cooked, increase the heat a little. Make sure the rice is kept below the liquid (the chicken can lie on the surface) and stir the rice occasionally if it seems to be cooking unevenly.

Chicken with Sloe Gin and Juniper

Juniper is used to make gin. The flavor of this dish is deliciously enhanced by using both sloe gin and juniper berries. Sloe gin is easy to make, but can also be bought ready-made.

INGREDIENTS

Serves 8

2 tablespoons butter

2 tablespoons sunflower oil

8 skinless, boneless chicken
    breast portions

12 ounces carrots, cooked

1 garlic clove, crushed

1 tablespoon finely chopped parsley

$^{1}/_{4}$ cup chicken stock

$^{1}/_{4}$ cup red wine

$^{1}/_{4}$ cup sloe gin

1 teaspoon crushed juniper berries

salt and ground black pepper

chopped fresh basil, to garnish

1 Melt the butter with the oil in a skillet, and cook the chicken until browned on all sides.

2 In a food processor or blender, combine all the remaining ingredients, except the basil, and blend to a smooth paste. If the mixture seems too thick, add a little more red wine or water.

3 Put the chicken breast portions in a clean pan, pour the sauce over the top, and cook over medium heat until the chicken is cooked through—about 15 minutes. Adjust the seasoning and serve garnished with chopped fresh basil.

Circassian Chicken

This is a Turkish dish, which is popular all over the Middle East. The chicken is poached and served cold with a flavorsome sauce.

INGREDIENTS

Serves 6

1 chicken, about 3 1/2 pounds
2 onions, quartered
1 carrot, sliced
1 celery stalk, trimmed and sliced
6 peppercorns
3 slices bread, crusts removed
2 garlic cloves, coarsely chopped
3 1/2 cups chopped walnuts
1 tablespoon walnut oil
salt and ground black pepper
chopped walnuts and paprika, to garnish

1 Place the chicken in a large pan, with the onions, carrot, celery, and peppercorns. Add water to cover, and bring to a boil. Simmer for 1 hour, uncovered, until the chicken is tender and cooked through. Let cool. Drain the chicken, reserving the stock.

2 Tear up the bread and soak in 6 tablespoons of the chicken stock. Transfer to a blender or food processor, with the garlic and walnuts, and add 1 cup of the remaining stock. Process until smooth, then transfer to a pan.

3 Over low heat, gradually add more chicken stock to the sauce, stirring constantly, until it is of a thick, pouring consistency. Season, remove from the heat, and let cool in the pan.

4 Skin and bone the chicken, and cut into bitesize chunks. Place in a bowl and add a little of the sauce. Stir to coat the chicken, then arrange on a serving dish. Spoon the remaining sauce over the chicken, and drizzle with the walnut oil. Sprinkle with walnuts and paprika and serve immediately.

Chicken with Red Wine Vinegar

This is a simple dish to prepare and tastes wonderful. It is an easy version of a modern classic in French cooking.

INGREDIENTS

Serves 4

4 skinless, boneless chicken breast
  portions, 7 ounces each

$1/4$ cup sweet butter

8–12 shallots, trimmed and halved

4 tablespoons red wine vinegar

2 garlic cloves, finely chopped

4 tablespoons dry white wine

$1/2$ cup chicken stock

1 tablespoon chopped fresh parsley

freshly ground black pepper

salad greens, to serve

1 Cut each chicken portion in half crosswise to make 8 pieces.

2 Melt half the butter in a large skillet over medium heat. Add the chicken and cook for 3–5 minutes, or until golden brown, turning once, then season with pepper.

3 Add the shallot halves to the skillet, cover, and cook over low heat for 5–7 minutes, shaking the skillet and stirring occasionally.

4 Transfer the chicken to a plate. Add the vinegar to the skillet and cook, stirring, for 1 minute, or until the liquid is almost evaporated. Add the garlic, wine, and stock and stir to blend.

5 Return the chicken to the skillet with any accumulated liquid. Cover and simmer for 2–3 minutes, or until tender and the juices run clear when pierced.

6 Transfer the chicken and shallots to a serving dish and cover to keep warm. Increase the heat and boil the cooking liquid until it has reduced by half.

7 Remove from the heat. Add the remaining butter, whisking until the sauce is thickened and glossy. Add the parsley. Pour the sauce over the chicken and shallots. Serve with salad greens.

VARIATIONS

You could try tarragon vinegar and substitute tarragon for parsley, or raspberry vinegar and garnish with fresh raspberries.

Broiled Cornish Hens with Citrus Glaze

The fresh flavor of citrus fruits complements young poultry perfectly. This recipe is suitable for many sorts of small birds, including squab, snipe, and grouse.

INGREDIENTS

Serves 4

2 Cornish hens, about 1^1/2 pounds each

^{1}/4 cup butter, softened

2 tablespoons olive oil

2 garlic cloves, crushed

^{1}/2 teaspoon dried thyme

^{1}/4 teaspoon cayenne pepper, or to taste

grated rind and juice of 1 lemon

grated rind and juice of 1 lime

2 tablespoons honey

salt and ground black pepper

fresh dill, to garnish

tomato salad, to serve

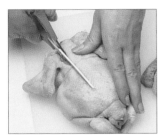

1 Using kitchen scissors or poultry shears, cut along both sides of the backbone of each bird; remove, and discard. Cut the birds in half along the breastbone, then, using a rolling pin, press down to flatten.

COOK'S TIP

If smaller Cornish hens, about 1 pound each, are available, serve one per person. Increase the butter to 6 tablespoons, if necessary.

---

2 Beat the butter in a small bowl, then beat in 1 tablespoon of the olive oil, the garlic, thyme, cayenne, salt, pepper, half the lemon and lime rind, and 1 tablespoon of combined citrus juice.

3 Loosen the skin of each hen breast. With a round-bladed knife, spread the butter mixture evenly between the skin and meat.

4 Preheat the broiler and line a broiling pan with foil. In a small bowl, combine the remaining olive oil, lemon and lime rind and juices, and the honey. Place the bird halves, skin side up, on the broiling pan and brush with t he juice mixture.

5 Broil for 10–12 minutes, basting once or twice with the juices. Turn over and broil for 7–10 minutes, basting once, until the juices run clear when the thigh is pierced. Serve with the tomato salad, garnished with dill.

Chicken with Apricot and Pecan Baskets

The potato baskets make a pretty addition to the chicken and could easily have different fillings when you feel like a change.

INGREDIENTS

Serves 8

8 skinless, boneless chicken breast
   portions, about 5 ounces each
2 tablespoons butter
$^3/4$ cup chopped mushrooms
1 tablespoon chopped pecan nuts
$^2/3$ cup chopped, cooked ham
1 cup whole-wheat
   bread crumbs
1 tablespoon chopped parsley, plus some
   whole leaves to garnish
salt and ground black pepper

For the potato baskets

4 large baking potatoes, about
   11 ounces each
6 ounces bulk pork sausage
8-ounce can apricots in natural juice,
   drained and quartered
$^1/4$ teaspoon ground cinnamon
$^1/2$ teaspoon grated orange rind
2 tablespoons maple syrup
2 tablespoons butter
$^1/4$ cup chopped pecan nuts, plus pecan
   halves to garnish

For the sauce

1 tablespoon cornstarch
$^1/2$ cup white wine
$^1/2$ cup chicken stock
$^1/4$ cup butter
scant $^1/4$ cup apricot chutney

1 Preheat the oven to 400°F. Put the potatoes in the oven to bake. Cook for 1½ hours, or until ready. Put the chicken between two sheets of plastic wrap and flatten with a meat pounder. Melt the butter in a pan and cook the mushrooms, pecan nuts, and ham. Stir in the bread crumbs, parsley, and seasoning. Divide the mixture among the chicken portions, roll up, and secure each one with a toothpick. Chill.

2 Mix the cornstarch for the sauce with a little of the wine and stock to make a smooth paste. Put the remaining wine and stock in a pan and add the paste. Cook, stirring, until smooth. Add the butter and chutney, and cook for 5 minutes, stirring. Turn the oven temperature down to 350°F.

3 Place the chicken in an oven-proof dish. Pour in the sauce. Cover with foil and bake for 20–25 minutes, until cooked.

4 When the potatoes are cooked, cut them in half, and scoop out the inside. Mash the potato in a mixing bowl.

5 Fry the bulk sausage and drain off any fat. Add the remaining ingredients and cook for 1 minute. Combine the bulk sausage mixture and potato and put in the potato shells. Sprinkle the pecans over the top, put in the oven with the chicken, and bake for 20–25 minutes.

6 When the chicken is cooked, remove the toothpicks, slice, and place on serving plates. Pour on the sauce, garnish with parsley, and serve with the potato baskets.

Chicken with Asparagus

Canned asparagus may be used instead of fresh, but will not require any cooking—simply add at the end to warm through.

INGREDIENTS

Serves 4

4 large, skinless, boneless chicken
    breast portions

1 tablespoon ground coriander

2 tablespoons olive oil

20 slender asparagus spears, cut
    into 3–4-inch lengths

1¹/₄ cups chicken stock

1 tablespoon cornstarch

1 tablespoon lemon juice

salt and ground black pepper

1 tablespoon chopped fresh parsley

3 Add the asparagus and chicken stock to the pan and bring to a boil. Cook for 4–5 minutes, or until just tender.

4 Mix the cornstarch to a paste with a little cold water, stir into the sauce, and cook, stirring, until thickened. Return the chicken to the pan, with the lemon juice, and reheat. Garnish with parsley and serve.

1 Divide each chicken portion into two natural fillets. Place each between two sheets of plastic wrap and flatten to a thickness of ¹/₄ inch with a rolling pin. Cut into 1-inch strips diagonally. Sprinkle with the coriander, and toss to coat each piece.

2 Heat the oil in a large skillet and cook the chicken very quickly, in small batches, for 3–4 minutes, until lightly colored and cooked through. Season each batch with a little salt and freshly ground black pepper. Remove and keep warm while cooking the rest of the chicken.

Chicken with Morels

Morels are among the tastiest of dried mushrooms and, although they are expensive, just a few will go a long way.

INGREDIENTS

Serves 4

3/4 cup dried morel mushrooms
1 cup chicken stock
1/4 cup butter
5 or 6 shallots, thinly sliced
1 1/2 cups white mushrooms,
    thinly sliced
1/4 teaspoon dried thyme
2–3 tablespoons brandy
3/4 cup heavy or
    whipping cream
4 skinless, boneless chicken breast
    portions, about 7 ounces each
1 tablespoon vegetable oil
3/4 cup champagne or dry
    sparkling wine
salt and ground black pepper

1 Put the morels in a strainer and rinse well under cold running water, shaking to remove as much grit as possible. Put them in a pan with the stock and bring to a boil over medium-high heat. Remove the pan from the heat and let stand for 1 hour.

2 Remove the morels from the cooking liquid, strain the liquid through a very fine strainer or a cheesecloth-lined strainer and reserve for the sauce. Reserve a few whole morels and slice the rest.

3 Melt half the butter in a skillet over medium heat. Add the shallots and cook for 2 minutes, or until softened, then add the morels and mushrooms, and cook, stirring frequently, for 2–3 minutes. Season and add the thyme, brandy and scant 1/2 cup of the cream. Reduce the heat to low and simmer gently for 10–12 minutes, or until any liquid has evaporated, stirring occasionally. Remove the morel mixture from the skillet and set aside.

4 Pull off the smaller fillets from the chicken portions (the finger-shaped piece on the underside) and reserve for another use. Make a pocket in each chicken portion by cutting a slit along the thicker edge, taking care not to cut all the way through.

5 Using a small spoon, fill each pocket with one-quarter of the mushroom mixture then, if necessary, close with a toothpick.

6 Melt the remaining butter with the oil in a heavy skillet over medium-high heat and cook the chicken portions on one side for 6–8 minutes, or until golden. Transfer to a plate. Add the champagne or sparkling wine to the skillet and boil to reduce by half. Add the strained morel cooking liquid and boil to reduce by half again.

7 Add the remaining cream and cook over medium heat for 2–3 minutes, or until the sauce thickens slightly and coats the back of a spoon. Adjust the seasoning. Return the chicken to the skillet with any accumulated juices and the reserved whole morels, and simmer for 3–5 minutes over medium-low heat until the chicken portions are hot and the juices run clear when the meat is pierced.

Chicken with Figs and Mint

The unusual combination of figs, orange, and mint makes a rich sauce to accompany tender chicken breast portions.

INGREDIENTS

Serves 4

3 1/3 cups dried figs

1/2 bottle sweet, fruity white wine

4 skinless, boneless chicken breast
    portions, about 6–8 ounces each

1 tablespoon butter

2 tablespoons dark orange marmalade

10 fresh mint leaves, finely chopped, plus a
    few extra to garnish

juice of 1/2 lemon

salt and ground black pepper

1 Place the figs in a pan with the wine and bring to a boil, then simmer very gently for about 1 hour. Let cool and chill in the refrigerator overnight.

2 Cook the chicken portions in the butter until they are tender. Remove and keep warm. Drain any fat from the pan and pour in the juice from the figs. Boil and reduce to about 2/3 cup.

3 Add the marmalade, chopped mint leaves, and lemon juice, and simmer for a few minutes. Season to taste. When the sauce is thick and shiny, pour it over the chicken. Garnish with the figs and mint leaves, and serve.

Guinea Fowl with Whiskey Cream Sauce

Served with creamy sweet potato mash and whole baby leeks, guinea fowl is superb with a rich, creamy whiskey sauce.

INGREDIENTS

Serves 4

2 guinea fowl, each weighing about
  $2^1/4$ pounds
6 tablespoons whiskey
$2/3$ cup chicken stock
$2/3$ cup heavy cream
20 baby leeks
salt and ground black pepper
fresh thyme sprigs, to garnish
mashed sweet potatoes,
  to serve

1 Preheat the oven to 400°F. Brown the guinea fowl on all sides in a roasting pan on the stovetop, then turn them breast uppermost, and transfer the pan to the oven. Roast for about 1 hour, or until the guinea fowl are golden and cooked through. Transfer the guinea fowl to a warmed serving dish, cover with foil, and keep warm.

2 Pour off the excess fat from the pan, then heat the juices on the stovetop, and stir in the whiskey. Bring to a boil and cook until reduced. Add the stock and cream and simmer again until reduced slightly. Strain and season to taste.

3 Meanwhile, trim the leeks so that they are about the same length as the guinea fowl breasts, then cook them whole in salted, boiling water for about 3 minutes, or until tender but not too soft. Drain the leeks in a colander.

4 Carve the guinea fowl. To serve, arrange portions of mashed sweet potato on warmed serving plates, then add the carved guinea fowl and the leeks. Garnish with sprigs of fresh thyme, and season with plenty of freshly ground black pepper. Spoon a little of the sauce over each portion and serve the rest separately.

VARIATION

If you prefer, you can substitute brandy, Madeira, or Marsala for the whiskey. Or, to make a nonalcoholic version, use freshly squeezed orange juice instead.

ONE POT
DISHES &
CASSEROLES

One of the best ways to blend the flavor of tender chicken with other ingredients is
to cook it slowly as a one-pot dish, casserole, or stew. In this chapter, you
will discover ingredients that you would rarely find accompanying chicken,
ranging from blackberries to cocoa and shrimp, as well as a host of
favorite flavorings, such as chiles, wine, mushrooms, garlic, and herbs. Many of the
dishes can be prepared in advance, and there are recipes suitable for everyday
cooking and for special occasions.

Chicken with Blackberries and Lemon

This delicious dish combines some wonderful flavors, and the red wine and blackberries give it a dramatic appearance.

INGREDIENTS

Serves 4

4 part-boned chicken breast
    portions, skinned
2 tablespoons butter
1 tablespoon sunflower oil
1/4 cup all-purpose flour
2/3 cup red wine
2/3 cup chicken stock
grated rind of 1/2 orange plus
    1 tablespoon juice
3 lemon balm sprigs, finely chopped,
    plus 1 sprig to garnish
2/3 cup heavy cream
1 egg yolk
1 cup fresh blackberries, plus 1/2 cup
    to garnish
salt and ground black pepper

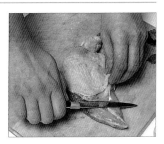

1 Preheat the oven to 350°F. Season the chicken breast portions. Heat the butter and oil in a skillet, cook the chicken to seal it, then transfer to a flameproof casserole. Stir the flour into the skillet, then add the wine and stock, and bring to a boil. Add the orange rind and juice, and the chopped lemon balm. Pour the mixture over the chicken.

2 Cover the casserole and cook in the oven for about 40 minutes.

3 Blend the cream with the egg yolk, add some of the liquid from the casserole, and stir back into the dish with the blackberries. Cover and cook for 10–15 minutes, until the chicken is cooked. Serve garnished with blackberries and the sprig of lemon balm.

Apricot and Chicken Casserole

This mildly curried fruity chicken dish served with almond rice makes a good winter meal.

INGREDIENTS

Serves 4

1 tablespoon oil
8 skinless, boneless chicken thighs
1 medium onion, finely chopped
1 teaspoon medium curry powder
2 tablespoons all-purpose flour
scant 2 cups chicken stock
juice of 1 large orange
8 dried apricots, halved
1 tablespoon golden raisins
salt and ground black pepper

For the rice

2 cups cooked long
    grain rice
1 tablespoon butter
¹/₂ cup toasted, sliced almonds

1 Preheat the oven to 375°F. Heat the oil in a large skillet. Cut the chicken into cubes and brown quickly all over in the oil. Add the chopped onion and cook gently until soft and lightly browned.

2 Transfer the chicken and onion to a large, flameproof casserole. Sprinkle in the curry powder and cook, stirring constantly, for a few minutes. Add the flour and blend in the stock and orange juice. Bring to a boil and season to taste with salt and freshly ground black pepper.

3 Add the apricots and golden raisins, cover, and cook gently for 1 hour, or until tender and cooked through, in the preheated oven. Adjust the seasoning to taste.

4 To make the almond rice, reheat the pre-cooked rice with the butter and season to taste. Stir in the toasted almonds just before serving.

Stoved Chicken

2 Heat the butter and oil in a large, heavy skillet, add the bacon and chicken, and brown on all sides, stirring frequently. Using a slotted spoon, transfer the chicken and bacon to the casserole. Reserve the fat in the skillet.

3 Sprinkle the remaining thyme over the chicken, season with salt and pepper, then cover with the remaining onion slices, followed by a neat layer of overlapping potato slices. Season the dish well.

This Scottish dish of slowly cooked potatoes layered with bacon and chicken has a lovely aroma of thyme and bay. It makes a perfect dish for cold fall and winter evenings.

INGREDIENTS

Serves 4

2^1/4 pounds baking potatoes, cut into ^{1}/4-inch slices

butter, for greasing

2 large onions, thinly sliced

1 tablespoon chopped fresh thyme

2 tablespoons butter

1 tablespoon vegetable oil

2 large bacon slices, chopped

4 large chicken pieces, halved

2^1/2 cups chicken stock

1 bay leaf

salt and ground black pepper

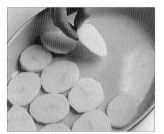

1 Preheat the oven to 300°F. Arrange a thick layer of half the potato slices in the base of a lightly greased, large, heavy casserole, then cover with half the onions. Sprinkle with half of the thyme, and season with salt and pepper to taste.

4 Pour the stock into the casserole, add the bay leaf and brush the potatoes with the reserved fat. Cover tightly and bake for about 2 hours, or until the chicken is very tender and cooked through.

5 Preheat the broiler. Take the cover off the casserole and place it under the broiler until the slices of potato begin to turn golden brown and crisp. Remove the bay leaf and serve hot.

Coq au Vin

This is a classic French country casserole, rich with the wonderful flavors of red wine and herbs.

INGREDIENTS

Serves 6

3 tablespoons light olive oil

12 shallots

8 ounces fatty bacon strips, chopped

3 garlic cloves, finely chopped

3 cups small mushrooms, halved

6 boneless chicken thighs

3 boneless chicken breast
   portions, halved

1 bottle red wine

salt and ground black pepper

3 tablespoons chopped fresh parsley,
   to garnish

boiled potatoes, to serve

For the bouquet garni

3 sprigs each of fresh parsley, thyme,
   and sage

1 bay leaf

4 peppercorns

For the beurre manié

2 tablespoons butter, softened

1/4 cup all-purpose flour

1 Heat the olive oil in a large, flameproof casserole and cook the shallots for 5 minutes, or until golden. Increase the heat, add the bacon, garlic, and mushrooms, and cook for 10 minutes more, stirring frequently.

2 Use a slotted spoon to transfer the cooked ingredients to a plate, then brown the chicken portions in the oil remaining in the pan, turning them until they are golden brown all over. Return the shallots, garlic, mushrooms, and bacon to the casserole and pour in the red wine.

3 Tie all the bouquet garni ingredients into a small piece of cheesecloth. Add to the casserole. Bring to a boil, reduce the heat, and cover the casserole, then simmer for 30–40 minutes, until the chicken is cooked through.

4 To make the beurre manié, cream the butter and flour together in a small bowl using your fingers or a spoon to make a smooth paste.

5 Add small lumps of this paste to the bubbling casserole, stirring well until each piece has melted into the liquid before adding the next. When all the paste has been added, simmer, stirring constantly, for 5 minutes.

6 Season the casserole to taste with salt and pepper and serve garnished with chopped fresh parsley and accompanied by boiled potatoes.

Chicken and Lentil Casserole

A casserole of wonderfully tender chicken, root vegetables, and lentils, finished with crème fraîche, mustard, and tarragon, makes a deliciously aromatic meal.

INGREDIENTS

Serves 4

12 ounces onions

12 ounces trimmed leeks

8 ounces carrots

1 pound rutabaga

2 tablespoons oil

4 chicken pieces, about 2 pounds
    total weight

$^1/_2$ cup green lentils

2 cups chicken stock

$1^1/_4$ cups apple juice

2 teaspoons cornstarch

3 tablespoons crème fraîche

2 teaspoons whole-grain mustard

2 tablespoons chopped fresh tarragon

salt and ground black pepper

fresh tarragon sprigs, to garnish

1 Preheat the oven to 375°F. Coarsely chop the onions, leeks, carrots, and rutabaga into similarly sized pieces.

2 Heat the oil in a large, flameproof casserole. Season the chicken pieces with salt and pepper and brown them in the hot oil until golden. Drain on paper towels.

5 Return the chicken to the pan. Add the stock, apple juice, and seasoning. Bring to a boil and cover tightly. Cook in the oven for 50–60 minutes, or until the chicken and lentils are cooked through.

3 Add the onions to the pan and cook for 5 minutes, stirring, until they begin to soften and color.

6 Place the casserole on the stovetop over medium heat. Blend the cornstarch with 2 tablespoons water and add to the casserole with the crème fraîche, mustard, and tarragon. Adjust the seasoning. Simmer gently for about 2 minutes, stirring, before serving garnished with tarragon sprigs.

4 Stir in the leeks, carrots, rutabaga, and lentils and stir over medium heat for 2 minutes.

Country Chicken Casserole

Succulent chicken pieces in a vegetable sauce are excellent served with brown rice or pasta.

INGREDIENTS

Serves 4

2 skinless, boneless chicken
    breast portions
2 chicken legs, skinned
2 tablespoons whole-wheat flour
1 tablespoon sunflower oil
1¼ cups chicken stock
1¼ cups white wine
2 tablespoons bottled strained tomatoes
1 tablespoon tomato paste
4 strips lean smoked back
    bacon, chopped
1 large onion, sliced
1 garlic clove, crushed
1 green bell pepper, seeded
    and sliced
3 cups white mushrooms
8 ounces carrots, sliced
1 bouquet garni
8 ounces fresh or frozen
    Brussels sprouts
1½ cups fresh shelled or frozen
    baby peas
salt and ground black pepper
chopped fresh parsley, to garnish

1 Preheat the oven to 350°F. Coat the chicken breast portions and legs with the flour seasoned with salt and pepper.

2 Heat the oil in a large, flameproof casserole, add the chicken, and cook until browned all over. Remove the chicken using a slotted spoon, and keep warm.

3 Add any remaining flour to the pan and cook for 1 minute. Gradually stir in the stock and wine, then add the bottled strained tomatoes and tomato paste.

4 Bring to a boil, stirring constantly, then add the chicken, bacon, onion, garlic, bell pepper, mushrooms, carrots, and bouquet garni, and stir. Cover and bake for 1½ hours, stirring once or twice.

5 Stir in the Brussels sprouts and baby peas, re-cover, and bake for 30 minutes more, until cooked.

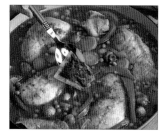

6 Remove and discard the bouquet garni. Add seasoning to the casserole, garnish with chopped fresh parsley, and serve immediately.

VARIATION

Red wine can be used instead of white for a delicious change.

Chicken Thighs with Lemon and Garlic

This recipe uses classic European flavorings for chicken. Versions of it can be found in Spain and Italy. This particular recipe, however, is of French origin.

INGREDIENTS

Serves 4

2 1/2 cups chicken stock
20 large garlic cloves
2 tablespoons butter
1 tablespoon olive oil
8 chicken thighs
1 lemon, rind and pith removed and
    sliced thinly
2 tablespoons all-purpose flour
2/3 cup dry white wine
salt and ground black pepper
chopped fresh parsley or basil, to garnish
new potatoes or rice, to serve

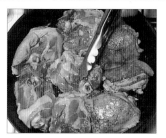

1 Put the stock into a pan and bring to a boil. Add the garlic cloves, cover, and simmer gently for 40 minutes. Heat the butter and oil in a sauté pan or skillet, add the chicken thighs, and cook gently on all sides until golden. Transfer to an ovenproof dish. Preheat the oven to 375°F.

2 Strain the stock and reserve it. Distribute the garlic and lemon slices among the chicken pieces. Add the flour to the fat in the pan in which the chicken was browned, and cook, stirring, for 1 minute. Add the wine, stirring constantly and scraping the base of the pan, then add the stock. Cook, stirring, until the sauce has thickened and is smooth. Season with salt and pepper.

3 Pour the sauce over the chicken, cover, and cook in the oven for 40–45 minutes, until cooked through. If a thicker sauce is required, lift out the chicken pieces, and reduce the sauce by boiling rapidly, until it is thick enough. Sprinkle over the chopped parsley or basil and serve with boiled new potatoes or rice.

Chicken with Garlic

In this recipe, garlic and onion are slowly cooked then puréed, making a fabulous sauce for the chicken. Use fresh new season's garlic if you can find it—there's no need to peel the cloves if the skin is not papery.

INGREDIENTS

Serves 8

4^1/$_2$ pounds chicken pieces

1 large onion, halved and sliced

3 large garlic bulbs (about 7 ounces),
    separated into cloves and peeled

^{2}/$_3$ cup dry white wine

^{3}/$_4$ cup chicken stock

4–5 thyme sprigs, or ^{1}/$_2$ teaspoon
    dried thyme

1 small rosemary sprig, or a pinch of
    ground rosemary

1 bay leaf

salt and ground black pepper

1 Preheat the oven to 375°F. Pat the chicken pieces dry with paper towels and season with salt and pepper.

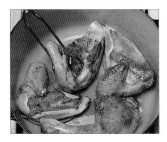

2 Put the chicken, skin side down, in a large, flameproof casserole and set over medium-high heat. Turn frequently and transfer the chicken to a plate when browned. Cook in batches, if necessary, and pour off the fat after browning.

3 Add the onion and garlic to the casserole, replace the lid, and cook over medium-low heat, covered, until lightly browned, stirring frequently.

4 Add the wine to the casserole, bring to a boil, and return the chicken to the casserole. Add the stock and herbs and bring back to a boil. Cover and transfer to the oven. Cook for 25 minutes, or until the chicken is tender and the juices run clear when the thickest part of the thigh is pierced.

5 Remove the chicken from the pan and strain the cooking liquid. Discard the herbs, transfer the solids to a food processor. and process until smooth. Remove any fat from the cooking liquid and return to the casserole. Stir in the garlic and onion purée, add the chicken, and reheat before serving.

Chicken with Chorizo

The additions of chorizo sausage and sherry give a warm, interesting flavor to this simple Spanish casserole. Serve with rice or boiled potatoes.

INGREDIENTS

Serves 4

1 medium chicken, cut into pieces, or
    4 chicken legs, halved

2 teaspoons ground paprika

4 tablespoons olive oil

2 small onions, sliced

6 garlic cloves, thinly sliced

5 ounces chorizo sausage

14-ounce can chopped tomatoes

12–16 bay leaves

5 tablespoons medium sherry

salt and ground black pepper

rice or potatoes, to serve

1 Preheat the oven to 375°F. Coat the chicken pieces in the paprika, making sure they are evenly covered, then season with salt. Heat the olive oil in a skillet and cook the chicken until brown.

2 Transfer to a large casserole. Add the onions to the pan and cook quickly. Add the garlic and sliced chorizo, and cook for 2 minutes.

3 Add the tomatoes, two of the bay leaves, and the sherry, and bring to a boil. Pour over the chicken and cover with a lid. Bake for 45 minutes. Remove the lid and season to taste. Cook for about 20 minutes more, or until the chicken is golden and cooked through. Serve with rice or potatoes, garnished with the remaining bay leaves.

Varna-style Chicken

In this tasty dish from Bulgaria, the chicken is smothered in a rich tomato and mushroom sauce.

INGREDIENTS

Serves 8

1 chicken, about 4 pounds, cut into
    8 pieces

$1/2$ teaspoon chopped fresh thyme

3 tablespoons butter

3 tablespoons vegetable oil

3–4 garlic cloves, crushed

2 onions, finely chopped

salt and ground white pepper

basil and thyme leaves, to garnish

freshly cooked rice, to serve

For the sauce

$1/2$ cup dry sherry

3 tablespoons tomato paste

a few fresh basil leaves

about 2 tablespoons white wine vinegar

generous pinch of granulated sugar

1 teaspoon mild mustard

14-ounce can chopped tomatoes

3 cups mushrooms, sliced

3 Add the sherry, tomato paste, seasoning, basil, vinegar, sugar, mustard, and tomatoes to the skillet and bring to a boil.

VARIATION

You could replace the cultivated mushrooms with wild ones.

4 Reduce the heat and add the mushrooms. Adjust the seasoning with more sugar or vinegar to taste.

5 Pour the tomato sauce over the chicken. Bake in the oven, covered, for 45–60 minutes, or until cooked thoroughly. Serve on a bed of rice, garnished with basil and thyme.

1 Preheat the oven to 350°F. Season the chicken with salt, pepper, and thyme. In a large skillet brown the chicken in the butter and oil. Remove from the skillet, place in a large casserole, and keep hot.

2 Add the garlic and onion to the skillet and cook for about 2–3 minutes, or until just soft.

Chicken with Chipotle Sauce

It is important to cook out chipotle chiles for this recipe, as they impart a wonderfully rich and smoky flavor to the chicken portions. The paste can be made ahead of time, making this a very easy recipe for entertaining.

INGREDIENTS

Serves 6

6 chipotle chiles

scant 1 cup water

chicken stock (see method)

3 onions

6 skinless, boneless chicken
  breast portions

3 tablespoons vegetable oil

salt and ground black pepper

fresh oregano, to garnish

2 Preheat the oven to 350°F. Coarsely chop the flesh of the chiles and put it in a food processor or blender. Add enough chicken stock to the soaking water to make it up to 1²/₃ cups. Pour the mixture into the food processor or blender and process until completely smooth.

1 Put the smoked chiles in a bowl and pour in hot water to cover. Let stand for about 30 minutes, or until very soft. Drain, reserving the soaking water in a measuring cup. Cut off the stalk from each chile, then slit them lengthwise, and scrape out the seeds with a small sharp knife.

3 Peel the onions. Cut them in half, then slice them thinly. Separate the slices.

4 Trim off any fat or membrane from the chicken portions.

5 Heat the oil in a large skillet, add the onions, and cook over low to medium heat for about 5 minutes, or until they have softened but not colored, stirring occasionally.

6 Using a slotted spoon, transfer the onion slices to a casserole that is large enough to hold all the chicken in a single layer. Season the onion slices.

7 Arrange the chicken on top of the onion slices. Season with salt and black pepper.

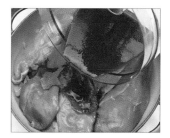

8 Pour the chipotle paste over the chicken, making sure that each piece is evenly coated.

9 Place the casserole in the preheated oven and bake for 45 minutes–1 hour, or until the chicken is cooked through, but is still moist and tender. Garnish with fresh oregano and serve.

COOK'S TIP

Chipotle chiles are dried and smoked chiles that are often used in Mexican cooking.

Guinea Fowl with Vegetable Stew

Mild, sweet leeks are excellent in this light stew of guinea fowl and spring vegetables. Chicken can be used instead of the guinea fowl.

INGREDIENTS

Serves 4

3 tablespoons olive oil

4 ounces pancetta, cut into lardons

2 tablespoons all-purpose flour

2 guinea fowl, about $2^1/2$–$3^1/2$ pounds
   each, cut into 4 portions each

1 onion, chopped

1 head of garlic, separated into cloves
   and peeled

1 bottle dry white wine

fresh thyme sprig

1 fresh bay leaf

a few parsley stalks

9 ounces baby carrots

9 ounces baby turnips

6 slender leeks, cut into 3-inch lengths

$1^3/4$ cups shelled fresh peas

1 tablespoon French herb mustard

$1/4$ cup fresh flat leaf
   parsley, chopped

1 tablespoon chopped fresh mint

salt and ground black pepper

1 Heat 2 tablespoons of the oil in a pan and cook the pancetta over medium heat until lightly browned, stirring occasionally. Remove from the pan and set aside.

2 Season the flour and toss the guinea fowl portions in it. Cook in the oil remaining in the pan until browned on all sides. Transfer to a flameproof casserole. Preheat the oven to 350°F.

3 Add the remaining oil to the pan and cook the onion gently until soft. Add the garlic and cook for 3–4 minutes, then stir in the pancetta and wine.

4 Tie the thyme, bay leaf, and parsley into a bundle and add to the pan. Bring to a boil, then simmer gently for 3–4 minutes. Pour the mixture over the guinea fowl and add seasoning. Cover and cook in the oven for 40 minutes.

5 Add the baby carrots and turnips to the casserole and cook, covered, for 30 minutes more, or until the vegetables are just tender.

6 Stir in the leeks and cook for 15–20 minutes more, or until all the vegetables and the guinea fowl are fully cooked.

7 Meanwhile, blanch the peas in boiling water for 2 minutes, then drain. Transfer the guinea fowl and vegetables to a warmed serving dish. Place the casserole over high heat and boil the juices vigorously, stirring, until they are reduced by about half.

8 Stir in the peas and cook gently for 2–3 minutes, then stir in the mustard, and adjust the seasoning. Stir in most of the parsley and the mint. Pour this sauce over the guinea fowl or return the pieces and vegetables to the casserole. Sprinkle the remaining parsley over the top and serve immediately.

Guinea Fowl with Cabbage

In this French recipe guinea fowl is cooked on a bed of cabbage, leeks, onions, and carrots, which give it a lovely flavor.

INGREDIENTS

Serves 4

1 guinea fowl, about 2$^1/_2$–3 pounds
1 tablespoon vegetable oil
1 tablespoon butter
1 large onion, halved and sliced
1 large carrot, halved and sliced
1 large leek, sliced
1 pound green cabbage, such as Savoy, sliced or chopped
$^1/_2$ cup dry white wine
$^1/_2$ cup chicken stock
1 or 2 garlic cloves, finely chopped
salt and ground black pepper

1 Preheat the oven to 350°F. Tie the legs of the guinea fowl with string.

2 Heat half the oil in a large, flameproof casserole over medium-high heat and cook the guinea fowl until golden brown on all sides. Transfer to a plate.

3 Pour out the fat from the casserole and add the remaining oil with the butter. Add the onion, carrot, and leek and cook over low heat, stirring, for 5 minutes. Add the cabbage and cook for about 3–4 minutes, or until slightly wilted, stirring occasionally. Season to taste.

4 Place the guinea fowl on its side on the vegetables. Add the wine and bring to a boil, then add the stock and garlic. Cover and transfer to the oven. Cook for 25 minutes, then turn the bird onto the other side, and cook for 20–25 minutes, or until it is tender and the juices run clear when the thickest part of the thigh is pierced.

5 Transfer the bird to a board and let stand for 5–10 minutes, then cut into four or eight pieces. With a slotted spoon, transfer the vegetables to a warmed serving dish and place the guinea fowl on top. Skim any fat from the cooking juices and serve separately.

Italian Chicken

Sun-dried tomatoes and pesto are a winning combination in this dish.

INGREDIENTS

Serves 4

2 tablespoons all-purpose flour

4 skinless chicken portions (legs, breast portions, or quarters)

2 tablespoons olive oil

1 onion, chopped

2 garlic cloves, chopped

1 red bell pepper, seeded and chopped

14-ounce can chopped tomatoes

2 tablespoons red pesto sauce

4 sun-dried tomatoes in oil, chopped

$2/3$ cup chicken stock

1 teaspoon dried oregano

8 black olives, pitted

salt and ground black pepper

chopped fresh basil and a few basil leaves, to garnish

tagliatelle, to serve

1 Place the flour and seasoning in a plastic bag. Add the chicken pieces and shake until coated. Heat the oil in a flameproof casserole, add the chicken, and brown quickly. Remove with a spoon and set aside.

2 Lower the heat, add the onion, garlic, and red bell pepper, and cook for 5 minutes.

3 Stir in all the ingredients, but not the olives. Bring to a boil.

4 Return the sautéed chicken portions to the casserole. Season lightly, cover, and simmer for 30–35 minutes, or until the chicken is cooked.

5 Add the olives and simmer for 5 minutes more. Transfer to a warmed serving dish, sprinkle with the chopped fresh basil, and garnish with a few basil leaves. Serve with tagliatelle.

Honey and Orange Glazed Chicken

This way of cooking chicken portions is not only popular in the United States, but also in Australia and Great Britain. It is ideal for an easy evening meal served with baked potatoes and salad.

INGREDIENTS

Serves 4

4 boneless chicken breast portions, 6 ounces each

1 tablespoon oil

4 scallions, chopped

1 garlic clove, crushed

3 tablespoons honey

4 tablespoons fresh orange juice

1 orange, peeled and segmented

2 tablespoons soy sauce

fresh lemon balm or flat leaf parsley, to garnish

baked potatoes and mixed salad, to serve

1 Preheat the oven to 375°F. Place the chicken in a shallow roasting pan. Set aside.

2 Heat the oil in a small pan, and cook the scallions and garlic for 2 minutes, or until softened. Add the honey, orange juice, orange segments, and soy sauce to the pan, stirring well until the honey has completely melted.

3 Pour the mixture over the chicken and bake, uncovered, for about 45 minutes, basting with the honey glaze once or twice, until the chicken is cooked. Garnish with the lemon balm or parsley and serve the chicken and its sauce with baked potatoes and a salad.

Chicken with Beans

This substantial casserole is rich with the flavors of wine, herbs, and sour cream.

INGREDIENTS

Serves 4–6

10 ounces dried kidney or other beans,
    soaked overnight
8–12 chicken portions, such as thighs
    and drumsticks
12 bacon strips
2 large onions, thinly sliced
1 cup dry white wine
$1/2$ teaspoon chopped fresh sage
    or oregano
$1/2$ teaspoon chopped fresh rosemary
generous pinch of freshly grated nutmeg
$2/3$ cup sour cream
1 tablespoon chili powder or paprika
salt and ground black pepper
sprigs of rosemary and lemon wedges,
    to garnish

1 Preheat the oven to 350°F. Cook the beans in fast-boiling water for 20 minutes. Rinse and drain the beans well and trim the chicken portions. Season the chicken with salt and pepper.

2 Arrange the bacon around the sides and base of an ovenproof dish. Sprinkle in half of the onion and then half the beans, followed by another layer of onion, and then the remaining beans.

3 In a bowl combine the wine with the sage or oregano, rosemary, and nutmeg. Pour over the onion and beans. In another bowl mix together the sour cream and the chili powder or paprika.

4 Toss the chicken in the cream mixture and place on top of the beans. Cover with foil and bake for $1^1/4$–$1^1/2$ hours, until done, removing the foil for the last 15 minutes. Garnish with rosemary and lemon.

Potted Chicken

This is a traditional Bulgarian way of cooking chicken—in a flameproof pot, on top of the stove—so that it cooks slowly and evenly in its own juices.

INGREDIENTS

Serves 6–8

8 chicken pieces
6–8 firm ripe tomatoes, chopped
2 garlic cloves, crushed
3 onions, chopped
4 tablespoons oil or melted white
    cooking fat
1 cup good chicken stock
2 bay leaves
2 teaspoons paprika
10 white peppercorns, bruised
handful of parsley, stalks reserved and
    leaves finely chopped
salt

1 Put the chicken, tomatoes, and garlic in a flameproof casserole. Cover and cook gently for 10–15 minutes.

VARIATION

For spicy chicken, add a seeded and chopped chile at Step 2.

2 Add the onions, oil or white fat, stock, bay leaves, paprika, peppercorns, and salt, and stir well.

3 Cover tightly and cook over very low heat, stirring occasionally, for about $1^3/4$–2 hours, or until the chicken is cooked through. Five minutes before the end of cooking, stir in the finely chopped parsley leaves. Serve hot.

Chicken Brunswick Stew

This chicken stew has a spicy bite.
It is warming and filling.

INGREDIENTS

Serves 6

1 chicken, about 4 pounds, cut
    into portions
paprika
2 tablespoons olive oil
2 tablespoons butter
1 pound chopped onions
8 ounces chopped green or yellow
    bell peppers
2 cups chopped peeled fresh or canned
    plum tomatoes
1 cup white wine
2 cups chicken stock
    or water
1/4 cup chopped fresh parsley
1/2 teaspoon hot
    pepper sauce
1 tablespoon Worcestershire sauce
2 cups corn kernels, fresh, frozen,
    or canned
1 cup wax beans, fresh or frozen
3 tablespoons all-purpose flour
salt and ground black pepper
bread rolls, rice, or potatoes, to
    serve (optional)

1 Pat the chicken pieces dry, then
sprinkle them lightly with salt
and paprika.

2 In a large, heavy pan, heat the
olive oil with the butter over
medium-high heat. Heat until the
mixture is sizzling and just starting
to change color.

3 Add the chicken pieces and
cook until golden brown on all
sides. Remove the chicken pieces
with tongs and set aside.

4 Reduce the heat to low and add
the chopped onions and bell
peppers to the pan. Cook for
8–10 minutes, or until softened.

5 Raise the heat. Add the tomatoes
and their juice, the wine, stock
or water, parsley, and hot pepper
and Worcestershire sauces. Stir and
bring to a boil.

6 Return the chicken pieces to the
pan, pushing them down in the
sauce. Cover, reduce the heat, and
simmer gently for 30 minutes,
stirring occasionally.

7 Add the corn and wax beans
and mix well. Partly cover and
cook for 30 minutes more.

8 Tilt the pan and skim off as
much of the surface fat as
possible. In a small bowl, mix the
flour with a little water to make
a smooth paste.

9 Gradually stir in about 3/4 cup
of the hot sauce from the pan.
Stir the flour mixture into the stew,
and mix well to distribute it evenly
and to thicken it. Cook for about
5–8 minutes more, stirring from
time to time.

10 Check the seasoning. Serve
the stew in shallow soup
plates or large bowls, with bread
rolls, rice, or potatoes, if you like.

Chicken with Sage, Prunes and Brandy

This stir-fry has a very rich sauce based on a good brandy—use the best you can afford.

INGREDIENTS

Serves 4

1/2 cup prunes, pitted
3 1/2 pounds skinless, boneless chicken
    breast portions
1 1/4 cups Cognac or brandy
1 tablespoon fresh sage, chopped
5 ounces smoked bacon, in one piece
24 pearl onions, peeled and quartered
salt and ground black pepper
fresh sage sprigs, to garnish

1 Cut the prunes into slivers. Cut the chicken breast portions into thin pieces.

2 Combine the prunes, chicken, Cognac or brandy, and chopped sage in a nonmetallic dish. Cover and leave overnight in the refrigerator to marinate.

3 Next day, strain the chicken and prunes, reserving the Cognac marinade mixture, and pat dry on paper towels.

4 Cut the smoked bacon into dice and set aside.

5 Heat a wok and add half the butter. When melted, add the onions and stir-fry for 4 minutes until crisp and golden. Set aside.

6 Add the bacon to the wok and stir-fry for 1 minute until it begins to release some fat. Add the remaining butter and stir-fry the chicken and prunes for 3–4 minutes, or until crisp and golden. Push the chicken mixture to one side in the wok, add the Cognac, and simmer until thickened. Stir the chicken into the sauce, season well with salt and pepper, and serve garnished with sage.

Chicken Chasseur

3 Pour off all but 1 tablespoon of fat from the pan. Add the onions or shallots, mushrooms, and garlic. Cook until golden, stirring frequently.

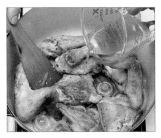

4 If using fresh tomatoes, plunge them into boiling water for 30 seconds, then refresh in cold water. Peel off the skins, remove the seeds, and chop the flesh. Return the chicken to the casserole with any juices. Add the wine and bring to a boil, then stir in the chicken stock and tomatoes.

5 Bring back to a boil, reduce the heat, cover, and simmer over low heat for about 20 minutes, or until the chicken is tender and the juices run clear when the thickest part of the meat is pierced. Tilt the pan and skim off any fat that has risen to the surface. Adjust the seasoning before serving.

A chicken sauté is one of the classics of French cooking. Quick to prepare, it lends itself to endless variation.

INGREDIENTS

Serves 4

^{1}/3 cup all-purpose flour
2^1/2 pounds chicken pieces
1 tablespoon olive oil
3 small onions or large
    shallots, sliced
2^1/2 cups mushrooms, quartered
1 garlic clove, crushed
4 tablespoons dry white wine
^{1}/2 cup chicken stock
12 ounces tomatoes or 1 cup canned
    chopped tomatoes
salt and ground black pepper
fresh parsley, to garnish

1 Put the flour into a plastic bag and season. Drop each chicken piece into the bag and shake to coat with flour. Tap off the excess.

2 Heat the oil in a flameproof casserole. Cook the chicken over medium-high heat until golden brown, turning once. Transfer to a plate and keep warm.

Chicken with Bell Peppers

This colorful dish comes from the south of Italy, where sweet bell peppers are plentiful.

INGREDIENTS

Serves 4

1 chicken, about 3 pounds,
    cut into portions
3 large bell peppers, red, yellow, or green
6 tablespoons olive oil
2 medium red onions, thinly sliced
2 garlic cloves, finely chopped
small piece of dried chile,
    crumbled (optional)
$^1/_2$ cup white wine
salt and ground black pepper
2 tomatoes, fresh or canned, peeled
    and chopped
3 tablespoons chopped fresh parsley

1 Trim any fat and skin from the chicken. Cut the bell peppers in half, discard the seeds and the stem. Slice into strips.

2 Heat half the oil in a large, heavy pan or flameproof casserole. Add the onions, and cook over low heat until soft. Remove to a side dish. Add the remaining oil to the pan, raise the heat to medium, add the chicken, and brown on all sides, about 6–8 minutes. Return the onions to the pan, and add the garlic and dried chile, if using.

3 Pour in the wine and cook until it has reduced by half. Add the bell peppers and stir well to coat them with the fats. Season. After 3–4 minutes, stir in the tomatoes. Lower the heat, cover the pan, and cook for 25–30 minutes, or until the bell peppers are soft and the chicken is cooked. Stir occasionally. Stir in the chopped parsley and serve.

Chicken Cooked in Butter

This simple and very delicious way of cooking chicken brings out all of its delicacy.

INGREDIENTS

Serves 4

4 small, skinless, boneless chicken
    breast portions
flour seasoned with salt and freshly
    ground black pepper
6 tablespoons butter
1 fresh parsley sprig, to garnish

1 Separate each chicken portion into two fillets. Lightly pound the larger fillets between two sheets of plastic wrap to flatten them. Dredge the chicken in the seasoned flour, shaking off any excess.

2 Heat the butter in a large, heavy skillet until it bubbles. Place all the chicken fillets in the pan, in one layer if possible. Cook over medium to high heat for 3–4 minutes, or until they are golden brown.

3 Turn the chicken over. Reduce the heat to medium-low, and continue cooking for 9–12 minutes, or until the fillets are cooked through but still springy to the touch. If the chicken begins to brown too much, cover the skillet for the final minutes of cooking. Serve immediately garnished with a little parsley.

Chicken in Creamed Horseradish

2 Wipe out the casserole, melt the butter, stir in the flour, and gradually blend in the stock. Bring to a boil, stirring constantly.

3 Add the horseradish sauce and season with salt and freshly ground black pepper. Return the chicken to the casserole, cover, and simmer for 30–40 minutes, or until the chicken is cooked through.

The piquancy of horseradish gives this dish a sophisticated taste. Replace with half the quantity of fresh horseradish, if you like.

INGREDIENTS

Serves 4

2 tablespoons olive oil

4 chicken portions

2 tablespoons butter

2 tablespoons all-purpose flour

scant 2 cups chicken stock

2 tablespoons creamed
   horseradish sauce

salt and ground black pepper

1 tablespoon chopped fresh parsley

mashed potatoes and green beans,
   to serve (optional)

1 Heat the oil in a large, flameproof casserole and gently brown the chicken portions on both sides over medium heat. Remove the chicken from the casserole and keep warm.

4 Transfer to a serving dish and sprinkle with fresh parsley. Serve with mashed potatoes and green beans, if you like.

Chicken in Green Sauce

Slow, gentle cooking makes the chicken succulent and tender.

INGREDIENTS

Serves 4

2 tablespoons butter

1 tablespoon olive oil

4 chicken portions

1 small onion, finely chopped

$^2/_3$ cup medium dry white wine

$^2/_3$ cup chicken stock

6 ounces watercress or arugula

2 fresh thyme sprigs

2 fresh tarragon sprigs

$^2/_3$ cup heavy cream

salt and ground black pepper

watercress leaves or arugula,
    to garnish

1 Heat the butter and olive oil in a heavy, shallow pan, then brown the chicken evenly. Transfer the chicken to a plate using a slotted spoon and keep warm in the oven.

2 Add the onion to the cooking juices in the pan and cook until softened but not colored.

3 Stir in the wine, boil for 2–3 minutes, then add the stock, and bring to a boil. Return the chicken to the pan, cover tightly, and cook very gently for about 30 minutes, or until the chicken juices run clear. Then transfer the chicken to a warm dish, cover the dish, and keep warm.

4 Boil the cooking juices hard until reduced to about 4 tablespoons. Remove the leaves from the watercress and herbs, tearing the arugula into small pieces, if using. Add the leaves to the pan with the cream and simmer over medium heat until the sauce has thickened slightly.

5 Return the cooked chicken to the pan, season, and heat through for a few minutes. Garnish with watercress leaves or arugula.

Chicken with Tomatoes and Shrimps

This tasty and unusual Piedmontese dish was created especially for Napoleon. Versions of it appear in both Italian and French recipe books.

INGREDIENTS

Serves 4

$^1/_2$ cup olive oil

8 skinless chicken thighs

1 onion, finely chopped

1 celery stalk, finely chopped

1 garlic clove, crushed

12 ounces ripe Italian plum tomatoes, peeled and coarsely chopped

1 cup dry white wine

$^1/_2$ teaspoon chopped fresh rosemary

1 tablespoon butter

8 small triangles thinly sliced white bread, without crusts

6 ounces large raw shrimp, peeled

salt and ground black pepper

finely chopped flat leaf parsley, to garnish

1 Heat 2 tablespoons of the oil in a skillet. Add the chicken and sauté over medium heat for about 5 minutes, or until it has changed color on all sides. Transfer to a flameproof casserole.

2 Add the onion and celery to the skillet and cook, stirring frequently, for about 3 minutes, or until softened. Add the garlic, tomatoes, wine, rosemary, and seasoning. Bring to a boil, stirring.

3 Pour the tomato sauce over the chicken. Cover and cook gently for 40 minutes, or until the chicken juices run clear when pierced.

4 About 10 minutes before serving, add the remaining oil and the butter to the skillet and heat until hot but not smoking. Add the triangles of bread and cook until crisp and golden on each side. Drain.

5 Add the shrimp to the casserole and heat until they are cooked. Taste the sauce for seasoning. Dip one of the tips of each fried bread triangle in parsley. Serve the dish hot, garnished with the crisp, fried bread triangles.

Chicken Pot au Feu

In France, a pot au feu traditionally contains beef simmered in a rich stock, although chicken is also used. In this recipe, a lovely wine and herb-scented stock contains tender morsels of chicken and spring vegetables.

INGREDIENTS

Serves 4

1 chicken, about 5 pounds

1 fresh parsley sprig

1 tablespoon black peppercorns

1 bay leaf

11 ounces baby carrots

6 ounces baby leeks

2 tablespoons butter

1 tablespoon olive oil

11 ounces shallots, halved if large

scant 1 cup dry white wine

$1^3/_4$ pounds baby new potatoes

$^1/_2$ cup heavy cream

salt and ground black pepper

small bunch of fresh parsley or tarragon, chopped, to garnish

1 Cut the chicken into eight pieces and place the carcass in a large stockpot. Add the parsley sprig, peppercorns, bay leaf, and the offcuts from the carrots and leeks. Cover with cold water and bring to a boil. Simmer for 45 minutes, then strain.

2 Meanwhile, melt the butter with the olive oil in a skillet, then add the chicken pieces, season with salt and pepper, and brown them all over. Lift out the chicken pieces onto a plate and add the shallots to the skillet. Cook over low heat for 20 minutes, stirring occasionally, until softened, but not browned.

COOK'S TIPS

• Any leftover stock can be kept in the refrigerator and used in other recipes.

• You could use large potatoes, but they will need to be par-boiled first so that they will cook in 10–15 minutes in the pot with the other ingredients.

3 Return the chicken to the skillet and add the wine. Scrape up any residue from the base of the skillet with a wooden spoon, then add the carrots, leeks, and potatoes with enough of the stock just to cover. Bring to a boil, then cover, and simmer for 20 minutes, or until the chicken is cooked through. Stir in the cream and serve, garnished with the chopped parsley or tarragon.

Chicken with Chianti

The robust, full-bodied red wine and red pesto give this sauce a rich color and almost spicy flavor, while the grapes add sweetness. Serve this Italian stew with broiled polenta or warm crusty bread, and accompany with a piquant salad, such as arugula or watercress, tossed with a tasty dressing.

INGREDIENTS

Serves 4

3 tablespoons olive oil

4 skinless, part-boned chicken
  breast portions

1 medium red onion

2 tablespoons red pesto

1¹/4 cups Chianti

1¹/4 cups water

4 ounces red grapes, halved lengthwise and
  seeded if necessary

salt and ground black pepper

fresh basil leaves, to garnish

arugula salad, to serve

1 Heat 2 tablespoons of the oil in a large skillet. Add the chicken portions and cook over medium heat for about 5 minutes, or until they have changed color on all sides. Remove with a slotted spoon and drain on paper towels.

2 Cut the onion in half, through the root. Trim off the root, then slice the onion halves lengthwise to create thin wedges.

3 Heat the remaining oil in the pan, add the onion wedges, and red pesto, and cook gently, stirring constantly, for about 3 minutes, or until the onion is softened, but not browned.

4 Add the Chianti and water to the skillet and bring to a boil, stirring, then return the chicken to the pan, and add salt and pepper to taste.

5 Reduce the heat, then cover the skillet, and simmer for about 20 minutes, or until the chicken is tender and cooked through, stirring occasionally.

COOK'S TIP
~
Use part-boned chicken breast portions, if you can get them, in preference to boneless chicken for this dish as they have a better flavor. Chicken thighs could also be cooked in this way.

6 Add the grapes to the skillet and cook over low to medium heat until heated through, then taste the sauce for seasoning. Serve the chicken hot, garnished with basil, and accompanied by the arugula salad.

VARIATIONS
~
Use green pesto instead of red, and substitute a dry white wine such as Pinot Grigio for the Chianti, then finish with seedless green grapes. A few spoonfuls of mascarpone cheese can be added at the end if you like, to enrich the sauce.

Chicken with Mushrooms

3 Add the mushrooms and cook them for 5 minutes. Remove and keep warm.

4 Increase the heat. Add the remaining oil and cook the chicken very quickly, in small batches, for 3–4 minutes, or until lightly colored. Season each batch with salt and pepper. Remove and keep warm on a plate while cooking the rest of the chicken.

Strips of succulent chicken are served in a cream, mushroom, and sherry sauce. Tagliatelle makes an ideal accompaniment.

INGREDIENTS

Serves 4

4 large, skinless, boneless chicken
   breast portions
3 tablespoons olive oil
1 onion, thinly sliced
1 garlic clove, crushed
3 cups white mushrooms, quartered
2 tablespoons sherry
1 tablespoon lemon juice
$^2/_3$ cup light cream
salt and ground black pepper

1 Divide each chicken portion into two natural fillets. Place each between two sheets of plastic wrap and flatten to a thickness of $^1/_4$ inch with the side of a rolling pin. Cut the chicken into 1-inch diagonal strips.

2 Heat 2 tablespoons of the oil in a large skillet and cook the onion and crushed garlic over low heat until tender.

5 Add the sherry and lemon juice to the pan and quickly return the chicken, onions, garlic, and mushrooms, stirring to coat.

6 Stir in the cream and bring to a boil. Adjust the seasoning to taste. Serve immediately.

VARIATIONS

White wine or brandy may be used to deglaze the pan in place of sherry.

Chicken Fricassée Forestier

The term fricassée is used to describe a light stew, which is first sautéed in butter. The accompanying sauce can vary, but here wild mushrooms and bacon provide a rich flavor.

INGREDIENTS

Serves 4

3 skinless, boneless chicken breast
    portions, sliced

$1/4$ cup sweet butter

1 tablespoon vegetable oil

4 ounces unsmoked fatty bacon, cut
    into pieces

5 tablespoons dry sherry or white wine

1 medium onion, chopped

12 ounces assorted wild mushrooms,
    trimmed and sliced

$1/3$ cup all-purpose flour

$2^{1}/4$ cups chicken stock

2 teaspoons lemon juice

4 tablespoons chopped fresh parsley

salt and ground black pepper

boiled rice, carrots, and baby corn, to serve

3 Cook the onion in the remaining butter until golden brown. Add the mushrooms and cook, stirring frequently, for 6–8 minutes, or until their juices begin to run. Stir in the flour, then remove from the heat. Gradually stir in the chicken stock until the flour is completely blended in.

4 Add the reserved chicken and bacon with the sherry juices, return to the heat, and stir to thicken. Simmer for 10–15 minutes and then add the lemon juice, parsley, and seasoning. Serve with plain boiled rice, carrots, and baby corn.

1 Season the chicken with pepper. Heat half of the butter and the oil in a large, heavy skillet or flameproof casserole and brown the chicken and bacon pieces. Transfer to a shallow dish and pour off any excess fat.

2 Return the skillet to the heat and brown the sediment. Pour in the sherry or wine and stir with a flat wooden spoon to deglaze the pan. Pour the sherry liquid over the chicken and wipe the skillet clean.

Tuscan Chicken

This simple chicken casserole has all the flavors of traditional Tuscan ingredients: sweet red bell peppers, tomatoes, and aromatic oregano.

Serves 4

8 skinless chicken thighs
1 teaspoon olive oil
1 medium onion, thinly sliced
2 red bell peppers, seeded
    and sliced
1 garlic clove, crushed
1¼ cups bottled strained tomatoes
⅔ cup dry white wine
large sprig fresh oregano, or
    1 teaspoon dried
14-ounce can cannellini beans, drained
3 tablespoons fresh bread crumbs
salt and ground black pepper

1 Cook the chicken in the oil in a heavy pan until golden brown. Remove and keep hot. Add the onion and bell peppers to the pan and cook until softened, but not brown. Stir in the crushed garlic.

2 Add the chicken, strained tomatoes, wine, and oregano. Season, bring to a boil, then cover.

3 Lower the heat and simmer gently, stirring occasionally, for 30–35 minutes, or until the chicken is tender and the juices run clear, when pierced with the point of a knife.

4 Stir in the cannellini beans and simmer for 5 minutes more, or until heated through. Sprinkle with the bread crumbs and cook under a preheated broiler until the topping is golden brown.

VARIATION

The wine can be replaced by chicken stock, if you like.

Chicken in Creamy Orange Sauce

This sauce is deceptively creamy—in fact it is made with low-fat farmer's cheese. The brandy adds a richer flavor, but is optional—omit it if you prefer and use orange juice alone.

INGREDIENTS

Serves 4

8 skinless chicken thighs or drumsticks

3 tablespoons brandy (optional)

1¹/₄ cups orange juice

3 scallions, chopped

2 teaspoons cornstarch

6 tablespoons low-fat farmer's cheese or
    plain yogurt

salt and ground black pepper

rice or pasta and salad greens,
    to serve

1 Cook the chicken pieces without adding any fat in a nonstick or heavy pan, turning until evenly browned.

COOK'S TIP

Cornstarch helps to stabilize the cheese or yogurt and stop it from curdling.

2 Stir in the brandy, if using, orange juice, and scallions. Bring to a boil, then cover, and simmer for 15 minutes, or until the chicken is tender and the juices run clear when pierced.

3 Blend the cornstarch with a little water, then mix into the farmer's cheese or plain yogurt. Stir this into the sauce and stir over medium heat until boiling.

4 Adjust the seasoning and serve with boiled rice or pasta and salad greens.

Chicken Liver Stir-fry

The final sprinkling of lemon, parsley, and garlic gives this dish a delightfully fresh flavor and a wonderful aroma.

INGREDIENTS

Serves 4

1¼ pounds chicken livers

6 tablespoons butter

2½ cups portabello mushrooms

1 cup chanterelle mushrooms

3 garlic cloves, finely chopped

2 shallots, finely chopped

⅔ cup medium sherry

3 fresh rosemary sprigs

grated rind of 1 lemon

2 tablespoons chopped fresh parsley

salt and ground black pepper

fresh rosemary sprigs, to garnish

4 thick slices of white toast,
   to serve

1 Clean and trim the chicken livers to remove any gristle or discolored parts.

2 Season the chicken livers generously with salt and ground black pepper, tossing well to coat them all thoroughly.

3 Heat a wok or large skillet and add 1 tablespoon of the butter. When it has melted, add the livers in batches (melting more butter when necessary but reserving 2 tablespoons for the vegetables) and flash-fry until golden brown on the outside. Drain using a slotted spoon and transfer to a plate, then place in a low oven to keep warm.

4 Cut the portabello mushrooms into thick slices. If large, cut the chanterelles in half.

5 Heat the wok and add the remaining butter. Stir in two-thirds of the chopped garlic and the shallots, and stir-fry for 1 minute, until golden brown. Stir in the mushrooms and continue to cook for 2 minutes more.

6 Add the sherry, bring to a boil, and simmer for 2–3 minutes, or until syrupy. Add the rosemary, seasoning, and livers to the wok or skillet. Stir-fry for 1 minute. Garnish with the rosemary, and sprinkle with a mixture of lemon, parsley and the remaining chopped garlic. Serve with slices of toast.

Chicken Braised in Red Wine

Red wine is a classic partner for chicken in French cooking. It gives the dish a lovely robust sauce. For a lighter sauce, you can use white wine instead of red, as in Alsace, where the local Riesling is often cooked with chicken.

INGREDIENTS

Serves 4

1 chicken, about 3½– 4 pounds, cut
   in pieces

1¹/₂ tablespoons olive oil

8 ounces pearl onions

1 tablespoon butter

8 ounces mushrooms, quartered if large

2 tablespoons all-purpose flour

3 cups dry red wine

1 cup chicken stock, or more
   to cover

bouquet garni

salt and ground black pepper

3 Melt the butter in the skillet over medium heat and cook the mushrooms, stirring, until golden brown.

4 Sprinkle the onions with the flour and cook for 2 minutes, stirring frequently. Add the wine, and boil for 1 minute, stirring. Add the chicken, mushrooms, stock, and bouquet garni. Bring to a boil, reduce the heat to very low, and simmer, covered, for about 45–50 minutes, or until the chicken is tender and the juices run clear when the thickest part of the meat is pierced with a knife.

5 Transfer the chicken pieces and vegetables to a plate. Strain the cooking liquid, skim off the fat, and return the liquid to the pan. Boil to reduce by one-third, then return the chicken and vegetables to the casserole, and simmer for 3–4 minutes to heat through.

1 Pat the chicken pieces dry and season with salt and pepper. Put the chicken in a large, heavy skillet, skin side down, and cook over medium-high heat for 10–12 minutes, or until golden brown. Transfer to a plate.

2 Meanwhile, heat the oil in a large, flameproof casserole over medium-low heat, add the onions, and cook, covered, until evenly browned, stirring frequently.

Chicken with Shrimp

This unusual combination of ingredients has its origins in a fish recipe. It is traditionally made with crayfish, although shrimp or chicken can work equally well and are often easier to obtain.

INGREDIENTS

Serves 4

1 chicken, about 3 pounds, cut into
    8 pieces
2 teaspoons vegetable oil
12 large raw shrimp, with heads if possible,
    or live crayfish
1 small onion, halved and sliced
2 tablespoons all-purpose flour
³/4 cup dry white wine
2 tablespoons brandy
1¹/4 cups chicken stock
3 medium tomatoes, cored and quartered
1 or 2 garlic cloves, finely chopped
bouquet garni
6 tablespoons whipping cream
salt and ground black pepper
fresh parsley, to garnish

1 Wash the chicken pieces, then pat dry with kitchen paper, and season with salt and pepper.

2 Heat the oil in a large, flameproof casserole and cook the shrimp or crayfish over high heat until they turn a bright color. Remove the shrimp or crayfish, cool slightly, and then peel off the heads and shells, and reserve. Chill the peeled tails.

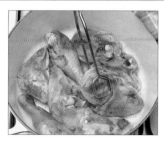

3 Add the chicken to the casserole, skin side down, and cook over medium-high heat for 10–12 minutes, or until golden brown all over, cooking in batches if necessary. Transfer the chicken to a plate and pour off all but 1 tablespoon of the fat.

4 In the same casserole, cook the onion over medium-high heat until golden, stirring frequently. Sprinkle with flour and continue cooking for 2 minutes, stirring frequently, then gradually add the wine and brandy, and bring to a boil, stirring constantly.

COOK'S TIP

To prepare ahead, cook as directed up to step 6. Cool and chill the chicken and sauce. To serve, reheat over medium-low heat for about 30 minutes. Add the shrimp or crayfish tails and heat through.

5 Add the stock, shrimp or crayfish heads and shells, tomatoes, garlic, and bouquet garni with the chicken pieces and any juices. Bring to a boil, then reduce the heat to very low. Cover the casserole and simmer for 20–25 minutes, or until the chicken is tender and the juices run clear when the thickest part of the meat is pierced with a knife.

6 Remove the chicken from the casserole and strain the cooking liquid, pressing down on the shells and vegetables to extract as much liquid as possible. Skim off the fat and return the liquid to the pan. Add the cream and boil until it is reduced by one-third and slightly thickened.

7 Return the chicken pieces to the pan and simmer for 5 minutes. Just before serving, add the shrimp or crayfish tails and heat through. Arrange on warmed plates, pour some of the sauce on top, and garnish with fresh parsley.

Burgundy Chicken

Chicken cooked in a rich wine sauce is a dinner-party classic. It is perfect accompanied by a bottle of good red wine.

INGREDIENTS

Serves 4

4 tablespoons all-purpose flour

3-pound chicken, cut into 8 portions

1 tablespoon olive oil

5 tablespoons butter

20 pearl onions

3-ounce piece of fatty bacon without rind, diced

about 20 white mushrooms

3 cups red Burgundy wine

bouquet garni

3 garlic cloves

1 teaspoon soft light brown sugar

salt and ground black pepper

1 tablespoon chopped fresh parsley and croutons, to garnish

1 Place 3 tablespoons of the flour and the seasoning in a large plastic bag and shake each chicken piece in it until lightly coated.

2 Heat the olive oil and ¼ cup of the butter in a large flameproof casserole. Add the pearl onions and bacon and cook gently for 3–4 minutes, or until the onions have browned lightly. Add the mushrooms and cook for about 2 minutes. Remove the bacon and vegetables with a slotted spoon, place in a bowl, and reserve.

3 Add the chicken pieces to the hot oil and cook until browned on all sides, about 5–6 minutes. Pour in the Burgundy wine and add the bouquet garni, garlic, soft light brown sugar, and seasoning.

4 Bring to a boil, cover, and simmer gently for 1 hour, stirring occasionally.

5 Return the reserved onions, bacon, and mushrooms to the casserole, cover, and cook for 30 minutes more until the chicken is cooked through.

6 Lift out the cooked chicken, vegetables, and bacon with a slotted spoon and arrange on a warmed dish. Remove the bouquet garni and boil the liquid rapidly for 2 minutes to reduce slightly. Cream the remaining butter and flour together and whisk in teaspoonfuls of the mixture until thickened slightly. Pour the sauce over the chicken and garnish with parsley and croutons.

Chicken Stew

This hearty Romanian stew traditionally uses a great variety of colorful seasonal vegetables and homegrown herbs, such as rosemary, marjoram, and thyme.

INGREDIENTS

Serves 6

4 tablespoons vegetable oil, or melted
    white cooking fat

1 mild onion, thinly sliced

2 garlic cloves, crushed

2 red bell peppers, seeded and sliced

1 chicken, about 3^1/$_2$ pounds

6 tablespoons tomato paste

3 potatoes, diced

1 teaspoon chopped fresh rosemary

1 teaspoon chopped fresh marjoram

1 teaspoon chopped fresh thyme

3 carrots, cut into chunks

^{1}/$_2$ small celery root, cut into chunks

^{1}/$_2$ cup dry white wine

2 zucchini, sliced

salt and ground black pepper

chopped fresh rosemary and marjoram,
    to garnish

dark rye bread, to serve

1 Heat the oil or white cooking fat in a large, flameproof casserole. Add the onion and garlic and cook for 1–2 minutes, or until soft; then add the red bell peppers.

2 Cut the chicken into six pieces, place in the casserole, and brown gently on all sides.

3 After about 15 minutes, add the tomato paste, potatoes, rosemary, marjoram, thyme, carrots, celery root, and white wine. Season to taste with salt and pepper. Cover and cook over low heat for 40–50 minutes, until the chicken is cooked through.

4 Add the zucchini 5 minutes before the end of cooking. Season. Garnish with the herbs and serve with dark rye bread.

COOK'S TIP

You could replace the fresh herbs with ^{1}/$_2$ teaspoon dried herbs.

Turkey Mole

In Mexico a mole is a rich stew, traditionally served on a festive occasion. The word comes from the Aztec "molli", a chili-flavored sauce. There are many different types— toasted nuts, fruit, and chocolate are among the classic ingredients.

INGREDIENTS

Serves 4

1 ancho chile, seeded
1 guajillo chile, seeded
$^3/_4$ cup sesame seeds
$^1/_2$ cup whole blanched almonds
$^1/_2$ cup shelled unsalted
   peanuts, skinned
$^1/_4$ cup white cooking fat or 4 tablespoons
   vegetable oil
1 small onion, finely chopped
2 garlic cloves, chopped
2 ounces canned tomatoes in
   tomato juice
1 ripe plantain
$^1/_3$ cup raisins
$^1/_3$ cup ready-to-eat pitted prunes
1 teaspoon dried oregano
$^1/_2$ teaspoon ground cloves
$^1/_2$ teaspoon crushed allspice berries
1 teaspoon ground cinnamon
$^1/_4$ cup unsweetened cocoa powder
4 turkey breast steaks
fresh oregano, to garnish (optional)
rice and warm tortillas, to serve

1 Soak both types of dried chile in hot water for 30 minutes, then lift them out, and chop them coarsely. Reserve 1 cup of the soaking liquid.

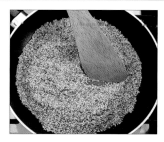

2 Spread out the sesame seeds in a heavy skillet. Toast them over medium heat, shaking the skillet lightly so that they turn golden all over. Do not let them burn, or the sauce will taste bitter. Set aside 3 tablespoons of the toasted seeds for the garnish and tip the rest into a bowl. Toast the almonds and peanuts in the same way and add them to the bowl.

3 Heat half the fat or oil in a skillet, cook the chopped onion and garlic for 2–3 minutes, then add the chiles and tomatoes. Cook gently for 10 minutes.

4 Peel the plantain and slice it into short diagonal slices. Add it to the onion mixture with the raisins, prunes, dried oregano, spices, and cocoa. Stir in the reserved soaking water. Bring to a boil, stirring, then add the toasted sesame seeds, almonds, and peanuts. Cook for 10 minutes, stirring, remove from the heat, and let cool.

5 Process the sauce, in batches, in a food processor or blender until smooth. The sauce should be fairly thick, but a little water may be added if necessary.

6 Heat the remaining fat or oil in a flameproof casserole. Add the turkey steaks and brown over medium heat.

7 Pour the sauce over the steaks and cover the casserole with foil and a tight-fitting lid. Cook over low heat for 20–25 minutes, or until the turkey is cooked. Sprinkle with sesame seeds and chopped oregano, and serve with a rice dish and warm tortillas.

Chicken and Egg One-pot Meal

This Ethiopian stew is traditionally served with a pancake-like flat bread, called injera. Rice is a good substitute for the flat bread, if you prefer. The eggs are an intrinsic part of the dish so make sure everyone receives one in their portion.

INGREDIENTS

Serves 4

6 tablespoons vegetable oil
6–8 onions, chopped
6 garlic cloves, chopped
2 teaspoons chopped fresh
    ginger root
1 cup water or chicken stock
1 cup bottled strained tomatoes or
    14-ounce can chopped tomatoes
1 chicken, about 3 pounds, cut into
    8–12 portions
seeds from 5–8 cardamom pods
$^{1}/_{2}$ teaspoon ground turmeric
large pinch of ground cinnamon
large pinch of ground cloves
large pinch of freshly grated nutmeg
cayenne pepper or hot paprika, to taste
4 hard-cooked eggs
salt and ground black pepper
fresh cilantro and onion rings,
    to garnish
flat bread or rice, to serve

1 Heat the oil in a pan, add the onions, and cook, stirring occasionally, for 10 minutes. Add the garlic and ginger and cook for 1–2 minutes.

2 Add the water or chicken stock and the bottled strained tomatoes or chopped tomatoes. Bring to a boil and cook, stirring constantly, for about 10 minutes, or until the liquid has reduced and the mixture has thickened. Season with salt and pepper.

3 Add the chicken and spices to the pan and turn the chicken in the sauce. Reduce the heat, then cover, and simmer, stirring occasionally, for about 1 hour, or until the chicken is cooked through. Add a little more liquid if the mixture seems too thick.

4 Remove the shells from the eggs and then prick the eggs once or twice with a fork. Add the eggs to the sauce and heat gently until warmed through. Garnish with cilantro and onion rings and serve with flat bread or rice.

Chicken with Baby Peas

This Italian dish strongly reflects the traditions of both Mediterranean and Jewish cooking. The fennel adds an anise flavor and the baby peas give the dish hearty substance.

INGREDIENTS

Serves 4

4 skinless, boneless chicken
  breast portions
all-purpose flour, for dusting
2–3 tablespoons olive oil
1–2 onions, chopped
$^1/4$ fennel bulb, chopped (optional)
1 tablespoon chopped fresh parsley, plus
  extra to garnish
$1^1/2$ teaspoons fennel seeds
5 tablespoons dry Marsala
$^1/2$ cup chicken stock
$2^3/4$ cups baby peas
juice of $1^1/2$ lemons
2 egg yolks
salt and ground black pepper

1 Season the chicken with salt and pepper, then generously dust with flour. Shake off the excess flour and set aside.

2 Heat 1 tablespoon of the oil in a pan, add the onions, fennel, if using, parsley, and fennel seeds. Cook for 5 minutes.

3 Add the remaining oil and the chicken to the pan and cook for 2–3 minutes on each side, until lightly browned. Remove the chicken and onion mixture from the pan and set aside.

4 Deglaze the pan by pouring in the Marsala and cooking over high heat until reduced to about 2 tablespoons, then pour in the stock. Add the peas and return the chicken and onion mixture to the pan. Cook over very low heat.

5 In a bowl, beat the lemon juice and egg yolks together, then gradually add ½ cup of the hot liquid from the chicken and peas, stirring well to combine.

6 Return the mixture to the pan and cook over low heat, stirring, until the mixture thickens slightly. (Do not let the mixture boil or the eggs will curdle.) Serve the chicken immediately, sprinkled with a little extra parsley.

Cubed Chicken and Vegetables

In this popular style of Japanese cooking, vegetables are simmered with a small amount of chicken in dashi stock—a traditional stock used in Japanese recipes. It is a light meal that looks attractive when served.

INGREDIENTS

Serves 4

2 boneless chicken thighs,
    about 7 ounces
1 large carrot, trimmed
1 konnyaku (black beancurd)
11 ounces satoimo (taro potato) or
    small potatoes
1¹/₄ pounds canned bamboo
    shoots, drained
2 tablespoons vegetable oil
1¹/₄ cups water mixed with 1¹/₂ teaspoons
    dashi-no-moto (dashi stock granules)
salt

For the simmering seasonings
5 tablespoons shoyu
2 tablespoons sake
2 tablespoons superfine sugar
2 tablespoons mirin (sweet rice wine)

1 Cut the chicken into bitesize pieces. Chop the carrot into ³/₄-inch triangular chunks by cutting the carrot slightly diagonally and turning it 90 degrees each time you cut.

2 Boil the konnyaku in rapidly boiling water for 1 minute and drain under running water. Cool, slice it crosswise into ¹/₄-inch thick strips. Cut a 1¹/₂-inch slit down the center of a strip without cutting the ends. Carefully push the top of the strip through the slit to make a decorative tie. Repeat with all the konnyaku.

3 Peel and halve the satoimo. Put in a colander and sprinkle with salt. Rub and wash under cold running water. Drain. If using, peel and halve the small potatoes.

4 Halve the canned bamboo shoots, then cut into the same shape as the carrot.

5 In a pan, heat the vegetable oil and stir-fry the chicken until the surface of the meat turns white. Add the carrot, konnyaku ties, satoimo, and bamboo shoots. Stir well with every new addition.

6 Add the water and dashi-no-moto and bring to a boil. Cook over high heat for 3 minutes, then reduce to medium-low. Add the simmering seasonings, cover, then simmer for 15 minutes, or until the liquid has evaporated, shaking the pan from time to time.

7 When the satoimo is soft, remove from the heat and transfer to a serving bowl. Serve immediately.

COOK'S TIP

When you cut satoimo, it produces a sticky juice. Rinsing with salt and water is the best way to wash it off.

Hijiki Seaweed and Chicken

The taste of hijiki is somewhere between rice and vegetable and is used in Japanese cooking. It goes well with chicken, especially when it's stir-fried with a little oil first.

INGREDIENTS

Serves 4

3^1/$_2$ ounces dried hijiki seaweed

5 ounces boneless chicken breast portion

^{1}/$_2$ small carrot, about 2 inches

1 tablespoon vegetable oil

scant ^{1}/$_2$ cup water mixed with
   ^{1}/$_4$ teaspoon dashi-no-moto (dashi
   stock granules)

2 tablespoons sake

2 tablespoons superfine sugar

3 tablespoons shoyu

a pinch of shichimi togarashi (seven-flavor
   spice) or cayenne pepper,
   to serve

1 Soak the hijiki in cold water for about 30 minutes. When it crushes between the fingers it is ready. Pour into a strainer and wash under running water. Drain.

2 Peel the skin from the chicken and par-boil the skin in rapidly boiling water for 1 minute, then drain. With a sharp knife, shave off all the yellow fat from the skin. Discard the clear membrane between the fat and the skin as well. Cut the skin into thin strips about ^{1}/$_4$ inch wide and 1 inch long. Cut the meat into small, bitesize chunks.

3 Peel and chop the carrot into long, narrow batons.

4 Heat the oil in a wok or skillet and stir-fry the strips of chicken skin for 5 minutes, or until golden and curled up. Add the chicken meat and keep stirring until the color changes.

5 Add the hijiki and carrot, then stir-fry for 1 minute more. Add the remaining ingredients. Lower the heat and cook for 5 minutes.

6 Remove the wok or skillet from the heat and let stand for about 10 minutes. Serve in small bowls. Sprinkle with shichimi togarashi or cayenne pepper.

Seafood, Chicken, and Vegetable Hotchpotch

This Japanese dish is cooked and eaten at the table, traditionally using a clay pot. You can use a flameproof casserole or fondue pot and will need a portable tabletop stove or burner.

INGREDIENTS

Serves 4

8 ounces salmon, scaled and cut into
  2-inch thick steaks with bones
8 ounces white fish (sea bream, cod,
  flounder, or haddock), cleaned and
  scaled, then chopped into 4 chunks
11 ounces chicken thighs, cut into large
  bitesize chunks with bones
4 hakusai leaves (Chinese cabbage), base
  part trimmed
4 ounces spinach
1 large carrot, cut into $1/4$-inch thick
  rounds or flower shapes
8 fresh shiitake mushrooms, stems
  removed, or 5 ounces oyster
  mushrooms, bases trimmed
2 thin leeks, washed and cut diagonally
  into 2-inch lengths
$10^{1}/4$-ounce packet beancurd block,
  drained and cut into 16 cubes
salt

For the hotchpotch liquid
$4^{1}/2$ x $2^{1}/2$ inches dashi-konbu
  (dried seaweed)
5 cups water
$1/2$ cup sake

For the condiments
$3^{1}/2$ ounces daikon, peeled
1 dried chile, halved and seeded
1 lemon, cut into 16 wedges
4 scallions, chopped
2 x $1/8$-ounce packets kezuri-bushi
  (bonito flakes)
1 bottle shoyu

1 Arrange the various prepared fish and chicken on a large serving platter.

2 Boil plenty of water in a large pan and cook the hakusai for 3 minutes. Drain in a strainer and let cool. Add a pinch of salt to the water and boil the spinach for 1 minute, then drain in a strainer under running water.

3 Squeeze the spinach and lay it on a sushi rolling mat, then roll it up firmly. Let rest, then unwrap and take the cylinder out. Lay the hakusai leaves next to each other on the mat. Put the cylinder in the middle and roll again firmly. Leave for about 5 minutes, then unroll and cut into 2-inch long cylinders.

4 Transfer the hakusai and spinach cylinders to the platter along with all the remaining vegetables and the beancurd.

5 Lay the dashi-konbu on the base of a flameproof casserole or fondue pot. Mix the water and sake in a small bowl.

6 Insert a skewer into the cut side of the daikon three times, and insert the chile pieces. Leave for 5 minutes, then grate finely. Drain and squeeze the liquid out. Shape the pink daikon into a mound and put in a bowl. Put all the other condiments into small bowls.

7 Fill the pot with two-thirds of the water and sake mix. Bring to a boil, then reduce the heat.

8 Transfer the casserole or fondue pot to a lighted burner at the table. Put the carrot, shiitake or oyster mushrooms, chicken, and salmon into the casserole. When the color of the meat and fish changes, add the rest of the ingredients in batches.

9 Guests pour soy sauce into small bowls, and squeeze in a little lemon juice, then mix with a condiment. Pick up the food with chopsticks and dip into the sauce. Cook more as you go, adding water and sake as the stock reduces.

Sichuan Chicken with Kung Po Sauce

This recipe, which hails from the Sichuan region of Western China, has become one of the classic recipes in the Chinese repertoire.

INGREDIENTS

Serves 3

2 skinless, boneless chicken breast
 portions, total weight about 12 ounces
1 egg white
2 teaspoons cornstarch
$1/2$ teaspoon salt
2 tablespoons yellow salted beans
1 tablespoon hoisin sauce
1 teaspoon light brown sugar
1 tablespoon rice wine or
 medium-dry sherry
1 tablespoon wine vinegar
4 garlic cloves, crushed
$2/3$ cup chicken stock
3 tablespoons peanut oil or
 sunflower oil
2–3 dried chiles, broken into small pieces
1 cup roasted cashew nuts
fresh cilantro, to garnish

1 Cut the chicken into neat pieces. Lightly whisk the egg white in a dish, whisk in the cornstarch and salt, then add the chicken, and stir until coated.

COOK'S TIP

Peanuts are the classic ingredient in this dish, but cashew nuts have an even better flavor.

2 In a separate bowl, mash the beans with a spoon. Stir in the hoisin sauce, brown sugar, rice wine or sherry, vinegar, garlic, and stock.

3 Heat a wok, add the oil, and then cook the chicken, turning constantly, for about 2 minutes, or until cooked. Drain over a bowl in order to collect the excess oil.

4 Heat the reserved oil and cook the chile pieces for 1 minute. Return the chicken to the wok and pour in the bean sauce mixture. Bring to a boil and stir in the cashew nuts. Spoon into a heated serving dish and garnish with cilantro leaves.

GRAINS, RICE, & PASTA

There are endless ways to enjoy chicken combined with pasta, grains, and rice.
This chapter offers recipes from around the globe, and includes traditional dishes
such as fried rice, paella, jambalaya, and risottos. These are hearty and filling
recipes, such as chicken and vegetable tagine, sophisticated pasta dishes, such as
pappardelle with chicken and mushrooms, as well as everyday favorites, such as
lasagne and cannelloni. Using combinations of herbs, spices, meats, seafood, and
dairy produce, the dishes in this chapter provide a wealth of choice for
adventurous eating.

Stuffed Chicken Rolls

These delicious chicken rolls are simple to make but sophisticated enough to serve at a dinner party. Slices are arranged on a bed of tagliatelle tossed with fried wild mushrooms.

INGREDIENTS

Serves 4

2 tablespoons butter

1 garlic clove, chopped

1¼ cups cooked white long grain rice

3 tablespoons ricotta cheese

2 teaspoons chopped fresh flat leaf parsley

1 teaspoon chopped fresh tarragon

4 skinless, boneless chicken
    breast portions

4 slices prosciutto

1 tablespoon olive oil

½ cup white wine

salt and ground black pepper

fresh flat leaf parsley sprigs, to garnish

cooked tagliatelle and sautéed wild
    mushrooms, to serve (optional)

1 Preheat the oven to 350°F. Melt about 2 teaspoons of the butter in a small pan and cook the garlic for a few seconds without browning. Spoon into a bowl.

COOK'S TIP

Risotto rice could be used in place of white long grain in this dish—it will make a denser stuffing for the chicken rolls.

2 Add the rice, ricotta, parsley, and tarragon and season with salt and pepper. Stir to mix.

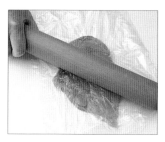

3 Place each chicken breast portion in turn between two sheets of plastic wrap and flatten by beating firmly with the side of a rolling pin.

4 Divide the slices of prosciutto among the chicken, trimming the ham to fit, if necessary.

5 Place a spoonful of the rice stuffing at the wider end of each ham-topped chicken portion. Roll up carefully and tie in place with cooking string or secure with a toothpick.

6 Heat the oil and the remaining butter in a skillet and lightly cook the chicken rolls until browned on all sides. Place side by side in a shallow ovenproof dish and pour in the white wine.

7 Cover the dish with baking parchment and cook in the oven for 30–35 minutes, or until the chicken is tender.

8 Cut the rolls into slices and serve on a bed of tagliatelle with sautéed wild mushrooms and a generous sprinkling of black pepper. Garnish with sprigs of flat leaf parsley.

Joloff Chicken and Rice

In West Africa, where this dish originated, it is usually made in large quantities, using cut-up whole chickens. This version is somewhat more sophisticated, but still has the traditional flavor.

INGREDIENTS

Serves 4

2 garlic cloves, crushed

1 teaspoon dried thyme

4 skinless, boneless chicken
    breast portions

2 tablespoons palm or vegetable oil

14-ounce can chopped tomatoes

1 tablespoon tomato paste

1 onion, chopped

scant 2 cups chicken stock

2 tablespoons dried shrimp or
    crayfish, ground

1 fresh green chile, seeded and chopped

1³/4 cups white long grain rice

3 cups water

salt and ground black pepper

chopped fresh thyme, to garnish

1 Combine the garlic and thyme in a bowl. Rub the mixture into the chicken breast portions. Heat the oil in a skillet.

2 Add the chicken breast portions to the skillet to brown in the oil, then remove to a plate. Add the chopped tomatoes, tomato paste, and onion to the skillet. Cook over medium-high heat for 15 minutes, or until the tomatoes are well reduced, stirring occasionally at first and then more frequently as the tomatoes thicken.

3 Lower the heat, return the chicken to the skillet, and stir well. Cook and stir for 10 minutes, then add the stock, the shrimp or crayfish, and the chile. Bring to a boil, then simmer for 5 minutes, or until the chicken is cooked, stirring occasionally. Season to taste.

4 Meanwhile put the rice in a separate pan. Pour in the water, and add some sauce from the chicken. Bring to a boil, then lower the heat, and cover the pan. Cook over low heat until the liquid has been absorbed and the rice is tender.

5 Pack the rice into four molds and set aside. Lift out the chicken from the sauce and put on a board. If the sauce is runny, cook it over high heat to reduce it. Unmold a rice timbale on each of four serving plates. Spoon the sauce around, then slice the chicken portions, and fan them on the sauce. Garnish with thyme sprigs and serve immediately.

Spanish Chicken

This colorful rice dish is ideal for entertaining. It is delicious served with crisp salad greens.

INGREDIENTS

Serves 8

2 tablespoons all-purpose flour

2 teaspoons paprika

$^1/_2$ teaspoon salt

16 chicken drumsticks

$^1/_4$ cup olive oil

about 5 cups chicken stock

1 onion, finely chopped

2 garlic cloves, crushed

$2^1/_3$ cups long grain rice

2 bay leaves

$1^1/_3$ cups diced cooked ham

1 cup pimiento-stuffed
   green olives

1 green bell pepper, seeded
   and diced

2 × 14-ounce cans chopped tomatoes, with
   the juice

4 tablespoons chopped fresh parsley

1 Preheat the oven to 350°F. Shake together the flour, paprika, and salt in a plastic bag, add the drumsticks, and toss well to coat.

2 Heat the oil in a large, flameproof casserole and, working in batches, brown the chicken drumsticks slowly on all sides. Remove and keep warm.

3 Meanwhile, bring the stock to a boil and add the onion, crushed garlic, rice, and bay leaves. Cook for 10 minutes. Remove from the heat and add the ham, olives, bell pepper, and canned tomatoes with their juice. Transfer to a shallow ovenproof dish.

4 Arrange the chicken on top, cover, and bake for about 30–40 minutes, or until tender. Add a little more stock if necessary to prevent the casserole from drying out. Remove the bay leaves and sprinkle with the chopped parsley to garnish before serving.

Chicken and Chorizo

2 Add the rice, chicken stock, tomato paste, and Tabasco sauce. Simmer, uncovered, for about 10 minutes.

3 Stir in the chicken, chorizo, and peas, and simmer for 5 minutes more. Switch off the heat, cover, and let stand for 5 minutes more before serving.

This spicy dish is a fast, fortifying meal for a hungry family and the perfect way to use up leftover chicken.

INGREDIENTS

Serves 4

3 tablespoons vegetable oil

1 medium onion, chopped

1 celery stalk, chopped

$^1/_2$ red bell pepper, seeded and chopped

2 cups long grain rice

4 cups chicken stock

1 tablespoon tomato paste

3–4 dashes of Tabasco sauce

8 ounces cold roast chicken,
   thickly sliced

4 ounces chorizo, sliced

$^3/_4$ cup fresh shelled or frozen peas

1 Heat the oil in a heavy pan. Add the onion, celery, and bell pepper and cook gently to soften without coloring.

VARIATION

You could use kabanos or any other cooked sausage instead of chorizo in this dish.

Chinese Special Fried Rice

Cooked rice fried with a selection of other ingredients is a staple Chinese dish. In this recipe a mixture of chicken, shrimp, and vegetables make a tasty combination.

Serves 4

scant 1 cup long grain white rice

3 tablespoons peanut oil

1 garlic clove, crushed

4 scallions, finely chopped

1 cup diced cooked chicken

1 cup cooked peeled shrimp, rinsed
   if canned

$^1/_2$ cup fresh shelled or frozen peas

1 egg, beaten with a pinch of salt

1 cup shredded lettuce

2 tablespoons light soy sauce

pinch of superfine sugar

salt and ground black pepper

1 tablespoon chopped roasted cashew
   nuts, to garnish

1 Rinse the long grain rice in two to three changes of warm water to wash away some of the starch. Drain well.

2 Put the rice in a pan and add 1 tablespoon of the oil and 1$^1/_2$ cups of water. Cover and bring to a boil, stir once, then cover, and simmer for 12–15 minutes, or until nearly all the water has been absorbed. Turn off the heat and leave covered for 10 minutes. Fluff up with a fork and let cool.

3 Heat the remaining oil in a wok or large, heavy skillet, add the garlic and scallions, and stir fry for 30 seconds.

4 Add the chicken, shrimp, and peas and stir-fry for 1–2 minutes, then add the cooked rice, and stir-fry for 2 minutes more. Pour in the egg and stir-fry until just set. Stir in the lettuce, soy sauce, sugar, and seasoning.

5 Transfer to a warmed serving bowl, sprinkle with the chopped roasted cashew nuts, and serve immediately.

Mushroom Picker's Chicken Paella

A good paella is based on a few well-chosen ingredients. Here, wild mushrooms combine with chicken and vegetables.

INGREDIENTS

Serves 4

3 tablespoons olive oil

1 medium onion, chopped

1 small bulb fennel, sliced

8 ounces assorted wild and cultivated
   mushrooms such as ceps, bay boletus,
   chanterelles, saffron milk-caps,
   hedgehog fungus, St George's, Caesar's,
   and oyster mushrooms, trimmed
   and sliced

1 garlic clove, crushed

3 chicken legs, chopped through
   the bone

$1^2/3$ cups Spanish rice or
   risotto rice

$3^3/4$ cups chicken stock, boiling

1 pinch of saffron threads or 1 envelope
   of saffron powder

1 fresh thyme sprig

14-ounce can lima
   beans, drained

$3/4$ cup frozen peas

salt and ground black pepper

1 Heat the olive oil in a 14-inch paella pan or a large skillet. Add the onion and fennel and cook over low heat for 3–4 minutes.

2 Add the mushrooms and garlic, and cook until the juices begin to run. Increase the heat to evaporate the juices.

3 Push both the onion and mushrooms to one side. Add the chicken and cook briefly.

4 Stir in the rice, add the stock, saffron, thyme, lima beans, and peas. Bring to a simmer and then cook gently for about 15 minutes without stirring.

5 Season with salt and pepper. Remove from the heat and cover the surface of the paella with a round of greased baking parchment. Cover the parchment with a clean dishtowel and let the paella finish cooking in its own heat for about 5 minutes. Bring to the table, uncover, and serve.

Chicken Paella

There are many variations of this basic recipe. Any seasonal vegetables can be added, together with mussels and other shellfish. Serve straight from the pan.

INGREDIENTS

Serves 4

4 chicken legs (thighs and drumsticks)

4 tomatoes

4 tablespoons olive oil

1 large onion, finely chopped

1 garlic clove, crushed

1 teaspoon ground turmeric

4 ounces chorizo sausage or smoked ham

generous 1 cup long grain rice

2¹/₂ cups chicken stock

1 red bell pepper, seeded and sliced

1 cup fresh shelled or
    frozen peas

salt and ground black pepper

1 Preheat the oven to 350°F. Cut the chicken legs in half. Plunge the tomatoes into boiling water for 30 seconds, then refresh in cold water. Peel off the skins, remove the seeds, and chop the flesh.

2 Heat the oil in a 12-inch paella pan or large, flameproof casserole and brown the chicken pieces on both sides. Add the onion and garlic and stir in the turmeric. Cook for 2 minutes.

3 Slice the sausage or dice the ham and add to the pan, with the rice and stock. Bring to a boil and season to taste, cover, and bake for 15 minutes.

4 Remove from the oven and add the chopped tomatoes, red bell pepper, and peas. Return to the oven and cook for 10–15 minutes more, or until the chicken is tender and the rice has absorbed the stock.

Cornish Hens with Dirty Rice

This rice is called dirty not because of its content (although the roux and chicken livers do "muss" it up a bit) but because jazz is called "dirty music" in New Orleans, and the rice in this recipe is certainly jazzed up.

INGREDIENTS

Serves 4

4 Cornish hens

2 bay leaves, halved

2 tablespoons butter

1 lemon

For the rice

4 tablespoons oil

$^1/_4$ cup all-purpose flour

$^1/_4$ cup butter

1 large onion, chopped

2 celery stalks, chopped

1 green bell pepper, seeded and diced

2 garlic cloves, crushed

scant 1 cup ground pork

8 ounces chicken livers, trimmed
    and sliced

Tabasco sauce

1$^1/_4$ cups chicken stock

4 scallions, shredded

3 tablespoons chopped fresh parsley

generous 1 cup American long grain
    rice, cooked

salt and ground black pepper

COOK'S TIP

You can substitute quails for the Cornish hens, in which case offer two per person and stuff each little bird with 2 teaspoons of the dirty rice before roasting for about 20 minutes.

---

1 In a small, heavy pan, make a roux by blending together 2 tablespoons of the oil and the flour. When it is a chestnut-brown color, remove the pan from the heat, and place it immediately on a cold surface.

2 Heat the remaining oil with the butter in a skillet and stir-fry the onion, celery, and green bell pepper for about 5 minutes until softened but not colored.

3 Add the garlic and ground pork and stir-fry for about 5 minutes, breaking up the pork and stirring well to cook it all over.

4 Add the chicken livers and cook for 2–3 minutes, or until they have changed color all over. Season with salt and black pepper and a dash of Tabasco sauce.

5 Stir the roux into the stir-fried mixture, then gradually add the stock. When it begins to bubble, cover, and cook for 30 minutes, stirring occasionally. Uncover and cook for 15 minutes more, stirring frequently.

6 Preheat the oven to 400°F. Mix the shredded scallions and chopped parsley into the meat mixture and stir it all into the cooked rice.

7 Put $^1/_2$ bay leaf and 1 tablespoons rice into each Cornish hen. Rub the outside with the butter and season with salt and pepper.

8 Put the birds on a rack in a roasting pan, squeeze the juice from the lemon over them, and roast in the oven for 35–40 minutes, basting twice during cooking with the pan juices.

9 Put the remaining rice into a shallow ovenproof dish, cover it, and place on a low shelf in the oven for the last 15–20 minutes of the birds' cooking time.

10 Serve the birds on a bed of dirty rice with the roasting juices—drained of fat— poured over them.

Louisiana Rice

Chicken livers are accompanied by pork, rice, vegetables, and an array of spices in this filling dish.

INGREDIENTS

Serves 4

4 tablespoons vegetable oil

1 small eggplant, diced

2 cups ground pork

1 green bell pepper, seeded and chopped

2 celery stalks, chopped

1 onion, chopped

1 garlic clove, crushed

1 teaspoon cayenne pepper

1 teaspoon paprika

1 teaspoon black pepper

$^1/_2$ teaspoon salt

1 teaspoon dried thyme

$^1/_2$ teaspoon dried oregano

2 cups chicken stock

8 ounces chicken livers, ground

$^2/_3$ cup long grain rice

1 bay leaf

3 tablespoons chopped fresh parsley

celery leaves, to garnish

1 Heat the oil in a large skillet until really hot, then add the diced eggplant and stir-fry for about 5 minutes.

2 Add the pork and cook for about 6–8 minutes, or until browned, using a wooden spoon to break up any lumps.

3 Add the chopped bell pepper, celery, onion, garlic, and all the spices and herbs. Cover and cook over high heat for 5–6 minutes, stirring frequently from the base to scrape up and distribute the crispy brown sediment.

4 Pour in the stock and stir to clean the base of the pan. Cover and cook for 6 minutes over medium heat. Stir in the chicken livers, cook for 2 minutes, then stir in the rice, and add the bay leaf.

5 Reduce the heat, cover, and simmer for about 6–7 minutes. Turn off the heat and let stand for 10–15 minutes more until the rice is tender. Remove the bay leaf and stir in the chopped parsley. Serve the rice hot, garnished with the celery leaves.

Risotto with Chicken

This is a classic Italian combination of chicken and creamy rice, cooked with prosciutto, white wine, and Parmesan cheese. It makes a great summertime meal.

INGREDIENTS

Serves 4

2 tablespoons olive oil

8 ounces skinless, boneless chicken breast
portions, cut into 1-inch cubes

1 onion, finely chopped

1 garlic clove, finely chopped

1/4 teaspoon saffron threads

2 ounces prosciutto, cut into
thin strips

2 1/4 cups risotto rice

1/2 cup dry white wine

7 1/2 cups simmering chicken stock

2 tablespoons butter (optional)

1/3 cup freshly grated Parmesan cheese,
plus extra to serve

salt and ground black pepper

1 Heat the oil in a wide, heavy pan over medium-high heat. Add the chicken cubes and cook, stirring, until they start to turn white.

2 Reduce the heat to low. Add the onion, garlic, saffron, and prosciutto. Cook, stirring, until the onion is soft. Stir in the risotto rice and mix well. Cook for 1–2 minutes, stirring constantly.

3 Add the wine and bring to a boil. Simmer gently until almost all the wine is absorbed.

4 Add the simmering stock, a ladleful at a time, and cook until the rice is just tender and the risotto creamy.

5 Add the butter, if using, and Parmesan cheese and stir in well. Season with salt and pepper to taste. Serve the risotto hot, sprinkled with extra Parmesan.

Chicken and Asparagus Risotto

Use thick asparagus for this recipe, as fine spears overcook in this risotto. The thick ends of the asparagus are full of flavor and they become beautifully tender in the time it takes for the rice to absorb the stock.

INGREDIENTS

Serves 4

1/4 cup butter
1 tablespoon olive oil
1 leek, finely chopped
1 1/2 cups oyster mushrooms, sliced
3 skinless, boneless chicken breast
    portions, cubed
12 ounces asparagus
1 1/4 cups risotto rice
3 3/4 cups simmering chicken stock
salt and ground black pepper
Parmesan cheese curls,
    to serve

1 Heat the butter with the oil in a pan until the mixture foams. Add the leek and cook gently until softened, but not colored. Add the mushrooms and cook for 5 minutes. Remove the vegetables from the pan and set aside.

2 Increase the heat and cook the chicken until golden. Do this in batches, if necessary, and then replace them all in the pan.

3 Meanwhile, discard the woody ends from the asparagus and cut the spears in half. Set the fine tips aside. Cut the thick ends in half and add them to the pan. Replace the leek and mushroom mixture and stir in the rice.

4 Pour in a ladleful of simmering stock and cook gently, stirring occasionally, until the stock is absorbed. Continue adding the stock a ladleful at a time, simmering until the stock is absorbed, the rice is tender, and the chicken is cooked.

5 Add the fine asparagus tips with the last ladleful of boiling stock for the final 5 minutes and continue cooking the risotto gently until the asparagus is tender. The whole process should take about 25–30 minutes.

6 Season the risotto to taste with salt and lots of freshly ground black pepper and spoon it into individual warm serving bowls. Top each bowl with curls of Parmesan, and serve.

COOK'S TIP

Use a cheese slicer to pare thin curls off a large piece of fresh Parmesan cheese.

Chicken Liver Risotto

The combination of chicken livers, bacon, parsley, and thyme gives this risotto a wonderfully rich flavor.

INGREDIENTS

Serves 2–4

1 tablespoon olive oil

2 tablespoons butter

1¹/₂ ounces pancetta, or speck, or
   3 rindless fatty bacon strips,
   finely chopped

2 shallots, finely chopped

1 garlic clove, crushed

1 celery stalk, thinly sliced

1¹/₂ cups risotto rice

³/₄ cup dry white wine

3³/₄–4 cups simmering chicken stock

1 teaspoon chopped fresh thyme

1 tablespoon chopped
   fresh parsley

salt and ground black pepper

parsley and thyme sprigs,
   to garnish

1 Clean the chicken livers, removing any fat or membrane. Rinse well, pat dry. and cut into small, even pieces.

2 Heat the oil and butter in a pan and cook the pancetta, speck, or bacon for 2–3 minutes. Add the shallots, garlic, and celery and continue cooking for 3–4 minutes over low heat until the vegetables are slightly softened. Increase the heat and add the chicken livers, stir-frying for a few minutes, or until they are brown all over.

3 Add the rice. Cook, stirring, for a few minutes, then pour in the wine. Let it boil so that the alcohol is driven off. Stir frequently, taking care not to break up the chicken livers. When all the wine has been absorbed, add the hot stock, a ladleful at a time, stirring constantly.

4 About halfway through cooking, add the thyme and seasoning. Continue to add the stock as before.

5 When the risotto is creamy and the rice is tender, stir in the parsley. Season. Remove from the heat, cover, and let rest for a few minutes before serving, garnished with the herbs.

Yogurt Chicken and Rice Cake

This Middle-Eastern specialty is traditionally flavored with small, dried berries called zereshk, but is just as delicious when made with fresh cranberries.

INGREDIENTS

Serves 6

3 tablespoons butter

1 chicken, about 3¹/₂ pounds, cut into pieces

1 large onion, chopped

1 cup chicken stock

2 eggs, beaten

2 cups plain yogurt

2–3 saffron threads, dissolved in 1 tablespoon warm water

1 teaspoon ground cinnamon

2¹/₄ cups basmati rice, soaked

5 cups boiling water

³/₄ cup cranberries or zereshk (see Cook's Tip)

¹/₂ cup sliced almonds

salt and ground black pepper

herb and radicchio salad, to serve

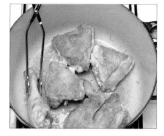

1 Melt two-thirds of the butter in a flameproof casserole. Cook the chicken pieces with the onion for 4–5 minutes, or until the onion is softened and the chicken has browned. Add the stock and season with salt and pepper. Bring to a boil, lower the heat, and simmer for 45 minutes, or until the chicken is cooked and the stock has reduced by half.

2 Drain the chicken, reserving the stock. Cut the flesh into large pieces, discarding the skin and bones, and place in a large bowl. In a separate bowl, combine the eggs with the yogurt. Add the saffron water and cinnamon. Season lightly. Pour this over the chicken and stir to coat. Cover and set aside to marinate for up to 2 hours.

3 Preheat the oven to 325°F. Grease a large, ovenproof dish, about 4 inches deep. Drain the rice and put it in a pan. Add the boiling water and a little salt, bring back to a boil, and then lower the heat, and simmer gently for 10 minutes. Drain, rinse thoroughly in warm water, and drain once more.

COOK'S TIP

If you use zereshk, wash them before use. Heat the berries, then layer them with the rice.

---

4 Using a slotted spoon, lift the chicken pieces out of the yogurt marinade and put them on a plate. Mix half the rice into the marinade. Spread the mixture on the base of the prepared dish. Arrange the chicken pieces in a single layer on top, then cover evenly with about half the plain rice. Sprinkle the cranberries or zereshk on top, then cover with the rest of the rice.

5 Pour the reserved chicken stock over the rice. Sprinkle with sliced almonds and dot with the remaining butter. Cover tightly with foil and bake in the oven for 35–45 minutes.

6 Leave the dish to cool for a few minutes, then place it on a cold, damp dishtowel (this will help to lift the rice from the base of the dish). Run a knife around the inside rim of the dish. Invert a large, flat plate over the dish and turn out the rice "cake". Cut into six wedges and serve hot, with a herb and radicchio salad.

Thai Fried Rice

This substantial dish is based on Thai fragrant rice, which is sometimes known as jasmine rice. Chicken, red bell pepper, and corn add color and extra flavor.

INGREDIENTS

Serves 4

2 cups water

$1/2$ cup coconut milk powder

$1^3/4$ cups Thai fragrant
    rice, rinsed

2 tablespoons peanut oil

2 garlic cloves, chopped

1 small onion, finely chopped

1-inch piece of fresh ginger root, grated

8 ounces skinless, boneless chicken breast
    portions, cut into $1^1/2$-inch dice

1 red bell pepper, seeded and sliced

$2/3$ cup drained canned corn kernels

1 teaspoon chili oil

1 teaspoon hot curry powder

2 eggs, beaten

salt

scallion shreds, to garnish

1 Pour the water into a pan and whisk in the coconut milk powder. Add the rice and bring to a boil. Lower the heat, cover, and cook for 12 minutes, or until the rice is tender and the liquid has been absorbed. Spread the rice on a cookie sheet and leave until cold.

2 Heat the oil in a wok, add the garlic, onion, and ginger and stir-fry over medium heat for 2 minutes.

3 Push the vegetables to the sides of the wok, add the chicken to the center, and stir-fry for 2 minutes. Add the rice and stir-fry over high heat for about 3 minutes more until the chicken is cooked through and tender.

4 Stir in the sliced red bell pepper, corn, chili oil, and curry powder, with salt to taste. Toss over the heat for 1 minute. Stir in the beaten eggs and cook for 1 minute more. Garnish with scallion shreds and serve.

Chicken Rice with Mint Relish

A fresh-tasting tomato and mint relish complements this dish perfectly.

INGREDIENTS

Serves 4

9 ounces chicken, skinned and diced
3 garlic cloves, chopped
1 teaspoon ground turmeric
2–3 tablespoons olive oil
2 small–medium carrots, diced or chopped
seeds from 6–8 cardamom pods
2³⁄4 cups long grain rice
9 ounces tomatoes, chopped
3 cups chicken stock
salt and ground black pepper

For the relish

3 tomatoes, diced
large handful of fresh mint, chopped
5–8 scallions, thinly sliced
juice of 2 lemons
salt

1 To make the relish, put all the ingredients in a bowl and mix together. Chill until ready to serve.

2 Mix the diced chicken with half the garlic and the turmeric. Heat a little of the oil in a pan, add the chicken, and cook briefly until the chicken has changed color and is almost cooked. Remove from the pan and set aside.

3 Add the carrots to the pan with the remaining oil, then stir in the remaining garlic, cardamom seeds, and the rice. Cook for 1–2 minutes.

4 Add the tomatoes and stock and bring to a boil. Cover and simmer for 10 minutes until the rice is tender. A few minutes before the rice is cooked, add the chicken. Season to taste. Serve with relish.

Chicken and Shrimp Jambalaya

The mixture of chicken, seafood, and rice suggests a close relationship to the Spanish paella, but the name is more likely to have derived from jambon *(the French for ham),* à la ya *(Creole for rice). Jambalayas are a colorful mixture of highly flavored ingredients, and are always made in large quantities for feasts and celebration meals.*

INGREDIENTS

Serves 10

2 chickens, about 3¹/₂ pounds each

1 pound piece raw smoked or cured ham

1¹/₂ pounds tomatoes

¹/₄ cup or white cooking fat or bacon fat

¹/₂ cup all-purpose flour

3 medium onions, thinly sliced

2 green bell peppers, seeded and sliced

2–3 garlic cloves, crushed

2 teaspoons chopped fresh thyme or
    1 teaspoon dried thyme

24 raw jumbo shrimp, peeled and deveined

2³/₄ cups white long grain rice

5 cups water

2–3 dashes Tabasco sauce

salt and ground black pepper

3 tablespoons chopped fresh flat leaf
    parsley, plus tiny fresh parsley sprigs,
    to garnish

COOK'S TIP
~
To devein a shrimp, make a shallow cut down the center of the curved back. Pull out the black vein with a toothpick or your fingers, then rinse the shrimp thoroughly.

1 Cut each chicken into ten pieces and season well. Dice the ham, discarding the rind and fat. Plunge the tomatoes into boiling water for 30 seconds, then refresh in cold water. Peel off the skins and chop the flesh.

2 Melt the white cooking fat or bacon fat in a large, heavy skillet. Add the chicken pieces, in batches, brown them all over, then lift them out with a slotted spoon, and set them aside.

3 Reduce the heat. Sprinkle the flour into the fat in the skillet and stir until the roux turns golden brown. Return the chicken pieces to the skillet.

4 Add the diced ham, onions, green bell peppers, tomatoes, garlic, and thyme. Cook, stirring frequently, for 10 minutes, then add the shrimp to the skillet and mix lightly.

5 Stir the rice into the skillet and pour in the water. Season with salt, pepper, and Tabasco sauce. Bring to a boil, then cook gently until the rice is tender, the chicken is cooked, and all the liquid has been absorbed. Add a little extra boiling water if the rice looks as though it is drying out before it is cooked.

6 Mix the parsley into the finished dish, garnish with tiny sprigs of flat leaf parsley, and serve immediately.

Lunch-box Rice with Three Toppings

In Japan, children will often be given a rice-based lunch box such as this one. Colorful toppings and a variety of tastes hold their attention so they don't get bored.

INGREDIENTS

Makes 4 lunch boxes

3 snow peas

scant 1¹/2 cups Japanese short grain
   rice cooked using scant 1²/3 cups
   water, cooled

3 tablespoons sesame seeds, toasted

salt

For the egg topping

2 tablespoons superfine sugar

1 teaspoon salt

3 extra large eggs, beaten

For the cod topping

4 ounces cod fillet, skinned and boned

4 teaspoons superfine sugar

1 teaspoon salt

1 teaspoon sake

2 drops of red vegetable coloring, diluted
   with a few drops of water (optional)

For the chicken topping

1³/4 cups ground raw chicken

3 tablespoons sake

1 tablespoon superfine sugar

1 tablespoon shoyu

1 tablespoon water

1 To make the egg topping, add the sugar and salt to the eggs in a pan. Cook over medium heat, stirring as if scrambling an egg. When it is almost set, remove from the heat and stir until the egg becomes slightly dry.

2 To make the cod topping, cook the cod fillet for 2 minutes in a large pan of boiling water. Drain and dry well with paper towels. Skin and remove all the fish bones.

3 Put the cod and sugar into a pan, add the salt and sake, and cook over low heat for 1 minute, stirring with a fork to flake the cod. Reduce the heat to low and add the coloring, if using. Continue to stir for 15–20 minutes, or until the cod flakes become fluffy and fibrous. Transfer to a plate.

4 To make the chicken topping, put the ground chicken, sake, sugar, shoyu, and water into a small pan. Cook over medium heat for about 3 minutes, then reduce the heat to medium-low, and stir with a fork or whisk until the liquid has almost evaporated.

5 Blanch the snow peas for about 3 minutes in lightly salted, boiling water, drain thoroughly, and then carefully slice into fine ⅛-inch sticks.

6 Mix the rice with the sesame seeds in a bowl. With a wet spoon, divide the rice among four 6¹/2 x 4¹/2-inch lunch boxes. Flatten the surface using the back of a wooden spoon.

7 Spoon a quarter of the egg topping into each box to cover one-third of the rice. Cover the next third with a quarter of the cod topping, and the last section with a quarter of the chicken topping. Garnish with the snow pea sticks.

Chicken and Split Pea Stew

This is a Californian version of the traditional Persian Koresh, a thick, saucy stew served with rice.

INGREDIENTS

Serves 4–6

3–4 tablespoons olive oil

1 large or 2 small onions, finely chopped

1¹/4 pounds boneless chicken thighs

¹/4 cup green split peas, soaked for 4 hours
then drained

2¹/4 cups chicken stock

1 teaspoon ground turmeric

¹/2 teaspoon ground cinnamon

¹/4 teaspoon freshly grated nutmeg

2 eggplant, diced

8–10 ripe tomatoes, diced

2 garlic cloves, crushed

2 tablespoons dried mint

salt and ground black pepper

fresh mint, to garnish

rice, to serve

1 Heat a little oil in a pan, add two-thirds of the onions, and cook for 5 minutes. Add the chicken and cook until golden.

2 Add the split peas to the pan, then the stock, turmeric, cinnamon, and nutmeg. Cook over medium-low heat for 40 minutes, or until the split peas are tender and the chicken is cooked.

3 Heat the remaining oil in a pan, add the eggplant and remaining onions, and cook until lightly browned. Add the tomatoes, garlic, and mint. Season.

4 Just before serving, stir the eggplant mixture into the chicken and split pea stew. Garnish the stew with fresh mint leaves and serve with rice.

Tagine of Chicken

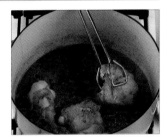

3 Add the onion and crushed garlic to the flameproof casserole and cook gently until tender. Add the spices and cook for 1 minute. Pour in the stock, bring to a boil, and return the chicken. Cover and bake for 45 minutes, or until cooked. Transfer the chicken to a dish, cover, and keep warm.

4 Remove any fat from the cooking liquid and boil to reduce by one-third. Meanwhile, blanch the olives and lemon slices in a pan of boiling water for 2 minutes, or until the lemon skin is tender. Drain and add to the cooking liquid, and adjust the seasoning to taste.

5 To cook the couscous, bring the stock to a boil in a large pan and sprinkle in the couscous slowly, stirring constantly. Remove from the heat, cover, and let stand for 5 minutes.

6 Meanwhile, cook the prepared vegetables, drain, and put them into a large bowl. Add the couscous and oil, and season to taste with salt and pepper. Stir the grains to fluff them up, add the garbanzos, and finally the chopped cilantro. Spoon onto a large serving plate, cover with the chicken, and spoon the liquid over it. Garnish with the fresh cilantro.

Chicken is cooked with spices and olives and served on a bed of vegetable couscous in this version of the Moroccan dish.

INGREDIENTS

Serves 8

8 chicken legs (thighs and drumsticks)
2 tablespoons olive oil
1 medium onion, finely chopped
2 garlic cloves, crushed
1 teaspoon ground turmeric
$^1/_2$ teaspoon ground ginger
$^1/_2$ teaspoon ground cinnamon
2 cups chicken stock
1$^1/_4$ cups pitted green olives
1 lemon, sliced
salt and ground black pepper
fresh cilantro sprigs, to garnish

For the couscous
2$^1/_2$ cups chicken stock
2$^2/_3$ cups couscous
4 zucchini, thickly sliced
2 carrots, thickly sliced
2 small turnips, peeled and cubed
3 tablespoons olive oil
1-pound can garbanzo beans, drained
1 tablespoon chopped fresh cilantro

1 Preheat the oven to 350°F. Cut the chicken legs into two through the joint.

2 Heat the oil in a large, flameproof casserole and, working in batches, brown the chicken on both sides. Drain well, remove to a dish, and keep warm.

Chicken and Vegetable Tagine

Moroccan tagines are usually served with couscous, but in this version couscous is stirred into rice for an unusual and tasty accompaniment for the chicken and vegetables.

INGREDIENTS

Serves 4

2 tablespoons peanut oil

4 skinless, boneless chicken breast portions, cut into large pieces

1 large onion, chopped

2 garlic cloves, crushed

1 small parsnip, cut into 1-inch pieces

1 small turnip, cut into $^3/_4$-inch pieces

3 carrots, cut into $1^1/_2$- inch pieces

4 tomatoes, chopped

1 cinnamon stick

4 cloves

1 teaspoon ground ginger

1 bay leaf

$^1/_4$–$^1/_2$ teaspoon cayenne pepper

$1^1/_2$ cups chicken stock

14-ounce can garbanzo beans, drained and skinned

1 red bell pepper, seeded and sliced

5 ounces green beans, halved

1 piece of preserved lemon peel, thinly sliced

20–30 pitted brown or green olives

salt

For the rice and couscous

3 cups chicken stock

generous 1 cup long grain rice

$^2/_3$ cup couscous

3 tablespoons chopped fresh cilantro

1 Heat half of the oil in a large, flameproof casserole and cook the chicken pieces for a few minutes, or until evenly browned. Transfer to a plate.

2 Heat the remaining oil and cook the onion, garlic, parsnip, turnip, and carrots together over medium heat for 4–5 minutes, or until the vegetables are lightly flecked with brown, stirring frequently. Lower the heat, then cover and cook the vegetables over very low heat for 5 minutes more, stirring occasionally.

3 Add the tomatoes, cook for a few minutes, then add the cinnamon stick, cloves, ginger, bay leaf, and cayenne. Cook for 1–2 minutes.

4 Pour in the chicken stock, add the garbanzo beans, and browned chicken pieces, and season with salt. Cover and simmer for 25 minutes.

5 Meanwhile, cook the rice and couscous mixture. Bring the chicken stock to a boil. Add the rice and simmer for about 5 minutes, or until almost tender. Remove the pan from the heat, stir in the couscous, cover tightly, and leave for about 5 minutes.

6 When the vegetables in the tagine are almost tender, stir in the bell pepper slices and green beans, and simmer for 10 minutes. Add the preserved lemon and olives, stir, and cook for 5 minutes more, or until the vegetables are tender and the chicken is cooked.

7 Stir the cilantro into the rice and couscous mixture and pile it onto a plate. Serve the chicken tagine in the traditional dish, if you have one, or in a casserole.

Conchiglie with Chicken Livers and Herbs

Fresh herbs and chicken livers are a good combination, often used together on crostini in Tuscany, Italy. Here they are tossed with pasta shells to make a very tasty supper dish.

INGREDIENTS

Serves 4

$^1/_4$ cup butter

4 ounces pancetta or fatty bacon, diced

9 ounces frozen chicken livers, thawed, drained and diced

2 garlic cloves, crushed

2 teaspoons chopped fresh sage

$2^3/_4$ cups dried conchiglie

$^2/_3$ cup dry white wine

4 ripe Italian plum tomatoes, peeled and diced

1 tablespoon chopped fresh flat leaf parsley

salt and ground black pepper

1 Melt half the butter in a pan, add the pancetta or bacon, and cook over medium heat for a few minutes, until it is lightly colored.

2 Add the livers, garlic, half the sage, and pepper. Increase the heat and toss the livers for about 5 minutes. Meanwhile, start cooking the pasta according to the packet instructions.

3 Pour the wine over the livers and let it sizzle, lower the heat, and simmer for 5 minutes until cooked. Add the remaining butter. When it melts, mix in the tomatoes, the remaining sage, and the parsley. Stir well. Add salt if needed.

4 Drain the pasta and tip it into a warmed bowl. Pour the sauce over it and toss well. Serve immediately.

Chicken and Rice Vermicelli

This delicious dish makes a filling meal. Take care when frying vermicelli as it has a tendency to spit when added to hot oil.

INGREDIENTS

Serves 4

1/2 cup vegetable oil

8 ounces rice vermicelli

5 ounces green beans, halved lengthwise

1 onion, finely chopped

2 skinless, boneless chicken breast
   portions, about 6 ounces each, cut
   into strips

1 teaspoon chili powder

2 cups cooked shrimp

3 tablespoons dark soy sauce

3 tablespoons white wine vinegar

2 teaspoons superfine sugar

fresh cilantro sprigs, to garnish

2 Heat the remaining oil, then add the green beans, chopped onion, and chicken strips and stir-fry together for 3 minutes, or until the chicken strips are cooked.

3 Sprinkle in the chili powder. Stir in the cooked shrimp, soy sauce, vinegar, and sugar, and stir-fry for 2 minutes.

4 Serve the chicken, shrimp, and vegetables on the fried vermicelli, garnished with sprigs of fresh cilantro.

1 Heat a wok or skillet, then add 4 tablespoons of the oil. Break up the rice vermicelli into 3-inch lengths. When the oil is hot, fry the vermicelli in batches. Remove from the heat and keep warm.

Farfalle with Chicken and Cherry Tomatoes

*Quick to prepare and easy to cook,
this colorful dish is full of flavor.
Serve it for a midweek supper, with
salad greens to follow.*

INGREDIENTS

Serves 4

12 ounces skinless, boneless chicken breast
    portions, cut into bitesize pieces
4 tablespoons Italian dry vermouth
2 teaspoons chopped fresh rosemary, plus
    4 fresh rosemary sprigs, to garnish
1 tablespoon olive oil
1 onion, finely chopped
3^1/$_2$ ounces piece of Italian salami, diced
2^1/$_2$ cups dried farfalle
1 tablespoon balsamic vinegar
14-ounce can Italian cherry tomatoes
good pinch of crushed dried red chiles
salt and ground black pepper

1 Put the chicken pieces in a large
bowl, pour in the vermouth,
and sprinkle with half the chopped
rosemary and salt and pepper to
taste. Stir well and set aside.

2 Heat the oil in a large pan, add
the onion and salami and cook
over medium heat for about
5 minutes, stirring frequently.

3 Cook the pasta according to
the instructions on the packet,
about 8–10 minutes.

4 Add the chicken and vermouth
to the onion and salami,
increase the heat to high, and cook
for 3 minutes, or until the chicken
is white on all sides. Sprinkle the
vinegar over the chicken.

5 Add the cherry tomatoes and
dried chiles. Stir well and
simmer for a few minutes more
until the chicken is cooked. Taste
the sauce for seasoning.

6 Drain the pasta and tip it into
the pan. Add the remaining
chopped rosemary and toss to mix
the pasta and sauce together. Serve
immediately in warmed bowls,
garnished with the rosemary sprigs.

Penne with Chicken, Broccoli, and Cheese

The combination of broccoli, garlic, and Gorgonzola is very tasty, and goes especially well with chicken.

INGREDIENTS

Serves 4

scant 1 cup broccoli flowerets, divided into tiny sprigs

$^1/_4$ cup butter

2 skinless, boneless chicken breast portions, cut into thin strips

2 garlic cloves, crushed

$3^1/_2$ cups dried penne

$^1/_2$ cup dry white wine

scant 1 cup panna da cucina or heavy cream

$3^1/_2$ ounces Gorgonzola cheese, rind removed and diced small

salt and ground black pepper

freshly grated Parmesan cheese, to serve

1 Plunge the broccoli into a pan of salted, boiling water. Bring back to a boil and boil for 2 minutes, then drain in a colander, and refresh under cold running water. Shake well to remove the surplus water and set aside to drain completely.

VARIATION

Use leeks instead of broccoli if you prefer. Cook them with the chicken strips.

2 Melt the butter in a large skillet or pan, add the chicken and garlic, with salt and pepper to taste, and stir well. Cook over medium heat for 3 minutes, or until the chicken becomes white. Meanwhile, start cooking the pasta for 8–10 minutes, or according to the instructions on the packet.

3 Pour the wine and cream over the chicken mixture in the pan, stir to mix, then simmer, stirring occasionally, for about 5 minutes, or until the sauce has reduced and thickened, and the chicken is cooked through. Add the broccoli, increase the heat, and toss to heat it through and mix it with the chicken. Taste for seasoning.

4 Drain the pasta and tip it into the sauce. Add the Gorgonzola and toss well. Serve immediately with grated Parmesan.

Pappardelle with Chicken and Mushrooms

Porcini mushrooms have a strong taste that goes particularly well with chicken and pasta. This is a rich and creamy dish.

INGREDIENTS

Serves 4

1/4 cup dried porcini mushrooms

3/4 cup warm water

2 tablespoons butter

1 garlic clove, crushed

1 small handful of fresh flat leaf parsley,
  coarsely chopped

1 small leek or 4 scallions, chopped

1/2 cup dry white wine

1 cup chicken stock

14 ounces fresh or
  dried pappardelle

2 skinless, boneless chicken breast
  portions, cut into thin strips

7 tablespoons mascarpone cheese

salt and ground black pepper

fresh basil leaves, shredded,
  to garnish

1 Put the dried mushrooms in a bowl. Pour in the warm water and soak for 15–20 minutes. Tip into a fine strainer set over a bowl and squeeze the mushrooms with your hands to release as much liquid as possible.

2 Chop the mushrooms finely and set aside the strained soaking liquid until required.

3 Melt the butter in a pan, add the mushrooms, garlic, parsley, and leek or scallions, with seasoning. Cook over low heat, stirring frequently, for about 5 minutes, then pour in the wine and stock, and bring to a boil. Lower the heat and simmer for about 5 minutes, or until the liquid has reduced and is thickened.

4 Meanwhile, start cooking the pasta in salted, boiling water for 8–10 minutes, or according to the packet instructions, adding the reserved soaking liquid from the mushrooms to the water.

5 Add the chicken and simmer for 5 minutes, or until just tender. Add the mascarpone, a spoonful at a time, stirring after each addition, then add one or two spoonfuls of the water used for cooking the pasta. Season to taste.

6 Drain the pasta and tip it into a warmed large bowl. Add the chicken and sauce and toss well. Serve immediately, topped with the shredded basil leaves.

VARIATION

Add 1 1/2 cups sliced white or chestnut mushrooms with the chicken.

Penne with Chicken and Ham Sauce

A meal in itself, this colorful pasta sauce is perfect for lunch or dinner.

INGREDIENTS

Serves 4

3 cups penne

2 tablespoons butter

1 onion, chopped

1 garlic clove, chopped

1 bay leaf

2 cups dry white wine

²/3 cup crème fraîche

8 ounces cooked chicken, skinned, boned, and diced

²/3 cup diced cooked lean ham

1 cup grated Gouda cheese

1 tablespoon chopped fresh mint

salt and ground black pepper

finely shredded fresh mint, to garnish

1 Cook the pasta in plenty of salted, boiling water following the instructions on the packet.

2 Heat the butter in a large skillet and cook the onion for 10 minutes, or until softened.

3 Add the garlic, bay leaf, and wine and bring to a boil. Boil rapidly until reduced by half. Remove the bay leaf, then stir in the crème fraîche, and bring back to a boil.

4 Add the chicken, ham, and cheese and simmer for 5 minutes, stirring occasionally until heated through.

5 Add the mint and seasoning. Drain the pasta and turn it into a large serving bowl. Toss with the sauce immediately and garnish with shredded mint.

> COOK'S TIP
>
> Crème fraîche is a richer, full-fat French cream with a slightly acidic taste. If you can't find any, substitute sour cream.

Tagliatelle with Chicken and Herb Sauce

Chicken and wine is always a winning combination. Serve this dish simply with salad greens.

INGREDIENTS

Serves 4

2 tablespoons olive oil

1 red onion, cut into wedges

12 ounces tagliatelle

1 garlic clove, chopped

$2^1/_2$ cups chicken, diced

$1^1/_4$ cups dry vermouth

3 tablespoons chopped fresh mixed herbs

$^2/_3$ cup plain yogurt or crème fraîche

salt and ground black pepper

shredded fresh mint, to garnish

1 Heat the oil in a large skillet and cook the onion for 10 minutes until softened and the layers have separated.

2 Cook the pasta in plenty of salted, boiling water following the instructions on the packet.

3 Add the garlic and chicken to the skillet and cook for 10 minutes, stirring occasionally until the chicken is browned all over and cooked through.

4 Pour in the vermouth, bring to a boil, and boil rapidly until reduced by about half.

5 Stir in the herbs, plain yogurt or crème fraîche, and seasoning and heat through gently, but do not boil.

6 Drain the pasta thoroughly and toss it with the sauce to coat. Serve immediately, garnished with shredded fresh mint.

COOK'S TIP

If you don't want to use vermouth, use dry white wine instead. Orvieto and Frascati are two Italian wines that are ideal to use in this sauce.

Fusilli with Chicken, Tomatoes, and Broccoli

This is a really hearty meal for a hungry family. Fusilli tricolore adds to the appearance as well as tasting great.

INGREDIENTS

Serves 4

1¹/₂ pounds ripe but firm
    plum tomatoes
6 tablespoons olive oil
1 teaspoon dried oregano
12 ounces broccoli flowerets
1 small onion, sliced
1 teaspoon dried thyme
1 pound skinless, boneless chicken breast
    portions, cubed
3 garlic cloves, crushed
1 tablespoon fresh lemon juice
4 cups fusilli
salt and ground black pepper

1 Preheat the oven to 400°F. Quarter the tomatoes.

2 Place the tomatoes in an ovenproof dish in a single layer. Add 1 tablespoon of the oil, the oregano, and ¹/₂ teaspoon salt, and stir to blend.

3 Bake until the tomatoes are just browned, about 30–40 minutes; do not stir.

4 Meanwhile, bring a large pan of salted water to a boil. Add the broccoli and cook until just tender, about 5 minutes. Drain and set aside. (Alternatively, steam the broccoli until tender.)

5 Heat 2 tablespoons of the oil in a large, nonstick skillet. Add the onion, thyme, chicken cubes, and ¹/₂ teaspoon salt. Cook over high heat, stirring often, for 5–7 minutes, or until the meat is cooked and beginning to brown. Add the garlic and cook for 1 minute, stirring.

6 Remove from the heat. Stir in the lemon juice and season with pepper. Keep warm until the pasta is cooked.

7 Bring another large pan of salted water to a boil. Add the fusilli and cook until just tender (check the instructions on the packet for timing). Drain and place in a large bowl. Toss with the remaining oil.

8 Add the broccoli to the chicken mixture. Add to the fusilli. Add the tomatoes and stir gently to blend. Serve immediately.

Pasta Sauce with Chicken and Tomato

Fusilli is good with a sauce as it clings to the ridges of the pasta. This deliciously rich tomato and chicken sauce is quick to make.

INGREDIENTS

Serves 4

1 tablespoon olive oil

1 onion, chopped

1 carrot, chopped

1 cup sun-dried tomatoes in olive
  oil, drained

1 garlic clove, chopped

14-ounce can chopped tomatoes, drained

1 tablespoon tomato paste

^{2}/3 cup chicken stock

3 cups fusilli

8 ounces skinless, boneless chicken breast
  portions, diagonally sliced

salt and ground black pepper

fresh mint sprigs, to garnish

5 Pour the sauce into a food processor or blender and process until smooth.

COOK'S TIP

Sun-dried tomatoes are sold soaked in vegetable or olive oil. The olive oil-soaked tomatoes have a superior flavor. If using, cook the onion and carrot in oil from the tomatoes.

---

6 Return the sauce to the pan and stir in the sun-dried tomatoes and chicken. Bring back to a boil, then simmer for 10 minutes, or until the chicken is cooked. Adjust the seasoning.

7 Drain the pasta thoroughly and toss it in the sauce. Serve immediately, garnished with sprigs of fresh mint.

1 Heat the oil in a large skillet and cook the chopped onion and carrot for 5 minutes, stirring from time to time.

2 Chop the sun-dried tomatoes and set aside.

3 Stir the garlic, canned tomatoes, tomato paste, and stock into the onions and carrots and bring to a boil. Simmer for 10 minutes, stirring occasionally.

4 Cook the pasta in plenty of salted, boiling water following the instructions on the packet.

Cannelloni al Forno

Chicken, mushroom, and a hint of tarragon make a light filling for cannelloni. Serve with a salad for a substantial meal.

INGREDIENTS

Serves 4–6

1 pound skinless, boneless chicken breast portions, cooked

3¹/4 cups mushrooms

2 garlic cloves, crushed

2 tablespoons chopped fresh parsley

1 tablespoon chopped fresh tarragon

1 egg, beaten

fresh lemon juice

12–18 cannelloni tubes

2 cups ready-made tomato sauce

²/3 cup freshly grated Parmesan cheese

salt and ground pepper

1 fresh parsley sprig, to garnish

1 Preheat the oven to 400°F. Place the chicken in a blender or food processor and process until finely ground. Transfer the ground chicken to a bowl.

2 Place the mushrooms, garlic, parsley, and tarragon in the food processor and process until finely ground. Add to the chicken mixture.

3 Thoroughly beat the mushroom mixture into the chicken, then add the egg, salt, pepper, and lemon juice to taste, and mix together well.

4 If necessary, cook the cannelloni in plenty of salted, boiling water according to the instructions on the packet, then drain well on a clean dishtowel.

5 Place the filling in a pastry bag fitted with a large plain nozzle. Use this to fill each tube of cannelloni once they are cool enough to handle.

6 Lay the filled cannelloni tightly together in a single layer in a buttered, shallow, ovenproof dish. Spoon the tomato sauce over them and sprinkle with Parmesan cheese. Bake in the oven for 30 minutes, or until brown and bubbling. Serve garnished with a sprig of parsley.

Chicken, Beef, and Pork Cannelloni

A rich mixture of chicken, beef, and pork with cream and a hint of brandy makes an extremely tasty filling for cannelloni. Crisp salad greens are all that is needed to accompany it.

INGREDIENTS

Serves 4

4 tablespoons olive oil

1 onion, finely chopped

1 carrot, finely chopped

2 garlic cloves, crushed

2 ripe Italian plum
    tomatoes, peeled and
    finely chopped

2^1/$_4$ cups ground skinless,
    boneless chicken

^{1}/$_2$ cup ground beef

^{1}/$_2$ cup ground pork

2 tablespoons brandy

2 tablespoons butter

6 tablespoons panna da cucina or
    heavy cream

1 cup freshly grated
    Parmesan cheese

salt and ground black pepper

salad greens, to serve

For the sauce

^{1}/$_4$ cup butter

^{1}/$_2$ cup all-purpose flour

3^3/$_4$ cups milk

freshly grated nutmeg

1 Heat the oil in a pan, add the onion, carrot, garlic, and tomatoes, and cook over low heat, stirring, for about 10 minutes.

2 Add all the ground meats to the pan and cook gently for about 10 minutes, stirring frequently to break up any lumps. Add the brandy, increase the heat, and stir until it has reduced, then add the butter and cream, and cook gently, stirring occasionally, for about 10 minutes. Let cool.

3 Preheat the oven to 375°F. To make the white sauce, melt the butter in a medium pan, add the flour, and cook, stirring constantly, for 1–2 minutes. Add the milk a little at a time, whisking vigorously after each addition. Bring to a boil and cook, stirring, until the sauce is smooth and thick. Grate in fresh nutmeg to taste, then season, and whisk well. Remove the pan from the heat.

4 Spoon a little of the white sauce into an ovenproof dish. Fill the cannelloni tubes with the meat mixture and place in a single layer in the dish. Pour the remaining white sauce over them, then sprinkle with the Parmesan cheese. Bake for 35–40 minutes, or until the pasta is tender when pierced with a skewer. Let stand for about 10 minutes before serving with salad greens.

Chicken Lasagne

Based on the Italian beef lasagne, this is an excellent dish for entertaining guests of all ages. Serve with salad greens.

INGREDIENTS

Serves 8

2 tablespoons olive oil

8 cups ground raw chicken

1^1/2 cups chopped fatty
   bacon strips

2 garlic cloves, crushed

1 pound leeks, sliced

8 ounces carrots, diced

2 tablespoons tomato paste

2 cups chicken stock

12 sheets no pre-cook
   lasagne verde

salt and ground black pepper

For the cheese sauce

^{1}/4 cup butter

^{1}/2 cup all-purpose flour

2^1/2 cups milk

1 cup grated sharp
   Cheddar cheese

^{1}/4 teaspoon dry hot mustard

1 Heat the oil in a large, flameproof casserole and brown the ground chicken and bacon briskly, separating the pieces with a wooden spoon. Add the crushed garlic cloves, sliced leeks, and diced carrots and cook for about 5 minutes, or until softened. Add the tomato paste, stock, and seasoning. Bring to a boil, cover, and simmer for 30 minutes.

2 To make the sauce, melt the butter in a pan, add the flour, and gradually blend in the milk, stirring until smooth. Bring to a boil, stirring constantly until thickened, and simmer for several minutes. Add half the grated cheese and the mustard, and season to taste.

3 Preheat the oven to 375°F. Layer the chicken mixture, lasagne, and half the cheese sauce in a 10-cup ovenproof dish, starting and finishing with a layer of chicken.

4 Pour the remaining half of the cheese sauce over the top to cover and sprinkle the remaining cheese over it. Bake in the preheated oven for 1 hour, or until bubbling and lightly browned on top.

Baked Turkey and Pasta

Slow-cooked turkey with vegetables make a well-flavored and low-fat sauce for pasta.

INGREDIENTS

Serves 4

2¹/₂ cups ground turkey

5 ounces smoked turkey
   strips, chopped

1–2 garlic cloves, crushed

1 onion, finely chopped

2 carrots, diced

2 tablespoons concentrated
   tomato paste

1¹/₄ cups chicken stock

8 ounces rigatoni

2 tablespoons freshly grated
   Parmesan cheese

salt and ground black pepper

3 Preheat the oven to 350°F. Cook the pasta in a large pan of salted, boiling water for 8–10 minutes, or according to the instructions on the packet, until *al dente*. Drain thoroughly and mix with the turkey sauce.

4 Transfer to a shallow ovenproof dish and sprinkle with grated Parmesan cheese. Bake in the preheated oven for 20–30 minutes, or until lightly browned.

1 Brown the ground turkey in a nonstick pan, breaking up any large pieces with a wooden spoon, until well browned all over.

2 Add the turkey strips, garlic, onion, carrots, paste, stock, and seasoning. Bring to a boil, cover, and simmer for 1 hour until tender.

Piquant Chicken with Spaghetti

A dash of vinegar adds piquancy to this herbed chicken sauce for spaghetti. Low-fat crème fraîche makes a creamy and healthy sauce.

INGREDIENTS

Serves 4

1 onion, finely chopped

1 carrot, diced

1 garlic clove, crushed

1¼ cups vegetable stock or water

4 small skinless, boneless chicken breast portions

bouquet garni (bay leaf, parsley stalks, and thyme)

1½ cups thinly sliced white mushrooms,

1 teaspoon wine vinegar or lemon juice

12 ounces spaghetti

½ cucumber, peeled and cut into batons

2 firm ripe tomatoes, skinned

2 tablespoons low-fat crème fraîche

1 tablespoon chopped fresh parsley

1 tablespoon chopped fresh chives

salt and ground black pepper

1 Put the onion, carrot, garlic, and stock or water into a pan with the chicken and bouquet garni. Bring to a boil, cover, and simmer gently for 15–20 minutes, or until tender.

2 Transfer the chicken to a plate and cover with foil. Strain the liquid, discard the vegetables, and return the liquid to the pan. Add the mushrooms and wine vinegar or lemon juice and simmer for 2–3 minutes, or until tender.

3 Cook the spaghetti in a large pan of salted, boiling water for 8–10 minutes, or according to the packet instructions. Drain.

4 Blanch the cucumber in boiling water for 10 seconds. Drain and rinse under cold water.

5 Cut the chicken into bitesize pieces. Boil the stock to reduce by half, then add the chicken, tomatoes, crème fraîche, cucumber, and herbs. Season to taste.

6 Transfer the spaghetti to a warmed serving dish and spoon the piquant chicken over it. Serve immediately.

Spaghetti and Turkey in Cheese Sauce

An American-Italian recipe, this dish, known as Spaghetti tetrazzini, makes an excellent family meal. It is quite filling and rich, so serve it with tossed salad greens.

INGREDIENTS

Serves 4–6

6 tablespoons butter

12 ounces turkey breast fillet, cut into thin strips

2 pieces bottled roasted bell pepper, drained, rinsed, dried, and cut into thin strips

6 ounces dried spaghetti

$1/2$ cup all-purpose flour

$3^3/4$ cups hot milk

$1^1/3$ cups freshly grated Parmesan cheese

$1/4$–$1/2$ teaspoon mustard powder

salt and ground black pepper

1 Melt 2 tablespoons of the butter in a pan, add the turkey, and season well. Toss the turkey over medium heat for 5 minutes, or until the meat turns white. Add the roasted bell pepper and toss to mix. Remove with a slotted spoon and set aside.

2 Preheat the oven to 350°F. Cook the pasta in salted, boiling water for 8–10 minutes, or according to the instructions on the packet.

3 Meanwhile, melt the remaining butter over low heat in the pan in which the turkey was cooked. Sprinkle in the flour and cook, stirring, for 1–2 minutes, then increase the heat to medium.

4 Add the hot milk, a little at a time, whisking vigorously after each addition. Bring to a boil and cook, stirring, until the sauce is smooth and thick. Add two-thirds of the grated Parmesan, then whisk in the mustard, salt, and pepper to taste. Remove the sauce from the heat.

5 Drain the pasta and return it to the pan. Mix in half the cheese sauce, then spoon the mixture around the edge of an ovenproof dish. Stir the turkey mixture into the remaining cheese sauce and spoon into the center of the dish. Sprinkle the remaining Parmesan evenly over the top and bake for 15–20 minutes, or until the cheese topping is just crisp. Serve hot.

Ravioli with Pork and Turkey

This Roman-style ravioli stuffed with ground meat and cheese is scented with fresh herbs. It makes a substantial main course.

INGREDIENTS

Serves 8

1 quantity pasta dough (see Cook's Tip)

all-purpose flour, for dusting

$^1/_4$ cup butter

large bunch of fresh sage, leaves removed and coarsely chopped

4 tablespoons freshly grated Parmesan cheese

extra sage leaves and freshly grated Parmesan cheese, to serve

For the filling

2 tablespoons butter

$1^1/_4$ cups ground pork

1 cup ground turkey

4 fresh sage leaves, finely chopped

1 fresh rosemary sprig, leaves removed and finely chopped

2 tablespoons dry white wine

generous $^1/_4$ cup ricotta cheese

3 tablespoons freshly grated Parmesan cheese

1 egg

freshly grated nutmeg

salt and ground black pepper

COOK'S TIP

To make pasta dough, sift 1¾ cups all-purpose flour and a pinch of salt onto a clean counter and make a well in the center with your fist. Pour 2 beaten eggs and 1 tablespoon oil into the well. Gradually mix in the eggs with your fingers. Knead the pasta until smooth, wrap in plastic wrap, and let rest for at least 30 minutes before rolling out.

1 To make the filling, melt the butter in a pan, add the pork, turkey, and herbs, and cook gently for 5–6 minutes, stirring frequently and breaking up any lumps in the meat with a wooden spoon. Season to taste and stir well to mix thoroughly.

2 Add the wine to the pan and stir again. Simmer for 1–2 minutes, or until reduced slightly, then cover, and simmer gently for about 20 minutes, stirring occasionally. With a slotted spoon, transfer the meat to a bowl and let cool.

3 Add the ricotta and Parmesan cheeses to the bowl with the egg and freshly grated nutmeg to taste. Stir well.

4 Using a pasta machine, roll out one-quarter of the pasta dough into a 36-inch strip. Cut the strip with a sharp knife into two 18-inch lengths.

5 Using a teaspoon, put 10–12 little mounds of the filling along one side of one of the pasta strips, spacing them evenly. Brush a little water onto the pasta strip around each mound, then fold the plain side of the pasta strip over the filling.

6 Starting from the folded edge, press down gently with your fingertips around each mound of filling, pushing the air out at the unfolded edge. Sprinkle lightly with flour.

7 With a fluted pasta wheel, cut along each long side, then in between each mound to make small square shapes. Dust lightly with flour.

9 Drop the ravioli into a large pan of salted, boiling water, bring back to a boil, and boil for 4–5 minutes until the filling is cooked.

10 While the ravioli are cooking, melt the butter in a small pan, add the fresh sage leaves, and stir over medium-high heat until the sage leaves are sizzling in the butter.

11 Drain the ravioli and pour half into a warmed large bowl. Sprinkle with half the grated Parmesan, then half the sage butter. Repeat with the remaining ravioli, Parmesan, and sage butter. Serve immediately, garnished with fresh sage leaves. Hand around more grated Parmesan separately.

8 Put the ravioli in a single layer on floured dishtowels and leave to dry while repeating the process with the remaining pasta to make 80–96 ravioli altogether.

Turkey Lasagne

2 Blanch the broccoli in a large pan of salted, boiling water for 1 minute, then drain, and rinse thoroughly under cold water to prevent the broccoli from over-cooking. Drain well and set aside.

3 To make the sauce, melt the butter in a pan, stir in the flour, and cook for 1 minute, still stirring. Remove from the heat and gradually stir in the milk. Return to the heat and bring the sauce to a boil, stirring constantly. Simmer for 1 minute, then add $^2/_3$ cup of the grated Parmesan and plenty of salt and pepper.

This easy pasta dish is delicious made with cooked turkey pieces and broccoli in a rich and creamy Parmesan sauce.

INGREDIENTS

Serves 4

2 tablespoons olive oil
1 onion, chopped
2 garlic cloves, chopped
1 pound cooked turkey meat, finely diced
1 cup mascarpone cheese
2 tablespoons chopped fresh tarragon
11 ounces broccoli, broken into flowerets
4 ounces no pre-cook lasagne verde
salt and ground black pepper

For the sauce
$^1/_4$ cup butter
2 tablespoons all-purpose flour
$2^1/_2$ cups milk
1 cup freshly grated
    Parmesan cheese

1 Preheat the oven to 350°F. Heat the oil in a pan and cook the onion and garlic until softened. Remove from the heat, stir in the turkey, cheese, and tarragon, with seasoning to taste.

VARIATION

This dish is also good made with half ham and half turkey.

4 Spoon a layer of the turkey mixture into a large, shallow ovenproof dish. Add a layer of broccoli and cover with sheets of lasagne. Coat with the cheese sauce. Repeat these layers, finishing with a layer of cheese sauce on top. Sprinkle with the remaining grated Parmesan cheese and bake for 35–40 minutes.

Bamie Goreng

*This Indonesian fried noodle dish is
wonderfully versatile. You can add
other vegetables, such as mushrooms,
broccoli, leeks, or bean sprouts; just
use whatever is at hand.*

INGREDIENTS

Serves 6–8

1 pound dried egg noodles

2 eggs

2 tablespoons butter

6 tablespoons vegetable oil

1 skinless, boneless chicken breast
   portion, sliced

4 ounces pork tenderloin, sliced

4 ounces veal liver, finely sliced (optional)

2 garlic cloves, crushed

4 ounces peeled cooked shrimp

4 ounces bok choy

2 celery stalks, thinly sliced

4 scallions, shredded

about 4 tablespoons chicken stock

dark soy sauce and light soy sauce

salt and ground black pepper

deep-fried onions and shredded scallions,
   to garnish (optional)

3 Heat the remaining oil in a wok
and cook the chicken, pork, and
liver (if using) with the garlic for
2–3 minutes, or until the meat has
changed color. Add the shrimp, bok
choy, sliced celery, and scallions
and toss to mix.

4 Add the noodles and toss over
the heat until heated through
and the bok choy is lightly cooked.
Add enough stock just to moisten,
and season with dark and light soy
sauce. Add the scrambled eggs and
toss to mix. Serve immediately,
garnished with onions, if you like.

1 Bring a pan of lightly salted
water to a boil, add the noodles,
and cook them for 3–4 minutes.
Drain, rinse under cold water, and
drain again. Set aside.

2 Put the eggs in a bowl, beat,
and season with salt and
pepper. Heat the butter with
1 teaspoon oil in a pan, add the
eggs, and stir over low heat until
scrambled but still quite moist.

Thai Fried Noodles

Chicken is combined with shrimp, pork tenderloin, and Thai flavorings to make this terrific fried-noodle dish.

INGREDIENTS

Serves 4

8 ounces thread egg noodles
4 tablespoons vegetable oil
2 garlic cloves, finely chopped
6 ounces pork tenderloin, sliced into
   thin strips
1 skinless, boneless chicken breast portion,
   about 6 ounces, sliced into thin strips
1 cup cooked peeled shrimp, rinsed
   if canned
3 tablespoons lime or lemon juice
3 tablespoons Thai fish sauce
2 tablespoons soft light brown sugar
2 eggs, beaten
$1/2$ red chile, seeded and finely chopped
$1/4$ cup bean sprouts
4 tablespoons roasted peanuts, chopped
3 scallions, cut into 2-inch lengths
   and shredded
3 tablespoons chopped fresh cilantro

1 Place the noodles in a large pan of boiling water and let stand for about 5 minutes.

2 Meanwhile, heat 3 tablespoons of the oil in a wok or large skillet, add the garlic, and cook for 30 seconds.

3 Add the pork and chicken to the wok or skillet and stir-fry over high heat until lightly browned, then add the shrimp, and stir-fry for 2 minutes.

4 Add the lime or lemon juice, Thai fish sauce, and sugar and stir-fry until the sugar has completely dissolved.

5 Drain the noodles and add to the pan with the remaining oil. Mix well. Pour in the beaten eggs. Stir-fry until almost set, then add the chile and bean sprouts. Add half the peanuts, scallions, and cilantro to the pan. Stir-fry for 2 minutes, then tip onto a serving platter. Sprinkle with the remaining ingredients, and serve immediately.

Sour Chicken Stir-fry

There are few cooking concepts that are better suited to today's busy lifestyle than the all-in-one stir-fry. This recipe has a Southeast Asian influence.

INGREDIENTS

Serves 4

10 ounces Chinese egg noodles

2 tablespoons vegetable oil

3 scallions, chopped

1 garlic clove, crushed

1-inch piece fresh root ginger, peeled
  and grated

1 teaspoon hot paprika

1 teaspoon ground coriander

3 skinless, boneless chicken breast
  portions, sliced

4 ounces sugar-snap peas

1 cup baby corncobs, halved

1 cup fresh bean sprouts

1 tablespoon cornstarch

3 tablespoons soy sauce

3 tablespoons lemon juice

1 tablespoon sugar

3 tablespoons chopped fresh cilantro or
  scallion tops, to garnish

1 Bring a large pan of salted water to a boil. Add the egg noodles and cook according to the instructions on the packet. Drain, cover, and keep warm.

2 Heat the oil. Add the scallions and cook over low heat. Mix in the next five ingredients, then stir-fry for 3–4 minutes. Add the next three ingredients and steam briefly. Add the noodles.

3 Combine the cornstarch, soy sauce, lemon juice, and sugar in a small bowl. Add to the wok and simmer briefly to thicken. Serve garnished with chopped cilantro or scallion tops.

CURRIES

Chicken is a popular choice to use in curried dishes and it's amazing how many different combinations of flavors there are. As well as recipes from India, there are dishes from all over Asia, including Malaysia, Vietnam, and Thailand. Mildly spicy curries sit alongside others that are extremely hot; and there are also many fragrantly spiced dishes and others that use fruit. There is even a selection of low-fat curries, so that you can enjoy the flavors and still eat healthily. With so many authentic and flavorsome recipes to choose from, this chapter will prove to be a curry-lover's paradise.

Thai Red Chicken Curry

Here chicken and potatoes are simmered in coconut milk spiced with red curry paste and Thai fish sauce, then garnished with shredded kaffir lime leaves and red chiles.

INGREDIENTS

Serves 4

1 onion
1 tablespoon peanut oil
1²/₃ cups coconut milk
2 tablespoons Thai red curry paste
2 tablespoons Thai fish sauce
1 tablespoon soft light brown sugar
8 ounces tiny new potatoes
1 pound skinless, boneless chicken breast
    portions, cut into chunks
1 tablespoon lime juice
2 tablespoons chopped fresh mint
1 tablespoon chopped fresh basil
2 kaffir lime leaves, shredded
1–2 fresh red chiles, seeded and
    finely shredded
salt and ground black pepper

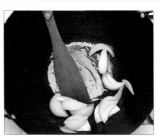

1 Cut the onion into wedges. Heat a wok until hot, then add the oil, and swirl it around. Add the onion and stir-fry for 3–4 minutes.

2 Pour in the coconut milk, then bring to a boil, stirring. Stir in the curry paste, fish sauce, and sugar.

3 Add the potatoes and seasoning and simmer gently, covered, for about 20 minutes.

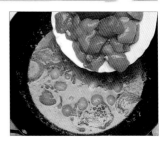

4 Add the chicken chunks, and cook, covered, over low heat for 5–10 minutes more, or until the chicken is cooked and the potatoes are tender.

5 Stir in the lime juice, chopped mint, and basil. Serve immediately, sprinkled with the shredded kaffir lime leaves and red chiles.

VARIATION

You can use boneless chicken thighs instead of breast portions. Simply skin them, cut the flesh into chunks, and cook in the coconut milk with the potatoes.

Fragrant Chicken Curry

In this dish, the mildly spiced sauce is thickened using lentils rather than the traditional onions fried in ghee.

INGREDIENTS

Serves 4

scant $^1/_2$ cup red lentils

2 tablespoons mild curry powder

2 teaspoon ground coriander

1 teaspoon cumin seeds

2 cups vegetable stock

8 skinless chicken thighs

8 ounces fresh or frozen shredded
   spinach, thawed and well drained

1 tablespoon chopped fresh cilantro

salt and ground black pepper

fresh cilantro sprigs,
   to garnish

white or brown basmati rice and broiled
   poppadums, to serve

1 Rinse the lentils under cold running water. Put into a large pan with the curry powder, ground coriander, cumin seeds, and stock.

2 Bring to a boil, then lower the heat. Cover and simmer gently for 10 minutes.

3 Add the chicken and spinach. Cover and simmer gently for 40 minutes more, or until the chicken is cooked.

4 Stir in the chopped cilantro and season to taste. Serve garnished with fresh cilantro and accompanied by the rice and broiled poppadums.

Coconut Rice with Green Chicken Curry

Use one or two fresh green chiles in this dish, according to how hot you like your curry. Remember that small, pointed chiles are usually fiery hot, while smaller, blunt ones tend to be milder. In any case, the mild aromatic flavor of the rice offsets the spiciness of the curry.

INGREDIENTS

Serves 3–4

4 scallions, trimmed and
    coarsely chopped

1–2 fresh green chiles, seeded and
    coarsely chopped

³/₄-inch piece of fresh ginger
    root, peeled

2 garlic cloves

1 teaspoon Thai fish sauce

large bunch of fresh cilantro

small handful of fresh parsley

2–3 tablespoons water

2 tablespoons sunflower oil

4 skinless, boneless chicken breast
    portions, cubed

1 green bell pepper, seeded and
    thinly sliced

1³/₄ cups canned coconut milk

salt and ground black pepper

For the rice

generous 1 cup Thai fragrant
    rice, rinsed

1³/₄ cups canned coconut milk

1 lemongrass stalk, quartered
    and bruised

COOK'S TIP

Lemongrass makes the perfect partner for coconut, especially when used with chicken. In this recipe, bruise the tough, top end of the lemongrass stalk with a mortar and pestle before use.

1. Put the scallions, chiles, ginger, garlic, Thai fish sauce, and fresh herbs in a food processor or blender. Pour in the water and process to a smooth paste.

2. Heat half the oil in large skillet. Cook the chicken cubes, stirring occasionally, until evenly browned. Transfer to a plate.

3. Heat the remaining oil in the skillet. Stir-fry the green bell pepper for 3–4 minutes, then add the chile and ginger paste. Cook, stirring, for 3–4 minutes, or until the mixture becomes fairly thick.

4. Return the chicken to the skillet and add the coconut milk. Season and bring to a boil, then lower the heat, half cover the pan, and simmer for 8–10 minutes.

5. When the chicken is cooked, transfer it with the bell pepper to a plate. Boil the cooking liquid for 10–12 minutes, or until it is well reduced and fairly thick.

6. Meanwhile, put the rice in a large pan. Add the coconut milk and the bruised pieces of lemongrass. Stir in a little salt, bring to a boil, then lower the heat, cover, and simmer very gently for 10 minutes, or for the time recommended on the packet. When the rice is tender, discard the pieces of lemongrass and fork the rice onto a warmed serving plate.

7. Return the chicken and bell peppers to the sauce, stir, and cook gently for a few minutes to heat through. Spoon the curry over the rice and serve immediately.

Fragrant Thai Chicken Curry

This flavorful and fragrant, creamy curry is quite simple to make even though it includes a variety of interesting ingredients.

INGREDIENTS

Serves 6

1³/4 cups canned coconut milk

6 skinless, boneless chicken breast
    portions, finely sliced

8 ounces can bamboo shoots, drained
    and sliced

2 tablespoons Thai fish sauce

1 tablespoon soft light brown sugar

scant 1 cup Thai jasmine rice

pinch of saffron threads

For the green curry paste

4 green chiles, seeded

1 lemongrass stalk, sliced

1 small onion, sliced

3 garlic cloves

¹/2-inch piece of galangal or fresh ginger
    root, peeled

grated rind of ¹/2 lime

1 teaspoon coriander seeds

1 teaspoon cumin seeds

¹/2 teaspoon shrimp or Thai fish sauce

For the garnish

1 red chile, seeded and cut into fine strips

finely pared rind of ¹/2 lime,
    finely shredded

fresh Thai purple basil or cilantro, coarsely
    chopped

1 To make the green curry paste, put the chiles, lemongrass, onion, garlic, galangal or ginger, lime rind, coriander seeds, cumin seeds, and shrimp or Thai fish sauce in a food processor or blender and process until they are reduced to a thick paste. Set aside.

2 Bring half the coconut milk to a boil in a large pan, reduce the heat, and simmer for about 5 minutes, or until reduced by half. Stir in the green curry paste and simmer for 5 minutes more.

3 Add the finely sliced chicken to the pan with the remaining coconut milk, bamboo shoots, fish sauce, and sugar. Stir well to combine all the ingredients and bring the curry back to simmering point, then simmer gently for about 10 minutes, or until the chicken slices are cooked through. The mixture will look grainy or curdled during cooking, but this is quite normal.

4 Meanwhile, add the rice and saffron to a pan of salted, boiling water. Reduce the heat and simmer for 10 minutes, or until tender. Drain the rice and serve it with the curry, garnished with the chile, lime rind, and Thai purple basil or cilantro.

Chicken with Spices and Soy Sauce

This simple but delicious Chinese-influenced dish comes from Malaysia. The combination of tamarind, nutmeg, cloves, and soy sauce is unusual and appetizing.

INGREDIENTS

Serves 4

1 chicken, about 3–3¹/₂ pounds,
   cut into 16 pieces

3 onions, sliced

about 4 cups water

3 garlic cloves, crushed

3–4 fresh red chiles, seeded and sliced, or
   1 tablespoon chili powder

3 tablespoons vegetable oil

¹/₂ teaspoon grated nutmeg

6 whole cloves

1 teaspoon tamarind pulp, soaked in
   3 tablespoons warm water

2–3 tablespoons dark or light soy sauce

salt

fresh green and red chile shreds, to garnish

plain boiled rice, to serve

1 Place the chicken pieces in a pan with one of the sliced onions. Pour in just enough water to cover. Bring to a boil, then reduce the heat, and simmer gently for about 20 minutes.

2 Grind the remaining onions with the garlic and chiles or chile powder to a fine paste in a food processor or using a mortar and pestle. Heat a little of the oil in a wok or skillet and cook the paste to bring out the flavor. Do not let the paste brown.

3 When the chicken has cooked for 20 minutes, lift it out of the stock and into the spicy mixture. Toss everything together over fairly high heat so that the spices permeate the chicken. Reserve 1¹/₄ cups of the stock to add to the pan later.

4 Stir in the nutmeg and cloves. Strain the tamarind and add the tamarind juice and the soy sauce to the chicken. Cook for 2–3 minutes more, then add the reserved stock.

5 Taste and adjust the seasoning. Cook, uncovered, for about 25–35 minutes more, or until the chicken pieces are tender and cooked through.

6 Transfer the chicken to a bowl, top with shredded green and red chiles, and serve with plain boiled rice.

Red Chicken Curry with Bamboo Shoots

Bamboo shoots have a lovely crunchy texture. It is quite acceptable to use canned whole bamboo shoots, which are crisper and of better quality than sliced shoots. Rinse before using.

INGREDIENTS

Serves 4–6

4 cups coconut milk
1 pound skinless, boneless chicken breast
  portions, cut into bitesize pieces
2 tablespoons Thai fish sauce
1 tablespoon sugar
8 ounces drained canned bamboo shoots,
  rinsed and sliced
5 kaffir lime leaves, torn
salt and ground black pepper
chopped fresh red chiles and kaffir lime
  leaves, to garnish

For the red curry paste
1 teaspoon coriander seeds
$1/2$ teaspoon cumin seeds
12–15 fresh red chiles, seeded and
  coarsely chopped
4 shallots, thinly sliced
2 garlic cloves, chopped
1 tablespoon chopped galangal
2 lemongrass stalks, chopped
3 kaffir lime leaves, chopped
4 fresh cilantro roots
10 black peppercorns
good pinch of ground cinnamon
1 teaspoon ground turmeric
$1/2$ teaspoon shrimp paste
1 teaspoon salt
2 tablespoons vegetable oil

VARIATION

You can use straw mushrooms instead of, or as well as, the bamboo shoots. These are available in cans from Asian stores and supermarkets. Drain well and then stir into the curry at the end of the recipe.

1 Make the curry paste. Dry-fry the coriander and cumin seeds for 1–2 minutes, then put in a mortar or food processor with the remaining ingredients, except the oil, and grind or process to a paste.

2 Add the oil, a little at a time, mixing or processing well after each addition. Transfer to a jar and chill until ready to use.

3 Pour half of the coconut milk into a large, heavy pan. Bring the milk to a boil, stirring constantly until it has separated.

4 Stir in 2 tablespoons of the red curry paste and cook the mixture for 2–3 minutes, stirring constantly. The remaining red curry paste can be kept in the refrigerator for up to 3 months.

5 Add the chicken pieces, Thai fish sauce, and sugar to the pan. Stir well, then cook for 5–6 minutes, or until the chicken changes color and is cooked through, stirring constantly to prevent the mixture from sticking to the base of the pan.

6 Pour the remaining coconut milk into the pan, then add the sliced bamboo shoots and torn kaffir lime leaves. Bring back to a boil over medium heat, stirring constantly to prevent the mixture sticking, then taste and add salt and pepper if necessary.

7 To serve, spoon the curry into a warmed serving dish and garnish with chopped chiles and kaffir lime leaves.

Chicken with Thai Spices

This is the perfect dish for a party, as the chicken and sauce can be prepared in advance and combined at the last minute.

Serves 4

3 tablespoons oil

1 onion, coarsely chopped

2 garlic cloves, crushed

1 tablespoon Thai red curry paste

3³/₄ cups canned coconut milk

2 lemongrass stalks,
    coarsely chopped

6 kaffir lime leaves, chopped

²/₃ cup strained plain yogurt

2 tablespoons apricot jelly

1 chicken, about 3¹/₂ pounds, cooked,
    boned, and skinned

2 tablespoons chopped
    fresh cilantro

salt and ground black pepper

kaffir limes leaves, shredded
    coconut, and fresh cilantro,
    to garnish

boiled rice, to serve

1 Heat the oil in a pan. Add the onion and garlic, and cook over low heat for 5–10 minutes, or until soft. Stir in the curry paste. Cook, stirring, for 2–3 minutes. Stir in the coconut milk, then add the lemongrass, lime leaves, yogurt, and apricot jelly Stir well. Cover and simmer for 30 minutes.

2 Process the sauce in a blender or food processor, then strain it back into a clean pan, pressing as much of the puréed mixture as possible through the strainer.

3 Cut the chicken into bitesize pieces. Add to the sauce.

4 Bring the sauce back to simmering point. Stir in the fresh cilantro and seasoning. Serve with rice, garnished with extra kaffir lime leaves, shredded coconut, and cilantro.

Chicken with Ginger and Lemongrass

This Vietnamese recipe contains the unusual combination of ginger and lemongrass with mandarin orange and chiles.

INGREDIENTS

Serves 4–6

3 chicken legs (thighs and drumsticks)
1 tablespoon vegetable oil
3/4-inch piece of fresh ginger root, finely chopped
1 garlic clove, crushed
1 small fresh red chile, seeded and finely chopped
2-inch piece of lemongrass, shredded
2/3 cup chicken stock
1 tablespoon Thai fish sauce
2 teaspoons sugar
1/2 teaspoon salt
juice of 1/2 lemon
1/2 cup raw peanuts
2 scallions, shredded
rind of 1 mandarin or satsuma, shredded
plain boiled rice or rice noodles, to serve

1 With the heel of a knife, chop through the narrow end of each of the chicken drumsticks. Remove the jointed parts of the chicken, then remove the skin. Rinse and pat dry with paper towels.

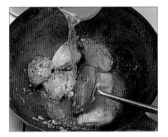

2 Heat the oil in a wok. Add the chicken, ginger, garlic, chile, and lemongrass and cook for 3–4 minutes. Add the stock, Thai fish sauce, sugar, salt, and lemon juice. Cover the pan and simmer for 30–35 minutes.

3 To prepare the peanuts, the red skin must be removed. To do this broil or roast the peanuts under medium heat until evenly brown, for about 2–3 minutes. Turn the nuts out onto a clean dishtowel and rub briskly to loosen the skins.

4 Transfer the chicken from the wok to a warmed serving dish, and sprinkle with the roasted peanuts, shredded scallions, and the rind of the mandarin or satsuma. Serve hot with plain boiled rice or rice noodles.

Chicken with Green Mango

Green, unripe mango is used for cooking various dishes on the Indian subcontinent, including pickles, chutneys, and some meat, chicken, and vegetable dishes. This is a fairly simple chicken dish to prepare and is served with rice and dhal.

INGREDIENTS

Serves 4

1 green mango
3¹/₄ cups cubed chicken
¹/₄ teaspoon onion seeds
1 teaspoon grated fresh ginger root
¹/₂ teaspoon crushed garlic
1 teaspoon chili powder
¹/₄ teaspoon ground turmeric
1 teaspoon salt
1 teaspoon ground coriander
2 tablespoons corn oil
2 onions, sliced
4 curry leaves
1¹/₄ cups water
2 tomatoes, quartered
2 green chiles, chopped
2 tablespoons chopped
   fresh cilantro

1 To prepare the mango, peel, pit, and slice the flesh thickly. Place the mango slices in a small bowl, cover, and set aside.

2 Place the chicken cubes in a bowl and add the onion seeds, ginger, garlic, chili powder, turmeric, salt, and ground coriander. Mix the spices into the chicken and then add half the mango slices.

3 In a medium pan, heat the oil and cook the sliced onions until they turn golden brown. Add the curry leaves.

4 Gradually add the spiced chicken pieces and mango slices, stirring constantly.

5 Pour in the water, lower the heat, and cook for about 12–15 minutes, stirring occasionally, until the chicken is cooked through and the water has been absorbed.

6 Add the remaining mango slices, the tomatoes, green chiles, and fresh cilantro. Serve hot.

Mughlai-style Chicken

This Mogul recipe, which comes from Andhra Pradesh, has a heady aroma of saffron and the captivating flavor of a silky almond and cream sauce.

INGREDIENTS

Serves 4–6

4 boneless chicken breast portions, rubbed all over with a little garam masala

2 eggs, beaten with salt and pepper

6 tablespoons ghee or vegetable oil

1 large onion, finely chopped

2-inch piece of fresh ginger root, finely crushed

4 garlic cloves, finely crushed

4 cloves

4 green cardamom pods

2-inch piece of cinnamon stick

2 bay leaves

15–20 saffron threads

$^2/_3$ cup plain yogurt, beaten with 1 teaspoon cornstarch

$^1/_3$ cup heavy cream

$^1/_2$ cup ground almonds

salt

1 Brush the chicken portions with the beaten eggs. In a wok or large pan, heat the ghee or vegetable oil and cook the chicken until cooked through and browned on both sides. Remove the chicken from the pan and keep warm.

2 In the same pan, cook the chopped onion, ginger, garlic, cloves, cardamom pods, cinnamon, and bay leaves. When the onion turns golden, remove the pan from the heat, let the contents cool a little, and add the saffron and yogurt mixture. Mix well to prevent the yogurt from curdling.

3 Return the chicken to the pan, along with any juices, and gently cook until the chicken is tender. Adjust the seasoning.

4 Just before serving, fold in the heavy cream and ground almonds. Make sure the curry is piping hot before serving.

Goan Chicken Curry

Coconuts grow in abundance in Goa, and so it is hardly surprising that coconut, in all of its forms, is widely used to enrich Goan cuisine.

INGREDIENTS

Serves 4

1¹/₂ cups dry unsweetened
    shredded coconut
2 tablespoons vegetable oil
¹/₂ teaspoon cumin seeds
4 black peppercorns
1 tablespoon fennel seeds
1 tablespoon coriander seeds
2 onions, finely chopped
¹/₂ teaspoon salt
8 small chicken pieces, such as thighs and
    drumsticks, skinned
fresh cilantro sprigs and lemon wedges,
    to garnish
chutney and plain boiled rice, to serve

1 Put the shredded coconut in a bowl with 3 tablespoons water. Leave to soak for 15 minutes.

2 Heat 1 tablespoon of the oil in a wok or large pan and cook the cumin seeds, peppercorns, fennel, and coriander seeds over low heat for 3–4 minutes, or until they begin to splutter.

3 Add the onions and cook for about 5 minutes, stirring occasionally, until the onion has softened and turned opaque.

4 Stir in the coconut, along with the soaking water and salt, and continue to cook for 5 minutes more, stirring occasionally to prevent the mixture from sticking to the pan.

5 Put the coconut mixture into a food processor or blender and process to form a coarse paste. Spoon into a bowl and set aside until required.

6 Heat the remaining oil and cook the pieces of chicken for 10 minutes. Add the coconut paste and cook over low heat for 15–20 minutes, or until golden and the chicken is cooked through.

7 Transfer to a warmed serving plate, and garnish with fresh cilantro and lemon wedges. Serve with chutney and plain boiled rice.

COOK'S TIP

If you prefer, make the spiced coconut mixture the day before and chill it in the refrigerator, then continue from step 6 when required.

Balti Chicken Tikka Masala

This recipe is based on makkhani murghi, a popular Balti dish. Serve with warm nan bread or fluffy basmati rice.

INGREDIENTS

Serves 4

4 skinless, part-boned chicken
    breast portions
²/3 cup plain yogurt
1-inch piece of fresh ginger root, grated
2 garlic cloves, crushed
1 teaspoon chili powder
1 tablespoon ground coriander
2 tablespoons vegetable oil
2 tablespoons lime juice
few drops each of yellow and red liquid
    food coloring, mixed to a bright
    orange shade

For the masala

1 pound tomatoes
6 tablespoons sweet butter
1 tablespoon vegetable oil
1 onion, chopped
1 teaspoon salt
1 fresh green chile, seeded and
    finely chopped
1 teaspoon garam masala
¹/4 teaspoon cayenne pepper
¹/2 cup heavy cream
3 tablespoons plain yogurt
2 tablespoons coarsely torn fresh
    cilantro leaves
1 teaspoon dry-roasted cumin seeds

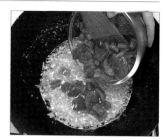

1 Cut each chicken portion into three or four pieces, then slash the meaty side of each piece. Put the chicken into a shallow dish. In a bowl, combine the yogurt, ginger, garlic, chili powder, ground coriander, oil, lime juice, and coloring. Pour this over the chicken and toss to coat completely, making sure that the marinade goes into the slits in the chicken. Cover and leave in the refrigerator for 6–24 hours, turning occasionally.

2 Preheat the oven to 450°F. Lift the chicken pieces out of the marinade, shaking off any excess, and arrange in a shallow baking pan. Bake for 15–20 minutes, or until golden brown and evenly cooked through.

3 Meanwhile, make the masala: plunge the tomatoes into boiling water for 30 seconds, then refresh in cold water. Peel off the skins, remove the seeds, and chop the flesh. Heat the butter and oil in a wok or large pan, add the onion, and cook for 5 minutes, or until softened. Add the tomatoes, salt, chile, garam masala, and cayenne pepper. Cook, covered, for about 10 minutes.

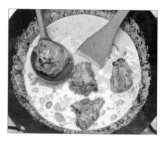

4 Stir in the cream and yogurt, then simmer over low heat for 1–2 minutes, stirring constantly. Add the chicken pieces, then stir to coat in the sauce. Serve the chicken immediately sprinkled with cilantro and roasted cumin seeds.

COOK'S TIP

If you can, leave the chicken to marinate for as long as possible to allow plenty of time for it to absorb the flavorings.

Chicken Korma

Although kormas are traditionally rich and high in fat, this recipe uses reduced-fat yogurt instead of cream, which gives the sauce a delicious flavor while keeping down the fat content. To prevent the yogurt from curdling, add it very slowly to the sauce and keep stirring until it is incorporated.

INGREDIENTS

Serves 4

1¹/2 pounds skinless, boneless chicken
 breast portions
2 garlic cloves, crushed
1-inch piece of fresh ginger root,
 coarsely chopped
1 tablespoon oil
3 green cardamom pods
1 onion, finely chopped
2 teaspoons ground cumin
¹/4 teaspoon salt
1¹/4 cups plain low-fat yogurt
toasted sliced almonds (optional)
 and a fresh cilantro sprig,
 to garnish
plain rice, to serve

1 Remove any visible fat from the chicken portions and cut the meat into 1-inch cubes.

2 Put the garlic and ginger into a food processor or blender with 2 tablespoons water and process to a smooth, creamy paste.

3 Heat the oil in a large, heavy pan and cook the chicken cubes for 8–10 minutes, or until browned on all sides. Remove the chicken cubes with a slotted spoon and set aside.

4 Add the cardamom pods and cook for 2 minutes. Add the onion and cook, stirring, for 5 minutes more.

5 Stir in the garlic and ginger paste, cumin, and salt, and cook, stirring constantly, for 5 minutes more.

6 Add half the yogurt, stirring in a tablespoonful at a time, and cook over low heat, until it has all been absorbed. Return the chicken to the pan.

7 Cover and simmer over low heat for 5–6 minutes, or until the chicken is tender. Add the remaining yogurt and simmer for 5 minutes more. Garnish with toasted sliced almonds, if using, and cilantro. Serve with rice.

COOK'S TIP
~
Traditionally, kormas are spicy dishes with a rich, creamy texture. They are not meant to be very hot curries.

Kashmiri Chicken Curry

Sliced apples give this low-fat yet flavorsome dish a subtle and fruity taste.

INGREDIENTS

Serves 4

2 teaspoons oil

2 medium onions, diced

1 bay leaf

2 cloves

1-inch cinnamon stick

4 black peppercorns

1 broiling chicken, about 1¹/₂ pounds,
    skinned and cut into 8 pieces

1 teaspoon garam masala

1 teaspoon grated fresh
    ginger root

1 teaspoon crushed garlic

1 teaspoon salt

1 teaspoon chili powder

1 tablespoon ground almonds

²/₃ cup plain low-fat yogurt

2 green eating apples, peeled, cored, and
    coarsely sliced

1 tablespoon chopped
    fresh cilantro

¹/₂ cup sliced almonds, lightly
    toasted, and fresh cilantro leaves,
    to garnish

1 Heat the oil in a wok or heavy skillet and cook the onions with the bay leaf, cloves, cinnamon, and peppercorns for about 3–5 minutes, or until the onions are beginning to soften but are not starting to brown.

2 Add the chicken pieces to the onions and continue to stir-fry for at least 3 minutes more.

3 Lower the heat and add the garam masala, ginger, garlic, salt, chili powder, and ground almonds and continue to stir for 2–3 minutes.

4 Pour in the yogurt and stir for 2 minutes more.

5 Add the apples and chopped cilantro, cover, and cook for about 10–15 minutes.

6 Check that the chicken is cooked through and serve immediately, garnished with the sliced almonds and whole cilantro leaves.

Mild Green Calcutta Curry

Coconut milk creates a rich sauce that is sweet with dried and fresh fruit and fragrant with herbs.

INGREDIENTS

Serves 4

4 garlic cloves, chopped
1 tablespoon chopped fresh ginger root
2–3 chiles, chopped
$1/2$ bunch of fresh cilantro leaves, chopped
1 onion, chopped
juice of 1 lemon
pinch of cayenne pepper
$1/2$ teaspoon curry powder
$1/2$ teaspoon ground cumin
2–3 pinches of ground cloves
large pinch of ground coriander
3 skinless, boneless chicken breast
    portions or thighs, cut into
    bitesize pieces
2 tablespoons vegetable oil
2 cinnamon sticks
1 cup chicken stock
1 cup coconut milk
1–2 tablespoons sugar
1–2 bananas
$1/4$ pineapple, peeled and chopped
handful of golden raisins
handful of raisins or currants
2–3 fresh mint sprigs, thinly sliced
juice of $1/4$–$1/2$ lemon
salt

1 Process the garlic, ginger, chiles, fresh cilantro, onion, lemon juice, cayenne pepper, curry powder, cumin, cloves, ground coriander, and salt in a food processor or blender.

2 Toss together the chicken pieces with about 1–2 tablespoons of the spice mixture and set aside.

3 Heat the oil in a wok or large skillet, then add the remaining spice mixture and cook over medium heat, stirring, for 10 minutes, or until the paste is lightly browned.

4 Stir the cinnamon sticks, stock, coconut milk, and sugar into the pan, bring to a boil, then reduce the heat, and simmer for 10 minutes.

5 Stir the chicken into the sauce and cook for 2 minutes, or until the chicken becomes opaque.

6 Meanwhile, thickly slice the bananas. Stir all the fruit into the curry and cook for 1–2 minutes. Stir in the mint and lemon juice. Check the seasoning and add more salt, spice, and lemon juice if necessary. Serve immediately with hot nan bread or steamed rice.

Chicken Saag

Here is a mildly spiced, low-fat dish using the popular combination of spinach and chicken. This recipe is best made using fresh spinach, but you can use frozen instead.

Serves 4

8 ounces fresh spinach leaves, washed but
    not dried

1-inch piece of fresh ginger root, grated

2 garlic cloves, crushed

1 green chile, coarsely chopped

scant 1 cup water

4 tomatoes

2 bay leaves

1 tablespoon oil

1/4 teaspoon black peppercorns

1 onion, finely chopped

2 teaspoons curry powder

1 teaspoon salt

1 teaspoon chili powder

3 tablespoons plain low-fat yogurt

8 chicken thighs, skinned

plain low-fat yogurt and chili powder, to
    garnish

nan bread, to serve

1 Cook the spinach leaves, without any extra water, in a tightly covered pan for 5 minutes. Put the cooked spinach, ginger, garlic, and chile with 1/4 cup of the water into a food processor or blender and process to a thick purée. Set aside. Plunge the tomatoes into boiling water for 30 seconds, then refresh in cold water. Peel off the skins and chop finely.

2 Heat the oil in a large, heavy pan, add the bay leaves and black peppercorns, and cook for 2 minutes. Add the onion and cook for 6–8 minutes more, or until the onion has browned.

3 Add the tomatoes and simmer for about 5 minutes. Stir in the curry powder, salt, and chili powder and cook for 2 minutes.

4 Add the spinach purée and 2/3 cup water, then simmer for 5 minutes.

5 Add the yogurt, 1 tablespoon at a time, and simmer for 5 minutes.

6 Add the chicken thighs. Cover and cook for 25–30 minutes, or until the chicken is cooked. Serve on nan bread, drizzle over some yogurt, and dust with chili powder.

Chicken Dhansak

Dhansak curries originate from the Parsee community and are traditionally made with a mixture of lentils and meat.

INGREDIENTS

Serves 4

scant $^1/_2$ cup green lentils

2 cups chicken stock

1 tablespoon oil

1 teaspoon cumin seeds

2 curry leaves

1 onion, finely chopped

1-inch piece of fresh ginger root, chopped

1 green chile, finely chopped

1 teaspoon ground cumin

1 teaspoon ground coriander

$^1/_4$ teaspoon salt

$^1/_4$ teaspoon chili powder

14-ounce can chopped tomatoes

8 chicken pieces, skinned

4 tablespoons chopped fresh cilantro

1 teaspoon garam masala

fresh cilantro, to garnish

plain and yellow rice,
   to serve

1 Rinse the lentils under cold running water. Put into a pan with the stock. Bring to a boil, cover, and simmer for about 15–20 minutes. Put the lentils and stock to one side.

2 Heat the oil in a large pan and cook the cumin seeds and curry leaves for 2 minutes. Add the onion, ginger, and chile and cook for about 5 minutes. Stir in the cumin, coriander, salt, and chili powder with 2 tablespoons water. Add the tomatoes and the chicken. Cover and cook for 10–15 minutes.

3 Add the lentils and stock, chopped fresh cilantro, and garam masala and cook for about 10 minutes more, or until the chicken is cooked through. Garnish with fresh cilantro and serve with spiced plain and yellow rice.

Chicken Bobotie

Perfect for a buffet party, this mild curry dish is set with savory custard, which makes serving easy. Serve with boiled rice and chutney.

INGREDIENTS

Serves 8

2 thick slices white bread

scant 2 cups milk

2 tablespoons olive oil

2 medium onions, finely chopped

3 tablespoons medium
   curry powder

10 cups ground chicken

1 tablespoon apricot jelly chutney, or
   superfine sugar

2 tablespoons wine vinegar or
   lemon juice

3 eggs, beaten

$^1/_3$ cup raisins or golden raisins

butter, for greasing

12 whole almonds

salt and ground black pepper

1 Preheat the oven to 350°F. Soak the bread in $^2/_3$ cup of the milk. Heat the oil in a skillet and gently cook the onions until tender, then add the curry powder, and cook for 2 minutes more.

2 Add the ground chicken, and brown all over, separating the grains of meat as they brown. Remove from the heat, season with salt and black pepper, add the apricot jelly, chutney, or superfine sugar, and the wine vinegar or lemon juice.

3 Mash the bread in the milk and add to the pan with one of the beaten eggs and the raisins.

4 Grease a 6$^1/_4$-cup shallow, ovenproof dish with butter. Spoon in the chicken mixture and level the top. Cover with buttered foil and bake in the oven for 30 minutes.

5 Meanwhile, beat the remaining eggs and milk. Remove the dish from the oven and lower the temperature to 300°F. Break up the meat using a fork and pour the egg mixture over it.

6 Sprinkle the almonds over the top and bake, uncovered, for 30 minutes, or until set and brown.

Hot Chicken Curry

This curry has a delicious thick sauce with extra color provided by chunks of red and green bell pepper.

INGREDIENTS

Serves 4

2 tablespoons corn oil

$^1/_4$ teaspoon fenugreek seeds

$^1/_4$ teaspoon onion seeds

2 onions, chopped

$^1/_2$ teaspoon chopped garlic

$^1/_2$ teaspoon chopped fresh ginger root

1 teaspoon ground coriander

1 teaspoon chili powder

1 teaspoon salt

14-ounce can tomatoes

2 tablespoons lemon juice

$2^1/_2$ cups cubed chicken

2 tablespoons chopped fresh cilantro

3 green chiles, chopped

$^1/_2$ red bell pepper, cut into chunks

$^1/_2$ green bell pepper, cut into chunks

fresh cilantro sprigs, to garnish

1 In a medium-size pan, heat the oil and cook the fenugreek and onion seeds until they turn a shade darker. Add the chopped onions, garlic, and ginger, and cook for about 5 minutes, or until the onions turn golden brown. Reduce the heat to very low.

2 Meanwhile, in a separate bowl, combine the ground coriander, chili powder, salt, tomatoes, and lemon juice.

3 Pour this mixture into the pan with the onions and increase the heat to medium. Stir-fry for about 3 minutes.

4 Add the cubed chicken and stir-fry for 5–7 minutes.

5 Add the cilantro, chiles, and bell peppers. Lower the heat, cover, and simmer for 10 minutes, or until the chicken is cooked.

6 Serve hot, garnished with fresh cilantro sprigs.

COOK'S TIP

For a milder version of this delicious curry, simply omit some or all of the green chiles.

Balti Chicken Curry

In this low-fat curry, tender pieces of chicken are lightly cooked with fresh vegetables and aromatic spices in the traditional Balti style.

INGREDIENTS

Serves 4

1¹/₂ pounds skinless, boneless chicken
    breast portions
1 tablespoon oil
¹/₂ teaspoon cumin seeds
¹/₂ teaspoon fennel seeds
1 onion, thickly sliced
2 garlic cloves, crushed
1-inch piece of fresh ginger root,
    finely chopped
1 tablespoon curry paste
8 ounces broccoli, broken into flowerets
4 tomatoes, cut into thick wedges
1 teaspoon garam masala
2 tablespoons chopped fresh cilantro
nan bread, to serve

1 Remove any visible fat from the chicken and cut the meat into 1-inch cubes.

2 Heat the oil in a wok or heavy skillet and cook the cumin and fennel seeds for 2 minutes, or until the seeds begin to splutter. Add the onion, garlic, and ginger and cook for 5–7 minutes. Stir in the curry paste and cook, stirring, for 2–3 minutes more.

3 Add the broccoli flowerets and cook for about 5 minutes. Add the chicken cubes and cook for 5–8 minutes.

4 Add the tomato wedges to the wok or skillet with the garam masala and the chopped fresh cilantro. Cook the curry for about 5–10 minutes more, or until the chicken cubes are tender. Serve with nan bread.

Chicken Jalfrezi

A Jalfrezi curry is a stir-fried dish cooked with onions, ginger, and garlic in a rich bell pepper sauce.

INGREDIENTS

Serves 4

1¹/₂ pounds skinless, boneless chicken
    breast portions
1 tablespoon oil
1 teaspoon cumin seeds
1 onion, finely chopped
1 green bell pepper, seeded and
    finely chopped
1 red bell pepper, seeded and
    finely chopped
1 garlic clove, crushed
³/₄-inch piece of fresh ginger root,
    finely chopped
1 tablespoon curry paste
¹/₄ teaspoon chili powder
1 teaspoon ground coriander
1 teaspoon ground cumin
¹/₂ teaspoon salt
14-ounce can chopped tomatoes
2 tablespoons chopped fresh cilantro
fresh cilantro sprig, to garnish
plain rice, to serve

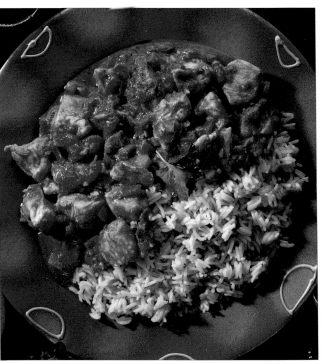

1 Remove any visible fat from the chicken and cut the meat into 1-inch cubes.

2 Heat the oil in a wok or heavy skillet and cook the cumin seeds for 2 minutes, or until they splutter. Add the onion, bell peppers, garlic, and ginger and cook for 6–8 minutes.

3 Add the curry paste and cook for about 2 minutes. Stir in the chili powder, coriander, cumin, and salt and add 1 tablespoon water. Cook for 2 minutes more.

4 Add the chicken cubes and cook for about 5 minutes. Add the chopped tomatoes and chopped fresh cilantro. Cover the wok or skillet with a lid and cook for about 15 minutes, or until the chicken cubes are cooked through. Garnish with a sprig of fresh cilantro and serve with rice.

Quick Chicken Curry

Curry powder can be bought in three different strengths—mild, medium, and hot. Use the type with the strength you prefer for this simple but tasty recipe.

INGREDIENTS

Serves 4

8 chicken legs (thighs and drumsticks)

2 tablespoons vegetable oil

1 onion, thinly sliced

1 garlic clove, crushed

1 tablespoon curry powder

1 tablespoon all-purpose flour

scant 2 cups chicken stock

1 beefsteak tomato

1 tablespoon mango chutney

1 tablespoon lemon juice

salt and ground black pepper

plain boiled rice and Indian pickles,
    to serve

4 Bring to a boil, replace the chicken pieces, cover, and simmer for 20–30 minutes, or until tender.

5 Peel the tomato by blanching in boiling water for 45 seconds, then run under cold water to loosen the skin. Peel and cut into small cubes.

6 Add to the chicken, with the mango chutney and lemon juice. Heat through gently and adjust the seasoning to taste. Serve with plenty of boiled rice and Indian pickles.

1 Cut the chicken legs in half. Heat the oil in a large, flameproof casserole and brown the chicken pieces on all sides. Remove and keep warm.

2 Add the onion and crushed garlic to the casserole and cook until soft. Add the curry powder and cook gently for 2 minutes.

3 Add the flour, and gradually blend in the chicken stock and the seasoning.

Hot Chili Chicken

Not for the faint-hearted, this fiery hot, low-fat curry is made with a spicy chili masala paste.

INGREDIENTS

Serves 4

2 tablespoons tomato paste
2 garlic cloves, coarsely chopped
2 fresh green chiles, coarsely chopped
5 dried red chiles
$^1/_2$ teaspoon salt
$^1/_4$ teaspoon sugar
1 teaspoon chili powder
$^1/_2$ teaspoon paprika
1 tablespoon curry paste
1 tablespoon oil
$^1/_2$ teaspoon cumin seeds
1 onion, finely chopped
2 bay leaves
1 teaspoon ground coriander
1 teaspoon ground cumin
$^1/_4$ teaspoon ground turmeric
14-ounce can chopped tomatoes
$^2/_3$ cup water
8 skinless chicken thighs
1 teaspoon garam masala
sliced green chiles, to garnish
chapatis and plain low-fat yogurt,
    to serve

3 Add the chili paste and cook for 2–3 minutes. Then add the coriander, cumin, and turmeric and cook for 2 minutes. Add the tomatoes and water. Bring to a boil and simmer for 5 minutes, or until the sauce thickens.

4 Add the chicken and garam masala. Cover and simmer for 25–30 minutes, or until the chicken is cooked. Garnish with sliced green chiles and serve with chapatis and yogurt.

1 Put the tomato paste, garlic, both types of chile, salt, sugar, chili powder, paprika, and curry paste into a processor or blender and process to a smooth paste.

2 Cook the cumin seeds in oil for 2 minutes. Add the onion and bay leaves and cook for 5 minutes.

Chicken Biryani

A deceptively easy curry to make, Chicken Biryani is a very popular dish with lots of flavor.

INGREDIENTS

Serves 4

1¹/₂ cups basmati rice, rinsed
¹/₂ teaspoon salt
5 whole cardamom pods
2–3 whole cloves
1 cinnamon stick
3 tablespoons vegetable oil
3 onions, sliced
1¹/₂ pounds skinless, boneless chicken
    breast portions, cubed
¹/₄ teaspoon ground cloves
5 cardamom pods, seeds removed
    and ground
¹/₄ teaspoon hot chili powder
1 teaspoon ground cumin
1 teaspoon ground coriander
¹/₂ teaspoon black pepper
3 garlic cloves, finely chopped
1 teaspoon finely chopped fresh
    ginger root
juice of 1 lemon
4 tomatoes, sliced
2 tablespoons chopped fresh cilantro
²/₃ cup plain yogurt
¹/₂ teaspoon saffron threads soaked in
    2 teaspoons hot milk
3 tablespoons toasted sliced almonds and
    fresh cilantro sprigs, to garnish
plain yogurt, to serve

1 Preheat the oven to 375°F. Bring a pan of water to a boil and add the rice, salt, cardamom pods, cloves, and cinnamon stick. Boil for 2 minutes and then drain, leaving the whole spices in the rice.

2 Heat the oil in a pan and cook the onions for 8 minutes, or until browned. Add the cubed chicken, followed by all the ground spices, the garlic, ginger, and lemon juice. Stir-fry for 5 minutes.

3 Transfer the chicken mixture to a casserole and lay the sliced tomatoes on top. Sprinkle with the fresh cilantro, spoon the plain yogurt over it, and top with the drained rice.

4 Drizzle the saffron and milk over the rice and the pour ²/₃ cup of water over it.

5 Cover tightly and bake in the oven for 1 hour. Transfer to a warmed serving platter and remove the whole spices from the rice. Garnish with toasted almonds and fresh cilantro and serve with extra plain yogurt.

Balti Chicken Madras

This is a fairly hot, low-fat chicken curry which is excellent served with either plain boiled rice, pilau rice, or nan bread.

INGREDIENTS

Serves 4

10 ounces skinless, boneless chicken
    breast portions
3 tablespoons tomato paste
large pinch of ground fenugreek
1/4 teaspoon ground fennel seeds
1 teaspoon grated fresh ginger root
1 1/2 teaspoons ground coriander
1 teaspoon crushed garlic
1 teaspoon chili powder
1/4 teaspoon ground turmeric
2 tablespoons lemon juice
1 teaspoon salt
1 1/4 cups water
1 tablespoon oil
2 medium onions, diced
2–4 curry leaves
2 green chiles, seeded and chopped
1 tablespoon fresh cilantro leaves

1 Remove any visible fat from the chicken breast portions and cut the meat into bitesize cubes.

COOK'S TIP

Always take care not to be over-generous when you are using ground fenugreek as it can be quite bitter.

2 Mix the tomato paste in a bowl with the fenugreek, fennel seeds, ginger, coriander, garlic, chili powder, turmeric, lemon juice, salt, and water.

3 Heat the oil in a wok or heavy skillet and cook the onions together with the curry leaves until the onions are golden brown.

4 Add the chicken pieces to the onions and stir for about 1 minute to seal the meat.

5 Pour in the prepared spice mixture and continue to stir the chicken for about 2 minutes.

6 Lower the heat and cook for 8–10 minutes until the chicken is thoroughly cooked. Add the chiles and fresh cilantro and serve immediately.

Karahi Chicken with Mint

For this tasty dish, the chicken is first boiled before being quickly stir-fried in a little oil.

INGREDIENTS

Serves 4

10 ounces skinless, boneless chicken breast
    portions, cut into strips

1¼ cups water

2 tablespoons soy oil

2 bunches of scallions, coarsely chopped

1 teaspoon grated fresh ginger root

1 teaspoon crushed dried red chile

2 tablespoons lemon juice

1 tablespoon chopped fresh cilantro

1 tablespoon chopped fresh mint

3 tomatoes, seeded and
    coarsely chopped

1 teaspoon salt

fresh mint and cilantro sprigs,
    to garnish

1 Put the chicken and water into a pan, bring to a boil, and lower the heat to medium. Cook for about 10 minutes, or until the water has evaporated and the chicken is cooked. Remove from the heat and set aside.

2 Heat the oil in a skillet or large pan, add the scallions, and stir-fry for about 2 minutes until soft.

3 Add the boiled chicken strips to the skillet or pan and stir-fry them for about 3 minutes over medium heat.

4 Gradually add the ginger, dried chile, lemon juice, fresh cilantro, fresh mint, tomatoes, and salt, and gently stir to blend all the flavors together.

5 Transfer to a serving dish and garnish with the fresh mint and cilantro sprigs.

Tandoori Chicken

A famous Indian chicken dish,
Tandoori Chicken is cooked in a clay
oven called a tandoor. This dish is
extremely popular in the West and
appears on many Indian restaurant
menus. Although the authentic
tandoori flavor is very difficult to
achieve in conventional ovens, this
version is delicious nevertheless.

INGREDIENTS

Serves 4

4 chicken quarters

3/4 cup plain low-fat yogurt

1 teaspoon garam masala

1 teaspoon chopped fresh
  ginger root

1 teaspoon chopped garlic

1 1/2 teaspoons chili powder

1/4 teaspoon ground turmeric

1 teaspoon ground coriander

1 tablespoon lemon juice

1 teaspoon salt

a few drops red food coloring

2 tablespoons corn oil

For the garnish

mixed salad greens

lime wedges

1 tomato, quartered

1 Skin, rinse, and pat dry the
chicken quarters. Make two slits
into the flesh of each piece, place in
a dish and set aside.

2 Combine the yogurt, garam
masala, ginger, garlic, chili
powder, turmeric, ground
coriander, lemon juice, salt, red
food coloring, and oil and beat
until well mixed together.

3 Cover the chicken with the
yogurt and spice mixture and
let marinate for 3 hours.

4 Preheat the oven to 475°F.
Transfer the chicken to an
ovenproof dish.

5 Bake the chicken in the oven for
20–25 minutes, or until it is
cooked right through and browned
on top.

6 Remove from the oven, transfer
to a dish, and garnish with the
salad greens, lime, and tomato.

Simple Curried Chicken

*A tasty curry that needs very little
time for preparation.*

Serves 4

1 pound tomatoes or canned
   chopped tomatoes
2 tablespoons vegetable oil
1 onion, chopped
1 green or red bell pepper, seeded
   and diced
1 garlic clove, finely chopped
1 $1/2$ tablespoons curry powder
$1/2$ teaspoon dried thyme
2 tablespoons lemon juice
$1/2$ cup water
scant $1/2$ cup currants or raisins
salt and ground black pepper
3 $1/2$-pound chicken, skinned and cut
   into 8 pieces
cooked rice, to serve

1 Preheat the oven to 350°F. If
you are using fresh tomatoes,
plunge them into boiling water for
30 seconds, then refresh in cold
water. Peel off the skins, remove
the seeds, and chop the flesh. Set
them aside.

2 Heat the oil in a flameproof
casserole or a deep skillet that
has a lid and an ovenproof handle.
Add the onion, diced green or red
bell pepper, and garlic. Cook,
stirring occasionally, until the
vegetables are soft but not
too brown.

3 Stir in the curry powder and
thyme, then add the tomatoes,
lemon juice, and water. Bring to a
boil, stirring frequently. Stir in the
currants or raisins. Season to taste.

4 Put the chicken pieces in the
skillet or casserole, arranging
them in one layer. Turn to coat
them with the sauce. Cover the pan
and transfer to the oven. Cook for
about 40 minutes, or until the
chicken is tender. Turn the pieces
halfway through cooking.

5 Remove the chicken and sauce
to a warmed serving platter.
Serve with freshly boiled rice.

VARIATION

For Curried Chicken Casserole,
omit the diced bell pepper and
cook 1 $1/2$ tablespoons finely
chopped fresh ginger and
1 green chile, seeded and finely
chopped, with the onion and
garlic. In step 3, stir in the curry
powder with scant 2 cups plain
yogurt; omit the tomatoes,
lemon juice, and water. Add
the chicken pieces, cover
and cook in the oven at a lower
temperature of 325°F for
1–1 $1/4$ hours.

Spicy Masala Chicken

These chicken pieces are marinated and then broiled and have a sweet-and-sour taste. They can be served hot or cold with a salad and rice.

INGREDIENTS

Serves 6

12 chicken thighs
6 tablespoons lemon juice
1 teaspoon chopped fresh
   ginger root
1 teaspoon chopped garlic
1 teaspoon crushed dried red chiles
1 teaspoon salt
1 teaspoon soft brown sugar
2 tablespoons honey
2 tablespoons chopped fresh cilantro
1 green chile, finely chopped
2 tablespoons vegetable oil
fresh cilantro sprigs, to garnish

1 Prick the chicken thighs with a fork, rinse, pat dry, and set aside in a bowl.

2 In a large mixing bowl, make the marinade by combining the lemon juice, ginger, garlic, crushed dried red chiles, salt, sugar and honey. Mix well.

3 Transfer the chicken thighs to the spice mixture and coat well. Set aside for about 45 minutes.

4 Preheat the broiler to medium. Add the fresh cilantro and chopped green chile to the chicken thighs and place them in a large, flameproof dish.

5 Pour any remaining marinade over the chicken and baste with the oil.

6 Cook the chicken thighs under the broiler for 15–20 minutes, turning and basting occasionally, until they are cooked.

7 Transfer the chicken to a serving dish and garnish with a few sprigs of fresh cilantro.

Karahi Chicken with Fresh Fenugreek

2 In a mixing bowl, combine the garlic, chili powder, and salt with the tomato paste.

3 Heat the oil in a large pan. Lower the heat and add the tomato paste and spice mixture.

4 Add the chicken pieces and stir-fry for 5–7 minutes. Lower the heat again.

5 Add the fenugreek leaves and fresh cilantro. Continue to stir-fry for 5–7 minutes.

6 Pour in the water. Cover and cook for about 5 minutes, and serve hot with rice or chapatis.

Fresh fenugreek is a flavor that not many people are familiar with. This recipe is a good introduction to this delicious herb.

INGREDIENTS

Serves 4

4-ounce skinless, boneless chicken thigh,
   cut into strips
4-ounce skinless, boneless chicken breast
   portion, cut into strips
$1/2$ teaspoon chopped garlic
1 teaspoon chili powder
$1/2$ teaspoon salt
2 teaspoons tomato paste
2 tablespoons soy oil
1 bunch of fenugreek leaves
1 tablespoon chopped fresh cilantro
$1^1/4$ cups water
rice or chapatis,
   to serve

1 Bring a pan of water to a boil, add the chicken, and cook for 5–7 minutes. Drain.

COOK'S TIP

When preparing fresh fenugreek, use only the leaves and discard the stems, which are very bitter.

Chicken in Cashew Nut Sauce

This chicken dish has a deliciously thick and nutty sauce, and it is best served with plain boiled rice.

INGREDIENTS

Serves 4

2 onions

2 tablespoons tomato paste

$1/2$ cup cashew nuts

$1^1/2$ teaspoons garam masala

1 teaspoon crushed garlic

1 teaspoon chili powder

1 tablespoon lemon juice

$1/4$ teaspoon ground turmeric

1 teaspoon salt

1 tablespoon plain
    low-fat yogurt

2 tablespoons corn oil

1 tablespoon chopped
    fresh cilantro

1 tablespoon golden raisins

$3^1/4$ cups cubed chicken

$2^1/4$ cups white mushrooms, halved

$1^1/4$ cups water

chopped fresh cilantro,
    to garnish

1 Cut the onions into quarters, then place them in a food processor or blender and process for about 1 minute.

2 Add the tomato paste, cashew nuts, garam masala, garlic, chili powder, lemon juice, turmeric, salt, and yogurt. Process for about $1–1^1/2$ minutes more.

3 In a pan, heat the oil, lower the heat to medium, and pour in the spice mixture from the food processor. Cook for 2 minutes, turning down the heat if necessary.

4 Add the fresh cilantro, golden raisins, and cubed chicken and continue to stir-fry for about 1 minute more.

5 Add the mushrooms, pour in the water, and bring to a simmer. Cover and cook over low heat for about 10 minutes, or until the chicken is cooked through and the sauce is thick. Cook for a little longer if necessary.

6 Serve garnished with chopped fresh cilantro.

Balti Chicken Vindaloo

This is rather a hot low-fat curry and is probably one of the best-known Indian dishes, especially in the West.

INGREDIENTS

Serves 4

1 large potato

$^2/_3$ cup malt vinegar

$1^1/_2$ teaspoons crushed coriander seeds

1 teaspoon crushed cumin seeds

$1^1/_2$ teaspoons chili powder

$^1/_4$ teaspoon ground turmeric

1 teaspoon crushed garlic

1 teaspoon grated fresh ginger root

1 teaspoon salt

$1^1/_2$ teaspoons paprika

1 tablespoon tomato paste

large pinch of ground fenugreek

$1^1/_4$ cups water

8 ounces skinless, boneless chicken breast portion, cubed

1 tablespoon oil

2 medium onions, sliced

4 curry leaves

2 green chiles, chopped

1 Peel the potato, cut it into large, irregular shapes, place in a bowl of water, and set aside.

COOK'S TIP

The best thing to drink with a hot curry is either ice water or a yogurt-based lassi.

2 In a bowl, combine the vinegar, coriander, cumin, chili powder, turmeric, garlic, ginger, salt, paprika, tomato paste, fenugreek, and water.

3 Pour this spice mixture over the chicken and set aside.

4 Heat the oil in a wok or heavy skillet and quickly cook the onions with the curry leaves for 3–4 minutes without burning.

5 Lower the heat and add the chicken mixture to the wok or skillet with the spices. Continue to stir-fry for 2 minutes. Drain the potato pieces and add to the pan. Cover and cook over medium-low heat for 5–7 minutes, or until the sauce has thickened slightly and the chicken and potatoes are cooked through.

6 Add the chopped green chiles before serving.

Chicken in a Spicy Lentil Sauce

Traditionally, this dish is made with lamb, but it is equally delicious, and low in fat, if chicken is substituted. The lentils are flavored with a tarka, which is poured over the dish just before serving.

INGREDIENTS

Serves 4

2 tablespoons chana dhal

¹/4 cup masoor dhal

1 tablespoon oil

2 medium onions, chopped

1 teaspoon crushed garlic

1 teaspoon grated fresh ginger root

¹/2 teaspoon ground turmeric

1¹/2 teaspoons chili powder

1 teaspoon garam masala

¹/2 teaspoon ground coriander

1¹/2 teaspoons salt

6 ounces skinless, boneless chicken breast
    portion, cubed

3 tablespoons fresh cilantro leaves

1–2 green chiles, seeded
    and chopped

2–3 tablespoons lemon juice

1¹/4 cups water

2 tomatoes, peeled and halved

For the tarka

1 teaspoon oil

¹/2 teaspoon cumin seeds

2 garlic cloves

2 dried red chiles

4 curry leaves

1 Boil the chana dhal and masoor dhal together in a pan of water until soft and mushy. Set aside.

2 Heat the oil in a wok or heavy skillet and cook the onions until soft and golden brown. Stir in the garlic, ginger, turmeric, chili powder, garam masala, ground coriander, and salt.

3 Next, add the chicken pieces and stir-fry for 5–7 minutes to seal in the juices and lightly brown the meat.

4 Add half the fresh cilantro, the green chiles, lemon juice, and water and cook for 3–5 minutes more until the chicken is cooked, before pouring in the chana dhal and masoor dhal, followed by the tomato halves.

5 Add the remaining cilantro. Remove the wok or skillet from the heat and set aside.

6 To make the tarka, heat the oil and add the cumin seeds, whole garlic cloves, dried chiles, and curry leaves. Heat for about 30 seconds and, while it is still hot, pour it over the top of the dhal. Serve immediately.

COOK'S TIP
Chana dhal is made from split, small garbanzos; masoor dhal is made from split lentils.

Balti Chicken in Orange and Pepper Sauce

Orange, ginger, coriander, garlic, and black pepper make a truly delicious sauce for chicken in this low-fat curry.

INGREDIENTS

Serves 4

1 cup low-fat ricotta cheese

$^1/_4$ cup plain low-fat yogurt

$^1/_2$ cup orange juice

$1^1/_2$ teaspoons grated fresh ginger root

1 teaspoon crushed garlic

1 teaspoon freshly ground black pepper

1 teaspoon salt

1 teaspoon ground coriander

1 chicken, about $1^1/_2$ pounds, skinned and cut into 8 pieces

1 tablespoon oil

1 bay leaf

1 large onion, chopped

1 tablespoon fresh mint leaves

1 green chile, seeded and chopped

1 In a small bowl whisk together the ricotta cheese, yogurt, orange juice, ginger, garlic, pepper, salt, and coriander.

COOK'S TIP

If you prefer the taste of curry leaves, you can use them instead of the bay leaf, but you need to double the quantity.

2 Pour this over the chicken and set aside for 3–4 hours.

3 Heat the oil with the bay leaf in a wok or heavy skillet and cook the onion until soft.

4 Pour in the chicken mixture and stir-fry for 3–5 minutes over medium heat. Lower the heat, cover, and cook for 7–10 minutes until the chicken is cooked through, adding a little water if the sauce is too thick. Add the fresh mint and chile, and serve.

Balti Chicken in Hara Masala Sauce

This fruity low-fat chicken dish has a creamy sauce with a kick of chile. It looks particularly attractive too, so it would be an excellent choice for informal entertaining.

INGREDIENTS

Serves 4

1 crisp green eating apple,
    peeled, cored, and cut
    into small cubes

4 tablespoons fresh cilantro leaves

2 tablespoons fresh mint leaves

$^{1}/_{2}$ cup plain low-fat yogurt

3 tablespoons low fat ricotta cheese

2 medium green chiles, seeded
    and chopped

1 bunch of scallions, chopped

1 teaspoon salt

1 teaspoon sugar

1 teaspoon crushed garlic

1 teaspoon grated fresh
    ginger root

1 tablespoon oil

8 ounces skinless, boneless chicken breast
    portion, cubed

2 tablespoons golden raisins

1 Place the apple, 3 tablespoons of the cilantro, the mint, yogurt, ricotta cheese, chiles, scallions, salt, sugar, garlic, and ginger in a food processor and process for about 1 minute, using the pulsing action.

2 Heat the oil in a skillet, pour in the yogurt mixture, and cook over low heat for 2 minutes.

3 Next, add the chicken cubes and blend everything together. Cook over medium-low heat for 12–15 minutes, or until the chicken is fully cooked through.

4 Finally, add the golden raisins and remaining 1 tablespoon fresh cilantro leaves before serving.

HOT & SPICY

Countries such as Mexico, Malaysia, Thailand, Indonesia, the Caribbean, and
Morocco are renowned for their use of spices and hot flavorings in everyday
dishes. In this chapter, chiles, turmeric, cumin, and garam masala come into their
own. These are just a few of the aromatic flavorings that are used to add color,
texture, and heat to a whole range of rice dishes, casseroles, taco and tortilla
fillings, roasts, pan-cooked dishes, fried dishes, and kebabs.

Chicken Piri-piri

This is a classic Portuguese African dish, based on a hot sauce made from Angolan chiles. Chicken and vegetables are layered over rice and casseroled with the spicy piri-piri sauce.

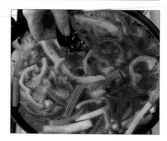

INGREDIENTS

Serves 4

4 chicken breast portions

2–3 tablespoons olive oil

1 large onion, thinly sliced

2 carrots, cut into thin strips

1 large parsnip or 2 small parsnips, cut
   into thin strips

1 red bell pepper, seeded and sliced

1 yellow bell pepper, seeded and sliced

4 cups chicken stock

3 tomatoes, peeled, seeded, and chopped

generous dash of piri-piri sauce

1 tablespoon tomato paste

$^1/_2$ cinnamon stick

1 fresh thyme sprig, plus extra fresh
   thyme, to garnish

1 bay leaf

$1^1/_2$ cups long grain rice

1 tablespoon lime or lemon juice

salt and ground black pepper

1 Preheat the oven to 350°F. Rub the chicken skin with a little salt and pepper. Heat 2 tablespoons of the oil in a large skillet and brown the chicken portions on all sides. Transfer to a plate.

2 Add some more oil to the skillet if necessary and cook the onion for 2–3 minutes, or until slightly softened. Add the carrots, parsnip, and bell peppers, stir-fry for a few minutes, and then cover and cook gently for 4–5 minutes, or until quite soft.

3 Pour in the chicken stock, then add the tomatoes, piri-piri sauce, tomato paste, and cinnamon stick. Stir in the thyme and bay leaf. Season to taste and bring to a boil. Using a ladle, spoon off $1^1/_4$ cups of the liquid and set aside in a small pan.

4 Put the rice in the base of a casserole. Using a slotted spoon, scoop the vegetables out of the pan and spread them over the rice. Arrange the chicken on top. Pour in the spicy chicken stock from the pan, cover the casserole tightly, and cook in the oven for about 45 minutes, or until both the rice and chicken are tender.

5 Meanwhile, heat the reserved chicken stock, adding a few more drops of piri-piri sauce and the lime or lemon juice.

6 To serve, spoon the piri-piri chicken and rice onto warmed serving plates. Serve the remaining sauce separately or poured over the chicken.

Chicken and Green Tomato Chimichangas

These rolled chicken pancakes are a common sight on street stalls along the Mexican border with Texas. Mexican green tomatoes are not, in fact, related to ordinary tomatoes, but have a similar flavor.

INGREDIENTS

Serves 4

2 skinless, boneless chicken
    breast portions
1 chipotle chile, seeded
1 tablespoon vegetable oil
2 onions, finely chopped
4 garlic cloves, crushed
$1/2$ teaspoon ground cumin
$1/2$ teaspoon ground coriander
$1/2$ teaspoon ground cinnamon
$1/2$ teaspoon ground cloves
scant 2 cups drained canned Mexican
    green tomatoes
$2^2/3$ cups cooked pinto beans
8–10-inch fresh wheat flour tortillas
oil, for frying
salt and ground black pepper

1 Put the chicken breast portions in a large pan, pour in water to cover, and add the chile. Bring to a boil, lower the heat, and simmer for 10 minutes, or until the chicken is cooked through and the chile has softened. Remove the chile and chop it finely. Lift the chicken portions out of the pan and put them on a plate. Let cool slightly, then shred with two forks.

2 Heat the oil in a skillet. Cook the onions until translucent, then add the garlic and ground spices, and cook for 3 minutes more. Add the Mexican green tomatoes and pinto beans. Cook over medium heat for 5 minutes, stirring constantly to break up the tomatoes and some of the beans. Simmer gently for 5 minutes more. Add the chicken and seasoning.

3 Wrap the tortillas in foil and place them on a plate. Stand the plate over a pan of boiling water for about 5 minutes, or until they become pliable. Alternatively, wrap them in microwave-safe wrap and heat them in a microwave on full power for 1 minute.

4 Spoon one-eighth of the bean filling into the center of a tortilla, fold in both sides, then fold the bottom of the tortilla up, and the top down to form a neat packet. Secure with a wooden toothpick. Make seven more.

5 Heat the oil in a large skillet and cook the chimichangas, in batches, until crisp, turning once. Remove them from the oil with a slotted spoon and drain on paper towels. Serve hot.

Chicken Pilau

This spicy dish is a complete meal on its own, but also makes a good accompaniment to curries.

INGREDIENTS

Serves 4

2 cups basmati rice

6 tablespoons butter

1 onion, sliced

$1/4$ teaspoon mixed onion and
    mustard seeds

3 curry leaves

1 teaspoon grated fresh ginger root

1 teaspoon crushed garlic

1 teaspoon ground coriander

1 teaspoon chili powder

$1^1/2$ teaspoon salt

2 tomatoes, sliced

1 potato, cubed

$1/2$ cup fresh shelled or
    frozen peas

$1^1/4$ cups cubed chicken

4 tablespoons chopped
    fresh cilantro

2 green chiles, chopped

3 cups water

1 Wash, then soak the rice in cold water for 30 minutes. Set aside in a strainer.

2 In a medium pan, melt the butter and cook the sliced onion until golden.

3 Add the onion and mustard seeds, the curry leaves, ginger, garlic, ground coriander, chili powder, and salt. Stir-fry for about 2 minutes.

4 Add the tomatoes, potato, peas, and chicken.

5 Add the drained rice and stir gently to combine.

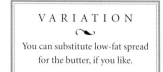

6 Add the cilantro and chopped green chiles. Mix and stir-fry for 1 minute more. Pour in the water. Bring to a boil and lower the heat. Cover and cook for about 20 minutes.

VARIATION

You can substitute low-fat spread for the butter, if you like.

Chicken in Green Almond Sauce

2 Put the onion, garlic, cilantro, green bell pepper, chile, Mexican green tomatoes with their juice, and the almonds in a food processor. Process to a coarse paste.

3 Heat the oil in a large skillet, add the almond mixture, and cook over low heat, stirring with a wooden spoon, for 3–4 minutes. Scrape into the casserole or pan with the chicken.

4 Make the stock up to 2 cups with water, if necessary. Stir it into the casserole or pan. Mix gently and simmer just long enough to blend the flavors and heat the chicken pieces through. Season with salt to taste. Serve, garnished with cilantro and accompanied by rice.

This casserole with its spicy sauce originates from Mexico.

INGREDIENTS

Serves 6

1 chicken, about 3¹/₂ pounds, cut into
   serving pieces

2 cups chicken stock

1 onion, chopped

1 garlic clove, chopped

2 cups coarsely chopped fresh cilantro

1 green bell pepper, seeded
   and chopped

1 jalapeño chile, seeded and chopped

10-ounce can Mexican
   green tomatoes

1 cup ground almonds

2 tablespoons corn oil

salt

fresh cilantro sprig, to garnish

rice, to serve

1 Put the chicken pieces into a flameproof casserole or shallow pan. Pour in the stock, bring to a simmer, cover, and cook for about 45 minutes, or until tender. Drain the stock into a measuring cup and set aside.

COOK'S TIP

If the color of the sauce seems a little pale, add 2–3 outer leaves of dark green romaine lettuce. Cut out the central veins, chop the leaves, and add at step 2.

Roast Spicy Chicken

An American favorite: crisp, roasted, spicy chicken with garlic.

INGREDIENTS

Serves 4

1 chicken, about 3¹/₂ pounds

juice of 1 lemon

4 garlic cloves, crushed

1 tablespoon cayenne pepper

1 tablespoon paprika

1 tablespoon dried oregano

¹/₂ teaspoon coarse black pepper

2 teaspoon olive oil

1 teaspoon salt

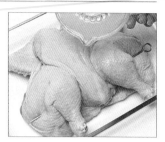

1 With a sharp knife or poultry shears, remove the backbone from the chicken. Turn it breast side up. With the heel of your hand, press down to break the breastbone, and open the chicken flat like a book. Insert a skewer through the chicken, at the thighs, to keep it flat during cooking.

2 Place the chicken in a shallow dish and pour the lemon juice over it to coat.

3 In a small bowl, combine the garlic, cayenne, paprika, oregano, pepper, and oil. Mix well. Rub evenly over the surface of the chicken.

4 Cover and leave to marinate for 2–3 hours at room temperature, or chill overnight (return to room temperature before roasting).

5 Season the chicken with salt on both sides. Transfer to a shallow roasting pan.

6 Put the pan in a cold oven and set the temperature to 400°F. Roast for about 1 hour, or until the chicken is cooked, turning occasionally and basting with the pan juices. To test, prick with a skewer: The juices that run out should be clear.

COOK'S TIP

Roasting chicken in an oven that has not been preheated produces a particularly crisp skin.

Sweet-spiced Chicken

Make sure you allow plenty of time
for the chicken wings to marinate
so the spicy flavors develop well,
then use a wok or a large skillet
for stir-frying.

INGREDIENTS

Serves 4

1 red chile, finely chopped

1 teaspoon chili powder

1 teaspoon ground ginger

finely grated rind of 1 lime

12 chicken wings

¹/₄ cup sunflower oil

1 tablespoon chopped
    fresh cilantro

2 tablespoons soy sauce

¹/₄ cup honey

lime rind and fresh cilantro sprigs,
    to garnish

1 Combine the fresh chile, chili
powder, ground ginger, and
lime rind. Rub the mixture into the
chicken skins and leave for at least
2 hours to let the flavors penetrate.

2 Heat a wok or large skillet and
add half of the oil. When the oil
is hot, add half the wings and stir-
fry for 10 minutes, turning
frequently until crisp and golden.
Drain on paper towels. Repeat with
the remaining wings.

3 Add the cilantro to the hot wok
or skillet and stir-fry for
30 seconds, then return the wings
to the pan and stir-fry for about
1 minute more.

4 Stir in the soy sauce and honey,
and stir-fry for 1 minute. Serve
the chicken wings hot with the
sauce drizzled over them, garnished
with lime rind and cilantro.

Chicken with Sauce Piquante

Sauce Piquante goes with just about everything that runs, flies, or swims in Louisiana—you will even find Alligator Sauce Piquante on menus. It is based on the brown Cajun roux and chile peppers give it heat: vary the heat by the number you use.

INGREDIENTS

Serves 4

4 chicken legs or 2 legs and 2
    breast portions
$^1/_3$ cup cooking oil
$^1/_2$ cup all-purpose flour
1 medium onion, chopped
2 celery stalks, sliced
1 green bell pepper, seeded and diced
2 garlic cloves, crushed
1 bay leaf
$^1/_2$ teaspoon dried thyme
$^1/_2$ teaspoon dried oregano
1–2 red chiles, seeded and
    finely chopped
14-ounce can tomatoes, chopped,
    with the juice
$1^1/_4$ cups chicken stock
salt and ground black pepper
watercress or arugula, to garnish
boiled potatoes, to serve

1 Halve the chicken legs through the joint, or cut the breast portions across the middle, to give eight pieces.

2 In a heavy pan, cook the chicken pieces in the oil until brown on all sides. Set aside.

3 Strain the oil from the pan into a flameproof casserole. Heat it and stir in the flour. Stir constantly over low heat until the roux is the color of peanut butter.

4 Tip in the onion, celery, and bell pepper and stir over the heat for 2–3 minutes.

5 Add the garlic, bay leaf, thyme, oregano, and chiles. Stir for 1 minute, then turn down the heat, and stir in the tomatoes with their can juice.

6 Return the casserole to the heat and gradually stir in the stock. Add the chicken pieces, cover, and simmer for 45 minutes, or until the chicken is cooked through.

7 If there is too much sauce or if it looks too runny, remove the lid for the last 10–15 minutes of the cooking time and turn up the heat a little to reduce and thicken the sauce.

8 Check the seasoning and serve garnished with watercress or arugula and accompanied by boiled potatoes.

COOK'S TIP

If you prefer to err on the side of caution with chili heat, use just 1 chile and pep up the seasoning at the end with a dash or two of Tabasco sauce.
The oil in chiles clings to your skin and could hurt if you then rub your eyes. Scrape out the seeds under cold running water and wash your hands after handling chiles.

Cajun Chicken

*Ham, chorizo, and shrimp
accompany chicken for this
wonderful spicy Cajun rice dish.*

INGREDIENTS

Serves 4

1 chicken, about 2^1/$_2$ pounds

1^1/$_2$ onions

1 bay leaf

4 black peppercorns

1 fresh parsley sprig

2 tablespoons vegetable oil

2 garlic cloves, chopped

1 green bell pepper, seeded,
    and chopped

1 celery stalk, chopped

generous 1 cup long grain rice

4 ounces chorizo sausage, sliced

^{2}/$_3$ cup chopped, cooked ham

14-ounce can chopped tomatoes
    with herbs

^{1}/$_2$ teaspoon hot chili powder

^{1}/$_2$ teaspoon cumin seeds

^{1}/$_2$ teaspoon ground cumin

1 teaspoon dried thyme

1 cup cooked, peeled shrimp

dash of Tabasco sauce

salt and ground black pepper

chopped parsley, to garnish

1 Place the chicken in a large,
flameproof casserole and pour
in 2^1/$_2$ cups water. Add the half
onion, the bay leaf, peppercorns,
and parsley, and bring to a boil.
Cover and simmer gently for about
1^1/$_2$ hours.

2 When the chicken is cooked,
lift it out of the stock, remove
the skin and carcass, and chop the
meat. Strain the stock, let cool,
and reserve.

3 Chop the remaining onion and
heat the oil in a large skillet.
Add the onion, garlic, green bell
pepper, and celery. Cook for about
5 minutes, then stir in the rice,
coating the grains with the oil.
Add the chorizo sausage slices,
ham, and reserved chicken and
cook for 2–3 minutes more,
stirring frequently.

4 Pour in the tomatoes and
1^1/$_4$ cups of the reserved stock,
and add the chile, cumin, and
thyme. Bring to a boil, then cover,
and simmer gently for 20 minutes,
or until the rice is tender and the
liquid absorbed.

5 Stir in the shrimp and Tabasco.
Cook for 5 minutes more, then
season well and serve hot,
garnished with chopped parsley.

Chicken with Cajun Sauce

Sizzling fried chicken served in a hot and tasty tomato sauce.

INGREDIENTS

Serves 4

1 chicken, 3 1/2 pounds, cut into 8 pieces
3/4 cup all-purpose flour
1 cup buttermilk or milk
vegetable oil, for frying
salt and ground black pepper
chopped scallions, and fresh cilantro
    sprigs, to garnish

For the sauce
1/2 cup vegetable oil
9 tablespoons all-purpose flour
2 onions, chopped
2–3 celery stalks, chopped
1 large green bell pepper, seeded
    and chopped
2 garlic cloves, finely chopped
8 ounces tomatoes
1 cup bottled strained tomatoes
scant 2 cups red wine or chicken stock
2 bay leaves
1 tablespoon soft brown sugar
1 teaspoon grated orange rind
1/2 teaspoon cayenne pepper

1 To make the sauce, heat the oil in a large pan and stir in the flour. Cook over medium heat, stirring for 15–20 minutes.

2 Add the onions, celery, green bell pepper, and garlic and cook, stirring, until softened.

3 Plunge the tomatoes into boiling water for 30 seconds, then refresh in cold water. Peel off the skins and chop the flesh. Stir in the tomatoes and remaining sauce ingredients and season with salt and pepper to taste. Bring to a boil and simmer for 1 hour, until rich and thick.

4 Meanwhile, prepare the chicken. Put the flour in a plastic bag and season with salt and pepper. Dip each piece of chicken in buttermilk or milk, then dredge in the flour to coat lightly all over. Shake off the excess flour. Set the chicken aside for 20 minutes to let the coating set before cooking.

5 Heat the vegetable oil 1 inch deep in a large pan until it is very hot and starting to sizzle. Cook the chicken pieces, turning them once, for about 30 minutes, or until deep golden brown all over and cooked through.

6 Drain the chicken on paper towels. Add them to the sauce and sprinkle with scallions.

Moroccan Spiced Roast Cornish Hens

Cornish hens taste great served with a spicy apricot and rice stuffing.

INGREDIENTS

Serves 4

3/4 cup cooked long grain rice

1 small onion, finely chopped

finely grated rind and juice of 1 lemon

2 tablespoons chopped fresh mint

3 tablespoons chopped dried apricots

2 tablespoons plain yogurt

2 teaspoons ground turmeric

2 teaspoons ground cumin

2 × 1-pound Cornish hens

salt and ground black pepper

lemon slices and mint sprigs, to garnish

1 Preheat the oven to 400°F. Combine the rice, onion, lemon rind, mint, and apricots. Stir in half each of the lemon juice, yogurt, turmeric, and cumin, and season with salt and pepper.

2 Stuff the Cornish hens with the rice mixture at the neck end only. Any stuffing left over can be served separately. Place the Cornish hens on a rack in a roasting pan.

3 Combine the remaining lemon juice, yogurt, turmeric, and cumin, then brush the mixture over the Cornish hens. Cover loosely with foil and cook the birds in the oven for 30 minutes.

4 Remove the foil and roast for 15 minutes more, or until golden brown and the juices run clear, not pink, when pierced.

5 Cut the Cornish hens in half with a sharp knife or poultry shears, and serve with any leftover rice stuffing. Garnish with lemon slices and fresh mint sprigs.

Sticky Ginger Chicken

This sweet, gingery glaze for chicken drumsticks turns dark and sticky under the broiler and tastes great.

INGREDIENTS

Serves 4

2 tablespoons lemon juice

2 tablespoons molasses sugar

1 teaspoon grated fresh ginger root

2 teaspoons soy sauce

8 chicken drumsticks, skinned

ground black pepper

lettuce and crusty bread, to serve

1 Combine the lemon juice, molasses sugar, grated ginger, soy sauce, and pepper to make a glaze for the chicken.

2 With a sharp knife, slash the chicken drumsticks about three times through the thickest part, then toss the chicken in the glaze.

3 Cook the chicken drumsticks under a hot broiler or on a barbecue, turning occasionally and brushing with the glaze, until the chicken is dark gold and the juices run clear, not pink, when pierced with a skewer. Serve on a bed of lettuce with crusty bread, if you like.

Moroccan Chicken Couscous

A subtly spiced and fragrant dish with a fruity sauce.

INGREDIENTS

Serves 4

1 tablespoon butter

1 tablespoon sunflower oil

4 chicken portions, about 6 ounces each

2 onions, finely chopped

2 garlic cloves, crushed

$1/2$ teaspoon ground cinnamon

$1/4$ teaspoon ground ginger

$1/4$ teaspoon ground turmeric

2 tablespoons orange juice

2 teaspoons honey

salt

fresh mint sprigs, to garnish

For the couscous

2 cups couscous

1 teaspoon salt

2 teaspoon superfine sugar

2 tablespoons sunflower oil

$1/2$ teaspoon ground cinnamon

pinch of freshly grated nutmeg

1 tablespoon orange flower water

2 tablespoons golden raisins

$1/2$ cup chopped blanched almonds

3 tablespoons chopped pistachio nuts

1 Heat the butter and oil in a large pan and add the chicken portions, skin side down. Cook for 3–4 minutes, or until the skin is golden, then turn them over.

2 Add the onions, garlic, spices, and a pinch of salt and pour in the orange juice and $1^1/4$ cups water. Cover and bring to a boil, then reduce the heat, and simmer for about 30 minutes.

3 Meanwhile, place the couscous and salt in a bowl and cover with $1^1/2$ cups water. Stir once and let stand for 5 minutes. Add the superfine sugar, 1 tablespoon of the oil, the cinnamon, nutmeg, orange flower water, and golden raisins, and mix well.

4 Heat the remaining 1 tablespoon of the oil in a pan and lightly cook the almonds until golden. Stir into the couscous with the pistachios.

5 Line a steamer with baking parchment and spoon in the couscous. Set the steamer over the chicken (or over a pan of boiling water) and steam for 10 minutes.

6 Remove the steamer and keep covered. Stir the honey into the chicken liquid and boil rapidly for 3–4 minutes. Spoon the couscous onto a warmed serving platter and top with the chicken, with a little of the sauce spooned over it. Garnish with fresh mint and serve with the remaining sauce.

Nasi Goreng

This dish is originally from Thailand. The bland flavor of crispy shrimp crackers makes exactly the right accompaniment to the spicy flavor of the dish.

INGREDIENTS

Serves 4

1 green chile
generous 1 cup long grain rice
2 eggs
2 tablespoons vegetable oil
2 scallions, coarsely chopped
2 garlic cloves, crushed
8 ounces cooked chicken, cut into strips
2 cups cooked shrimp
3 tablespoons dark soy sauce
shrimp crackers, to serve

1 Remove he seeds from the chile. Chop the flesh finely.

2 Rinse the rice and then cook for 10–12 minutes in 2 cups water in a pan with a tight-fitting lid. When cooked, refresh under cold water and drain.

3 Lightly beat the eggs. Heat 1 tablespoon of the oil in a small skillet and swirl in the beaten egg. When cooked on one side, flip over, and cook on the other side. Remove from the pan and let cool. Cut the omelet into strips.

4 Place the scallions, chile, and garlic in a blender or food processor and blend to a paste.

5 Heat a wok and then add the remaining oil. When the oil is hot, add the chile paste and stir-fry for 1 minute. Stir the chicken and shrimp into the chile paste, and cook until heated through.

6 Add the rice and stir-fry for 3–4 minutes. Stir in the soy sauce. Serve with shrimp crackers, and the strips of omelet.

Chicken Satay

Here is one of the classic spicy foods of the East. The chicken pieces should be large, otherwise they will not absorb the marinade satisfactorily.

INGREDIENTS

Serves 4

4 skinless, boneless chicken
   breast portions
2 teaspoons light brown sugar

For the marinade
1 teaspoon cumin seeds
1 teaspoon fennel seeds
1 $^1/_2$ teaspoons coriander seeds
6 shallots or small onions, chopped
1 garlic clove, crushed
1 lemongrass stalk, root trimmed
3 macadamia nuts or 6 cashew nuts
$^1/_2$ teaspoon ground turmeric

For the sauce
4 shallots or small onions, sliced
2 garlic cloves, crushed
$^1/_2$-inch cube shrimp paste
6 cashew nuts or almonds
2 lemongrass stalks, trimmed, lower
   2 inches sliced
3 tablespoons sunflower oil
1–2 teaspoons chili powder
1 $^3/_4$ cups canned coconut milk
4–5 tablespoons tamarind water or
   2 tablespoons tamarind concentrate
   mixed with 3 tablespoons water
1 tablespoon soft brown sugar
$^1/_2$ cup crunchy peanut butter

1 Cut the chicken into thin strips and sprinkle with the sugar.

2 Make the marinade. Dry-fry the spices, then grind them to a powder. Put the shallots or onions in a mortar or a food processor and add the garlic. Coarsely chop the lower 2 inches of the lemongrass and add it to the onions with the nuts, ground spices, and turmeric. Grind or process to a paste.

3 Add the chicken pieces and stir well until coated. Cover loosely with plastic wrap and let marinate for at least 4 hours.

4 Prepare the sauce. Pound or process the shallots or onions with the garlic and shrimp paste. Add the nuts and the lower parts of the lemongrass stalks. Process to a fine paste. Heat the oil in a wok and cook the paste for 2–3 minutes. Add the chili powder and cook for 2 minutes more.

5 Stir in the coconut milk and bring slowly to a boil. Reduce the heat and stir in the tamarind water and brown sugar. Add the peanut butter and cook over low heat, stirring gently, until fairly thick. Keep warm. Soak 16 bamboo skewers in water for 30 minutes. Prepare the barbecue, if using.

6 Thread the chicken onto the bamboo skewers. Barbecue or broil for about 5 minutes, or until golden and tender, brushing with oil occasionally. Serve with the hot peanut sauce.

Chicken Rendang

This spicy Malaysian dish is marvelous as part of a buffet. Serve it with shrimp crackers or with boiled rice and deep-fried anchovies.

INGREDIENTS

Serves 4

1 chicken, about 3 pounds
1 teaspoon sugar
1 cup dry unsweetened
   shredded coconut
4 small red or white onions,
   coarsely chopped
2 garlic cloves, chopped
1-inch piece of fresh ginger root, peeled
   and sliced
1–2 lemongrass stalks, root trimmed
1-inch piece of fresh galangal, peeled
   and sliced
5 tablespoons peanut oil or
   vegetable oil
2–3 teaspoons chili powder or to taste
$1^3/_4$ cups canned coconut milk
2 teaspoons salt
fresh chives and deep-fried anchovies,
   to garnish

1 Cut the chicken into 8 pieces and remove the skin, sprinkle with the sugar, and let stand for 1 hour.

2 Dry-fry the coconut in a wok or large skillet over medium heat, turning constantly until it is crisp and golden. Transfer the fried coconut to a food processor and process to an oily paste. Transfer to a bowl and reserve.

3 Add the onions, garlic, and ginger to the processor. Cut off the lower 2 inches of the lemongrass, chop, and add to the processor with the galangal. Process to a fine paste.

4 Heat the oil in a wok or large pan and cook the onion mixture for a few minutes. Reduce the heat, stir in the chili powder, and cook for 2–3 minutes, stirring constantly. Spoon in $^1/_2$ cup of the coconut milk and season with salt to taste.

5 As soon as the mixture bubbles, add the chicken pieces, turning them until they are well coated with the spices. Pour in the coconut milk, stirring constantly to prevent curdling. Bruise the top of the lemongrass stalks and add to the wok or pan. Cover and cook gently for 40–45 minutes, or until the chicken is tender.

6 Just before serving, stir in the coconut paste. Bring to just below boiling point, then simmer for 5 minutes. Transfer to a serving bowl and garnish with fresh chives and deep-fried anchovies.

Chicken and Mushroom Donburi

"Donburi" means a one-dish meal that is eaten from a bowl, and takes its name from the eponymous Japanese porcelain food bowl. The rice here is completely plain but is nevertheless an integral part of the dish and offsets the spicy ingredients.

INGREDIENTS

Serves 4

$1^1/_2$ cups Japanese rice or Thai fragrant
    rice, rinsed
2 teaspoons peanut oil
$^1/_4$ cup butter
2 garlic cloves, crushed
1-inch piece of fresh ginger root, grated
5 scallions, diagonally sliced
1 green fresh chile, seeded and finely sliced
3 skinless, boneless chicken breast
    portions, cut into thin strips
5 ounces beancurd, cut into
    small cubes
$1^3/_4$ cups shiitake mushrooms, stalks
    discarded and cups sliced
1 tablespoon Japanese rice wine
2 tablespoons light soy sauce
2 teaspoons granulated sugar
$1^2/_3$ cups chicken stock

1 Put the rice in a pan, and add $2^1/_2$ cups water. Bring to a boil, then lower the heat, cover, and simmer for 8–10 minutes or according to the instructions on the packet. Remove the pan from the heat and let stand, covered, for 5 minutes.

2 While the rice is cooking, heat the oil and half the butter in a large skillet. Stir-fry the garlic, ginger, scallions, and chile for about 1–2 minutes, or until slightly softened. Add the strips of chicken and cook, in batches, until all the pieces are evenly browned.

3 Transfer the chicken mixture to a plate and add the beancurd to the pan. Stir-fry for a few minutes, then add the mushrooms. Stir-fry for 2–3 minutes over medium heat until the mushrooms are tender.

4 Stir in the rice wine, soy sauce, and sugar and cook briskly for 1–2 minutes, stirring constantly. Return the chicken to the pan, toss over the heat for about 2 minutes, then pour in the stock. Stir well and cook over low heat for 5–6 minutes, or until bubbling.

5 Spoon the rice into individual serving bowls and pile the chicken mixture on top, making sure that each portion gets a generous amount of chicken sauce.

Stir-fried Chicken with Basil and Chiles

This quick and easy chicken dish is an excellent introduction to Thai cuisine. Thai basil, which is sometimes known as holy basil, has a unique, pungent flavor that is both spicy and sharp. Deep-frying the leaves adds another dimension to this dish.

INGREDIENTS

Serves 4–6

3 tablespoons vegetable oil

4 garlic cloves, thinly sliced

2–4 fresh red chiles, seeded and
　finely chopped

1 pound skinless, boneless chicken breast
　portions, cut into bitesize pieces

3 tablespoons Thai fish sauce

2 teaspoons dark soy sauce

1 teaspoon sugar

10–12 Thai basil leaves

2 fresh red chiles, seeded and finely
　chopped and about 20 deep-fried Thai
　basil leaves, to garnish

1 Heat the oil in a wok or large skillet. Add the garlic and chiles and stir-fry over medium heat for 1–2 minutes, or until the garlic is golden brown.

COOK'S TIP

To deep-fry Thai basil leaves, first make sure that the leaves are completely dry or they will splutter when added to the oil.

2 Add the pieces of chicken to the wok or skillet and stir-fry until the chicken changes color.

3 Stir in the Thai fish sauce, soy sauce, and sugar. Continue to stir-fry the mixture for 3–4 minutes, or until the chicken is fully cooked with the sauce.

4 Stir in the fresh Thai basil leaves. Spoon the entire mixture onto a warm serving platter or individual serving dishes and garnish with the sliced chiles and deep-fried Thai basil.

Chicken and Basil Coconut Rice

For this dish, the rice is simmered with coconut so it absorbs the flavor of the chiles, basil, and spices.

INGREDIENTS

Serves 4

1³/₄ cups Thai fragrant rice, rinsed

2–3 tablespoons peanut oil

1 large onion, finely sliced into rings

1 garlic clove, crushed

1 fresh red chile, seeded and
  finely sliced

1 fresh green chile, seeded and
  finely sliced

generous handful of basil leaves

3 skinless, boneless chicken breast
  portions, about 12 ounces,
  finely sliced

¹/₄-inch piece of lemongrass, pounded or
  finely chopped

1¹/₄ cups coconut milk mixed with
  1¹/₄ cups water

salt and ground black pepper

1 Bring a pan of lightly salted water to a boil. Add the rice to the pan and boil for about 6 minutes, or until partially cooked. Drain.

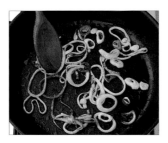

2 Heat the oil in a skillet and cook the onion rings for 5–10 minutes, or until golden and crisp. Lift out, drain on paper towels, and set aside.

3 Cook the garlic and chiles in the oil remaining in the pan for 2–3 minutes, then add the basil leaves, and cook briefly until they begin to wilt. Remove a few leaves and set them aside for the garnish, then add the chicken slices with the lemongrass, and cook for 2–3 minutes, or until golden.

4 Add the rice. Stir-fry for a few minutes to coat the grains, then pour in the coconut milk. Cook for 4–5 minutes, or until the rice is tender, adding a little more water if necessary. Adjust the seasoning. Pile the rice into a warmed serving dish, sprinkle with the fried onion rings and basil leaves, and serve immediately while still hot.

Indonesian Pineapple Rice

This way of presenting rice not only looks spectacular, but it also tastes so good that it can easily be served solo.

INGREDIENTS

Serves 4

³/₄ cup raw peanuts

1 large pineapple

3 tablespoons peanut or sunflower oil

1 onion, chopped

1 garlic clove, crushed

2 boneless chicken breast portions, about 8
  ounces

generous 1 cup Thai fragrant rice, rinsed

2¹/₂ cups chicken stock

1 lemongrass stalk, bruised

2 thick slices of ham

1 fresh red chile, seeded and very
  finely sliced

salt

1 Dry-fry the peanuts in a nonstick skillet until golden. When cool, grind one-sixth of them in a coffee or herb mill, and chop the remainder.

2 Cut a lengthwise section of pineapple, slicing through the leaves, then cut out the flesh to leave a neat shell. Chop 4 ounces of the pineapple into cubes, saving the remainder for another dish.

3 Heat the oil in a pan and cook the onion and garlic for 3–4 minutes, or until soft. Cut the chicken into thin strips, add to the pan, and stir-fry over medium heat for a few minutes, or until evenly golden brown.

4 Add the rice to the pan. Toss with the chicken mixture for a few minutes, then pour in the stock, with the lemongrass and a little salt. Bring to just below boiling point, then lower the heat, cover the pan, and simmer gently for 10–12 minutes, or until the rice and the chicken pieces are tender.

5 Cut the ham into julienne strips. Stir the chopped peanuts, the pineapple cubes, and the ham into the rice, then spoon the mixture into the pineapple shell. Sprinkle the ground peanuts and the sliced chile over the top and serve immediately.

Bang Bang Chicken

Use toasted sesame seed paste to give an authentic flavor to the sauce for this Sichuan dish.

INGREDIENTS

Serves 4

3 skinless, boneless chicken breast
    portions, about 1 pound
1 garlic clove, crushed
$^1/_2$ teaspoon black peppercorns
1 small onion, halved
1 large cucumber, peeled, seeded, and cut
    into thin strips
salt and ground black pepper

For the sauce

3 tablespoons toasted sesame paste
1 tablespoon light soy sauce
1 tablespoon wine vinegar
2 scallions, finely chopped
2 garlic cloves, crushed
2 x $^1/_2$-inch piece of fresh ginger root,
    peeled and cut into batons
1 tablespoon Sichuan peppercorns,
    dry-fried and crushed
1 teaspoon light brown sugar

For the chili oil

4 tablespoons peanut oil
1 teaspoon chili powder

1 Place the chicken in a pan. Just cover with water, add the garlic, peppercorns, and onion and bring to a boil. Skim the surface, stir in salt and pepper to taste, then cover the pan. Cook for 25 minutes, or until the chicken is cooked through. Drain, reserving the stock.

2 Make the sauce by mixing the toasted sesame paste with 3 tablespoons of the chicken stock, saving the rest for soup. Add the soy sauce, vinegar, scallions, garlic, ginger, and crushed peppercorns to the sesame mixture. Stir in sugar to taste.

3 Make the chili oil by gently heating the oil and chili powder together until foaming. Simmer for 2 minutes, cool, then strain off the red-colored oil, and discard the sediment.

4 Spread out the cucumber strips on a platter. Cut the chicken portions into pieces of about the same size as the cucumber strips and arrange them on top. Pour the sauce over the chicken, drizzle with the chili oil, and serve.

Caribbean Chicken with Pigeon Pea Rice

Golden, spicy, caramelized chicken tops a richly flavored vegetable rice in this hearty and delicious supper dish. Pigeon peas are a common ingredient in Caribbean cooking.

INGREDIENTS

Serves 4

1 teaspoon allspice

$^1/_2$ teaspoon ground cinnamon

1 teaspoon dried thyme

pinch of ground cloves

$^1/_4$ teaspoon freshly grated nutmeg

4 skinless, boneless chicken
   breast portions

3 tablespoons peanut or sunflower oil

1 tablespoon butter

1 onion, chopped

2 garlic cloves, crushed

1 carrot, diced

1 celery stalk chopped

3 scallions, chopped

1 fresh red chile, seeded and thinly sliced

14-ounce can pigeon peas

generous 1 cup long grain rice

$^1/_2$ cup coconut milk

$2^1/_2$ cups chicken stock

2 tablespoons raw sugar

salt and cayenne pepper

1 Combine the allspice, cinnamon, thyme, cloves, and nutmeg. Rub the mixture all over the pieces of chicken. Set aside for 30 minutes.

2 Heat 1 tablespoon of the oil with the butter in a pan. Cook the onion and garlic over medium heat until soft and beginning to brown. Add the carrot, celery, scallions, and chile. Cook for a few minutes, then stir in the pigeon peas, rice, coconut milk, and chicken stock. Season with salt and cayenne pepper. Bring to a boil, then cover, and simmer over low heat for about 25 minutes.

3 About 10 minutes before the rice mixture is cooked, heat the remaining oil in a skillet, add the sugar, and cook, but do not stir, until it begins to caramelize.

4 Carefully add the chicken to the skillet. Cook for 8–10 minutes, or until the chicken has a browned, glazed appearance and is cooked through. Transfer the chicken to a board and slice it thickly. Serve the pigeon pea rice in individual bowls, with the chicken on top.

Caribbean Peanut Chicken

Peanut butter is used a lot in Caribbean dishes. It adds richness, as well as a delicious depth of flavor.

INGREDIENTS

Serves 4

4 skinless, boneless chicken breast
  portions, cut into thin strips
generous 1 cup white long
  grain rice
2 tablespoons peanut oil
1 tablespoon butter, plus extra
  for greasing
1 onion, finely chopped
2 tomatoes, peeled, seeded, and chopped
1 fresh green chile, seeded and sliced
4 tablespoons smooth peanut butter
scant 2 cups chicken stock
lemon juice, to taste
salt and ground black pepper
lime wedges and fresh flat leaf parsley
  sprigs, to garnish

For the marinade
1 tablespoon sunflower oil
1–2 garlic cloves, crushed
1 teaspoon chopped fresh thyme
1 1/2 tablespoons medium curry powder
juice of 1/2 lemon

1 Combine all the marinade ingredients in a bowl and stir in the chicken. Cover with plastic wrap and set aside in a cool place for 2–3 hours.

2 Cook the rice in lightly salted, boiling water. Drain and transfer to a buttered casserole.

3 Preheat the oven to 350°F. Heat 1 tablespoon of the oil with the butter in a flameproof casserole and cook the chicken pieces, stirring frequently, for about 4–5 minutes, or until brown.

4 Transfer the chicken to a plate. Add the remaining oil to the casserole and cook the onion for 5–6 minutes. Stir in the tomatoes and chile. Cook over low heat for 3–4 minutes, stirring occasionally. Remove the pan from the heat.

5 Mix the peanut butter with the chicken stock. Stir into the tomato and onion mixture, then add the chicken. Stir in the lemon juice, season to taste, then spoon the mixture over the rice.

6 Cover the casserole. Cook in the oven for 15–20 minutes, or until piping hot and cooked through. Use a large spoon to toss the rice with the chicken mixture. Serve immediately, garnished with the lime wedges and parsley sprigs.

Chicken with Spiced Rice

*This hot dish is ideal for midweek
entertaining. It can be prepared in
advance and reheated in the oven.
Serve with all the traditional curry
accompaniments.*

INGREDIENTS

Serves 8

2 pounds boneless chicken thighs

4 tablespoons olive oil

2 large onions, thinly sliced

1–2 green chiles, seeded and
    finely chopped

1 teaspoon grated fresh
    ginger root

1 garlic clove, crushed

1 tablespoon hot curry powder

²/₃ cup chicken stock

²/₃ cup plain yogurt

2 tablespoons chopped
    fresh cilantro

salt and ground black pepper

For the rice

2¹/₄ cups basmati rice

¹/₂ teaspoon garam masala

3³/₄ cups chicken stock or water

scant ¹/₂ cup raisins or golden raisins

¹/₄ cup toasted chopped almonds

1 Put the rice into a strainer and
wash under cold running water
to remove any starchy powder
coating the grains. Then put into a
bowl, cover with cold water, and let
soak for 30 minutes. The grains will
absorb some water so that they
will not stick together in a solid
mass while cooking.

2 Preheat the oven to 325°F.
Cut the chicken into 1-inch
cubes. Heat 2 tablespoons of the
olive oil in a large, flameproof
casserole. Add one onion and cook,
stirring occasionally, until softened.
Add the finely chopped chiles,
ginger, garlic, and curry powder
and continue cooking for 2
minutes more, stirring from time
to time.

3 Add the stock and seasoning, and
bring slowly to a boil. Add the
chicken. Cover and cook in the oven
for 20 minutes, or until tender.

4 Remove from the oven and stir
in the yogurt.

5 Meanwhile, heat the remaining
oil in a flameproof casserole
and cook the remaining onion
gently until tender and lightly
browned. Add the drained rice,
garam masala, and stock or water.
Bring to a boil, cover, and cook in
the oven with the chicken for
20–35 minutes, or until tender and
all the stock has been absorbed.

6 To serve, stir the raisins and
toasted almonds into the rice.
Spoon half the rice into a large,
deep serving dish, cover with the
chicken and then the remaining
rice. Sprinkle with chopped
cilantro to garnish.

Balti Chicken with Green and Red Chiles

Ground chicken is seldom cooked in Indian or Pakistani homes. However, it works very well in this recipe.

INGREDIENTS

Serves 4

10 ounces skinless, boneless chicken
    breast portions, cubed

2 thick red chiles

3 thick green chiles

2 tablespoons oil

6 curry leaves

3 medium onions, sliced

1 1/2 teaspoons crushed garlic

1 teaspoon chili powder

1 1/2 teaspoons ground coriander

1 1/2 teaspoons grated fresh ginger root

1 teaspoon salt

1 tablespoon lemon juice

2 tablespoons chopped fresh cilantro

chapatis and lemon wedges,
    to serve

2 Place the chicken in a food processor to grind.

5 Add the ground chicken and stir-fry for 3–5 minutes.

1 Boil the cubed chicken in water for about 10 minutes, or until soft and cooked through. Remove with a slotted spoon.

3 Halve the chiles lengthwise and remove the seeds, if you like. Cut the flesh into strips and set aside.

4 Heat the oil in a wok or skillet and cook the curry leaves and onions until the onions are a soft golden brown. Lower the heat and add the garlic, chili powder, ground coriander, ginger, and salt.

6 Add the lemon juice, the prepared chile strips, and most of the fresh cilantro. Stir-fry for 3–5 minutes more, then serve, garnished with the remaining fresh cilantro and accompanied by warm chapatis and lemon wedges.

COOK'S TIP

Taste this dish during cooking as it is quite mild, especially if you seed the chiles, and you may find that it needs some additional spices to suit your palate.

Chicken with Panir and Peas

This is something of an unusual combination, but it really works well. Serve with plain boiled rice.

INGREDIENTS

Serves 4

1 chicken, about 1¹/₂ pounds
2 tablespoons tomato paste
3 tablespoons plain
    low-fat yogurt
1¹/₂ teaspoons garam masala
1 teaspoon crushed garlic
1 teaspoon grated fresh
    ginger root
pinch of ground cardamom
1 tablespoon chili powder
¹/₄ teaspoon ground turmeric
1 teaspoon salt
1 teaspoon sugar
2 teaspoons oil
1-inch cinnamon stick
2 black peppercorns
1¹/₄ cups water
1 cup cubed panir
2 tablespoons fresh cilantro leaves
2 green chiles, seeded and chopped
¹/₄ cup low-fat ricotta cheese
³/₄ cup fresh shelled or thawed
    frozen peas

1 Skin the chicken and cut it into 6–8 equal pieces.

COOK'S TIP

~

Panir is an Indian cheese made from whole milk.

2 Combine the tomato paste, yogurt, garam masala, garlic, ginger, cardamom, chili powder, turmeric, salt, and sugar in a bowl.

3 Heat the oil with the whole spices in a wok or heavy skillet, then pour the sauce mixture into the oil. Lower the heat and cook gently for about 3 minutes, then pour in the water, and bring to a gentle simmer.

4 Add the chicken pieces and stir-fry for about 2 minutes, then cover the wok or skillet, and cook over medium heat for about 15 minutes.

5 Add the panir cubes to the pan, followed by half the cilantro and half the green chiles. Mix well and cook for 5–7 minutes more.

6 Stir in the ricotta cheese and peas, heat through, and serve garnished with the reserved cilantro and chiles.

Chicken and Cilantro Potatoes

The potatoes are cooked separately in the oven before being added to spicy chicken. Make sure you start the preparation in good time, as the chicken takes 2 hours to marinate.

INGREDIENTS

Serves 4

^{2}/3 cup plain low-fat yogurt
^{1}/4 cup ground almonds
1^1/2 teaspoons ground coriander
^{1}/2 teaspoon chili powder
1 teaspoon garam masala
1 tablespoon coconut milk
1 teaspoon crushed garlic
1 teaspoon grated fresh
   ginger root
2 tablespoons chopped
   fresh cilantro
1 red chile, seeded and chopped
8 ounces skinless, boneless chicken breast
   portion, cubed
1 tablespoon oil
2 medium onions, sliced
3 green cardamom pods
1-inch cinnamon stick
2 cloves
salt and ground black pepper

For the potatoes
1 tablespoon oil
8 baby potatoes, thickly sliced
^{1}/4 teaspoon cumin seeds
1 tablespoon finely chopped
   fresh cilantro

VARIATION
Any variety of fresh mint may also be added to the potatoes, if you like.

1 In a bowl, combine the yogurt, ground almonds, ground coriander, chili powder, garam masala, coconut milk, garlic, ginger, half the fresh cilantro, and half the red chile.

2 Place the chicken pieces in the mixture, mix well, and let marinate for about 2 hours.

3 Meanwhile, start to prepare the potatoes. Heat the oil in a wok or heavy skillet. Add the sliced potatoes, cumin seeds, and fresh cilantro and quickly stir-fry for 2–3 minutes. Season with salt and pepper to taste.

4 Transfer the potatoes to a heatproof dish, cover, and cook in a preheated oven at 350°F for about 30 minutes, or until the potatoes are cooked through. Test with a skewer.

5 About halfway through the potatoes' cooking time, heat the oil with the onions, cardamom pods, cinnamon, and cloves for about 1^1/2 minutes.

6 Add the chicken mixture to the onions and stir-fry for 5–7 minutes. Lower the heat, cover, and cook for 5–7 minutes. Season to taste. Top with the potatoes and garnish with cilantro and chile.

Indian Spiced Chicken

These tender marinated chicken
pieces can be served hot or cold.

INGREDIENTS

Serves 4

1 chicken, about 4 pounds
mixed salad greens and lemon wedges,
    to serve

For the marinade
$^2/3$ cup plain low-fat yogurt
1 teaspoon ground paprika
2 teaspoons grated fresh
    ginger root
1 garlic clove, crushed
2 teaspoons garam masala
$^1/2$ teaspoon salt
red food coloring (optional)
juice of 1 lemon

1 Cut the chicken into eight
pieces, using a sharp knife.

2 Combine all the marinade
ingredients in a large dish, add
the chicken pieces, and mix to coat
with the marinade. Chill for
4 hours or overnight to let the
flavors penetrate the flesh.

3 Preheat the oven to 400°F.
Remove the chicken pieces
from the marinade and arrange
them in a single layer in a large,
ovenproof dish. Bake for about
30–40 minutes, or until cooked
through. Reserve the marinade.

4 Baste with a little of the
marinade while cooking.
Arrange on a bed of salad greens
and serve hot or cold, with wedges
of lemon.

Red-hot Chicken

A good party dish. The chicken is marinated the night before so all you have to do on the day is to cook it in a very hot oven and serve with wedges of lemon and salad greens.

INGREDIENTS

Serves 4

1 chicken, 4 pounds, cut into 8 pieces

juice of 1 large lemon

$^2/_3$ cup plain low-fat yogurt

3 garlic cloves, crushed

2 tablespoons olive oil

1 teaspoon ground turmeric

2 teaspoons paprika

1 teaspoon grated fresh ginger root or
 $^1/_2$ teaspoon ground ginger

2 teaspoon garam masala

1 teaspoon salt

a few drops red food
 coloring (optional)

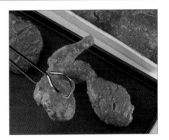

3 Combine all the remaining ingredients and pour the sauce over the chicken pieces, turning them to coat thoroughly. Cover with plastic wrap and chill in the refrigerator overnight.

4 Preheat the oven to 425°F. Remove the chicken from the marinade and arrange in a single layer on a shallow cookie sheet. Bake for 15 minutes, turn over, and cook for 15 minutes more, or until cooked through and tender.

1 Skin the chicken pieces and cut two slits in each piece.

2 Arrange in a single layer in a glass or ceramic dish and pour the lemon juice over them.

Chili Chicken

Serve as a simple supper dish with boiled potatoes and broccoli, or as a party dish with rice.

INGREDIENTS

Serves 4

12 chicken thighs
1 tablespoon olive oil
1 onion, thinly sliced
1 garlic clove, crushed
1 teaspoon chili powder or 1 red
    chile, chopped
14-ounce can chopped tomatoes
1 teaspoon superfine sugar
15-ounce can red kidney beans, drained
salt and ground black pepper

1 Cut the chicken into large cubes, removing all skin and bones. Heat the oil in a large, flameproof casserole and brown the chicken on all sides. Remove with a slotted spoon. Keep warm.

2 Add the onion and garlic to the casserole and cook gently until soft. Stir in the chili powder or chopped red chile and cook for 2 minutes. Add the tomatoes with their juice, seasoning, and sugar. Bring to a boil.

3 Replace the chicken, cover the casserole, and simmer for about 30 minutes, or until cooked through.

4 Add the red kidney beans and gently cook for 5 minutes more to heat them through before serving.

Ginger Chicken Wings

Here is a really quick dish that is full of flavor. Chicken wings coated in a spicy yogurt sauce are quickly cooked and then sprinkled with ginger.

INGREDIENTS

Serves 4

10–12 chicken wings, skinned

³/4 cup plain low-fat yogurt

1¹/2 teaspoons grated fresh
   ginger root

1 teaspoon salt

1 teaspoon Tabasco sauce

1 tablespoon tomato ketchup

1 teaspoon crushed garlic

1 tablespoon lemon juice

1 tablespoon fresh cilantro leaves

1 tablespoon oil

2 medium onions, sliced

1 tablespoon shredded fresh
   ginger root

1 Place the chicken wings in a glass or china bowl. Pour the yogurt into a separate bowl with the ginger, salt, Tabasco sauce, tomato ketchup, garlic, lemon juice, and half the cilantro leaves. Whisk everything together, then pour the mixture over the chicken wings, and stir gently to coat.

2 Heat the oil in a wok or heavy skillet and cook the onions until soft.

3 Add the chicken and cook over medium heat, stirring occasionally, for 10–15 minutes, or until cooked through.

4 Add the remaining cilantro and the shredded ginger, and serve the chicken wings hot.

VARIATION

You can substitute other cuts of chicken for the wings, but increase the cooking time.

Jeera Chicken

This aromatic dish has a delicious, distinctive taste of cumin. Serve simply with cooling cucumber raita.

3 Add the chiles, garlic, and ginger and cook for about 2 minutes.

4 Add the ground coriander, ground cumin, and salt and cook for 2–3 minutes more.

INGREDIENTS

Serves 4

3 tablespoons cumin seeds

1 tablespoon oil

$^{1}/_{2}$ teaspoon black peppercorns

4 green cardamom pods

2 green chiles, finely chopped

2 garlic cloves, crushed

1-inch piece of fresh ginger root, grated

1 teaspoon ground coriander

2 teaspoons ground cumin

$^{1}/_{2}$ teaspoon salt

8 chicken pieces, such as thighs and
   drumsticks, skinned

1 teaspoon garam masala

fresh cilantro and chili powder,
   to garnish

cucumber raita, to serve

1 Dry-roast 1 tablespoon of the cumin seeds in a small, heavy skillet for 5 minutes, or until they turn a few shades darker and give off a roasted aroma. Set aside.

2 Heat the oil in a large, heavy pan and cook the remaining cumin seeds, black peppercorns, and cardamom pods for about 2–3 minutes.

5 Add the chicken. Cover and simmer for 20–25 minutes.

6 Add the garam masala and reserved toasted cumin seeds and cook for 5 minutes more. Garnish with fresh cilantro and chili powder and serve with cucumber raita.

Chicken Dopiazza

*Dopiazza translates literally as
"two onions" and describes this
chicken dish in which two types of
onion—large and small—are used
at different stages during the
cooking process.*

INGREDIENTS

Serves 4

2 tablespoons oil

8 small onions, halved

4 tomatoes

2 bay leaves

8 green cardamom pods

4 cloves

3 dried red chiles

8 black peppercorns

2 onions, finely chopped

2 garlic cloves, crushed

1-inch piece of fresh ginger root,
    finely chopped

1 teaspoon ground coriander

1 teaspoon ground cumin

$1/2$ teaspoon ground turmeric

1 teaspoon chili powder

$1/2$ teaspoon salt

$1/2$ cup water

8 chicken pieces, such as thighs and
    drumsticks, skinned

plain rice, to serve

1 Heat half the oil in a large,
heavy pan and cook the small
onions for 10 minutes, or until
golden brown. Remove and set
aside. Plunge the tomatoes into
boiling water for 30 seconds, then
refresh in cold water. Peel off the
skins and finely chop the flesh.

2 In the remaining oil cook the
bay leaves, cardamom pods,
cloves, chiles, and peppercorns for
2 minutes. Add the onions, garlic,
and ginger and cook for 5 minutes.
Stir in the spices and salt.

3 Add the tomatoes and water
and simmer for 5 minutes, or
until the sauce thickens. Add the
chicken and cook for 15 minutes.

4 Add the reserved onions, then
cover, and cook for 10 minutes,
or until the chicken is cooked
through. Serve with boiled rice.

COOK'S TIP

To make the onions easy to peel,
quickly soak them in boiling water.

Index

Acknowledgments

The publishers would like to thank the following contributors:

Recipe creators: Catherine Atkinson, Michelle Berriedale-Johnson, Angela Boggiano, Ruby le Bois, Carla Capalbo, Lesley Chamberlain, Jacqueline Clark, Maxine Clark, Carole Clements, Andy Clevely, Elizabeth Wolf-Cohen, Trish Davies, Roz Denny, Sarah Edmonds, Joanna Farrow, Christine France, Yasuko Fukuoka, Sarah Gates, Shirley Gill, Brian Glover, Rosamund Grant, Caroline Handslip, Deh-Ta Hsiung, Shehzad Husain, Christine Ingram, Peter Jordan, Manisha Kanani, Emi Kazuko, Lucy Knox, Elisabeth Lambert Ortiz, Lesley Mackley, Norma MacMillan, Sue Maggs, Kathy Man, Sally Mansfield, Elizabeth Martin, Jane Milton, Sallie Morris, Katherine Richmond, Keith Richmond, Anne Sheasby, Marlena Spieler, Jenny Stacey, Liz Trigg, Laura Washburn, Steven Wheeler, Kate Whiteman and Jeni Wright.

Photographers: Karl Adamson, Edward Allwright, David Armstrong, Steve Baxter, Nicki Dowey, James Duncan, Rafi Fernandez, John Freeman, Ian Garlick, Michelle Garrett, John Heseltine, Amanda Heywood, Janine Hosegood, Dave Jordan, Dave King, Don Last, Clare Lewis, Sara Lewis, William Lingwood, Patrick McLeavy, Thomas Odulate, Peter Reilly, Craig Robertson, Simon Smith, Sam Stowell and Sunil Vikayaki.